THE JUSTICE OF ISLAM

THE JUSTICE OF ISLAM

Comparative Perspectives on
Islamic Law and Society

LAWRENCE ROSEN

OXFORD
UNIVERSITY PRESS

OXFORD

UNIVERSITY PRESS

Great Clarendon Street, Oxford OX2 6DP

Oxford University Press is a department of the University of Oxford.
It furthers the University's objective of excellence in research, scholarship,
and education by publishing worldwide in

Oxford New York

Athens Auckland Bangkok Bogotá Buenos Aires Calcutta
Cape Town Chennai Dar es Salaam Delhi Florence Hong Kong Istanbul
Karachi Kuala Lumpur Madrid Melbourne Mexico City Mumbai
Nairobi Paris São Paulo Singapore Taipei Tokyo Toronto Warsaw
with associated companies in Berlin Ibadan

Oxford is a registered trade mark of Oxford University Press
in the UK and in certain other countries

Published in the United States
by Oxford University Press Inc., New York

British Library Cataloguing in Publication Data

Data available

Library of Congress Cataloging in Publication Data
Rosen, Lawrence, 1941–
The justice of Islam: comparative perspectives on Islamic law
and society/Lawrence Rosen.
p. cm.—(Oxford socio-legal studies)
Includes bibliographical references and index.
1. Islamic law. 2. Sociological jurisprudence. I. Title. II. Series.
LAW
340´.115—dc 21 99–049281
ISBN 0–19–829884–6 (hb)
ISBN 0–19–829885–4 (pb)

1 3 5 7 9 10 8 6 4 2

Typeset in Garamond by
Cambrian Typesetters, Frimley, Surrey

Printed in Great Britain
on acid-free paper by
Biddles Ltd., Guildford and King's Lynn

For Jeanne

Contents

Introduction

One out of every five people in the world is a Muslim. To some degree each of them is emotionally, morally, or administratively attached to Islamic law. The sacred law, the shari'a, is, of course, meant as an overarching guide to everyday conduct, a way that will lead the believer to the benefits accorded by Allah, an idea bound up even in the earliest meaning of the Arabic term as 'a path leading to a source of water.' Islamic law summarizes the ethos of the faith, the standards of specific conduct, and the practical implications of its own promise.

But Islamic law is also a living system of everyday adjudication. Indeed, its qualities as a moral code, a field of abstract theological investigation, and a process of addressing the relationships and conflicts that may arise among the faithful are not fully separable. However much the different faces of the shari'a may, at times, take on institutional distinctiveness or doctrinal individuality, common features run through all of its manifestations—and through the societies and cultures of which they are a part. It is these common threads—repeated, interwoven, reinforcing—that will, in a similar fashion, describe and link each of the chapters in this book.

To many Westerners the image of Islamic law is often that of the enforcement arm of a strict system of acceptable behavior, the remnant of a once encompassing system of regulation whose scope has been reduced to the domain of the familial by nations bent on modernization through adoption of foreign codes, or the theological musings of scholars whose doctrines bear little relation to law as a system of actual adjudication. To some extent each of these conclusions is understandable: Fundamentalists have tried to use the sacred law as a vehicle for asserting both authenticity and control; Western codes have significantly displaced precursor laws in the commercial, penal, and civil domains of many Arab states, the influence on family matters remaining widely variant; and the doctors of Islamic law have a long history of separating the chair from the bench (and both from the throne), giving great care to issues that might never arise in practice or emphasizing the literary form, rather than the practical import, of their readings of sacred texts. But as with many such views of highly developed systems of theology and law, projections from the West, coupled with the sociology of Western knowledge itself, have sometimes obscured deeper connections and more ramified implications.

Islamic law, in all its manifestations, is intimately entwined with other portions of Islamic culture and society. Such a position is, of course, virtually a given for an anthropologist, for it is at the heart of our enterprise to assert that the different domains of a people's life always have some bearing on one another, and that a significant portion of the force that a cultural system has in convincing its adherents of its truth lies precisely in its being replicated in so many domains that its precepts and directions appear both immanent and natural. From this perspective, one is, therefore, necessarily led to explore connections across the lines some disciplines have reified. Thus, in the study of Islamic law it is central to our present concerns to consider how law is connected to various social practices, how cultural assumptions suffuse the law and give it legitimacy, how attachments that may not seem obvious reveal themselves when any feature is followed to its next set of entanglements. In doing so, three themes begin to emerge: that Islamic law is not simply a matter of substantive rules or moral musings, but part of a cultural process that becomes more evident the more we seek its reverberations in related domains; that only by taking a comparative approach can we see what sort of process this is and how its distinctively Islamic aspects are given expression; and that as we traverse a series of substantive issues the sheer vitality of law as a contributor to this cultural process furnishes us with an excellent entrée to the wider understanding of Islamic cultures past and present.

These themes will continue to cross-cut each of the separate topics of the present work thus forming the fundamental framework of which each is intended as a specific exemplification. The chapters in Part 1 explore the social and cultural logic of Islamic law, first by seeing how judicial discretion—that 'qadi justice' made famous to the West by colonizers and comparativists—actually partakes of standards found in the larger domains of culture and legal reasoning. Indeed, the reasoning style is one in which cases are explored for the consequences that the actions of the litigants may have for the larger society. As each litigant is seen as a socially constructed person the system as a whole displays the characteristic features of a common law system of legal reasoning—one in which a moving system of classifying concepts (in this case of 'persons' rather than 'facts') becomes the focus of judicial attention. When one looks at Islamic law in this fashion one is, moreover, moved to rethink the whole taxonomy of legal systems and to recon-ceptualize the criteria on which such a classificatory scheme may be composed. Islamic law thus becomes the basis, as well as the subject, for reconsidering the whole comparative law project. Similarly, Islamic law approaches to responsibility and compensation for injury demonstrate not only the emphasis on the situated person, so crucial to an understanding of cultural orientations in the Arab world generally, but how a style of legal reasoning connects everyday cultural assump-tions through their legal articulation.

The law, however conceived, is no more restricted to courts than it is to docu-ments, and the chapters in Part 2 move us in and out of the courts, tracing implica-tions of courtroom and courtyard on one another. Here we see that 'custom' for the contemporary Muslim—and probably throughout Islamic history—is not some-thing completely separated from law. To the contrary, so long as fundamental Quranic precepts are not violated, local practice is seen as itself Islamic, an orienta-tion that is vital to the emphasis in Islamic law on the local articulation of the accept-able. By reviewing changes in the docket and courtroom practice of a single Moroccan court over the past thirty years one can, moreover, see precisely how social standards precipitating courtroom battles have altered and how the courts have changed as the surrounding society has changed. Then, by looking in detail at an alternative court set up by the Moroccan government, where no specific body of law is operative and cases are meant to be handled quickly according to local standards, the features that connect the regular courts to society are highlighted by the new courts' failure to satisfy popular ideas about appropriate legal process. Indeed, how people structure their trust in one another becomes the issue of the final chapter in this section, precisely because the regularization of obligation has a profound effect on the peaceful relationships or potential litigation that may move in and out of the courts for years to come.

Part 3 takes the focus back and forth across time as well as space. One of the benefits of studying contemporary Islamic courts is that one can look back at the documentary evidence for earlier times and try to fill in some of the blanks by careful interpolation rather than mere projection or speculation. The ways in which Muslims articulate their sense of justice and injustice over time is especially important here. The argument is put forth that justice in Islamic cultures does not mean equality but equivalence, and that it is precisely in formulating equivalencies that the larger cultural context is revealed. Although many scholars have argued that Islamic law was only formed a century or more after the Prophet's death, it can be suggested that in fact the Prophet did have a well-developed jurisprudential theory—what I call a sociological jurisprudence—fully informed by a vision of what human interaction was like and what criteria should be applied to address its consequences. These features show themselves as well when we look at the specific instance of tolerance for various forms of speech. There we can see that within Islamic cultures the key axis is not that of liberty or constraint, but the relation of the private to the public, an emphasis that, once again, recalls the importance of seeing how law and culture mutually assist one another in the conceptualization of what people and social relationships are really like. To see, finally, how the courts of the United States, faced with a religion at once familiar and distant, are testing and being modified by the cases involving Muslims that are increasingly appearing before them is to see how two cultures' assumptions interact and how each can form a test case for the analyst of some of the most central features of a cultural system.

The study of Islamic law is intrinsically comparative. Spanning numerous centuries and cultures, the shape and alteration of Islamic law is, whatever its shared theological underpinnings, remarkably variant. Most of the research on which this book is based has been conducted over several decades in Morocco, with additional work in Tunisia and Malaysia. No single place or time can stand for all instances, but it will form a not insignificant part of the thesis of this book that, using both fieldwork and documentary sources, one can indeed speak of themes and variations in Islamic law, gaining in one's understanding of the particular from one's understanding of the range of variation of the similar. The more we understand this practical variation the more we are challenged to explore the reciprocal relation of a universalizing law and its local manifestations. And the more Islamic law is drawn upon for comparative studies—in anthropology, law, and Oriental scholarship—the more we learn to see aspects of the particular that may have escaped notice and to apply this most fascinating of instances to our broader understanding of the nature of legal and cultural forms.

I have built up numerous debts over the years to those who have encouraged and supported my research. The Moroccan Ministry of Justice and the judges, administrators, and office staff of the many courts in which I have worked have been most generous in their permissions and their assistance. So, too, as regards various government ministries and research institutes: The Fulbright Program in Morocco, CERES in Tunisia, and MACEE in Malaysia. Conversations over the years with Taoufik Agoumy, Mustafa Benyakhlef, Yaghnik Driss, Abdellah Hammoudi, and Muhammad Zwitun have greatly enriched my understanding of North African law and culture. As an adjunct professor of law at Columbia Law School, and a visiting professor at the law schools of the University of Pennsylvania, Northwestern, and Georgetown Universities, I have had the benefit of students and colleagues whose knowledge of Western law has added immeasurably to my comparative project. I have received helpful comments over the years from lecture audiences at the European University Institute (Florence), the Center for Advanced Study in the Behavioral Sciences (Palo Alto), the French and Dutch Research Institutes in Cairo, and the Universities of Michigan, Birmingham, Cardiff, and the Aegean. I also benefited greatly from the audiences who discussed portions of several chapters during my tenure as a Phi Beta Kappa Visiting Lecturer. I am grateful for generous support at various stages of my work from Princeton University, the National Science Foundation, the Fulbright Program, and the John D. and Catherine T. MacArthur Foundation, as well as to the Masters and Fellows of Wolfson College, Oxford, and Corpus Christi College, Cambridge, where various portions of the manuscript were written. My colleagues Clifford Geertz, Hildred Geertz, and Avram Udovitch, along with Baber Johansen and David Powers, continue to enhance my understanding of Morocco and Islamic law, and I am delighted to remain so much in their debt. Much as I should like to blame others for any shortcomings in this book, I cannot very well write about responsibility and intention, much less custom and justice, without accepting all such culpability as my own.

Several of the chapters have been significantly revised since their appearance in earlier publications, and are reprinted here by agreement with the initial publishers. Portions of Chapter 1 were published in Rosen (1980–1); Chapter 2 in Rosen (1989b); Chapter 3 in Rosen (1996) and Rosen (1998); Chapter 4 in Rosen (1989c); Chapter 5 in Rosen (1995d); Chapter 6 in Rosen (1997); Chapter 9 in Rosen (1995c) and Rosen (1995b); and Chapter 12 in Rosen (2000). Many of the arguments are intimately connected to my interpretation of Moroccan society and law, as developed in Rosen (1984) and Rosen (1989), to which readers may wish to turn for both broader and more particular development of issues raised in these chapters.

Finally, it should be noted that Arabic spellings, with allowance for Moroccan dialect where appropriate, broadly follow the system used by Hans Wehr in *A Dictionary of Modern Written Arabic*, with some significant modifications: ǰ will be

<u>sh</u>, <u>k</u> will be <u>kh</u>, and <u>ḡ</u> will be <u>gh</u>, <u>t</u> will be <u>th</u>, and <u>d</u> will be <u>dh</u>. Each term will be transcribed with full diacritics only the first time it appears in the text. Terms that have gained currency in English, such as Quran, qadi and shari'a, will be presented in recognizable spellings rather than with precise Arabic diacritics. The index will also serve as a glossary inasmuch as a brief translation of each term is indicated while the number in bold type will direct attention to the place in the text where the term is most fully defined.

L.R.

Part 1

The socio-logic of Islamic legal reasoning

1

Equity and discretion in Islamic law

In Terminiello v. Chicago, Mr Justice Frankfurter, commenting on the United States Supreme Court, said: 'This is a court of review, not a tribunal unbounded by rules. We do not sit like a kadi under a tree dispensing justice according to considerations of individual expediency.'[1] For Justice Frankfurter, as for many others, the image of the Islamic law judge, the qadi, is often that of a man sitting barefoot and turbaned under a tree or in the corner of a mosque dispensing justice off the top of his head. Even Max Weber, who appreciated that actual Islamic adjudication was neither capricious nor unrestrained, chose the term Kadijustiz *to refer to a type of legal system in which judges have recourse to a general set of ethical precepts unevenly employed on a case-by-case basis rather than to a series of rules abstractly formulated and uniformly applied.[2] Although the traditional role of the qadi has been greatly altered by the introduction of Western codes and the development of bureaucratic structures, the quest in many Muslim countries for an authentically Islamic way of life has given renewed emphasis to classic precepts of Islamic jurisprudence. It is important, therefore, to appreciate that, far from being arbitrary or unsystematic, qadi justice partakes of regularities that not only run through the course of Islamic legal history but also reveal the interplay of Islamic law and the societies in which it is rooted.*

Justice Frankfurter's statement, however, points up more than the limitations in our understanding of contemporary Islamic adjudication: It also raises fundamental questions about the nature of discretion and equity within a given legal tradition. Notwithstanding the existence of a body of legal rules or acceptable judicial procedures, the qadi, like his colleagues elsewhere, is often called upon to give substantive content to principles that cannot be mechanically implemented. How, under such circumstances, is the judge to define what shall for purposes of adjudication be regarded as a fact? By what means is he (or, in the Moroccan case, sometimes she) to choose among competing solutions? In what way is he to render a decision when the proper justification for his action is not immediately apparent from prior cases or guidelines? And where shall he turn for help when confronted with a situation in which rules, principles, or doctrines of law, if strictly applied, would lead to a result which seems contrary to his own comprehension of what is fair or just for all concerned?

Faced with these problems of equity and discretion, the Islamic judge finds considerable guidance in the precepts, procedures, and forms of judicial reasoning that have shaped the tradition within which he works. But this tradition, from its most settled rules to its most idiosyncratic decisions, is deeply suffused by a set of assumptions and concepts that have currency and implications in the wider cultural context. Thus, in his assumptions about human nature and social relationships, in his comprehension of the role of

---

[1] United States Supreme Court (1949: 11).
[2] Weber (1954: 351). See generally Turner (1974: 107–21) and Powers (1994).

language and social discourse, and in his perception of recognizable modes of rational decision-making, the qadi is affected not only by substantive and procedural elements distinctive to Islamic legal thought but also by a set of cultural propositions that render his actions comprehensible, if not universally acceptable, to the society he serves.

Admittedly, within the expansive realm of Islamic law, no single court or local tradition can fully represent all instances. In order to show how the justice of the qadi may be at once institutionally distinctive and culturally characteristic—how, in short, law is suffused by culture and culture is integral to law—the close analysis of a particular jurisdiction may prove most illuminating. The present study will, therefore, focus on the qadi's court in the Moroccan city of Sefrou and its surrounding countryside. In this ancient city of 70,000 people lying just south of Fez, and in the portion of the hinterland of the Middle Atlas Mountains that it serves, one can see themes that have analogs throughout the Islamic world while gaining an appreciation of the way qadi justice is embedded in local society and culture.

FACTUAL DETERMINATIONS AND LEGAL REASONING: THE NEXUS OF
LAW AND CULTURE

'It is a feature of the human predicament,' says H. L. A. Hart, 'that we labour under two connected handicaps whenever we seek to regulate, unambiguously and in advance, some sphere of conduct by means of general standards. . . . The first handicap is our relative ignorance of fact; the second is our relative indeterminacy of aim.'[3] For the qadi, no less than for judges elsewhere, the dual predicament of factual assessment and purposeful adjudication turns, initially, on the way in which an issue is framed for judicial consideration, the procedures available for assessing proffered facts, and the acceptable style of judicial reasoning and justification.

A. Pleading and proof: the social construction of a legal case

In Morocco, the litigants and lower court personnel are primarily responsible for framing an issue for decision. The petitioner's complaint, whether made out by the court clerk, a public scribe, or the plaintiff, must set forth the nature of the case, the identity of the defendant, and the precise remedy sought. If the complaint lies within the subject-matter jurisdiction of the qadi—presently limited to those matters covered by the Code of Personal Status[4] (marriage, divorce, filiation, inheritance,

---

[3] Hart (1961: 125).

[4] The Code was first adopted in 1958: It has received some minor, but not insignificant changes, most recently in 1993. The Arabic and French versions of the revised Code (*Mudawwana*) are available in Royaume du Maroc (1993). The Arabic text of the unrevised Code, together with an occasionally misleading French version, is available in Colomer (1963) and Colomer (1967). Portions of the unrevised Code also appear in English in Mahmood (1972). For analyses of the original Code, see Anderson (1958); Borrmans (1977); Lapanne-Joinville (1959); and Gallagher (1959). On the 1993 revisions, see Essaid (1998: 101–6), and Khachani (1998).

child custody), civil suits for which the amount in controversy does not exceed the statutory limit, or issues involving documents signed by the court notaries—the case will be listed on the court docket. The central concern for court and litigant alike will, however, be the construction of appropriate evidence. Here, the nature of persuasive evidence, the role of the court notaries, and the cultural creation of binding assertions become vital.

In a sense, all evidence that comes before the court, regardless of its form, is treated as if it were oral in nature. From the point of view of classical Islamic legal theory, documents are regarded simply as written reminders of individual witnesses' statements, reminders that will serve to recall their testimony in any future dispute.[5] In actual practice this theory has long since given way to the use of documents as sufficient in themselves for purposes of evidentiary presentation.[6] Nevertheless, the qadis' courts in Morocco still tend to scrutinize documents for probative value in terms of the courts' perception of the nature of oral assertions and to consider documents, regardless of the literacy of those involved, as embodying and supplementing that which has been uttered before appropriate court personnel.

The most persuasive evidence a litigant can produce on trial is a document signed by two notaries that supports the litigant's factual claim. However, such a document is regarded as simply the reduction to writing of oral evidence presented to the notaries. Thus, in a marriage contract or a deed—the two kinds of documents that appear most frequently in litigation—the notaries merely inscribe the terms that have been orally presented to them by the parties involved. While the notaries may refuse to certify a relationship which is contrary to law—for example, a marriage contract lacking some transfer of wealth from the groom to the bride or her marital guardian, or a business agreement for an illicit purpose—it is less in their control over the content of such documents than in the form of validation supplied by such a document that the importance of the notarization process lies.[7] To appreciate this point one must understand the nature of binding obligations in the structure of Moroccan social life.[8]

To many Westerners, Moroccan society appears reassuringly exotic and disconcertingly familiar. That women should appear veiled in public, that an ancient walled city should enclose a featureless maze of byways and blind alleys, that the marketplace should be a cacophony of hawking and haggling is somehow more easily comprehended simply for being so different. More troubling, because superficially more recognizable, is the schema of social relationships. Notwithstanding references to tribe or urban quarter, genealogy or religious brotherhood, Moroccan society is

[5] Schacht (1964: 193). See also, Brunschvig (1960b) and Linant de Bellefonds (1965: 130).
[6] Cf. Wakin (1972).
[7] By telling potential litigants that their case is of dubious merit, notaries may significantly affect the kinds of cases that come before the court. For an example of a notary discouraging litigation, see Wigmore (1936: 587).
[8] The following analysis of Moroccan society is developed more fully in Geertz et al. (1979), Rosen (1984); and Rosen (1989a).

not built up of a series of corporate groups membership of which alone might define one's place in society or one's expectable behavior. Quite the contrary, Moroccan society evokes a sense of the familiar by being constructed of a series of interpersonal ties, freely negotiated and highly expedient, which center on each individual. Associations of residence or kinship, identities of interest and occupation, affiliations of friendship and common experience constitute not a binding set of relationships but a repertoire of relational possibilities to be drawn upon in the formation of a personal network of relations. But whereas the individualism and instrumentalism of this social organization strike a recognizable chord for many Westerners, the nature and implications of the ways in which such ties are conceptualized and formed make easy identity more elusive. For at the heart of Moroccan personal ties are a series of unapparent assumptions about the order and meaning of social life, assumptions that deeply affect the course and content of judicial decision making.

For Moroccans, every relationship implies an obligation. To be related in a particular degree of kinship, to be another's neighbor, to be the client of a merchant in the bazaar carries with it certain idealized expectations of mutual aid and potential recompense. Of crucial importance, however, is the fact that the specific content, the meaning, of each of these relationships is highly negotiable. Even within a family, for example, one can choose to have closer economic and political ties with some individuals than with others, or with outsiders than with family members. It is, however, clearly understood that every action one takes creates an obligation in the other, and the key to the formation of a network of personal ties, as well as to a sense of how others are most likely to act toward oneself, is to organize and learn about such obligations in the most effective way possible. This sense of mutual ingratiation and indebtedness is broadly subsumed by Moroccans under the central Arabic concept of *ḥaqq*.

The term haqq has a variety of interconnected meanings.[9] It means 'right,' 'duty,' 'truth,' 'reality,' and 'obligation.' In one context it can mean 'you are right,' in another, 'you are wrong.' Al-Haqq is one of the ninety-nine names of Allah known to man. (The hundredth, it is said, is known but to the camel, hence his enigmatic smile!) To speak of haqq is, in short, to convey that sense of mutual obligations which bind men to men, and man to God. What is 'true' or 'real' is the web of indebtedness that links sentient beings to one another in a chain of obligations. But since each obligation, of kinship or contract, residence or political aim, is itself subject to negotiation, and since each obligation formed may be fulfilled in a variety of reciprocating forms, each Moroccan must try to get his or her definition of a situation—as implying some specific form of obligation—to prevail. In this highly flexible and manipulable system, this running imbalance of one-upmanship and ingratiation, one tries to add a degree of certainty by employing some of the recognized social conventions through which particular ties may be given more concrete definition and networks of affiliation an air of predictability.

---

[9]   See Rosen (1984: 60–70); Macdonald and Calverley (1971: 126).

Thus, one might make a form of ritual sacrifice (*'ār*) the doorway of a particular individual or at the threshold of a saintly shrine, a form of ingratiation which implies that failure to fulfill the request may call forth supernatural sanction. Or one may seek out an intermediary who, because of his own network of ties, can act as an agent for one's present request. One can bargain over the applicable term to characterize a given bond—as a tie among close kinsmen, or as a pact between neighboring tribes—in an attempt to make the broader ideals of these affiliations govern the relationship and its forms of reciprocation. Whether it is in the request to a dependant for a woman in marriage or for help in contacting a government official, the governing factors are the terms by which action will proceed, the knowledge that an obligation formed for one purpose can be called up for quite another, and the recognition that all men and women are bound up in such personal and ephemeral webs of indebtedness.

But if such obligations are indeed so flexible and changing, how are people to gain a sense of order in their relationships and how is a court of law to recognize a binding tie of a particular sort to which judicial sanction may be applied? The answer, of course, lies in the conventions by which particular obligations are given a degree of fixity in ordinary social life and in a series of mechanisms, consonant with social practice, by which the courts can give concrete meaning to such a bond. If two litigants disagree over their perception of the sort of tie they have indeed negotiated, the court, like the participants, will look to the social conventions characterizing their relation and to the means by which their bond may be said to have taken on concrete obligations. In doing so the court will be mindful of the central importance of language in defining relationships in Morocco.

For Moroccans, no utterance can by itself create a binding obligation. Indeed, because individuals constantly try to get a relationship defined in a personally convenient way, it is well understood that where relationships of obligation are being formed, mere utterances imply nothing about the truth of the thing asserted.[10] For one man to say that his bond to another incorporates a mutual right and duty does not of itself convey any implication of its truth. What is crucial is that his assertion be validated. Here certain social conventions come into play. An assertion may be validated by formal agreement in front of others, by virtue of specific actions by both parties to demonstrate the particular meaning of their statements, or by means of one or both taking an oath. In a sense, therefore, mutual expressions mean nothing until something more has happened—until the haqq, in the sense of 'obligation,' has been sufficiently validated to render it capable of being assessed as 'true' or 'real.'

One of the primary mechanisms for validating assertions is having some individual who is in a position to do so verify such utterances. In ordinary social relations this may, for example, involve the use of a go-between who, because of his domi-

---

[10] I am indebted to Clifford Geertz for drawing my attention to this issue. See, Rosen (1984: 117–33). For data supporting the assertion, see Bourgeoise (1959–60: fascicule no. 3, 80); and the discussion of truth in Crapanzano (1980: 80–1).

nance in the network of obligations he possesses to both parties, will be regarded by them and others as a guarantor of the facts asserted. In other domains, this role is more formalized. Thus, in the marketplace most occupational groupings choose one individual, called the *amīn* who because of his knowledge and the respect of his colleagues, acts as the articulator of acceptable standards and the verifier of commercial relationships. Overseeing the market as a whole stands another official (the *muḥtasseb*) who, like the amin, acts both as a regulator of market practice and a person who may be called upon to give acknowledged credence to what he has heard or seen.

It is in the broader context of seeking individuals who may validate actions and statements that the role of the notaries and other court officials is to be understood. The Arabic term for notaries, *'adūl,* from a root meaning 'just' or 'equitable,' has been wisely translated by Tyan as 'reliable witness.'[11] For when a document has been signed by the requisite pair of notaries, they are really doing in the realm of the law what is sought, though not always with such formality, in other relationships: They are adding their stature, their word, as reliable witnesses to a bond that only takes on implications of truth, of interrelationship, by virtue of having received some form of validation. Along with court-appointed experts, who possess special knowledge on such diverse topics as construction, boundaries, or pregnancy, the notaries perform an indispensable function for the qadi: They create things as 'facts' in order that they may be judicially recognized as facts.

There is, however, quite a range of documents a litigant may obtain from the notaries in order to make the oral testimony embodied by these documents more persuasive. Consonant with the emphasis on face-to-face evaluations of testimony, a litigant will often try to support his claim by having three, or preferably twelve, eligible witnesses come before two notaries and give testimony in support of the litigant's claims. The resultant document (called a *teleqiya,* if at least three witnesses testify; a *lafīf,* if twelve or more do so) may be given still greater force by having each witness appear before two separate pairs of notaries. If the testimony of all witnesses remains consistent, the notaries will certify this in a document called a *stifsār* (Cl. Ar. *istifsār*). This practice bears some similarities to the custom of co-swearing among the Berbers, in which a man chosen by the plaintiff swears to the truthfulness of the defendant's assertions, and an additional ten men add their voices in support of the reliability of the lead oath-taker.[12] To paraphrase Aeschylus, perhaps in this instance it is not the oath that makes the man believable, but the man the oath. The use of group witnessing in the qadi's court, however, is directed toward the question of actual occurrences rather than character, and the court will subject even the testimony sworn separately before two sets of notaries to rational scrutiny. The unpublished case of Hussaini v.

---

[11] Tyan (1960: 239). On the notarization process generally, see Tyan (1945). On the related role of experts, see Dwyer (1977).
[12] See Brunschvig (1963: 180); Milliot (1953: 737).

Alahami, dating from 1965 and involving the presentation of documents by both sides, will help illustrate this point.[13]

(4 March 1965: Complaint) The plaintiff claims that his wife, the defendant, left their home five months ago and that although he has sent members of their tribe to request her return she has refused to come back. He wants the court to make her return.

(13 July 1965) The defendant's father, appearing as his daughter's legal representative, says that the plaintiff divorced his wife seven months ago, and he presents a document in which fifty people testify to this effect. The document was not made out before notaries. The plaintiff denies having divorced his wife and says the defendant's witnesses are ineligible because they are all her close relatives. The qadi says that if the plaintiff wishes to contest the testimony of the witnesses he may request that they submit to a stifsar examination.

(26 October 1965) The qadi states that a valid divorce must be conducted before notaries. Article 48 of the Code says that if there are witnesses to a divorce that is said to have occurred in the absence of notaries this testimony must itself be notarized. Since the defendant has not produced a stifsar, judgment must be entered for the plaintiff. Pending the introduction of any new evidence on appeal, the defendant must return to her husband.

(19 July 1966: Before the Appellate Court) Two documents are presented. The defendant presents a notarized document in which twelve witnesses state that they know the couple were married for a little over one year, after which the husband repudiated his wife. The second document, presented by the plaintiff, contains the notarized testimony of twelve witnesses who state that the couple have been married for four years, that a brideprice of 750 dirhams was paid at the time of the marriage, and that all of the witnesses were present at the wedding and took part in the festivities. They further assert that at no time has the plaintiff divorced his wife.

The appellate court, reviewing the documents, rules that whereas all of the plaintiff's witnesses come from the settlement in which he and his wife lived, while those of the defendant live some distance away, and whereas it is more likely that those living in the same village would know if a divorce had been uttered, the ruling of the qadi is upheld. The woman must return to her husband's home, be a good wife, and pay court costs.

Confronted with two sets of witnesses, the court chose to assume that those living

---

[13] Sefrou, Morocco Qadi's Court, Dossier No. 1965/65. Cases from the qadi's court in Sefrou are not published. The citation system employed here is the same as that used by the court itself: The year litigation began is indicated to the left of the stroke, the docket number to the right. As presented here, the cases are summaries rather than verbatim translations of the records. Occasionally, cases from different levels of the judicial hierarchy have appeared in the *Révue Algérienne, Tunisienne, et Marocaine de Legislation et de Jurisprudence*, the *Révue Marocaine de Droit*, the *Révue Juridique, Politique et Economique du Maroc*, and *L'Actualité Juridique*. A unique collection of cases from the Protectorate period will be found in Milliot (1920); Milliot (1924); and Milliot and Lapanne-Joinville (1952). For a full translation of a case drawn from the Milliot collection, see Wigmore (1936: 593–614). Examples of various notarized documents can also be found in Zeys and Said (1946).

in the same settlement as the couple were more likely than those living at some distance to know the actual state of their relationship. But this was not the only assumption at work. Officials in the qadi's court told me that in a case like this the burden of proof is largely placed on the wife. Obviously, they argued, the husband is eager to live with his wife or he would exercise his legally recognized right to divorce her unilaterally. And since no charges of mistreatment were made, the qadi might well suspect that the wife's family had played a significant role in creating the dispute. Moreover, they said, it was unlikely that the husband was holding out for a settlement in which he would receive some consideration for divorcing his wife, since he was willing to expend a good deal of time and money litigating his claim. Whatever the merits of these arguments, they demonstrate the kinds of cultural assumptions and legal presumptions that shape the qadi's discretionary powers.

The testimony of the litigants and their witnesses, as well as the notarized documents they introduce, may be totally contradictory. Or there may simply be no evidence on either side to support the parties' assertions. In such a situation the court has the power to require that one or both of the litigants support his or her claims with a holy oath. The oath itself has no set form and may be taken anywhere, although most commonly it is taken in the presence of two notaries at a mosque, a saintly shrine, or in the lodge of a religious brotherhood.[14]

The most interesting feature of these oaths, however, is the apportionment of the burden of swearing and the legal presumptions that accompany its use.[15] The burden of oath-taking is not consistently placed on either the plaintiff or the defendant in the case, and indeed the burden may shift within any one proceeding, depending on the subject matter involved in the oath. The standard procedure is for the plaintiff or the court to demand that the defendant take the oath, swearing, for example, that he did not take any of his wife's belongings with him upon their divorce. If the defendant takes the oath, he or she will be presumed innocent. If, however, the defendant refuses to swear, the plaintiff must take the oath; and if the latter does so, the case will be awarded to him or her. Should both parties take oaths—and only one such case has been found in the records of the Sefrou court—the qadi will dismiss the suit outright. The roles of plaintiff and defendant in this sequence may, however, be reversed when the matter involves an object of knowledge that the court regards as more likely to lie within the competence or control of only one of the parties involved. Thus, if a wife claims that her husband took something that would normally belong to a woman and it is she who is the plaintiff in the case, the burden of oath-taking will fall first to her and to her husband only if she refuses.

[14]   See generally, Westermarck (1926: 493–505, 564–9), where it is noted that both oaths and solemn promises usually begin with the word haqq.

[15]   On the importance of oaths in Islamic society, see Mottahedeh (1980: 42–52). On the order of oath-taking in various Islamic jurisdictions and periods, see Berque (1944: 24); Brunschvig (1963: 177–80; Jennings (1979); Kellal (1958); Liebesny (1975: 243–54); Chraa (1956); and Westermarck (1926: 510). Agmon (1999) also describes a similar pattern of distributing the burden of proof in Ottoman-period courts. It is interesting to note, incidentally, that in American law as well it is established doctrine that in civil cases the party that has control of the facts has the burden of proof.

The importance of all this is related to the power that the oaths themselves are believed to contain. For the overwhelming majority of people in the Sefrou region I have interviewed there is a real fear that a false oath will result in harsh supernatural punishment, and it is not at all unusual for an individual to maintain a particular testimony right up to the moment of oath-taking and then to stop, refuse the oath, and surrender the case. Even the fear of mistakenly swearing what the person thinks is true but about which he possesses some slight doubt may prevent an innocent party from taking the oath. Thus the presumptions and the order of oath-taking may, in certain circumstances, be the deciding factor in the case.

For present purposes, however, the point that bears stressing is simply that while the qadi may exercise some discretion in the matter, oath-taking itself places a significant limitation on the extent to which the qadi will have to rely on his personal judgment in deciding cases where no clear line of evidence has been established. Custom—and in a few instances the Code of Personal Status (e.g., Article 39)—indicates the order of swearing and the nature of the presumptions involved. But as a release from the burden of adjudication and as a limitation on fact-finding procedures, the oath is a vital factor in confining and structuring the procedural and evidentiary discretion of the Moroccan religious lawcourt judge.

B. Inquiry and procedure: the case in court

Once a complaint has been filed and any pre-trial documents acquired, the case is brought before the qadi. The following description, derived from notes taken during a visit to the qadi's court in Sefrou, will give some flavor of the proceeding.

The qadi's court meets in a long narrow room at the side of the city hall. The qadi, a clerk by his side, sits behind an expansive desk at one end of the room while litigants mill about in a courtyard just beyond the door at the other end. A uniformed aide ushers parties in as their case is called. This aide serves as a translator for Berbers who cannot understand the qadi's Arabic and as a monitor of courtroom order, although his embellishment of the court's inquiries and his patronizing choreography of litigants lends an air of self-aggrandizement to these otherwise modest tasks. The qadi first determines who is who and how, if at all, they are related to one another. His first substantive question is usually the signal for the shouting to begin. The parties begin by talking to the qadi but often end by addressing the aide, the clerk, others crowded into the courtroom, and even the stray anthropologist. The qadi mutters, nods, and questions; the principals sit, stand, shout, and cry; the aide tries to quiet people by pinning down their hands, in the certain knowledge that no Moroccan can speak if his hands are not free; and the clerk rushes to finish writing up the last case and find the correct dossier for the present one. Eventually one person gets to tell a more or less coherent story, and women no less than men speak with great verve and style. Most cases are treated very rapidly. In one case a woman and her son appeared before the qadi. The woman, quite old and sick, claimed that her husband—the man's father—left her some land when he died and that she later sold it to her son with the understanding that a share of the income from its use would be given her as support. There were no witnesses or documents to support her claim. The woman kept interrupting her son as he denied that any support agreement was attached to the land sale. The woman kept trying to swear that what she said was true, but the qadi cut her off and summarily ordered the man to pay some 40 dirhams (about 8 dollars) per month in support. Turning to the clerk, the qadi said that the father would certainly not have wanted his wife to be dispossessed by the son. The aide shouted out the qadi's judgment almost before the latter had finished and, with the litigants still shouting, hustled mother and son out of the courtroom in one great sweeping motion.

Almost twenty cases were heard in the two-hour court session—cases of inheritance and divorce predominating—and in each instance the qadi seemed most concerned with the relationships of the parties, the documents they presented, and only rarely with a detailed examination of the elaborate arguments each person seemed eager to present. Little deference was shown to the qadi, and the style of discourse reminded one of the public marketplace or a neighborhood dispute more than the forum of a high religious and legal official.

Throughout this seemingly chaotic proceeding there runs both method and purpose. Qadis in Sefrou, as well as in other parts of the country, are intent on determining certain basic factors about the people who come before them and initially give them wide latitude in arguing their case. Social background is especially important, and its relevance to judicial decision making is not unrelated to its role in general social interaction. The constant focus in Moroccan society is on the individual as the locus of a series of distinctive ties of obligation. Each of the social traits the individual possesses—place of origin, kin connections, residence, and occupation—contributes both to the repertoire he or she may draw upon in establishing a network and to the series of traits which others may use to predict his or her most likely affiliations, customary ways of forming ties to others, and the probable course and consequences of any relationship with the interlocutor. The extent to which any relationship may be governed by the stereotype of a person as Berber or Arab, townsman or countryman, member of a given tribal faction or practitioner of a given trade will vary with the situation and the parties. But this information is invariably regarded as useful to the overall assessment of one individual by another. For the qadi, the relevance of this information goes not to the question of any potential tie of his own to the litigant but to two related points. First, such information is taken as an indicator of a person's most likely ways of acting in any situation. To comprehend who someone is, say qadis, is to know what he may have done. And second, it is assumed that, within certain broad limits, it is only fair to gauge the standard of conduct to which an individual should be held according to what sort of person he is. To hold an educated man to the same standards as one who is unlettered, or a woman to the same standards as a man, would, most qadis insist, be grossly unjust.[16]

---

[16] On the relation between social position and duty, see Yamani (1968: 17). On the role of character evidence in Moroccan criminal proceedings, see Morère (1961).

Just as in ordinary social life the constant focus is on what a person does and the range of relationships it affects, so in the judicial context it is through an assessment of the consequences of one's actions, measured against the traits and ties by which one is identified, that the qadi gains insight into the claims and actors before him.

Awareness of a critical feature of personal identity, therefore, leads to a series of cultural implications which, for all their variation within the society and across time, provide a code for the assessment of both character and action. It is broadly assumed, for example, that women are more likely to be guided by passion and men by reason, that these motivating forces structure one's knowledge of the world, that knowledge is what sets one person's social stature above that of another, that stature is broadly related to particular types of obligational networks, and that interrelationships of various kinds entail qualities of social responsibility and harm on which the evaluation of social and legal repercussions may be based. The locus of these implications resides in neither a set of roles nor institutions, but in the individual as a concatenation of traits and ties, and hence this implicational code operates as both a cultural guide and a malleable gauge. Faced with the task of interpreting motives and acts, however, the code of cultural entailment becomes a tool of major significance in the qadi's determination of facts and choice of legal remedies.

That there exists, in the qadi's perception and evaluation of others, considerable scope for discrimination and injustice is a point not lost on many Moroccans. Yet the line of inquiry the qadi follows is so similar and the data he appears to seek so familiar from everyday life that approbation for his way of proceeding broadly outweighs criticism of particular results. This point is brought home both in the style of discourse between judge and witness and in the characterization of wise adjudication.

We noted earlier the importance of validating assertions in Moroccan life and the institutionalization of this process in the role of the notaries. The style of questioning and the modes of response often follow a common pattern. After his initial inquiry into social background, the qadi will ask the plaintiff to tell his story. Almost invariably, the plaintiff will be interrupted midway by the defendant, and both parties will begin to argue with one another. When asked, most qadis say that they want to see the two parties interact and want to gauge the intensity of their attachment to the issue. Moreover, the qadi is trying to determine how widely or narrowly to set the bounds of relevance in the case. If, for example, a woman has run away from her husband in part as the culmination of a property dispute between two kin groups, the qadi may or may not take this into consideration in his decision. His discretion in this matter is limited by the specific rules of the Code—for example, a runaway wife must return to her husband unless severely mistreated and then file a separate suit seeking his proper behavior—but the boundaries he sets may also be influenced by his perception of how people of the sort before him are expected by him to comport themselves. Thus he may simply chide an unlettered country woman for running away but seek out the full nature of an educated urbanite's dispute while reminding him of the example he should set.

Often, too, a litigant will use a style of argument common to the broader social process of validating assertions. To get another to accept one's own definition of a situation, it is common to engage the other in a kind of Socratic dialogue in which a set of questions is posed to which the other is forced to respond on a yes or no basis. In court, litigants will often use this style with the judge. Accused of beating his wife, a man may say to the judge, 'Is she not a woman? Doesn't the Quran say a man is the "governor" of a woman? Is it not shameful for a woman to say these things to a man?' At each point he seeks to get the qadi to affirm his statement in the presence of others, just as he might in his ordinary social discourse.

In short, for the qadi the 'facts' are estimations of character, assumed by social background and displayed by courtroom encounter, as much as they are weighings, based on related considerations, of the notarized documents presented. It is interesting in this regard to note that when stories are told of really clever qadis they often involve the qadi trapping one of the parties in a display of his true character. Thus, a story may be recounted of how, as recently as the 1940s, a qadi disguised himself and entrapped the person in a relationship similar to the sort he denies ever having formed, or how a qadi will have provoked a person in court until the litigant does or says what was earlier denied. Interestingly, too, no penalties exist for perjury, even if a person has taken an oath, it being assumed that the harm to one's reputation as one who stands by a validated assertion, the loss of the case, or supernatural sanction will suffice as punishment.[17]

In his evaluation of conflicting evidence the qadi may also have recourse to certain established presumptions. In line with Moroccan legal tradition, he may, for example, presume that testimony asserting a positive fact is more reliable than assertions about a negative—for example, that a sale took place rather than that it never occurred— since every change of obligation, each shift in the distribution of haqq, constitutes an act, and acts have greater consequences than forbearance.[18] Here, as in ordinary social relations, the focus is not on a person's state of mind as such but on those actions which only a sane and competent adult must have intended to perform in such an act. And here, too, since consequence is perceived to vary with social characteristics, the qadi believes he can gauge his remedy according to the harm done by such a person acting in such a way. As in any judgment his decision embodies elements of the arbitrary, though his discretion is clearly bounded by law and culture alike.

LAW AND EQUITY: THE NEXUS OF REASONING AND JUSTICE

The Code of Personal Status controls a substantial proportion of the cases that come before the qadi. For issues not dealt with by the Code, as well as for some aspects of

---

[17] Schacht (1964: 159) and Westermarck (1926: 509).

[18] For a detailed listing of presumptions in the Maliki school of Islamic law, see Lapanne-Joinville (1957).

those that are, the qadi may utilize concepts and modes of analysis that contribute significantly to the shape of his discretionary and equitable powers. In particular, he may look for substantive guidance in local custom or past decisions and for legal justification in the concepts of analogic reasoning and the public good.

Most of the present-day creative use of custom is associated with the laws of personal status, and it is, therefore, to this domain that the present discussion will be limited. For example, in the formation of any marriage in Morocco the husband must pay to his wife or her marital guardian (*walīy*) a sum of money or quantity of goods agreed upon by the parties as a bridewealth payment (*ṣdāq*). It is usually the wife's father who serves as her marital guardian—generally seeking the husband as well as negotiating the marriage contract—and although local customs vary he will generally add at least an equivalent sum to the bridewealth and then use the entire amount to purchase the girl's dowry (*aṭāṭ l-bit*). This dowry remains the wife's property and will leave the marriage with her in the event of a divorce. The brideprice is always recorded in the marriage contract, but the recordation of the dowry is a matter of local custom, personal preference, and judicial discretion. It is a matter of some importance, too, because, in the absence of any record to the contrary, the legal fiction obtains that all the 'furnishings of the household' (the literal meaning of the Arabic term for 'dowry') belong to the wife even though they may have been purchased during the course of the union. And since much of a woman's marital security in this society, which still grants the husband the right of unilateral divorce, resides in the threat to the husband of the financial loss he stands to suffer in the event of a divorce, the recording of a dowry may play an important role in the stability of the marriage itself.[19]

The qadi also possesses the power to order a girl's marital guardian to agree to a given marriage, and if the guardian refuses, the qadi may himself give the girl in marriage. The purpose of this provision, coupled with that which grants a woman freedom from arbitrary actions by her own marital guardian, is to insure that girls are not prevented, in effect, from contracting their own marriages if they choose to do so. This provision is often employed in cases where a girl has been raped and her marital guardian opposes a subsequent marriage, or where the girl herself has developed a bad reputation and it is thought best to situate her in a respectable marriage. Moreover, Article 13 of the Code says that in such a situation the girl should be married 'by means of an equivalent brideprice to a man of equal condition,' which 'condition,' according to Article 14–2°, is to be determined 'by reference to local custom (*'urf*).' The determination of 'equal condition' is thus left to the qadi and his sense of local custom to determine.[20] On the few occasions in which Sefrou qadis have exercised this power, they have proved to be as sensitive to criteria of ethnicity, skin color, and familial reputation as to the financial status of the principals and their respective families.

---

[19] For an example, see Rosen (1970). See also my essay 'Marriage Stories' in Rosen (forthcoming).
[20] On the legal concept of 'marital equality' generally, see Ziadeh (1957).

One final example also concerns marital relations. The Code provides that when a man divorces his wife he must pay her a sum in compensation. This sum, the so-called 'gift of consolation'(*muta'a*), is left to the qadi to set; and in Sefrou, where such payments were often employed before the advent of the Code, the figure has customarily been set at one-third of the brideprice. However, if the marriage occurred long ago or involved a particularly high or low brideprice, the qadi will vary the amount due according to his own discretionary judgment. Under a 1993 amendment to the Code, the qadi may also vary the consolation payment depending on whether the husband has acted 'without good reason' in divorcing his wife.[21]

In sum, the qadi possesses some leeway in utilizing local custom in his decisions. His perception of local custom may be highly idiosyncratic or represent the perspective of only one segment of the population. Custom, like prior cases, may serve as persuasive evidence or as the basis for a legal presumption, but even where the present code permits resort to custom, qadis appear to avoid controversy by relying on court experts and notaries to indicate the acceptable forms of local customary practice.[22]

In classical Islamic legal theory, a qadi was expected to justify his interpretation of novel facts or situations by means of an analogy firmly rooted in Quranic precept, the practices of the Prophet and his companions, or the consensus of scholars or notables. Early Islam permitted the exercise of personal reasoning (*ijtihād*) by those who were so knowledgeable in the sacred sources that they might penetrate to the correct solution of a problem when the answer was not immediately evident by strict analogy. By the tenth century, however, opinion hardened against new interpretations, and distinct schools of legal doctrine crystallized around notable scholars. Since Islamic law has long been an object of ethical contemplation as much as an instrument of adjudication, one or more legal scholars might be asked by a litigant to supply an advisory opinion to the court. Although the opinions of qadis were almost never published or cited in subsequent decisions, the views of respected scholars were more frequently collected and distributed.

Contemporary Moroccan jurisprudence is heir to this tradition in several key respects. Like his predecessors, the modern qadi may ignore analogic reasoning by basing his decision on an approach known to have been preferred by the consensus of earlier scholars. He may also rely on the principle of public utility (*istislaḥ*), arguing, for example, that it is better for society to force a man into marriage with a girl he has molested than to impose the penalties and shame of a criminal accusation on

---

[21] Royaume du Maroc (1993), Article 52b. There is some ambiguity in the second section of this amended article, however, inasmuch as it allows an adjustment of the payment based on 'the situation of the divorced wife.' Some husbands wish to see this as a basis for taking the woman's own assets into account, while wives argue that the general requirement for support by a husband in Article 35, by not mentioning a woman's assets or duties to support her husband, means that her assets are not relevant to the question of support. For a case involving just such an argument in divorce litigation, see my essay 'Marriage Stories' in Rosen (forthcoming).

[22] The relation of Islamic law to custom and case law is discussed in Coulson (1959) and Ziadeh (1960), as well as in Ch. 5.

the man.[23] He may also turn to a body of legal literature unique in Islamic law to Morocco, the 'amal, which are collections of actual judicial practice that often did not correspond with the preferred opinion of scholars. This latter body of literature has some of the qualities of both case law and substantive law, even though it lacks binding force and internal consistency.[24] Reference to 'amal decisions serves primarily to support the stature of individual judgments and adds to the flexibility and creativity by which judicial powers may be exercised.

Custom, prior opinions, analogic reasoning, and public interest evaluations all constitute sources of principles used by the qadi where code and text may be wanting. Coupled with his use of social perception and the modes of determining facts, they give substantive shape to discretionary power. But what happens when the law on a matter is quite clear, when there is no lacuna that would legitimize recourse to these other mechanisms, but the qadi nevertheless feels that justice would be violated by strict application of the law? This may be particularly true when the case involves a wife who possesses insufficient grounds to obtain a judicial remedy to her marital situation but who is clearly suffering some hardship as a result of her husband's actions. A single unreported case from 1961, al-Haji v. Hedraz,[25] will serve to illustrate this point.

(19 September 1961: Complaint) The plaintiff states that her husband, the defendant, has been sent to jail for two years. For three years and two months prior to that he did not support her or their young daughter. She requests that the qadi divorce her because she cannot wait until her husband gets out of jail to support her and because a woman needs a husband to support her. Twice, she says, she has filed suits against her husband: The first case was thrown out on a technicality, and in the second the court ruled that the defendant should pay her support for the period of one year and four months, but he has not paid anything on this judgment. The plaintiff therefore also asks that the earlier judgment be enforced.

(16 October 1961) A summons for the defendant has been sent to the jail in which he is incarcerated, but no answer has been received. The plaintiff tells the court that she knows her husband does not have the money with which to pay the support judgment leveled against him.

(19 February 1962) Defendant absent. Public prosecutor in Fez claims communication foul-up between his office and the court. Delay ordered.

---

[23] Obviously, the assessment of what serves the public weal can yield both varied and amusing results. Yamani cites as an 'excellent example of public interest consideration' the following story: 'Ibn Al-Kayem related that his teacher Ibn Taimiah passed a group of Tatar drinking wine. His disciples wanted to forbid them from doing so, but Ibn Taimiah did not allow this, his reasoning being that God prohibited wine because it distracts from prayer and devotional rituals, but in the case of the Tatars wine distracts them from murder, loot, and rape' (Yamani (1968: 11)). On the principle of istislah generally, see Kerr (1968).

[24] On the role of 'amal as case law or substantive law, compare Berque (1944: 33–42, 119–32) with Milliot (1953: 167). For an analysis of one of the leading collections of 'amal, see Toledano (1974). The issue of Islamic law as case law is analyzed in Ch. 2.

[25] Sefrou Qadi's Court, No. 1961/262.

(12 March 1962, 21 June 1962, 12 September 1962, 24 September 1962) Each time the chief of the Fez court district has been asked to send the defendant for trial of the suit, but each time the defendant is absent.

(29 October 1962) Again the defendant is absent. The court says it has communicated by letter and phone with the warden of the jail, the prosecutor, and the chief of the Fez court district asking for the man to be presented, and each time they have failed to bring him. As always, the plaintiff is present. She says she mainly wants a divorce. Her husband still has a year to serve.

(21 January 1963) The qadi notes that the defendant is in jail for theft. He says that the plaintiff is always present, that the court itself is at fault for not presenting the defendant, and that a special effort must be made to help the plaintiff in reaching a decision on her petition. The qadi notes the defendant's admission in the earlier case that he did not support his wife and that he has since failed to obey the judgment entered against him. It is not right, says the qadi, for a woman to be alone while her husband is in jail: Allah considers marriage to be of great importance and wants the children of a marriage to be raised properly. Divorce is preferable to the continuation of the sort of situation with which we are presented here. The defendant has failed to support his family and has twice failed to obey the court order to do so. The defendant is therefore acting against the defining principles of a marriage and the laws of support. The law gives the qadi the right to divorce a couple if the husband cannot or will not support his wife. (A quotation from the Quran is cited here.) The qadi says that he knows the plaintiff's condition and that she has lived as a good woman throughout this period. Moreover, the defendant is a convicted thief. One school of law, says the qadi, says that a woman cannot request a divorce until she has lived one year without her husband ever being present, while another school sets the minimum period at three years. Both schools would be satisfied by the circumstances of the present case. Finally, says the qadi, a judicial divorce in this kind of case would be irrevocable (*b'ain*). A revocable kind of judicial divorce (*rja'i*) would be less preferable anyway because the husband might take the plaintiff back as his wife again before the divorce became final thus granting him the opportunity to bring further hardships on his wife. There are, says the qadi, so many reasons to favor such a divorce that even if the defendant should appear in court it would not alter his decision. Therefore, the qadi pronounces an irrevocable judicial divorce. This judgment may, he concludes, be appealed.

(14 August 1963: Before the appellate court) The court notes that the defendant has not paid the proper costs necessary to appeal the case within the allotted time. The defendant says he does not know the law. The appellate court dismisses the appeal.

It is important in analyzing the above case to understand that in Morocco there are two different kinds of divorces, revocable and irrevocable. Briefly, a man may repudiate the same woman three different times. After the first repudiation he may take her back as his wife within three months whether or not she wishes to return to him. After the second repudiation she must consent to being reunited within the three-month period. And after the third repudiation no direct reunion is permissible. Thus, only if the three-month separation period has elapsed and the man has twice previously repudiated the wife, or the wife has forgiven the husband some obligation in order to obtain the divorce, or the qadi has granted the woman a judicial divorce for cause is an irrevocable divorce recorded. Absence of more than a year is sufficient grounds for an irrevocable divorce. Imprisonment of the husband does not constitute grounds for any kind of judicial divorce. Thus, as a matter of strict law the qadi could only grant the plaintiff a revocable form of divorce, one which would leave her husband free to reclaim her as his lawful wife any time within the following three months. The qadi, however, clearly felt that it would be unfair to the plaintiff to subject her to this possibility.

Two questions of central importance to our study of Islamic law must therefore be considered. First, on the basis of what information and through the medium of what processes did the qadi decide that in this case it would be more equitable to violate the strict letter of the law than to obey it? And second, in terms of what principles did he construct the justification for his result? In order to answer the first of these questions we must have recourse to certain additional information; in order to answer the second we must relate this particular situation to those fundamental legal concepts mentioned earlier in our study.

To the extent that it is possible to reconstruct the history of this judicial decision and others like it, it is necessary to take into account the social positions of the participants and the process of decision-making in which the qadi himself engaged. In his opinion the qadi points not only to the husband's bad record but also to the fact that he has acquainted himself with the circumstances in which the plaintiff lives and knows that she has constantly displayed the characteristics of a respectable woman. In cases of this sort the qadi obtains such information through two main sources. First, he may inquire, directly or through others, into the plaintiff's habits and condition from the head of the urban quarter (*muqaddem al-ḥuma*) or sheikh of the rural settlement in which the plaintiff resides. These government-appointed officials have no formal ties with the judicial system, but may be used by the court to inform it on matters of this sort. In this particular case, the qadi learned that the plaintiff was from a good family of the city, that the husband had proved to be a scoundrel of uncertain background, and that the plaintiff's neighbors regarded her as circumspect, well-behaved, and long-suffering.

In addition to inquiry through the local officials, the qadi relied for information and general advice on several other persons in the community. In Morocco, as throughout the Arab world, people will often refer to certain individuals as 'the notables of the area' (*a'yān al-bilād*). These community leaders possess no formal organization or recognition: They are merely those persons who, by general reputation, familial background, or position, are generally regarded as the standard-bearers of the distinctive customs and highest values of their region. They are at once the unofficial arbiters of local propriety and the embodiment—at least ideally—of the distinctive characteristics of the community as a whole. Many of these 'notables' come into regular contact with the qadi or his closest associates and may be officials in the local court system itself. Indeed, since they form no corporate group or institutionalized entity, the determination of who is a 'notable of the area' is neither regular in its process nor subject to precise and uniform interpretation. The fact remains, nevertheless, that in some situations the qadi will consult informally with some of these persons in an attempt to determine certain facts about the litigants and—more importantly—what local practice, as articulated by these community leaders, is and should be in a given case. This is, then, a kind of informal consultation rather than a formal concilium, by means of which the qadi can determine the practice and sentiments of the community as articulated by some of its more notable citizens and diminish the exercise of his individual discretion through a process of consultation with important community leaders.[26]

In the present case the qadi did indeed consult with such 'notables' about the disposition of the matter. He was apparently convinced that the equity of the woman's case was very substantial and that a decision granting her an irrevocable divorce would be regarded favorably by all knowledgeable persons. There remained only the determination of a proper rationale for such a decision.

Earlier in our discussion, reference was made to the concept of istislah, the implementation for reasons of public utility of a judicial approach which, though not based on strict analogies with formal legal sources, is adopted as the preferred approach to a given problem. The qadi in the present case clearly relied on this traditional form of Moroccan legal reasoning in reaching his decision. He refers in his opinion to the reasons why an irrevocable divorce should be granted the plaintiff and why it is better for her, her family, and society as a whole to dissolve her union irrevocably. The qadi was doubtless aware that the present Code allows reference to such sources and reasoning in the absence of an applicable statutory provision, but he was apparently willing to argue its importance even when there is an appropriate provision if the equities of the case appear overwhelming. The fact that the appellate court, which could have chosen not to enforce the technicalities of filing dates, did not choose to overrule his decision indicates that the qadi's argument was convincingly presented. Although no formal confrontation of the rule of law and the role of equity was joined in this case, it appears that by using his powers of consultation and utilitarian reasoning, the present-day qadi may indeed be able to render an essentially lawless decision justified in terms of countervailing equities.

THE NATURE OF QADI JUSTICE

In his critique of Weber's concept of Kadijustiz, Max Rheinstein wrote:

Case law may tend toward irrationality, but even in that most extreme form in which it appears, that is, the practice of the khadi, it does not lack all rationality. Neither the

---

[26]   On the concept of concilium, see Tyan (1955: 245–7).

Mohammedan khadi nor his counterpart, the English (or American) justice of the peace, is expected to administer justice according to his own arbitrary whim or momentary fancy. The 'good' khadi is the one whose decision is in accordance with popular conviction, that is, with the religious or ethical value system prevailing at the time and place. In primitive or archaic circumstances this value system may be more felt than consciously known, but it exists wherever there exists a society and it is the very art of the khadi to articulate it as it applies to a concrete case. He is the one who is able to express in words, although of concrete application, what the common man but vaguely feels but cannot so easily apply and even less put into words. Only where he has succeeded in articulating in his decision the 'sound feeling of the people', will the khadi's decision meet with that approval without which he cannot permanently maintain his authority. This practice will often contain a good measure of irrationality, but basically his thought is of the pattern of the substantively rational, although largely inarticulate, kind.[27]

In fact, the equitable and discretionary powers of the contemporary Moroccan qadi are shaped as much by the sources of his legitimacy and the similarity of legal and cultural reasoning as by the articulation and enactment of assumptions that are characteristic of his society. Traditionally, the power of the qadi to interpose his own judgment was legitimized by the belief that adjudication in conformity with divine law is one of those duties which some individual must perform on behalf of all if the society is to remain a proper community of believers in the eyes of Allah.[28] In the past, men have been known to refuse judicial appointment for fear that they might inadvertently mislead their fellow believers or be corrupted by deriving their powers from necessarily tainted secular officials.[29] For those who did serve, however, the burden of spiritual guardianship legitimized the search for morally correct decisions. Although classical Islamic ethical thought turned, in part, on the categorization of all acts as obligatory, recommended, permissible, blameworthy, or forbidden, Moroccan juridical thought eschewed the elaboration of abstract concepts of right action in favor of more pragmatic evaluations of human relationships and the common weal. As Schacht noted generally for Islamic law, 'considerations of good faith, fairness, justice, truth, and so on play only quite a subordinate part in the system.'[30] Rather, it has been in the assessment of the features characterizing those who come before them and in the role of procedural constancy that one finds the distinctive qualities of qadi justice.

Moroccan jurisprudence, like Moroccan society, focuses on a series of human

---

[27]　Weber (1954: xlvii).

[28]　See Juynboll (1961a); Schacht (1964: 206); and Tyan (1955: 243).

[29]　So onerous is the responsibility of the qadi said to be that even pious men might refuse to accept the post. 'The *qadi* of Spain, Muhâjir b. Naufal, who . . . is supposed to have spoken from his grave of the evil outcome of the office of *qadi*, used to weep and lament for his soul when he recalled the "reckoning which awaits the *qadi* in the world to come for the discretionary choice and the *ijtihad* (personal interpretations) he is forced to employ" ' (Coulson (1956: 219)). More indicative of the potential entanglement with civil authorities may be the story of the man who was dissuaded from accepting a post as qadi when his traveling companion said: 'Are you not then aware that when Allah has no more use for a creature He casts him into the circle of officials?' Coulson (1956: 212).

[30]　Schacht (1974: 397).

characteristics as they cohere in particular individuals. Notwithstanding the provisions of the Code, the qadi, once he has determined to keep the bounds of relevance widely set, probes for the background and relationships that bear on the network of obligations between or among the parties. Although qadis undoubtedly vary in their assessment of these factors and weigh them differently in setting the boundaries of the case or their depth of inquiry, each of the factors involved entails certain consequences. It is interesting to note in this regard that the term *asel*—which refers to one's origins, background, set of presumed associations, and customs—also refers to that form of legal reasoning by entailment which a judge may rely upon in the implementation of legal presumptions. Thus, as we have seen, the qadi may legally presume who is most likely to possess certain knowledge in assigning the order of oath-taking. Or he may invoke a form of that implicational code which suggests that gender implies motivation; motivation, knowledge; knowledge, social position; position, network; and network, repercussions. Here, too, one may be able to discern significant shifts in the code of cultural entailment over time. It may be said of Moroccans, as of Saudi Arabians, that theirs is a world 'in which people define tasks, roles, and institutions, not the other way around.'[31] What may be changing is not the overall tendency toward personalism but the fact that in the past a man's occupation, residence, kin group, and religious brotherhood ties cumulated such that knowledge of any one feature implied a series of others, whereas now the set of implications may be less tightly integrated or the need to consider it rendered less pressing because of the Code. Stereotypes, loosed from their cultural context, may now come to serve judicial efficiency more than the articulation of community norms.[32]

Indeed, it may be argued that Islamic law is, to borrow John Dewey's distinction, based on a logic of consequence rather than a logic of antecedent.[33] Instead of considering prior cases or similar examples, the qadi focuses on the consequence of actions as the index of validated assertions and as the criterion for judging social implications. It is in the harm done or the alteration in relationships that the critical point lies. Thus, as in everyday social perceptions, the court ignores intent as an independent factor and concentrates instead on occurrences. The more serious the impact on society, the more serious are the legal implications. The requirement, for example, of four eyewitnesses to an act of fornication is not solely an evidentiary burden of extraordinary weight: It is also an assertion that if, contrary to the tradition (*hadīth*) that 'God loves those who hide their sins,' one commits an act in so blatant a fashion that four people may have seen it, the harm to society must be serious indeed.[34] Similarly, the use of numerous witnesses to a man's mistreatment of his wife is a statement about social consequence converted into a legally recognizable infraction.

[31] Iseman (1978: 50).
[32] On related factors affecting changes in judicial procedure see Ch. 6.
[33] Dewey (1924).
[34] This interpretation is taken from Yamani (1968: 34). The internal reference to the Prophet is elaborated in Juynboll (1961a).

Justice, then, lies not in the simple invocation of rights and duties but in their contextual assessment and the mode of analysis. Procedure and reasoning are central. Asked how similar cases which result in divergent judgments can be justified, qadis invariably offer two answers. First, that no two individuals are identical and hence no two cases are the same. But more importantly, they insist that the same reasoning process—of drawing analogies, of weighing moral implications, of adducing evidence, of assessing entailments, of gauging the social interest—may reasonably lead to different conclusions, but that if the procedures are the same, the most important criterion for treating similar cases similarly will have been met.[35]

The emphasis on the form of procedure as opposed to its momentary result and the concern with individual assessment over routinized processing is closely related to the second handicap noted by Hart for the establishment of general rules: namely, the relative indeterminacy of aim. In the qadi's court, the aim is neither the strict enforcement of rights nor the reconciliation of the parties, however much each of these elements may play a role in some cases. Rather, the aim is to give at least momentary order to shifting relationships and to validate their present status long enough to avoid violence and to set people back on a social course of negotiating their own ties peaceably. It is more than mere cynicism, therefore, that leads many Moroccans, when discussing the nature of qadi justice, to refer to the popular saying: 'When the times are just, one day is for me and one day is against me.'

Qadi justice in Morocco gives the appearance ultimately of an entity constructed around an elaborate exoskeleton. Rather than being built up from within by a series of rules and regulations, the system is bounded by a structure of assumptions and conventions by which the non-legal world is set apart from the legal but within which both that outside world and the peculiar institutions of the law itself have merged to form an entity of enormous cohesion and resilience. The presence of statutes and appellate courts may contribute to greater rigidity or, as the authors of the original 1958 Code hoped, to a new body of flexible judicial practice (*'amal*). Whatever its particular course, it is clear that legal precepts and procedures will continue to be influenced by changing cultural and moral ideas. Just as in American law where, for example, a witness may testify that someone was 'drunk' but may not conclude that a person was 'in love,' so, too, in Moroccan law evidentiary standards and modes of legal reasoning partake of everyday assumptions about human conduct and fairness. For the student of law, a close analysis of qadi justice may demonstrate that the goal need not be that posed by the legal realists (the prediction of what judges will do) nor that suggested by the legal positivists (the enumeration of specific rules). Rather, one can show that discretionary judgments and equitable assessments are suffused by principles and standards which are as incomprehensible without an understanding of how cultural precepts shape them as would the study of social relations be incomplete without an understanding of their judicial articulation.

---

[35] Berque (1944: 21) places particular emphasis on contradictory judicial results being understood as linked by common procedures.

2

Islamic case law and the logic of consequence

Social scientists have frequently asserted that the conjuncture of cultural concepts and social relations can be seen with great clarity in even the most arcane aspects of religious, economic, and political life. Whole visions of the worldview of a people have been found in an isolated rite of passage, an entire ethos in the complex exchange of shells, and complete cosmologies in the struggle for transient elective office. Yet with few exceptions the operations of formal courts of law have been treated by anthropologists either as peculiar domains whose untypical language, rules, and procedures somehow remove them from the mainstream of cultural life, or as microcosmic realms beyond which one need seldom stray in order to understand how conflicts may be authoritatively composed. The tendency of anthropologists to avoid formal courts of law in the societies they study may be due in part to the distance with which courts and lawyers are viewed in Western culture—a domain seen to be fraught with professionally skewed assumptions and far from disinterested goals—or with an antiquated desire to show, contrary to colonial ideology, that native peoples possess law in every bit as refined a sense as do Western societies. The result has been a valuable acknowledgment of the non-judicial modes of dispute management, but a sometimes inappropriate avoidance of the courts themselves.

However, the modes of thought or forms of interaction found in courts are not necessarily any less culturally characteristic of the broader societies than the modes of thought or forms of interaction found in a monastery, a market center, or a men's club—all of which anthropologists readily enter without further specialized study or fear of professional disapproval. Therefore, in what follows I want to consider a distinctly legal topic— the nature of case law in the courts of modern Morocco—and use this as a vehicle to show how, in this society, law pervades culture and culture informs law. As with a single ritual, a network of exchange, or a contest for political leadership, one cannot hope to see all of a society through such a limited focus. But an example of this sort can point out the implications and benefits of approaching any legal system as part of a larger cultural system.

THE COLLECTIONS OF ISLAMIC JUDICIAL OPINIONS

Earlier in the twentieth century a difference in interpretation arose between two of France's foremost scholars of Islamic law.[1] The dispute centered on a body of writings, collectively known as the 'amal literature, which consists of the opinions of Islamic judges on a wide variety of issues they have been called on to decide. On one

---

[1] The key sources in this discussion are Berque (1944); Berque (1960); Milliot (1918: 13–21); and Milliot and Lapanne-Joinville (1952: v–xix). See also Toledano (1981), and Schacht (1956).

side stood Louis Milliot, the dean of French Islamic law scholars, who first brought
to Western attention the 'amal collections that formed a part of the legal literature of
Morocco. Milliot argued that these opinions constitute a set of doctrinal propositions that function like a body of positive law. Some years later, Jacques Berque, a
former Affaires Indigènes officer and later professor at the Collège de France,
suggested that the collections of judicial practice, far from being the functional
equivalent of a code of law, might operate instead as a kind of case law, a series of
opinions used to guide rather than settle certain cases coming before a court. The
issue has considerable significance for the study of Islamic law not only in North
Africa but elsewhere in the Islamic world where scholar and judge, legal doctrine and
judicial practice, may compete for authoritative voice. But beyond the historical and
practical concerns that the 'amal literature provides for Islamic law studies, a larger
set of questions arises that is relevant to the comparative study of legal development.
What, we may ask, does it mean to speak of a body of writing as constituting either
a code-like set of rules or a system of particularizing case law when participants in
the system have not themselves clearly calculated the respective importance of
general rules and individual cases? How, in the absence of historical or anthropological examples, may we envision the use of actual court decisions in the Islamic law
development of North Africa, and against what broader cultural features may we
interpolate their role? Indeed, in what ways do the construction and implementation
of doctrine and practice become clear when viewed in the light of those cultural
assumptions that appear to suffuse the entire process of judicial reasoning and judicial fact-finding in the context of modern Islamic law?

In order to answer these questions, it may be helpful to describe briefly the nature
of the 'amal literature and the specific ways in which Milliot and Berque came to
interpret it. Then, standing back from the 'amal itself, it will be necessary to indicate
how the larger background of cultural assumptions and modes of reasoning informs
Islamic law and the uses to which actual judicial opinions are put by contemporary
judges. Finally, a particular interpretation will be offered of the role and meaning of
case law in the Moroccan context, and of the role it may play in the development of
Islamic law in a modern nation-state.

The collection of 'amal writings that Louis Milliot first described in his
Démembrements consists primarily of a series of works drawn up in the fifteenth
through seventeenth centuries. Unlike some other sources of Islamic law—particularly the Quran and the traditions concerning the Prophet's utterances and acts—or
the treatises and later commentaries that set forth the approach of notable scholars
around whom particular schools of thought developed, the 'amal rest on the actual
practice of judges of Islamic law. Some, such as the *Lamiyya* of Ali al-Zaqqaq, were
composed as procedural guides that judges could consult to see how earlier jurists
approached issues that came before them; others, like the *'Amal al-Muṭlaq*, encouraged judicial use by presenting their materials as mnemonic poems or practical
manuals. In each instance the approaches of named jurists are mentioned in the
context of a series of distinct issues, though neither the details of particular cases nor

the factual bases for distinguishing one type of case from another are elucidated. Rather, the presentation of opinions turns on the nature and range of acceptance of one approach over another. Because this rather technical factor is important to the relationship Moroccan culture has to Moroccan law, it is worth noting how this form of presentation and legal reasoning operates.

Faced with an issue not squarely covered by Quranic injunction, the 'amal authors instructed judges to follow what is called the 'dominant opinion' (*mashhur*)—the approach taken by most jurists in a given area and incorporated as such in most collections of judicial practice. However, a 'preferred approach' (*rajih*), one based on what is socially desirable or customarily done, or even an 'isolated approach' (*shadd*), one based on necessity, custom, or the approach of a well-known jurist, could be used in place of the predominant approach. While no specific techniques were established for distinguishing precisely when each of these approaches could be invoked, much less for distinguishing cases by their facts, it is clear that the overall orientation implied by the 'amal is itself entwined with the added concepts of public welfare and custom, ideas that are themselves grounded on a series of broader cultural assumptions.

Although classical Islamic law allowed no specific place to custom as a source for judicial decision-making, the existence and shape of the opinions collected in the 'amal writings clearly demonstrate that these collections themselves served as a vehicle for legitimizing local custom. Not only do preferred opinions appear to acquire their status because numerous judges have taken the same approach, but also their wide acceptance is often based directly on local practice. Working from the tradition that 'what the faithful regard as good is good in the sight of God,' Islamic judges have long incorporated the actual practices of those they serve as legitimate in the sight of the law. Indeed, preserving existing practice has long been recognized as one of the indispensable necessities for the preservation of communal harmony against that chaos and strife (*fitna*) that hang as an ever-present threat over human society. Yet instances may arise in which even the approach preferred by many, if not indeed the most distinguished, judges may need to give way in the face of a broader harm that may result from the strict application of doctrine. In such an instance, a judge may turn to the concept of the 'public interest' (*istislah*) or to the idea of a solution appropriate to the circumstance (*istihsan*) to resolve the issue at hand. Whether it is a case in which the court rules that it is unfair to make a custodial mother move as frequently as her soldier husband even though the formal law requires her to remain near her former husband, or (as we saw in the last chapter) a case in which the judge grants the wife of an imprisoned man an irrevocable divorce because the sole form of divorce to which she is legally entitled would allow her husband to recall her to a life of continuing hardship, judges have available to them techniques articulated and legitimized in these early collections of judicial practice that allow both custom and circumstance to inform specific judgments. To understand the way the choice of approaches and rationales operates at present and may have operated when these practices were themselves being collected, it will, however, be valuable to recapitulate some elements of that larger set of cultural circumstances on which the actual practice of Moroccan law rests.

THE CULTURAL CONTEXT OF ISLAMIC LEGAL THOUGHT

For Westerners first coming in contact with Moroccan society—or for that matter, societies throughout the Arab world—the institution of the marketplace, the bazaar, often serves to establish a general perception of the culture. It is there that one encounters a domain where prices are not fixed and bargaining is ever-present, where the absence of clear indicators of quality, quantity, and availability leads to a constant quest for information or for personally reliable suppliers, and where the lines of competition run less between one seller and another than between any given seller and the buyer who stops for a moment before his or her shop or stall. If this image is extended beyond the marketplace to the broader realm of social relations, it becomes possible to grasp certain essential features of Moroccan social and cultural life. For just as in the bazaar, it is through a constant process of negotiation and contracting that Moroccans form relationships with one another. Family, tribe, or neighborhood may offer bases from and within which to fashion one's affiliations, but it is only through a constant process of constructing a network of obligations that each person can seek relationships in which security may be found. And just as in the marketplace, where conventions and institutions, shared concepts and recognizable tactics give shape and order to the constant process of negotiation, so, too, in the realm of constructing social ties wherever they may prove most desirable, individuals operate through a set of common assumptions and institutions. For our purposes, three such socio-cultural constellations are important.

The first relates to the central importance of the individual in Moroccan life. For Moroccans each individual stands at the center of a web of obligations and incorporates, in his or her own set of characteristics and network of ties, the features of social background (*asel*) and situated encounters (*ḥāl*) by which he or she will be known to others. As each person tries to predict how another will act, and how he or she may fit into their own network of affiliations, attempts will be made, as in the marketplace, to find out things about the other's associations and personal characteristics. A wide range of cultural concepts is geared to this emphasis on knowing another's situated ties. Thus, if one looks at Moroccan narrative styles one sees that the constant emphasis is on knowing the host of situations in which one has encountered others. Because people do not fashion their individuated selves any more than humanity may fashion the moral precepts by which it must live, emphasis is not on the individual as the possessor of a psychic structure that generates a self that is, whatever its overt manifestations, most authentic where it is most private. Rather, emphasis is placed on the person as the embodiment of traits and ties that are discernible and subject to incorporation in one's own realm of affiliations. The narration of a story thus focuses on the situated encounters of the individuals involved rather than on inner states or implacable forces of nature or circumstance. Even time is seen less as the movement of events in conformity with an underlying design or revelatory direction and more as the encapsulation of affiliations as they exist at any given instant. A believable account therefore relies not on chronological ordering but on seeing the person through the various encounters he or she has with others. Understanding a person is like understanding a gem not by its geological history but by the aspects it reveals as it is turned to catch the light at different angles.

This stress on the contextualized person is itself connected to the Moroccan concept of truth, for truth is seen not as something that inheres in an utterance or an act, but as a process by which human beings bring otherwise neutral statements into the realm of human relationships and consequence. Just as a price mentioned in the marketplace is not true or false until an agreement—a relationship—is formed with reference to it, so too in the realm of social relations a statement about an attachment to another does not become subject to evaluation as true or false until it has been validated. Such validation may occur by using an oath, by marshaling public opinion to one's own view of the asserted relationship, or by confirming the relationship by acting as if it were indeed so. Thus, just as one keeps bargaining options open in the bazaar until an agreement receives accepted confirmation, so, too, one keeps open the possibility of forming ties wherever they may prove most advantageous by not holding another's statements about his relation to you to its normal consequences until an institutionalized mode of validation brings it into the realm of the true, where it may be subject to the criteria and sanctions of the true.

If the situated individual and the validated utterance are two key ingredients of the Moroccan vision of reality, a third aspect is bound up in the idea of consequence. In the Moroccan view, one can identify and assess a person, an utterance, or an act only by their consequences in the world of human relations. Thus it is not a person's inner state separate from his or her overt acts, or that person's claims to reciprocity apart from their validated status, that matter; it is the impact each person has on various networks of obligation that serve to place and measure him. And because the repercussions of one person's acts may differ markedly from those of another, the assessment of a person's deeds is an integral feature of determining that person's importance and reliability. So, for example, it is believed that a rich man can have a greater impact on relationships than a poor man, or a learned man can have a greater impact than one whose ignorance is less likely to make him a model to be followed or an ally to be sought out, and therefore that the harm that people of various categories may do suggests the standard of responsibility to which they should be held. An elaborate calculus of consequence thus serves to place actors and their attendant acts in context and to render them subject to evaluation as members of various social networks.

Each of these factors—of person, truth, and consequence—takes particular shape and implication in various situational and institutional settings. Because truth must be personal to have any consequence in the world of relations, it is to the reliable witness that one turns for authentication of a tradition of the Prophet, a claim to the occurrence of an act in the world, or the existence of a legally cognizable relationship. Just as it is the person who makes the assertion believable, so, too, it is the consequences a person may have in the world that makes the weight of that person's claim assessable. Just as it is the repercussions of one's acts that do not simply reveal but actually comprise the qualities associated with character and background, so, too, it is only within their personalized embodiment that significant social features possess meaning in the world. And just as one can trace the implications of this dynamic—of the individual unit set in an organizing but not governing framework—in the realm of social relations, artistic production, and religious rite, so, too, one can discern its role in the structure and process of Islamic adjudication.[2]

Islamic law courts in contemporary Morocco are characterized by several distinctive institutional features. As in earlier times, it is still the single judge, the qadi, who decides each case, and though his jurisdiction has been circumscribed by the creation of other courts within the unified legal system, and his place has been settled within the hierarchy of a national bureaucratic structure, it remains true, as we saw in the previous chapter, that his is a very traditional court both in the law it applies and in the process by which his judgment is brought to bear on individual cases. To recapitulate, it is to the qadi that cases are brought that involve matters of personal status or property matters in which the basis of one's claim is a document made out by notaries of the court. This latter feature would appear to suggest that written documents are the central form of proof in the qadi's court, when in fact quite the reverse is true. Oral evidence is what really counts, the personal presentation before the court or its personnel of an individual's asserted claim. The notaries ('adul) are simply the institutionalization, within the legal setting, of those reliable witnesses who, as in any social relationship, can serve to validate an utterance by the force of their own reputation as reliable actors in a network of consequential ties. It is before such notaries—who always work in pairs—that a litigant will therefore appear, often with a significant number of fellow witnesses, to make assertions that can be assessed as true or false only when the court personnel have transformed mere utterances into legally cognizable claims. In the role of notaries and in the emphasis on oral testimony we thus see, in the domain of the law, the centrality to Moroccan concepts of reality and credibility that the ideas of the person and the impact of speech have on the meaning of relationships. But the notaries are not alone in shaping issues for adjudication; courts also use various experts who come from the local area and who have been engaged in the craft or trade in which their expertise lies. At the judge's direction they may be sent to determine boundaries, the quality of construction, the costs of living for wives and children, and the like. Through them important aspects of local standards are brought before the court by people designated as personally knowledgeable about such matters.

When, therefore, a case actually comes up for a hearing, the mode of fact-finding and the form of judicial reasoning employed by the qadi reveal that they are closely

---

[2] On the analogies to architecture, mathematics, and music, see Gittes (1983).

related to the patterns of thought and action found in the culture at large. For example, at the outset of each case the qadi is very careful to determine the social background of each of the parties, for such information offers him, as any Moroccan, a clue as to the customary ways that such people enter into relations with one another and their most likely ties to one another. Moreover, he requires oral testimony, either by the parties or by their spokesmen, since it is only by such statements that one can probe for another's believability. Considerable discretion is involved in drawing bounds of relevance around the issue presented, and it is not uncommon for the qadi to consider a wider range of relationships and issues when rich or important people, or populous or prestigious groups, are involved simply because the repercussions of such people's acts are regarded as more critical to the preservation of social harmony. But perhaps the most striking features of the qadi's proceeding are the emphasis on local circumstances and the style of judicial reasoning.

As already suggested, the qadi relies heavily on the notaries and the experts for determination of facts. Indeed, it can be argued that unlike many complex legal systems that propel investigation and decision-making up to the higher reaches of the legal order, in Morocco the process of adjudication continually pushes matters down and away from the qadi—down to the level where local custom and circumstance can become most significant. The use of multiple witnesses appearing before the notaries for certification of their oral claims, the frequent recourse to those who are experts on local matters, and a legal order in which the rules set down by authoritative sources are few and the scope for local practice is explicitly sanctioned, all contribute to the centrality of local customs and standards in the process of adjudication. The emphasis on the local is also evident in the judge's evaluation of oral evidence. For example, if the oral or notarized testimonies of witnesses conflict, the qadi will often turn to assumptions about what people of a given background or personal circumstances are thought to be knowledgeable about or, as a matter of human nature, what they are expected to have done. Thus, it is generally assumed that neighbors are more reliable than witnesses living at a greater distance, that relatives are more likely to lie on behalf of kinsmen than strangers are, and that a transaction is most likely to have occurred if people have operated as if it had existed for some time. Even when the evaluation of oral testimony or the discernment of local facts by experts cannot resolve a matter, a strong element of the rational and customary enters into the use of the ultimate vehicle of fact-finding, namely the decisional oath.

Oath-taking in Moroccan law, like the remnant still found in some European systems, allows the defendant to swear to his or her statements, and thus bring the case to an end favorable to the oath-taker. However, the defendant may choose to refer the oath back to the plaintiff, who can successfully conclude the case by then swearing to his or her claims. Whoever takes the oath first wins. Where the element of rational, local practice enters is in the designation of the plaintiff and the defendant for purposes of oath-taking. It is not necessarily the one who files the case or answers it who plays each of these roles when oath appointment is at issue. Rather, the defendant is whichever party the court believes is most likely to possess knowledge of the issue at hand and thus most able to swear to the matter. For example, a husband who sues his wife for return of their household goods may be designated the defendant when the question as to who owns articles that are normally associated with a man can be resolved by no other means than a decisory oath. If one traces the presumptions built into this system of oath-taking, it is clear that, far from being an 'irrational' mode of proof, the process incorporates a broad range of cultural assumptions about who is most likely to know what, and thus have the first right (and the initial burden should they swear falsely) to conclude the case with an oath.

Similarly, the modes of legal reasoning employed suggest similar attention to local detail and broadly shared assumptions. Consider, for example, several elements of Moroccan judicial reasoning. There exists in Islamic law, not only as practiced in Morocco, the idea that positive assertions should take precedence over negative ones. Put differently, all other things being equal, testimony about something having occurred should be favored over testimony that it did not occur. Thus, testimony that a sale occurred is seen as positive, and a claim that nothing has occurred to alter prior circumstances is designated negative, while testimony impeaching another's character is taken as positive, and testimony tending to support one's character is demarcated negative. The law therefore seems to recognize that shifts in the balance of obligations among people are indeed the normal course of things and that such alterations should be given judicial sanction. Consequently, sales are taken as probable occurrences, disputed marriages are confirmed, and the assumption reinforced that a man who has not been able to establish his reputation for credibility before a dispute arises will be of poor moral character and an unreliable witness to events.

Judges may also draw together a series of features about background and circumstances to draw conclusions of legal import. Knowing that a person is from a given social background, that one is a man or a woman, or that one is learned or illiterate often implies, for judges as for others, a set of entailments that are taken as indicative of the impact of one's actions. In Morocco, the reference point in judicial logic, as in cultural logic, is therefore not so much to an antecedent set of rules or stereotyped categories of role or social position. Rather, the focus is on what John Dewey once called a 'logic of consequence,' in which the effects of another's acts are of central concern and prior data is marshaled toward the evaluation of one or another action in the world rather than to the application of a set of rules.[3] Thus, in the Moroccan case, knowledge about others cumulates into a conception of what a particular person is expected, by acts or utterances, to bring about in the world. It is not a system of social or legal perception that concentrates on judging individuals by standardized behavior or idealized roles, but one that assesses individual impact as a result of individuated circumstance. And it is against this background that the last feature of legal reasoning, and the one that will lead us back to an understanding of the literature on judicial practice, comes into play, namely, the role of analogic reasoning.

[3]   Dewey (1924).

Qiyas, or analogic reasoning, is one of the acknowledged sources of law in Islam, a vehicle by which extensions could be made from the limited number of Quranic rules and Prophetic traditions to those circumstances that had never been addressed. Although individual authority to engage in extensions of the Sacred Law through such analogic reasoning was ostensibly circumscribed in the early centuries of Islam as a result of the formation of specific schools of thought and the closure of 'the gates of independent reasoning,' analogic reasoning has in fact continued to develop, often in arcane and scholastic ways, to present times.[4] For our purposes, two points need to be underscored.

The first point concerns the materials used in constructing analogies. Traditionally, litigants submitted to the judge the opinions of scholars who themselves developed analogies that were proffered as solutions to the case at hand. These scholars distinguished cases not by reference to one another but against a general proposition embodied in a concrete circumstance. Thus, an argument in favor of holding a son to the payment of bridewealth when only his father had contracted for the payment would be analogized to the kind of unjust enrichment involved in lending money for interest. Analogic reasoning thus worked through broad concepts exemplified by specific situations, rather than by eliciting detailed rules from acknowledged precepts or by recourse to a logical principle by means of which a series of individual instances would have to be regularized in order to maintain doctrinal consistency.[5] The second point to underscore is that analogies are, as we implied earlier, framed in terms of repercussions rather than antecedent precepts. Thus, a judge will compare outcomes rather than prior rules, results rather than causes. To decide that reopening a long-closed passageway is like perpetuating avenues of trade and intercourse, or that ongoing injury to a wife can be stopped by granting an irrevocable divorce where only a revocable one is allowed, is to focus one's comparisons on a local outcome and repercussion rather than on the refinement of a doctrine or code.

It is here, then, that we can recapture the role of the literature on judicial practice and the debate over its role as positive law or case law. The collections of 'amal writings depend, both in their structure and—we may conjecture—their acceptance, on many of the social and cultural features to which we have been referring. As one analyzes these collections, it becomes evident that the judicial choice among conflicting scholarly opinions is itself informed through the principle of the socially useful, by the articulation to local practice. Examples of this process abound. For instance, one can point to 'amal interpretations that say that even though the clause in a marriage contract allowing a woman to initiate a divorce is granted by the husband voluntarily, it should receive the stricter enforcement of an agreement that was actually bargained for because local custom regards it as something given in exchange for a lower bridewealth payment. Or one could point to modern usages where the qadi

---

[4] See generally, Hallaq (1984).
[5] On analogic reasoning, see Makdisi (1985a); Schacht (1964); and Yamani (1968).

refuses a rural woman's claim against her former husband for the cost of hospital delivery of their child because birth at home is customary for such women, even though most commentators include all birth expenses among those to which a woman is entitled.[6] In each instance the focus of judges, both historically and at present, is not on principles or doctrines as such, or on the factual differentiation of cases, but on an assessment of consequences, on the repercussions for the networks of ties that people possess, or should be free to contract, in face-to-face dealings. Just as the thrust of judicial organization and the determination of facts constantly involve the tendency to propel matters down to the locally defined and locally derived, so, too, the mode of judicial reasoning represented in the 'amal literature, as in current practice, channels the judge's thinking not to the level of ever more refined doctrinal analysis or to the elaboration of legally distinct modes of reasoning, but to filling up propositions with local meaning.

Indeed, the study of contemporary judicial decision-making suggests that the goal of the law, now as at an earlier time, contributes greatly to the way it is formulated and implemented. As we have seen, it can be argued that the primary goal of the Islamic law judge is to put people back into a position of negotiating their own arrangements within the broad bounds laid down in the canon of Islamic law. If we look at Islamic law as a whole, as well as at collections of early and recent judicial practice, we can see that most critics are wrong when they claim that Islamic law, unlike other highly developed systems, lacks doctrinal refinement and consistency.[7] Such a criticism misses the point that Islamic law is consistent with those very relationships and assumptions of local society that the courts are seeking to reinforce. The role of the qadi, rather like that of Islam in general, is thus to set the general parameters of conduct, not to govern every detail of daily life. Just as in Islamic architecture, music, mathematics, and social organization, the law forms an organizing framework, not a governing force, and harmony lies in allowing such lines of individual-centered affiliation to work themselves out by the free arrangement of units according to local circumstance. That is why, in the context of the literature on judicial practice, one finds an early jurist emphasizing local consequences over the retention of doctrinal consistency when he says: 'Once the argument of the opinion adopted in judicial practice becomes clear to you (O judge!) it becomes your duty to issue judgment in accordance with it, for adjudicating contrary to the judicial practice leads to civil strife and great corruption.'[8]

---

[6] These and many similar examples from the writings of Sijilmasi are elaborated in Toledano (1981).

[7] See Schacht (1964: 199–211). Among other misplaced criticisms of Islamic law, probably derived from his European-based assumptions about how legal systems 'ought' to work, Schacht castigates Islamic law for mingling rules of procedure and substantive law. Not only is the distinction overdrawn but, it can be argued, since person-assessment and consequences are central, it is precisely in connecting these two domains that Islamic law as a practical law, rather than a scholar's rarefied domain, finds its great strength.

[8] Toledano (1981: 167).

CASE LAW, CODE, OR CULTURAL PROCESS?

Interpolating from contemporary social, culture, and legal features to the meaning and role of the practice contained in the 'amal writings thus leads to a view of this literature that is slightly different from that offered by either Milliot or Berque. Milliot saw in the collections of judicial practice the articulation of specific ways of resolving concrete situations.[9] He distinguished these writings from form books and the opinions of scholars, and equated the function of the 'amal with that of legal opinions as used by lawyers in France. By seeing the 'amal as tantamount to positive law, however, Milliot mistook a result for a process. He saw these opinions as a source used to fill the lacunae in the Sacred Law rather than as an example of a mode of reasoning by which custom is drawn into the law not to develop a body of doctrine but to allow local circumstance judicial legitimacy. And by not probing for the highly personalistic way in which the opinion of one person may take precedence over that of another, he gave insufficient attention to the process by which particular opinions, which might otherwise seem to be on an equal footing, have widely differing effects. Thus, while Milliot was able to see that Islamic law was not the functional equivalent of the French code, he mistakenly believed that a rule-like set of propositions emanates from Islamic judicial practice and that the publication of contemporary opinions would succeed in establishing a new body of positive law that, under the French protectorate, would allow Islamic law to cope with modern circumstances.

By contrast, Jacques Berque never believed that our understanding of the 'amal allows for a definitive evaluation of its role. However, he did on several occasions suggest that the 'amal appears to have functioned as a set of specific solutions that could be adopted or rejected in case-law fashion by subsequent jurists. He found no evidence that the 'amal was meant to yield a set of rule-like propositions. In order to constitute positive law, the 'amal would have to be based on a stable set of underlying precepts, when in fact, Berque argued, it has no such normative reference point. Instead, he characterized Islamic judicial practice as pragmatic case law.[10] But Berque was not entirely clear about what he meant by case law. If he meant that the 'amal— or any modern Islamic law judgment—may be used in the same way that French lawyers use cases, he would have been suggesting that while such cases lack any precedent value and may not even be frequently cited by judges in subsequent cases, they do suggest concrete solutions to cases that possess some authority for having been used by well-known judges or in important jurisdictions. By his reference to case law, Berque presumably did not mean that opinions in Islamic law operate as they do in Anglo-American law, where, to borrow Edward Levi's formulation, categorizing principles developed out of the factual circumstances of one case are extended or distinguished by application to the facts of new cases. Berque's vision of judicial practice as

[9]   Milliot (1920: 15–21).
[10]   See Berque (1944: 33–50) and Berque (1960). See also the discussion of Islamic case law in Coulson (1959).

pragmatic guidance nevertheless appears close to the mark. What is, I believe, necessary in order to see more fully the role of the 'amal literature—and to offer a more accurate interpretation of its role in the past—is to see how this pragmatic tool operated in the larger context of Moroccan social and cultural life.

Seen from this vantage, decisions in prior cases replicate a process of fact-finding and reasoning whose goal is to put litigants back in a position of negotiating their own relationships. Islamic courts have the broad duty of retaining control over the practices specifically addressed by the Quran and of fulfilling, on behalf of all, those duties incumbent on the community of believers if the community is to remain a moral body in the eyes of God. By constantly drawing the local into the ambit of the judicial, and by emphasizing the perception of social utility as seen by a judge who, like others in society, can make his the accepted view not by force alone but by conducing the acceptance of those affected by his judgment, the pattern of Islamic judicial decision-making replicates social practice and thereby adds to its own legitimacy. Prior decisions thus do not work like European positive law in their orientation toward the formation of a body of doctrinally consistent rules, nor are they isolated practices that should be treated as discrete artifacts, the traces of the passing of the law. Instead, the 'amal and contemporary Moroccan opinions partake of a common process, and by the different ways they are applied in the ongoing nature of that process they can be attended to, ignored, adduced, or avoided with the same force and in the same manner as any other human view. Because the law is regularized by reference to local practice rather than to doctrine, the 'amal and current opinions make sense only as seen in light of the local. And because local law is itself not a body of artificial reason or professionalized doctrine so much as it is the articulation of the accepted, Islamic law makes sense, in turn, only as part of a larger social and cultural scheme.

Such an interpretation of Islamic law in Morocco, in the past as in the present, finds confirmation in the course of legal development in recent decades. In the first years following national independence in 1956, the Moroccan government formulated a new Code of Personal Status. This code, which remains very close to traditional Islamic law, states that in the event that judges do not find guidance for a particular issue in the statute they may turn to local custom and the 'amal writings. Indeed, there is some indication that the authors expected the Code would contribute to the development of a new body of 'amal writings.

But during the decades since the Code was adopted this has not proved to be true. The reason for this may be, first, that there is now an appellate hierarchy, which did not exist in pre-colonial times. In classical Islamic practice the idea of an appellate structure was contrary to the idea that no one could claim to speak definitively for the Sacred Law and, as our earlier analysis would suggest, the use of appeals might contradict the emphasis on local practice over the establishment of universal rules.[11]

---

[11] The emphasis on the personalistic aspect of judicial decision-making is also evident in the traditional approach to dealing with qadis' errors inasmuch as attention focused on how to choose better qadis or on the examination of a present qadi's integrity more than on the procedures applied or the role of witnesses and litigants. See Rebstock (1999).

And while appeals could certainly be used to create a body of substantive national law, the appellate courts have not proceeded in that direction. Instead they have acted like *de novo* review boards rehearing many facts and directing attention to code provisions that lower court judges may have missed. Thus we see that opinions in specific cases have not changed their role, even with the introduction of a national code or appellate structure.

The existence of the Code has, however, changed something else. In the past, qadis seem to have set the general terms of many issues, while local practice set the particulars. But now the Code has taken on some of the functional role of general guidance, and qadis appear less ready than some of their precursors to enunciate broad standards. Moreover, there has been a significant increase in the number of lawyers in Morocco, and their role may ultimately affect the use of judicial opinions too. So far, however, it is my impression that lawyers do not frequently bring the decisions of other courts to the attention of qadis, as the 'amal and scholarly briefs once did. Instead, lawyers are serving to regularize and facilitate the production of evidence to the court. Berque's suggestion that progress in Islamic law would come not through the perfection of positive law but through greater efficiency in the procedures and techniques employed in adjudication remains insightful if as yet unproved.[12] What does seem clear thus far is that the process by which Islamic judicial decision-making operates—with its emphasis on reconstituting interpersonal negotiation and its orientation to the consequences of individuals' acts—continues to play a conservative role in Moroccan legal development. Instead of becoming a vehicle for social reform by particular interest groups or an instrument for limiting or extending government control, case law serves to replicate local standards, at least as articulated by those chosen to give them voice, and thus to repeat, rather than challenge, existing patterns.[13] Regularity in Islamic law, at least as presently practiced in Morocco, lies not in the similarity of results in cases that appear to be similar, but in the constancy of the mode of analysis—of employing reliable witnesses, focusing on oral testimony, weighing the social interest, and relying on local experts. The logic of the case is the logic of one of various alternative ways of reading local consequence, and an array of cases proves the array of possible alternatives. As the movement of population blurs regional distinctiveness, particularly in the cities, the emphasis on the local is not, in fact, reduced, but expanded, the bounds of any given domain being enlarged to account for a kind of homogenized localism. Moroccans can therefore see in the range of judicial decisions what they are wont to see in their social lives generally—that consistency and harmony are not to be found in reducing differences to single propositions, or varied judgment to uniform antecedents. Rather, the appreciation of security and the avoidance of chaos will be further assured by cases that bespeak a common goal and a common process more than a common result;

---

[12] Berque (1944: 28).
[13] Compare this interpretation with the image of Islamic law as a patrimonial system in Weber (1954). See also the discussion of Weber's interpretation in Turner (1974: 107–21).

that way lies conformity to the way people truly are and how God intended they should conduct themselves. It is therefore very likely that, short of a major upheaval in the body politic, Islamic law in Morocco will continue its conservative course and that individual opinions will contribute not to the development or regularization of doctrine but to the mutually reinforcing legitimization of interpersonal negotiation within a framework that partly for that very reason is regarded as authentically Islamic.

Law is, of course, only one domain in which a culture may reveal itself. But like politics, marriage, and exchange, it is an arena in which people must act, and in doing so they must draw on their assumptions, connections, and beliefs to make their acts effective and comprehensible. In the Islamic world, as in many other places, the world of formal courts offers a stage—as intense as ritual, as demonstrative as war—through which a society reveals itself to its own people as much as to the outside world.

3

Islamic law as common law: Power, culture, and the reconfiguration of legal taxonomies

Comparativists often rely on a taxonomy of legal systems to place any given legal order in relation to others, to assist in understanding the influences one system may have on another, and to specify some of the purposes or functions by which to characterize a particular legal regime in the first place. In the vast majority of instances, however, scholars have constructed typologies in ways that vitiate the stated goals, with the result that the commentators themselves commonly regard their own systems as muddled. 'All in all,' say the authors of the leading casebook in the field, 'in spite of valiant efforts to identify "determinative elements" of world legal systems, the taxonomic fundamentals of comparative law are still in their infancy.'[1]

The classificatory systems that have been proposed range from the historically imprecise to the patently useless. The usual scheme thus includes such categories as common law, civil law, socialist (or nowadays, post-socialist) law, religious law, primitive law (with or without quote marks), traditional law, and—my own favorite— René David's 'other conceptions of law (residual classification).'[2] *It is rare to find any consistent analysis of the criteria for constructing categories: Even if one leaves aside the older classifications based on race, language, or presumed origins, present-day systems display just as much inconsistency when they employ such organizing rubrics as 'legal style,' 'legal tradition,' or 'socio-economic formation.'*[3] *The resultant categories often replicate—in the reasons for their construction no less than in their humorous outcomes—many of the same problems confronted in the history of biology, where one encounters such wonderful taxonomic categories as placental animals who were educable* (Educabilia) *or uneducable* (Ineducabilia), *'fruits ordinary' and 'fruits outlandish,' and (a category distinction perhaps only a department chair can fully appreciate) 'animals unsuspicious' and 'animals infuriate.'*[4] *Notwithstanding such results the value—heuristic rather than positivistic—of specifying criteria and group-*

---

[1] Schlesinger et al. (1988: 311).

[2] R. David and C. Jauffret Spinosi, *Les Grands Systemes de Droit Contemporains*, 10th edn, 1992, cited in Mattei (1997: 8).

[3] See Schlesinger et al. (1988: 310–12); 'Legal systems may be classified in a tripartite scheme according to the source of social behavior that plays the leading role in them' (Mattei (1997: 13)). Although I shall be arguing that taxonomies of law do have their value, it may be well to keep in mind Locke's famous statement: 'this whole mystery of Genera and Species, which make such a noise in the Schools, and are, with Justice, so little regarded out of them, is nothing else but abstract Ideas, more or less comprehensive, with names annexed to them' (Locke (1975: Bk. 3, Ch. 3, § 9)).

[4] See Ritvo (1997: 36–9, 21, 189).

ing instances may be as significant in legal studies as in the elucidation of various political, kinship, or economic institutions.[5]

In the course of studying Islamic law in its everyday practice I have been increasingly struck with its similarities to the common law form in which I have also been trained in the United States. At some point, however, one begins to ask whether what one is encountering is like something else or is itself an instance of that other thing. I want, therefore, to outline some of these similarities, then to propose and apply a set of criteria for classifying legal systems—an enterprise that entails recasting the taxonomy of legal systems generally—and only at that point to return to the question of what value is gained by thinking about legal systems in such classificatory terms. This may seem the reverse of how one ought to go about such an effort, but until the process of reclassification begins to hint at certain insights it may be difficult to assess the general value in thinking about law taxonomically. Such an approach also replicates my own thought process in arriving at this reclassification, a procedure which is not intended as a brief excursion into my own intellectual biography but as an indication of how the evidence with which I am working may conduce others to think about their own materials as we contemplate shifting the paradigm of legal classification.

ISLAMIC LAW AS COMMON LAW

Common law systems contain an inherent contradiction. On the one hand they seek to draw upon the common culture as a prominent, though by no means exclusive, mechanism for the determination of facts and, on the other, find that the inherent ambiguities of most cultural forms pose obstacles to the definitiveness required of legal assertions. This ironic relation of the common law to the common culture is, however, not unique to Anglo-American systems of law. As we try to understand how, in any given system, culture is drawn upon by the law the ethnographic approach has much to commend it. To ask how, for example, Americans construct their assessments of another's believability and then ask how that squares with evidentiary assumptions about character or credibility is to touch upon the law at precisely one of those points where law and culture intersect: To ask how our form of legal reasoning partakes simultaneously of the logic of a culture and the logic of the law is to ask how each domain lends credence to the other. And to seek, in ethnographically contrastive examples, how these same features play themselves out when, to borrow Wigmore's metaphor,[6] the kaleidoscope of any legal form is turned, may afford us some insight into the scope and pattern of common law as a general form of cultural and legal organization.

---

[5] As in many other domains one is always comparing things that are not identical but whose range of similarities reveal central organizing features. As Clifford Geertz has put it: 'Santayana's famous dictum that one compares only when one is unable to get to the heart of the matter seems to me, here at least, the precise reverse of the truth: it is through comparison, and of incomparables, that whatever heart we can actually get to is to be reached' (Geertz (1983: 233)).

[6] Wigmore (1941).

A useful starting point for the consideration of Islamic law as a common law system is Edward Levi's characterization of common law reasoning.[7] Levi speaks of American common law as a system of 'moving categorizing concepts,' a system in which each court has the ability to regroup the facts of present and past cases in such a way as to shift or extend prior categories to meet current instances. This is, however, accomplished with such linkage to the terms of the prior set of categories as to give a restrained sense of continuity even where significant departure may be present. It is a mode of reasoning that fits well with a system of law that, as one commentator has put it, 'glorifies the particular situation.'[8]

By comparison, I would suggest, Islamic law also displays a system of moving classifications. But unlike the Western common law, which has sought regularity in the institutions and conceptions by which the legal system tries to capture and comprehend cultural change without appearing to be divorced from it, Islamic law tries to capture the cultural forms directly without appearing to affect them through its own institutional structure. Let me try to exemplify what I mean.

Anglo-American common law has developed elaborate techniques by which it is imagined to be extremely good at assessing facts, the use of scientific techniques being only one of the more recent manifestations of this cultural emphasis. By contrast, Islamic law prides itself on elaborate techniques for assessing persons. The Anglo-American emphasis relates to a political history of indirect control which operated, archetypally, through jurors who once knew those before them but later developed into a more anonymized, rights-based set of protections against the state. It also connects to a cultural emphasis on the individual as the creator of his or her own circumstances, a religious emphasis on interiority as the mark of moral meaning, and the development of concepts of probability, natural progression, and time as a vehicle through which the essence of any person is revealed. Each of these concepts has lent emphasis to the idea that truth is best acquired through an account of occurrence.

The contrast to North African Muslim cultural history is quite sharp. Here, individuals are thought to stand at the center of personally constructed networks of affiliation which they must service and sustain through an elaborate calculus of reciprocating, negotiated, bargained-for relationships. In this sociological bazaar the focus is constantly on who the person is in any given circumstance, and assessment of that person is itself largely a function of determining the consequences brought about in the world by the network of ties he or she constructs.[9] Not surprisingly, under such circumstances, elaborate techniques have developed for assessing persons.

---

[7] Levi (1948), and Levi (1965).

[8] Howard (1994). The analogy to Kuhnian paradigms, which may in this context come to the mind of many readers, was actually drawn by Kuhn himself when he wrote that a paradigm, 'like an accepted judicial decision in the common law, . . . is an object for further articulation and speculation under new or more stringent conditions' (Kuhn (1970: 23)).

[9] Both men and women create networks of obligation, though to different degrees, with different resources, and to different effects. For a more developed discussion of this issue see Rosen (1984).

Thus North Africans characteristically want to know about a person's social origins—since they supply the baseline for how a person constructs his attachments—and who owes what to whom: Such information is vital if one is to calculate the impact of one's own ties to such a person. Unlike the West, where time reveals the truth of persons, in the Arab world it is, rather, nested bonds of obligation—like some elaborate map, or the diagram of an electrical system—that shows where another is located in social space and what forces keep a person attached, consequent, identified.

When they are brought into court these cultural orientations take on an aspect at once distinct to the law's need for definitive results and the cultural propulsion to maintain the room for maneuver that is seen as an inherent aspect of social order. The qadi will, in most instances, thus try to determine who a person is, not just what happened in the circumstance at issue: He (or sometimes now, she) will try to assess the variety of a person's relationships, may inquire into the person's tribal or local origins, will ask how the person has acted in a range of contexts, and will pay attention to how a person talks about the people to whom he or she is attached. Modern qadis consistently claim to be able to tell if people are lying by comparing their responses to what a person of such a background is characteristically like in his network formation. In the past, there were even court personnel who were experts on physiognomy, thus helping to establish the truth of claimed social origins as evidence of how one most likely negotiates ties and possesses relationships. Moreover, witnesses had to be certified as reliable—in the sense of having proven relationships of consequence and predictable implications—before being allowed to testify, and this element is still present in the attempt to calculate interpersonal attachments more than events as a primary vehicle for determining truth.

This emphasis on contexts of relationship for determining legal issues is itself deeply connected to the aims of the law. Whereas Western common law courts may boast of determining the truth and letting the chips fall where they may, Muslim judges characteristically insist that their goal is to get people back into working relationships—contentious as they may be—rather than to solve matters in a way that ignores future ties. It thus makes a good deal of sense—cultural sense—for the law to use techniques of person perception that are seen as consistent with this goal. There are few people who believe that disputes are 'solved' when rights are determined to the detriment of what the consequences will be for ongoing relationships, and fewer still who believe that one court case constitutes the boundary to any interpersonal dispute. The best one can hope for is that if negotiated ties are still possible some degree of overall social peace can be maintained.

Given this aim, the courts have institutionalized many of the cultural orientations found in other domains of society—as, for example, in the use of notaries as official 'reliable witnesses,' whose documents are presumptively dispositive, or through court-attached experts, who determine what a person of such circumstances can expect by way of support or remedy. More importantly, the process of determining truth has continued to emphasize features of person assessment: Most procedural elements focus on social context and social consequence rather than on specific occurrences. Or, more precisely, it is believed—culturally and legally—that to know the person is to know the event: To place an individual—or to see through a person's attempts to hide who they are sociologically—*is*, in large measure, to get at the facts.

We may treat these and other features as a set of cultural postulates that are simulated in the legal domain as a correlative set of legal postulates.[10] As a suggestive rather than exhaustive list one might indicate these postulates along the following lines:

Table 1 Comparison of Islamic socio-cultural and legal postulates

Socio-cultural postulates	Legal postulates
Humans are reasoning creatures responsible for developing their knowledge.	Causal chains trace to the acts of the nearest sentient being involved in their own effects.
All forms of knowledge have value, so those who possess knowledge should be carefully attended to.	Experts should supply the court with local knowledge to supplement the testimony of reliable witnesses.
Actions do not exist separate from their intentions.	No separate intent inquiry is needed if the person and the context are known.
A person is constructed by obligational bonds to others and the peopled environment that nurtures him.	To know what someone has done one needs to know his network of indebtedness.
All relationships are essentially negotiable.	Judicial inquiry should look for actual not idealized relationships.
People stand at the center of greater or lesser constellations of bargained-for relationships.	The bounds of relevance of a legal dispute are a function of the network of ties involved.
One must seek extensive bonds of obligation to secure oneself in an uncertain world.	Greater legal harm attends wider and more consequent networks of affiliation.

[10] The idea of jural postulates, derived from Stone (1950), is developed in Hoebel (1954), and Hoebel (1965). By using the idea of postulates I would not want to be understood to be agreeing with the proposition that such foundational concepts generate and account for the structure of a society or culture. In this I agree with Clifford Geertz (1983: 186–7), that one should concentrate on the sets of meanings by which people orient themselves rather than posit certain foundational concepts. Indeed, my use of postulates is intended as a form of summarizing some of these orienting ideas, not a comprehensive description of the structure of Arab society and law.

Table 1 (*continued*)

Socio-cultural postulates	Legal postulates
One assesses another by the way he uses words to create bonds of obligation.	Documents are the reduction to writing of the oral and should be evaluated for the truth of the person represented therein.
Utterances are binding only when validated by oath or reliance enforced by webs of obligation.	Agreements must be validated by reliable witnesses.

Thus a system has developed which assumes that persons are, to borrow the image of an Arab poet, known by the traces they leave, the effects they have on others' nego-tiated relationships. As changes occur they are brought into judicial cognizance by a form of organization and reasoning that pushes fact-finding down to the level of local determination through court-appointed local experts, reliable witnesses, and a set of assumptions about human relationships that accords with—indeed is an integral part of—the commonsense assumptions about how people conduct themselves in the world. For example, as we shall see in Chapter 5, it can be argued that a move has begun in Islamic law toward more use of circumstantial evidence, concepts of proba-bility, and the notion that things—and not only sentient beings—can cause things to happen.[11] These apparent shifts have occurred in such diverse realms as the explana-tion of agricultural success, the circumstances of local history, and the efficacy of reli-gious acts. Such changes appear to have been drawn into the law through the same modes of assessing local circumstance that applied to their precursors. But Islamic law not only provides us with a number of intriguing indications that, on more than intu-itive grounds alone, it shares a number of features with common law systems: It also forces us to reconsider the very factors by which we shall form our classifications in the first place. It is to that consideration that we must now turn our attention.

RECONFIGURING LEGAL TAXONOMIES: COMMON LAW SYSTEMS

A. Criteria of Comparison

Societies, it can be argued, are held together when the categories by which people divide and orient their experiences are replicated in so many domains that they appear to be both immanent and natural. Law, then, figures prominently in a culture when the reverberations carried in its proceedings and results also partake of cultural orien-tations that converge and resonate in religion, politics, the economy, the family, and many other areas. There are certainly those societies, or portions of them, in which the law is so much a cultural domain of its own that it is less well connected to the

[11]   See Rosen (1995a).

assumptions and orientations that resound through other aspects of the society. But any consideration of common law systems must suggest—and indeed lead us to investigate—precisely those ways in which the common culture and the common law are defined by the very ways in which they partake of one another's orientations. Looked at in this fashion, a detailed consideration of Islamic law and Western common law suggests some intriguing possibilities for categorizing and studying socio-legal systems. But any such classification must first be freed from some of its historic baggage.

Unfortunately, the fabrication of legal taxonomies continues to remain largely mired in nineteenth-century formulations and errors. When the First International Congress of Comparative Law convened in Paris in 1900 several distinct trends in legal analysis were brought together. On the one hand there was the idea that evolutionism pointed the way to the mechanisms by which that 'science of law' envisioned by continental legal scholars of the seventeenth and eighteenth centuries could actually proceed. Joined with this was the belief that, since all humans were of a single species and law was a 'necessary manifestation' of that unitary human nature, diverse laws would ultimately converge into a single system.[12] But the categories of 'legal families' set in train by these assumptions never came to reflect a focus on the mechanisms of change since the issue was prejudged by the self-satisfied knowledge that all was to a purpose, and that purpose was convergence in a Eurocentric form of law. Though shorn of the language of race and *volksgeist*, contemporary taxonomies continue to reflect this history.

Thus, we continue to be told, as part of the distinction between civil and common law systems, that continentals are given to abstract thought while the English favor the concrete. 'As a generalisation, civil law or Germanic and Romanistic legal families tend to think in abstract, conceptual and symmetrical terms . . . whereas the English common law is typical for its concrete, court-based approach seeking pragmatic answers to issues before the court' (Cruz (1995: 36)). 'On the Continent lawyers think abstractly, in terms of institutions; in England, concretely, in terms of cases, the relationship of the parties, "rights and duties" ' (Zweigert and Kotz (1998: 70));[13] we are also told that civilians plan while common lawyers improvise: 'Another conse-

---

[12] Hyland (1996: 186), citing G. del Vecchio's 1910 reference to 'the profound unity of human nature of which the law is a necessary manifestation.' The purposeful nature of the evolutionism of comparative lawyers is also neatly captured in a statement by Josef Kohler, also cited in Hyland (1996: 186): 'Comparative legal investigation deals with the evolutionary side of the law; by no means, however, with that desolate and sterile kind of evolution which derives each development from an accidental and external coincidence of particular fact; but, on the contrary, with the spiritual point of view which assumes that the world-process involves an inherently reasonable course of development, an evolutionary struggle which employs the mechanical factors only for the attainment of its ends.'

[13] Such stereotypes are not limited to cross-Channel examples: 'Thus in the Far East law does not lead to a judicial decision in favour of one party, but to a peaceable settlement or amicable composition. There is much of the wisdom of the Orient here . . . [I]n the West man naturally fights for his rights and seeks a clear decision, treating a compromise as a thing perhaps to be settled for, and in the East the face-saving compromise is the ideal and a firm decision only a necessary evil' (Zweigert and Kotz (1998: 72)).

quence of the historical development which is reflected in the mode of legal thinking is the civil law penchant for planning, systematising, and regulating everyday matters as comprehensively as possible. In contrast, the classic common law characteristic is to improvise' (Cruz (1995: 36)).[14] We are even told (in the words of the latest edition of a leading text in the field) that: 'Convinced, *perhaps from living by the sea*, that life will controvert the best-laid plans, the Englishman is content with case law as opposed to enactments.'[15] Most systems of legal classification remain extraordinarily vague and circular,[16] the functionalist emphasis on purpose[17] still being equated with convergence toward a basically Western model.[18] Although a few comparative lawyers appreciate that law is part of culture rather than some separable and refined essence of it, little advantage has been taken of social science understanding about ideology, the role of elites, or law as an instrument of political order.

In part, the problem with most legal classifications stems from a more widespread misunderstanding of how the study of taxonomy has developed in modern times. For as Stephen Jay Gould reminds us, in his essay on how Alfred Kinsey's Ph.D. dissertation on the taxonomy of wasps affected his later work on human sexuality, classical taxonomy was essentialist in nature. It viewed the world as a series of pigeonholes defined by fundamental features separating one species from another. Variation was treated as a necessary evil, a kind of scattering out from the essential form. Modern taxonomists, by contrast, appreciate that 'variation is primary; essences are illusory,' a view in which 'shadings and continua' must be accepted as fundamental. Such a taxonomy focuses on the uniqueness of individual systems while noting the existence of 'islands of form,' 'ranges of irreducible variation,' that derive from no immutable essence.[19] Obviously one's categories are meant to reveal central features: Men and mice and insects may all have hairy legs, but having or lacking backbones or exoskeletons may be the more valuable category for sorting instances. In the study of legal systems this suggests that we could approach common law systems not against the background of some essential feature of precedent or case distinction but as a range of processes by means of which variant, indeterminable, and shifting cultural concepts give substance, meaning, and legitimacy to relatively more fixed judgments, and do so in ways that contrast with other systems of legal reasoning and institutionalization.

[14] 'If we may generalize, the European is given to making plans, to regulating things in advance, and therefore, in terms of law, to drawing up rules and systematizing them. He approaches life with fixed ideas, and operates deductively. The Englishman improvises, never making a decision until he has to' (Zweigert and Kotz (1998: 71)).

[15] Zweigert and Kotz (1998: 71; emphasis added).

[16] 'We make these groupings primarily for taxonomic purposes, so as to arrange the mass of legal systems in a comprehensible order' (Zweigert and Kotz (1998: 63)).

[17] '[T]he comparativist can rest content if his researches . . . lead to the conclusion that the systems he has compared reach the same or similar results, but if he finds that there are great differences or diametrically opposed results, he should be warned and go back to check again whether the terms in which he posed his original question were indeed purely functional, and whether he has spread the net of his researches quite wide enough' (Zweigert and Kotz (1998: 36)).

[18] See Hyland (1996: 190).

[19] Stephen Jay Gould, 'Of Wasps and WASPS,' in Gould (1985: 155–66, at 160–1). See also Gould (1978).

'Surprisingly,' says one legal writer, 'comparativists rarely find it worth mentioning by which criteria they select their material.'[20] Often internally contradictory and disowned as quickly as they are enunciated,[21] the criteria for legal classification, as for any other typology, are inseparable from the purposes to which they are applied and the broader theories that, for the moment, they may entail. Anthropologists and creative writers have noted categories that represent much of the experience of the people who use them—whether it be that of a real tribe which groups certain animals and plants together because they have a similar fleshy taste or, as in the case of Borges' zoological classification from a mythical Chinese encyclopedia, to reveal the reader's own limited perceptions.[22] Serious taxonomists appreciate that even though Linnaeus grouped things together just because they looked alike, such systems still have value after the Darwinian revolution if they focus on multiple characteristics and/or adaptive functions.[23] Although, as we shall see, one must be careful in drawing analogies between biological and socio-legal classification, and notwithstanding the risks attendant on any classification of replicating the problems separating the lumpers from the splitters or the proponents of analogy from those of homology, one can forge categories on the basis of particular features and then test their heuristic value against the widening range of experience to which they point us.

Bearing such considerations in mind, I want to propose two distinct yet related features as the defining characteristics by which to reconfigure a system of legal classification. These two criteria are:

(1) the place that law occupies in the overall distribution of power within the society and polity at large, in the face of

(2) fundamentally unstable and indeterminate cultural conceptualizations which must be taken into consideration by the legal system.

---

[20]   Frankenberg (1985: 430). Just as bad, if not worse, are the numerous instances in which the criteria keep being changed in the course of a single discussion (Mattei (1997)), or instances in which the criteria are so poorly defined as to defy regularized application (Sacco (1991)).

[21]   See, e.g., Mattei (1997: 17, n. 52): 'Some of my choices are based mostly on intuition and sensibility rather than on measuring devices unavailable at this point. Thus many readers may challenge and feel little sympathy for my choices. However, I must clearly state at the outset that the actual content of the taxonomy and the choices I make are aimed mostly to clarify my taxonomy and I am not particularly fond of any one of the dubious ones that I have entered.' On the problems comparativists have with their own categories, see Frankenberg (1985: 411–12, 426–9).

[22]   Borges writes of a Chinese encyclopedia in which animals are divided into the following groups: '(a) belonging to the Emperor, (b) embalmed, (c) tame, (d) suckling pigs, (e) sirens, (f) fabulous, (g) stray dogs, (h) included in the present classification, (i) frenzied, (j) innumerable, (k) drawn with a very fine camelhair brush, (l) et cetera, (m) having just broken the water pitcher, (n) that from a long way off look like flies.' Cited in Foucault (1970: xv).

[23]   The approach known as 'cladistics' relies primarily on anatomically unique features shared by different lines. As a result, it is now argued that a taxon like that of reptiles has no validity, despite Linnaeus' use of it, whereas the existence of well over a hundred distinctive features shared by dinosaurs and birds, most of them based on homologous functioning rather than analogous structures, leads many to group these two categories more closely than in the past. On the approach of numerical taxonomy, see Sokal (1966). On modern systems of biological classification, see generally Cain (1993: 15–26), and n. 71 below.

The choice of the first criterion, even though rarely addressed by comparativists, is rather straightforward. Law is clearly a mechanism through which the terms and values of a society are articulated and given legitimate backing, and, as such, law, however defined, is undeniably part of the equation of power at work in the community. This power may, of course, range from the draconian to the ancillary, but it is neither irrelevant to nor divorced from the overall way in which power is itself organized. The main question, then, is not whether power is a key aspect of the type of legal system at work or a function of the enforcement of a sovereign, but how the distribution of power operates through the law in ways that are deeply intertwined with the overall distribution of power within a given society.

The choice of the second criterion is integral to the theory of culture to which many anthropologists subscribe. In this view, human beings are essentially category-creating creatures; indeed, it is one of the great discoveries of the age that we achieved our present speciation only *after* we acquired the capacity to create the categories of our own experience. Moreover, these cultural conceptualizations are essentially open-ended, unstable, and indeterminate; indeed, the capacity to reconfigure experience in order to adapt to changing circumstances is vitally connected to the malleability of the cultural categories themselves. Legal systems, like any other domain of life, must contend with these fundamentally incomplete and unstable cultural conceptualizations. How this problem is approached varies from indirect absorption through localized legal institutions to direct attempts to limit the changeable nature of such cultural concepts. By seeing if there are, in effect, a limited set of characteristic 'solutions' to these twinned problems of power and culture we may be able to sort the multiplicity of legal systems into discrete categories and sharpen both our criteria of selection and the insights we hope to gain through them.

Unlike other classificatory systems that rely on such features as the presence or absence of case law, codes, precedent, or supernatural sanction, the two features noted here focus on the legal system as part of a larger socio-cultural–political order. Accordingly, the resultant categories seek to organize types of responses to the issues of power and culture. Codes, precedent, and the like are specific ways of addressing both power and culture, but they are second-order mechanisms through which primary factors—how power itself is distributed and how culture is dealt with by law—are approached. Relying on second-order features would indeed be like creating a category based on whether things have hair on their legs or go bump in the night, rather than getting at the features—the attendance to power and culture—which specific mechanisms further in a categorically distinctive way. To test for the usefulness of these criteria let me, then, first indicate what I see as the characteristic responses that common law systems—both Anglo-American and Islamic—have to these issues, and, secondly, elaborate the other two categories of my overall typology. Only after addressing both of these concerns do I want to consider the utility of constructing a legal taxonomy in the first place.

B. Common law systems

Common law systems address each of the criteria with which we are working in a highly characteristic fashion: They address the first criterion

(*a*) by dispersing power to the local level through various mechanisms of indirect control, while still retaining ultimate power at the apex;

and they address the second

(*b*) by letting local cultural conceptualizations and information fill up much of the content of the law through indirectly administered mechanisms of incorporation.

Numerous commentors have, at least implicitly, remarked on these features as they apply to the case of the Anglo-American variants of common law. From the time when a relatively small number of Norman invaders found themselves in charge of an island people who vastly outnumbered them, to the control of the Indian subcontinent by a handful of British troops and bureaucrats, law has served the British as a vehicle for political centralization. Since at least the time of Henry II the keystone to the political control of the many by the few lay in the institutions of indirect political control.[24] From the Norman institution of collective liability (the 'hue and cry') to the elaboration of the jury of presentment into a full-scale trial jury, the British used institutions that pushed the administration of everyday legal matters back to the local level, while retaining ultimate administrative control through the oversight of the judiciary and the issuance of necessary writs for legal actions. At the same time, this system of indirect rule was able to absorb changing cultural norms through local institutions in such a way that the values and orientations of concepts and procedures applied by the law remained both recognizable and legitimate to the populace at large. That the legal regime was, at different moments, identified with the interests of invaders, gentry, or particular elites is of secondary importance: What mattered was that, through a legal system of indirect rule—a system of rule by indirection—power was dispersed to the local and culture was not sharply demarcated in the law from the local.

Indeed, it is against these criteria that we can perhaps best read some of the features often ascribed to common law regimes. Justice Benjamin Cardozo summarized the view of many when he wrote that '[t]he common law is at bottom the philosophy of pragmatism; its truth is relative, not absolute.'[25] Brian Simpson elaborates:

[I]t is a feature of the common law system that there is no way of settling the correct text or formulation of the rules, . . . in 'any authentic form of words'. . . . Nor does the common law

---

[24] On Henry II's reforms see van Caenegem (1987: 114–17).
[25] Quoted in Howard (1994: 205).

system admit the possibility of a court, however elevated, reaching a final, authoritative state-ment of what the law is in a general abstract sense.[26]

Simpson can thus conclude that:

The point about the common law is not that everything is always in the melting-pot, but that you never quite know what will go in next. . . . We must start by recognizing what common sense suggests, which is that the common law is more like a muddle than a system, and that it would be difficult to conceive of a less systematic body of law.[27]

That this quality of indeterminacy inheres in common law systems follows from the criteria I have described: Since power is dispersed yet held by the center through mechanisms of indirect control, and since the changing concepts of the culture are a major source of the law itself, it comes as no surprise that the mode of reasoning should stress a high degree of relativization and conceptual openness. Levi's 'moving system of categorizing concepts' makes perfect sense when structural form and pliant response are attended to through such a political-cultural approach.

Similarly, Melvin Eisenberg has argued that common law is characterized not by the application of binding doctrinal propositions, the application of general rules to hard cases, or the ultimate invocation of the judge's own moral or political convic-tions. Rather, he sees as central the application of those 'social propositions'—those propositions that encompass the moral, political, and world-ordering ('experiential') norms—which grant both regularity and responsiveness to the system.[28] While Eisenberg's idea of 'social propositions' is quite vague and his characterization of Levi's analogic reasoning misplaced,[29] his formulation implicitly acknowledges that the boundary between culture and legal application is kept structurally open-ended in common law systems: The dispersal of power through indirect control forms a backbone to a structure that can incorporate changing social and cultural life while still retaining an identifiable form.

Analogic reasoning has, as we saw in Levi's own formulation, played a key role for many commentators in assessing the nature of common law systems. Cass Sunstein, for example, reasserts the common law's emphasis on the particular, but goes on to say that in common law 'analogical reasoning operates without a comprehensive theory that accounts for the particular outcomes it yields.'[30] As we shall see, in both the American and Islamic variants of common law, such incomplete theorizing is

---

[26] Simpson (1973: 89, 90). The internal quote is from Frederick Pollock.

[27] Simpson (1973: 91, 99). Simpson sees the common law as a customary system inasmuch as it is a set of practices and beliefs received by 'a caste of lawyers.' Clearly, much of the common law may, in its Anglo-American variant, be shaped, if not created, by lawyers—or by other legal figures in the Islamic world—but this does not reduce it to the culture of the legists. Much of what is received is the common sense of the broader culture (e.g., how persons and situations are perceived), and common law is thus much more than positivistic assertions fabricated within the legal domain alone.

[28] Eisenberg (1988: 44–5).

[29] Eisenberg (1988: 84–7) reduces Levi's argument to nothing more than reasoning by example, never mentioning the idea of a 'moving system of categorizing concepts' which is a far more subtle and different notion.

[30] Sunstein (1993: 747). See, generally, White (1996).

attendant on the common law mimicking that same quality which inheres in cultural concepts themselves, the very concepts that are, in turn, integral to any common law system's claim to legitimacy. To speak of the open texture of common law legal reasoning—whether as part of its capacity for 'moral evolution' or its ability to gather divergent views under shared outcomes[31]—is to speak of a defining typological characteristic in common law systems, namely, the direct embrace of unstable cultural concepts through a system of indirect and localized application.

How then do these features that we are identifying with the whole class of common law systems show themselves in Islamic law? As to the first criterion, indirect political control, Islamic legal regimes, despite their organizational and doctrinal variation, have—both historically and in most instances through to the present— characteristically propelled matters down to local experts and reliable witnesses to determine the facts, sought to fashion settlements among the parties (sometimes even by having the parties meet informally at a notary's home or with go-betweens encouraged by the court to intervene), aimed at putting parties back into negotiable relationships with one another, and largely avoided appellate structures until they were forced on them in colonial times. Muftis (jurisconsults) varied in the extent to which they explicated their reasoning, their connection to the locality in which they worked, and the check they provided between state-approved approaches and local decision-making.[32] But increasingly it is clear that their role was not simply that of literary stylist or abstract theorizing: In many instances they articulated the principle of a case, which, even though it might not be applied to any other case, thus served, like Anglo-American courts of appeal, to establish regularizing concepts and modes of reasoning, placing a kind of upper limit to the lower one established by local adjudication. In various ways, then, these legal consultants contributed to that form of indirect control involvement that is represented in other common law variants by such professionals as the bar, the academy, and even the appellate structure.[33] Even penal laws that distinguish between punishments that are mandated by the Quran (*ḥuddud*) and those that are deemed discretionary (*ta'zir*) represent a distribution of power between the sovereign and the courts. From the earliest days of the 'constitution' of the Caliphal period, a clear distinction existed between matters that involved the political powers and those that were of concern to the Sacred Law, and while this

---

[31] '[A]nalogical reasoning does not require people to develop full theories to account for their convictions; it promotes moral evolution over time; it fits uniquely well with a system based on principles of stare decisis; and it allows people who diverge on abstract principles to converge on particular outcomes' (Sunstein (1993: 790–1)).

[32] See, for example, the discussion in Tucker (1998: 15–22).

[33] Scholars of the classical and medieval period disagree on the relation of fatwas to developments in the law applied in actual cases. Johansen (1993) emphasizes the range of maneuverability demonstrated by the fatwa literature while seeing literature, rather than court cases, as the locus of doctrinal change; Tucker (1998: 21–2) acknowledges that most of a mufti's fatwas outside the core region of the Ottoman empire were not directly connected to court proceedings, but does indicate the absence of real disjuncture between the two and the connection they made between local practice and central authority. As research begins to assume greater connections the use and interpretation of court records may further affect our views of the structural forms of power and culture in these systems.

was neither a simple balance of powers nor a demarcation of precise design it was an expression of the devolution of power to multiple legitimate sources.[34] The result, in quite varied forms, has been a politico-juridical scheme in which the overall distribution of power incorporated a strong element of indirect control and localized determination.[35]

As to the criterion of addressing unstable cultural concepts, Islamic law has long evinced the characteristics of common law regimes. Consider, for example, Levi's distinction. Anglo-American common law imagines itself to be exquisitely sophisticated in the determination of facts—whether by adversarial inquiry, statistical analysis, or forensic investigation. By comparison, Islamic law officials imagine they are particularly adept at the determination of persons: They believe that if they know a person's origins they can describe his characteristic relationships and actions, and, as we have seen, experts in physiognomy were even attached to the courts to help determine where a person really came from. If the Anglo-American variant is, in Levi's terms, a moving system of classifying *facts*, Islamic law courts utilize a system of moving *person* perception in the same fashion. So, for example, it was common in the past for a distinction to be made between 'clean' and 'dirty' trades, the practitioners of the former (cloth merchants, food distributors, etc.) being more readily able to perform the five-times-daily ritual ablutions necessary for prayer. But when a new trade comes along that is lucrative but 'dirty,' like that of automobile mechanic, the law—which uses such criteria, for example, to set bridewealth payments for women under its aegis—has had to revise its categories accordingly. Or if a woman holds a good position in the civil service and earns more than her husband, courts, which otherwise would favor the husband, have often revised their categories in order to grant to the mother custody of a minor child. Islamic law, then, is a moving system of person classification that is structurally and functionally quite similar to the fact-oriented pattern to which Levi addressed himself in American law.

Similarly, analogic reasoning was by no means simply a matter of whatever appealed to the judge any more than it was a mechanical operation amenable to predictable outcomes. Rather, as in Anglo-American law, Islamic legal reasoning involves reference to the purposes, similarities, and public value of drawing one or another link among instances.[36] Historical and contemporary evidence continues to

---

[34] See Serjeant (1964).

[35] Many students of Muslim political organization, as it existed until the Ottoman and colonial periods, have noted that Islamic law was really a negation of the state, an attempt to keep the two separate—in bodies of law (qanun being applied by secular officials, shari'a by specialists in the sacred law) as well as in those enforcing such laws. Islamic law was not meant to further the state: It is a law that focuses on the individual and asks whether what any individual does is good or bad for society. Although he puts the matter too strongly and too much in Western terms, it is also worth noting Adam Mez's emphatic statement, referring to all of the court personnel: 'This body of learned men, *absolutely independent of the State*, thus constitute the highest tribunal. Through them democracy, the sovereignty of the community of the faithful, maintained its position in the important sphere of the law' (Mez (1937: 230); original italics).

[36] On the varieties and commonalities of Islamic analogic reasoning, see Hallaq (1987) and Hallaq (1997).

grow suggesting that not only were the 'gates of independent reasoning' (the ability of earlier commentors to add to the body of religious law through their own interpretative powers) never really closed but that Islamic law judges have frequently exercised their own reasoning powers to reach decisions that have been creative and even contrary to established tradition.[37] In the determination of which judges should be regarded as most worthy of being followed; in the development of the concept of consensus (*ijmā'*), which, for most scholars and judges, implied that once agreed upon even an approach that originated from a 'weak' source should be applied; and in the recourse to concepts of the public interest (*maṣlaḥa*), Islamic law has pursued a highly relativistic mode of incorporating the ever-variable social and cultural standards of the community as integral to the law itself.[38]

A number of the features of these two variants of common law—American and Islamic—may be summed up in the following table:

Table 2 Comparison of American and Islamic common law variants

American common law	Islamic common law
Assessment of *facts* through moving classificatory concepts	Assessment of *persons* through moving classificatory concepts
Reasoning by analogy favored	Reasoning by analogy (*qiyas*) as one of the sources (*'usul*) of law
Morality may be brought in by analogic reasoning	Moral precepts may be recognized from respected sources unless clearly limited by Quranic prescription.

[37] See, e.g., Hallaq (1994) (showing that a fatwa was not only brought to bear on an actual case but that the style of reasoning is typical of many such instances); Layish (1991: 83–4) (showing the creative extension of the concept of 'injury' (*darar*) to a wife suffering psychological abuse and insult); Johansen (1995) (arguing that casuistic reasoning allowed judges a greater range of creativity in response to changing social differentiation in the post-classical Hanifi period); Tucker (1998: 143–5) (describing instances in which mothers are appointed guardians of their children even when the standard rules require appointment of someone from the father's kin group); and Tucker (1998: 160–7) (describing extension of the concept of 'judicial doubt' (*shubha*)—really a kind of mistake of law argument—to situations that would have yielded a result no longer regarded as appropriate).

[38] Accommodation to change in Islamic law, while varying over time and in the theories of various legal scholars, has incorporated several important elements. Although the Quran and Traditions of the Prophet (*sunna*) were inviolate, various forms of analogy developed—from strict analogy when the purpose of the foundational text was indisputable, to the search for a sound analogy (*tawil*) when either purpose or text were open to different views. Characteristically, all such reasoning comes down to the person who is doing the interpreting: It must either be a 'qualified person' or a body of scholars, but the focus is always on a person or persons who marshal opinion rather than on the office a person holds. The same is true when the concept of the 'public interest' is involved: Whether the reasoning follows the 'preferred' course or the course of general benefit to the community, the emphasis comes back to the person who gains sufficient repute to make his view prevail. On the concept of necessity in Islamic law, see Muslehuddin (1975).

Table 2 (*continued*)

American common law	Islamic common law
Cases or controversies have distinct boundaries	The 'bounds of relevance' are situational; cases are not necessarily expected to end disputes
Similar cases should be decided similarly	No two people or situations are alike, so no two cases are alike
Justice means equality	Justice means equivalence
The goal is to establish rights and duties	The goal is to return people to negotiating permissible relations among themselves
Custom may be accepted by the court as part of the common law	Local custom *is* Islamic law unless it violates Quranic prescriptions
Later judges determine the range of what prior cases say	Prior cases decided by respected judges provide insight but do not form the backdrop to each unique case
Judges are constrained by a prior court's construction of a statute more than by factual situations	Judges are now constrained by appellate structures whereas traditionally no judge could speak with final authority
Movement in the law is often not apparent or is justified obliquely, so that explicit policy does not appear to be made by the courts	Judges may, without acknowledging that they are changing the law, look to public interest (*maṣlaḥa*) in individual instances and to preferred opinions of scholars (*istiḥsan*) where codes or the Quran are silent
No elaborated set of principles needs to be worked out in advance to guide later decisions	Future decisions depend on code and/or individual contexts for whose assessment the process is the principle
'Judges are not behavioral scientists' (Levi 1965: 407)	Judges bespeak local standards that set the terms by which relationships can be permissibly formed

Again, from this rather stylized comparison we may perhaps see that both of these systems share a certain family resemblance; they belong in the same taxonomic category. Both emphasize process over form, both utilize moving socio-cultural categories, both limit the power of judges by degrees of uncertainty about the range and force of their rulings for future cases. Far from being autocratic or arbitrary ('the qadi under the tree dispensing justice for each case without recourse to general rules') Islamic common law constrains by its emphasis on local person perception and local sources of knowledge; far from being a veil behind which judges can do whatever they personally think fit, American common law constrains by its style of acceptable argument. That the one should ground its ultimate legitimacy in religious precept and the other in the will of the people may matter far less than the similarity of their emphasis on the circumstantial and their extraction of guidance from broader socio-political orientations. Unlike systems of law that are predominantly arms of the state or that concentrate on replicating existing social relations, these two systems share a focus on the distribution and limitation of power within processes that continually move between general principle and local circumstance. However, in order to test for the utility of our chosen criteria for categorizing legal systems and the actual group-ings that result, it will be necessary, next, to consider the other two taxonomic cate-gories that form our overall classification, the civil law and reciprocity-based systems.

ELABORATING THE TAXONOMY: CIVIL LAW AND RECIPROCITY-BASED LAW SYSTEMS

In the formulation of a taxonomic scheme the analyst has several classic choices avail-able. Facing the problem of whether to concentrate on differences among entities, and hence proliferate categories, or focus on their common points, thus claiming greater validity through elegance and parsimony, the investigator replicates the usual dilemma of the taxonomic 'lumpers' and 'splitters.' The choice is also influenced by public relations: Will people adopt a system replete with neologisms and multiple categories, or will they more likely adopt the proffered system if it employs (indeed, appropriates) familiar terms and an economy of forms? On the assumption that truth and wisdom (to say nothing of simple advertising advantage) are to be served by brevity and familiarity, I have chosen to keep my taxonomic categories to just three groupings, each of which has a terminology and a *locus classicus* I shall cheer-fully appropriate. We have already looked at the first, the category of the common law: We may now add the other two, civil law systems and reciprocity-based legal systems.

A. Civil law systems

'Civil law' systems are usually associated with continental Europe, its former colonies, and those nations that chose to fashion their laws after the codes or procedural systems of eighteenth- and nineteenth-century European nation-states. The features usually associated with civil law systems are those of elaborated legal codes (often modeled on the archetypal Justinian and Napoleonic Codes); the avoidance of prece-dent and case law in favor of reference to the code and scholarly opinion; and the formation of a professional judiciary, separated from the members of the bar, who conduct investigations by direct inquiry and are dependent for their advancement on the government-controlled bureaucracy. Such features, while important, are, however, indicative rather than definitive of more central criteria: Like hairy-leggedness, codes and state-directed inquiry are features that cross-cut legal taxa and constitute partial instances, not central solutions, to the problems of power and culture.

Those analysts who have attended to aspects of power, even if only implicitly, come closer to the mark, though not without some value judgments influencing their work. Thus, civil law systems are frequently equated with authoritarianism and the absence of a strict separation of powers. Van Caegenem, for example, asks frankly whether civil law is authoritarian and common law democratic, and while he offers a somewhat equivocal affirmation of the latter proposition he gives, in the scope of a few pages, a resounding yes to the former.[39] Others put the matter just as bluntly: '[W]hat is the philosophy of the Civil law?' asks A. G. Chloros. 'In this respect, it can be argued that the Civil law is on the side of authority and order. . . . [I]n the field of human relations . . . the Civil law carries a strong element of paternalism.'[40] Similarly, Norman F. Cantor says: 'The fundamental principles of Roman law in the Justinian code are absolutism and rationality.'[41] He points to the lack of independence of the judiciary in the Roman-law system and the continuing role of Roman law as a 'powerful contributor to a continental culture of conformity and regulation and close control over society by a self-perpetuating elite.'[42]

Such comments could be dismissed as part of the continuing battle between the civilians and the common law lawyers that has characterized so much of continental versus Anglo-Saxon antipathy in the past. For purposes of thinking through the characteristics of legal systems, however, it is necessary to sort out these and other factors from the brickbats that often accompany them. Bearing in mind our own criteria—how is power organized and how are unstable cultural concepts utilized— several factors warrant attention. Politically, civil law systems do indeed conceive of the law as an arm of the central state. This does not mean that there may be no independence to the judiciary; that may fluctuate with history and the particular variant of civil law. What it does mean, though, is that the law is not imagined primarily as a counterbalance to central authority, and it is not organized so that it performs its work separate from that which the state furthers directly. Thus power is not, as in common law systems, dispersed: Where, for example, lay jurors in civil law systems sit with professional judges they still do not see the official dossier nor do they commonly expect to act independently of the judges; where judges fail to

---

[39] van Caegenem (1987: 73–83).

[40] Chloros, like many commentors, is being descriptive, rather than simply evaluative, but, like many, finds himself having to temper the characterization of authoritarianism with the argument that this is just another way of organizing a polity. He says: 'It was a Roman principle to be found in Justinian's Institutes that *quod principi placuit legis habet vigorem* [what pleases the prince has the force of law]. If this principle is alarming, we need not be unduly worried about the philosophy of the Civil law as a whole. For order and discipline are essential elements if liberty is not to give way to anarchy. What the Civil law has sometimes found difficult is to draw the line which will permit a right mixture between liberty and order' (Chloros (1978: 17)).   [41] Cantor (1997: 33).

[42] Cantor (1997: 44). The remark about judicial independence is on p. 40.

find guidance in the code they are characteristically instructed to do what the legislator would have done had he but got round to writing an applicable provision.[43] The result is a set of legal regimes in which substantive law is managed at the center in furtherance of a state whose organizing principle is one of predictable application of authoritative views.

This orientation is, of course, connected with the second leg of our test, the way culture is inscribed in the law. Civil law systems are basically amalgamative, absorptive: Culture is subject to reception by the legal system, which receives it not through the direct invocation of an oracular jury or an analogizing judiciary but, reluctantly if at all, by being the one that declares it to have an existence beyond mere opinion and by direct judicial action through which it is raised to the position of law. Thus a sharp distinction can be made conceptually between law and custom, the latter having no force unless marked as part of the former, thereby losing its separable identity. So, too, for changing conceptualizations in general: They should come through the legislature, not through the people or the court. The larger orientation of which this constitutes one aspect has been remarked by Cantor:

What distinguishes Roman law from Anglo-American common law is that at the bottom they represent two very different cultures. Roman law was a culture of closure. Knowing what was good and right in society, it wanted to create a judicial structure that would confirm this goodness and rightness and make their operations in society easier and more evident. What was useful and applicable about the law had already been discovered and written down. After that, as social and economic change occurred, it was only necessary to make adjustments at the margin within a preexisting system.[44]

Once again, the contrast to common law systems is striking. Allison, for example, has argued that the attempt to make the distinction between private and public law found in continental systems apply in common law regimes has failed precisely because the expectations of independence and expertise are quite different in each of these regimes. 'Legal transplants' cannot, he argues, be thought of simply as the transfer of rules from one system to another: 'Without a study of effect or interpretation one cannot draw inferences concerning the success of transplantation.'[45] Indeed, much of the angst concerning the role of the European Court in British law arises out of the quite different political implications that a common code of human rights or regulatory schemes have for the political culture of Britain versus the continental countries.

---

[43] Aristotle had pointed out this precept: 'When the law lays down a general rule, and a later case arises that is an exception to the rule, it is then appropriate, where the lawgiver's pronouncement was too unqualified and general, to decide as the legislator himself would decide if he were present on this occasion' (cited in Jonsen and Toulmin (1988: 68)). Aristotle is not, however, proposing authoritarianism: His argument is that rules must be supplemented by equitable precepts that are sufficiently flexible to fit quite different situations.

[44] Cantor (1997: 44). See also Varga (1977) on the quest for the singular embodiment of the law in a readily accessible code.

[45] Allison (1996: 6–7). Allison is particularly responding to the argument of Watson (1974).

Islamic law clearly does not fit the pattern of civil law systems as defined here. Codes have been adopted in most Islamic countries for a variety of matters, but the United States certainly has more statutes than any other nation and that alone does not qualify it as a civil law system.[46] Similarly, Islamic courts often seek resolution of their differences among the parties themselves, but again that feature (like 'hairy-leggedness') is found in other regimes and is not a defining criterion. More crucially, Islamic law embraces the cultural quite directly. Muslims consistently say that their customs do not stand apart from or alongside Islamic law; rather, they see their customs *as* Islamic law, provided they do not contravene a clear Quranic precept.[47] The style of reasoning is also crucial. Whereas civil law systems work against an ideal of certainty, common law systems are intensely relativistic. Indeed, the mode of reasoning is not simply based on case law but is an example of the larger category of casuistic reasoning. That is, instead of agreed general principles or rules there exists, as Jonsen and Toulmin put it, 'a shared perception of what [is] *specifically* at stake in particular kinds of human situations.'[48] The recognition of a multiplicity of concrete situations that do not require certitude for an orderly political dispersal of power to operate consistent with changing cultural circumstances takes different expression in different variants of common law. In Anglo-American law it is represented in the trial jury and private prosecutions, the focus on procedures that imply the presence of a jury, and the modes of distinguishing precedents; in Islamic regimes it is represented in the traditional absence of appeals, the use of analogy, public interest, and preferred or minority opinions, and the popular conception of Islam as that which Muslims do.[49] Casuistry in Islamic law, as Baber Johansen points out, serves to reconcile the practices of important social and professional groups with doctrine and to create more scope for judicial action. 'In this way, casuistry helps to underline the differentiation between the various legal spheres of Islamic law and to enlarge the judge's margin of action. The integration of new forms of casuistically examined social practices into the law is an ongoing process that enables the jurists to amend and develop their doctrine on specific points.'[50]

[46] It is not, therefore, accurate to say, as Judith Tucker does, that: 'Codified law cannot, by definition, be flexible and fluid law. Legal codes no longer offer a variety of possible interpretations; rather they work to standardize cases and minimize the element of judicial subjectivity' (Tucker (1998: 184)). Rather, codes as used in civil law systems tend towards this characterization and the modern Turkish situation is indeed one in which the most thoroughgoing attempt has been made at replacing Islamic law with a European-style civil law system. Tucker (1998: 184–5) goes on to wonder, 'whether or not such codification actually violates the Islamic legal traditions to such an extent as to rob it of fundamental coherence.' The response offered here is that where codes have been introduced into Islamic countries they have (with a few exceptions, of which Turkey is the most noticeable) not replaced Islamic law—in the sense of the procedural, cultural, and political rather than just substantive law aspects of the system—and thus it is not the presence or absence of codes that is critical but how they fit in with the broader concerns of power and culture.

[47] See the discussion in Ch. 5. On custom as an implicit source of law in Islam, see Libson (1997) and Rosen (1989a: 42). [48] Jonsen and Toulmin (1988: 18).

[49] An-Naim has said: 'Islam is what Muslims believe and [the way they] behave' (Hammoudi (2000)).

[50] Johansen (1995: 155–6). See also the discussion of Islamic law in Jonsen and Toulmin (1988: 366–7, n. 19).

Similarly, the very image of Islamic law is consistent with its being categorized as a common law variant. For while it may seem that Islamic law, as a 'religious law system' must be grounded in certainty, such a characterization misses the point. Not only is there an in-built indeterminacy to Islamic law—there being few actual Quranic prescriptions and no single authoritative voice to fill the interstices—but the very absence of elaborated code-like formulations conveys the sense of law being immanent rather than, as in civil law systems, manifest. The shari'a, like Anglo-American common law, hovers over society, legitimizing not centrality through its own certitude but, ironically, its opposite—the dispersion of power to local practice.[51] Just as '[t]he immemorial and unwritten character of common law allowed its origin to be placed, beyond memory, in the realm of nature and not of man,'[52] so too Islamic law is projected not simply as natural—which is simply a feature of all cultural conceptualizations—but as a phantom mediator between the certainty that pulls toward categorical acceptance and the struggle against the collapse toward the center in favor of a centrifugal dispersal.[53] Civil law systems posit law as certain and perpetuate the image that judges discover it as proof of its very existence; common law regimes posit an ontological law but, in disagreeing over it, focus on the process of working through its indeterminacy. It is this latter approach to power and culture, not the existence of a religious base or utilization of precedent, that gives Islamic law its family resemblance to other forms of common law.

B. Reciprocity-based legal systems

The third of our major legal taxonomic categories approaches power and culture in a somewhat different fashion than either the common or civil law systems. Here, power is oriented toward reinforcing the social system by which human interactions take place. Legal institutions do not assert a moral order separate from social practice nor seek to incorporate its changing concepts as the source for their own enforced precepts. Rather, legal spokesmen articulate standards of behavior within a larger cosmological order, and are both limited and empowered in their involvement by the quest to make parties and their supporters work out their own differences along the lines of accepted convention. Cultural concepts are brought in directly, by legal personnel and parties speaking for themselves or through spokesmen, but since the focus is on how people respond to various social situations cultural ideas are given the appearance of unmediated cosmological propositions.

The term 'reciprocity-based' is used to describe this family of legal systems because, in the sense in which anthropologists work with the term, such legal systems reinforce

[51] This image of Islamic law hovering over society can, of course, get indefensibly romanticized. Coulson writes: 'Floating above Muslim society as a disembodied soul, freed from the currents and vicissitudes of time, it represents the eternally valid ideal towards which society must aspire' (Coulson (1964: 2)).   [52] Goodrich (1994: 75).
[53] The self-image of law as immanent and natural is explored in the American context in Schlag (1996).

mutual interconnections that, at any given moment, constitute the basis for distribut-ing power within these societies. 'Reciprocity,' of course, does not necessarily mean equal any more than it implies stasis: As anthropologists use it, it means the exchange of goods and services, expectations and obligations that stitch together relationships in a society. The exchanges can be quantitatively and qualitatively equal or dispropor-tionate; they can be immediate in time or delayed to best advantage.[54] But even when highly manipulated or egregiously one-sided there is always an element of give *and* take, of mutuality, of relationship by means of which at least the ideals of social and moral behavior are most often expressed. The term fits for this class of legal systems, too, insofar as it describes systems that reinforce relationships of reciprocity in what-ever form they take and bespeak (rather than merely enforce) its canonical standards.

Put somewhat differently, reciprocity-based legal systems do not break into the cultural web of reciprocity (however configured among negative, generalized, or balanced forms) through a separate (and separating) legal institution, but seek to uphold the social conventions by drawing on the multiple roles their articulators possess to effect the expression and, one hopes, the realization of the generalized forms of social reciprocity. Such systems are by no means static: The creativity of the Cheyenne or the Kapauku, the Tiruray or the Busoga are well-documented. This creativity may, I suspect, be seen by members of the society not as change but as the conserving force of re-reading existing standards to assert the mix of reciprocity forms that are thought to hold the society and the cosmos together.

Reciprocity-based systems vary widely but always display characteristic features. Although it may seem that they simply reinforce the status quo—a feature that may, of course, be attributed to other families of law as well—in fact, given the emphasis on reciprocity, this social conservatism has a distinctive shape. Here social conven-tions, not those of the law, are primary and litigants are commonly propelled back into their relationships with little interference by legal personnel on the shape of those relationships. Indeed, whether it is the archetypal judge in Brecht's *Caucasian Chalk Circle* taking handouts from each side before punishing both, or the Indonesians' image of the law as a bird that swoops down to take the object in dispute away from both parties,[55] penalties may be exacted from both sides for fail-ure to work things out according to the criteria appropriate to their relationships and positions in the social and cosmological orders. The law may act in this regard like those teachers who punish both children who are fighting, in order to teach them to settle their differences—even by schoolyard tussle or lumping their felt sense of injury—rather than risk the possibility of greater social disorder.

Similarly, such systems are sometimes described as aimed at the production of social harmony. This is often coupled with an image of the preservation of society from something akin to illness. Here is René David on the subject:

---

[54] See generally, Sahlins (1972), especially the chapter entitled 'On the Sociology of Primitive Exchange' (pp. 185–275). See also Price (1980) on the cultural variability of the mix of reciprocity forms.
[55] Geertz (1983).

The FAR EAST and BLACK AFRICA reject the idea of law as a principle. For the people of these countries it is sadly necessary in some cases to pronounce a sentence, to impose a solution on someone who has not respected the rules in use in society, but the delivery of a judgment providing a sanction cannot be regarded as normal; still less does it deserve to be advocated as a desirable means of settlement in human relationships. Disputes and crimes are looked on as sicknesses disturbing the proper functioning of the social 'body' . . . [T]hey do not call for authoritarian solutions; conflicts, when they occur, must not be resolved, but 'dissolved' by conciliation procedures. In all circumstances the essential is to restore harmony, for harmony among men, linked to the harmony of the cosmos, is something which must be ensured if it is desired that the world live in peace according to the natural order. . . . [M]any factors are taken into consideration to make both sides accept a solution, whose merit lies in its 'just,' not its 'legal' nature.[56]

Like so many statements of this sort, David's is a mixture of insight and error, especially when, as in this case, it is used to characterize so broad a portion of the world as 'the Far East and Black Africa.' 'Harmony,' which certainly means very different things to different groups in different societies, may indeed be an expressed goal, just as it might be in some common or civil law systems. But this misses the point. More often than not harmony is neither achieved nor is it a sufficiently subtle concept for grasping the actual goal. Indeed, as Elizabeth Colson has said (in a criticism aimed at Victor Turner's idea of *communitas*, but equally applicable to the arguments of many comparative lawyers):

However much disputes and their settlement are conducted in a rhetoric of community values appealing to something like *communitas*, what people learn from them is much more pragmatic information: the limits of community tolerance for different kinds of behaviour under a variety of circumstances, an appreciation of how particular individuals respond to provocation, and some mapping of the changing alliances that form the basis for daily interaction.[57]

In reciprocity-based systems strained relationships are no more solved by law than by social processes at large. Indeed, it is the replication of the pattern of reciprocity in the one that is mimicked in the other, with all the attendant uncertainties and lack of resolution this may entail. Similarly, the image of illness may indeed be the operative metaphor in some variants, and may be appropriate inasmuch as the stress is on the social and cultural 'body' being the unit that is being directed to 'heal thyself.'

There are also characteristic limits in reciprocity-based systems to the role of legal personnel. Whether it is the Barotse judge who cannot use his legal role alone to conduce an ungenerous husband to act like a good man[58] or the legal spokesmen of a Philippine group who give direct articulation of appropriate moral precepts to a person's subjective sense of injury,[59] power is displaced onto social forces and cultural concepts are left largely unaffected by direct articulation. Justice, then, may lie not in process or professionally developed or extracted law, but in assessing a person's

---

[56] David (1975: p. 5, capital letters as in original).
[57] Colson (1995: 80).
[58] See 'The Case of the Ungenerous Husband' in Gluckman (1955: 172–3).
[59] Schlegel (1970).

proper place in the scheme of things. This may be as true for an Indic kingdom as in a socialist republic seeking to educate those who come before the law to their proper roles.[60] The family resemblance in each instance speaks of a legal order that uses power to support social convention and approaches unstable cultural concepts by reinforcing their inscription in conventional behavior.

APPLYING THE TAXONOMY

Earlier legal taxonomies have not worked very well for two main reasons. One is the confusion of purpose: They have been almost entirely the handiwork of continental comparativists who could offer little *raison d'être* for their efforts beyond classification for its own sake. Others, even when favoring a view of law in evolutionary terms, never took the concept seriously enough to demonstrate the mechanisms through which such evolution is supposed to operate, their use of quasi-Darwinian terminology never really transcending the metaphorical to require serious consideration of the criteria for classification.[61] Before turning to the uses of classification, though, it may be well—in testing for that utility—to take one last step in which we continue to assume its worth in order to see how the proposed system plays out over a range of legal systems.

The following table summarizes the criteria applied to each of the three main orders of law that have been discussed:

Table 3 Summary of legal systems' approaches to power and culture

Legal system	Power	Culture
Common law	Indirect, dispersed, localized	Open-ended, moving classificatory system
Civil law	Direct, centralized	Amalgamative, absorptive, subject to legal reception
Reciprocity-based	Supports social conventions, limited by quest for social solutions	Articulates concepts inscribed in conventional behavior

---

[60] Geertz (1983), Engel (1978), and Feifer (1964).

[61] On evolutionary views see Richard Schwartz (1986). Sally Falk Moore (1986) properly criticizes Roberto Unger's typology of customary, bureaucratic, and legal orders for its essentializing assumptions. While Unger is at least focusing on political power, he also is not comparing similar things to one another—legal systems—but whole political orders.

By these criteria, we can see, for example, that the old category of religious law drops out altogether. Jewish law (at least since the destruction of the Second Temple), like Islamic law, fits well as a common law system; Hindu and Buddhist law as reciprocity-based systems; Confucian law (about whose actual operations we need to know more) probably as a civil law system. Some so-called primitive systems may fruitfully be thought of as variants of common law (the Iroquois, perhaps, demonstrating some of the reasons they may have been a model for a few aspects of American law); some systems of antiquity (Babylonia, Greece) as civil law variants. It is also interesting to think of such legal forms as university disciplinary proceedings and labor/management grievance procedures in these terms; to do so shifts our focus to the broader distribution of power within these institutions and the ways in which cultural concepts are or are not shared by those living within the same enterprise.

Concentrating on power and culture as central criteria also moves us away from too great an emphasis on the role of legal professionals in legal systems. Weber's famous fourfold division of legal systems along the axes of those concentrating on formal rules as opposed to substantive results, and those employing greater or lesser degrees of rationality, fits almost no cases precisely and, oddly for Weber, makes few direct connections to the larger cultural context.[62] And while Mirjan Damaska gives noteworthy attention to the relation of law to the organization of authority, he, too, cannot get us to the actual operation and cultural placement of law in particular cultures.[63] The legal taxa described here, by contrast, are neither ideal types nor self-contained: They are entities tied to their cultures and polities without reductionism on either side.

It has been argued, too, that legal systems, like their attendant cultural systems, 'skeletalize' information, taking from the vast array of potential information certain aspects which then receive emphasis in everything from linguistic constructs to ritual performances.[64] The three families of law analyzed here may also be thought of as basic skeletal patterns: They are not ideal types that do not exist in actual form in any situation but are themselves the result of skeletalizing processes, winnowed down and applied to their worlds, in variant forms, precisely in order to fashion power and culture to a given image. Whether they are effective or in tune with the realities of their situations is no more relevant than asking whether one or another religion is truer to human nature or human 'flourishing': They are, in their own contexts, models of and for the lives of their people, quite aside from any question of their success or failure.

Setting up a system of legal categorization can also attune us to features to watch for as systems undergo alteration. It has been argued, for example, that 'the statement that post-socialist law has simply returned within the Roman-Germanic family from

---

[62] Weber (1954). Mattei's classification, which includes, as one of its three categories, professionalized law, is even less defensible. Mattei (1997).   [63] Damaska (1986).
[64] Geertz (1983: 167–234).

where it originated is open to . . . challenge.'[65] Systems change, hybrids form, new variants appear.[66] Some countries (Hungary) may well become common law variants of an altogether new type; others (Bulgaria) may well follow civil law models. But if we see socialist law not as a civil law form gone wrong but as a reciprocity-based system in which the governing powers sought to gain conformity of social behavior and to be the spokesman for acceptable cultural concepts, we may be able to chart the changes that have occurred since the fall of communism more precisely than if we misperceive their earlier form.[67]

ON THE USES OF LEGAL TAXONOMY

'Taxonomy, or the study of classification, is generally accorded low status among the sciences—too often it is seen as an exercise in mere ordering, fit only for bookkeepers, and roughly equivalent to pasting stamps in prearranged spaces in nature's album. This attitude is both arrogant and false. Nature is full of facts, but any 'album' for their arrangement must record human decisions about order and cause. Thus, taxonomies represent the height of human creativity, and embody our most fundamental ideas about the causes of natural order. Taxonomies also channel our thinking into fruitful paths when a classification properly captures causes of order, but often into ludicrous error (older racial taxonomies, for example) when we mistake thoughtless prejudice for objective truth.'[68]

Given the taxonomy thus far described we must now return to a consideration of the value of thinking taxonomically about law in the first place. What exactly is the value of such a taxonomy? What insights does it purport to offer? What theoretical implications are associated with choosing one or another system? And what further considerations will establish the validity or usefulness of any proffered classification?

We can begin with the proposition that, as is the case with any classificatory system, pathways and attachments that might not previously have been appreciated

---

[65] Ajani (1995: 117).

[66] 'Mixed' or 'hybrid' systems in legal, as in biological, classifications must neither be ignored nor be used to undermine an overall taxonomy. Integration with other elements of the entity must not be replaced with notice of a singular feature. 'Turkey,' says Örücü (1996: 338), 'did not become a Middle Eastern Switzerland by simply borrowing the Swiss Civil Code in 1926.' What needs to be understood is the way that changes in law, as in other domains, fit into the overall cultural pattern, and how the law now comes to address the questions of power and culture we have emphasized. It may also be that systems that appear to be on the fence between legal styles are there precisely because they have not, in the larger political and cultural domain, resolved the issues of how power will be distributed and on what, if any, basis a common culture will be posited.

[67] Chloros (1978: 22), for example, characterizes socialist law by two criteria: 'The first is that the total good is better than the good of the individual. The individual, in other words, has, in the main, value in himself but only to the extent that he is part of the whole. The second proposition is that government, and therefore law, based upon discretionary power, is better than the rule of law.' This appears to me to be an example of a reciprocity-based variant rather than a separable category.

[68] Gould (1989).

are revealed when the criteria of common grouping strips away irrelevant features. In the case of Islamic law, for example, seeing it as a variant of common law systems helps us to see why, as a matter of fact, the strict application of Islamic law by fundamentalist regimes has consistently failed in modern times. Whether in the Sudan or Pakistan or Iran, in each instance governments have failed to turn Islamic law into an arm of the state. To the contrary, in each instance the courts have slipped out of centralized control and created a number of approaches that are quite inconsistent with what the governing regime imagined would be the simple imposition of the Sacred Law. In post-revolutionary Iran, as Mir-Hosseini has demonstrated, the courts have developed such concepts as the best interests of the child in custody cases or have recognized women's rights in ways that strict views of Islamic law administered on behalf of the state would not sustain.[69] Similarly, in Pakistan and the Sudan the simple use of Islamic law as an arm of the state has slipped through the fingers of those at the center.[70] The reason, I believe, is that these regimes have been trying to apply a common law variant as if it were a civil law system: Islamic law, with its emphasis on incorporating cultural conceptualizations that are inherently unstable and dispersing power through localized institutions, is a very different system than that which can simply be controlled from the center. So long as the procedures, the assumptions, and the modes of reasoning themselves remain unchanged, Islamic law remains a system that is not, and never was, set up for the furtherance of state policy.

A second advantage of rethinking legal taxa concerns the pathways through which influences themselves may operate. Without turning the analogy into a homology, it is rather like looking at the way in which viruses spread: It is much easier, we now know, for viruses to spread across more closely related species than between and among those that are more distantly related. To know the degree of relationship as it pertains to an important criterion at the genetic and microbiological level is not only to recast the taxa along the lines of this more useful criterion but to further our understanding, in turn, of the etiology of disease itself.[71] Similarly, in legal studies, the focus on how rules are drawn from one system and applied to another has not produced very useful results because it is not a useful criterion. However, if we look

[69] See Mir-Hosseini (1993), where she demonstrates that women in Iran who pursue their legal cases to judgment win almost 90% of the time.

[70] See Fluehr-Lobban (1987).

[71] A new botanical classification, to be published in the *Annals of the Missouri Botanical Garden*, uses 3 genes from 565 flowering plants to formulate a system of classification that does away completely with the morphologically based Linnaean system. Under the new system it has been learned, for example, that papayas are not related to passion fruit but to cabbages; that roses are related to nettles and figs. The genetic relations have convinced researchers that, in the words of one newspaper report, 'at last, 200 years after Linnaeus, they have the true picture of how all the world's plants are related' (McCarthy (1998)). The non-specialist may, however, be forgiven for wondering if, when the question is indeed one of genetics, this classification may prove most efficacious, but when it is a question of some other issue (e.g., adaptability to a given environment) a morphological feature shared with a genetically unrelated plant (e.g., heat resistance as a function of leaf surface) may not remain relevant. The lesson for legal taxonomies, too, may be that we must constantly ask what our purpose is as we weigh the merits of alternative classificatory schemes.

toward issues of power and culture other connections make more sense. Several examples may help.

Some years ago the Moroccan government introduced a jury system into the legal order. It was, however, modeled on the European system of lay jurors: Several laymen sat together with the judge in the case and voted with him on the outcome. People I have spoken with who served on these juries were favorably disposed to the idea but found the actuality unsatisfying, and within a few years these juries were dropped altogether. The reasons participants gave reinforced the sense that the form did not fit the overall thrust of the legal system: The jurors were not independent, they did not have the power to invoke local circumstances, they felt they were simply tools in the hands of the court, and they were not allowed to ask for information in the ways that would have made sense of things to them. We may never know whether a common law-type jury system would have felt more compatible, but clearly this civil law institution did not fit with the Moroccans' form of inquiry and decision-making.[72]

Similarly, the repercussions of colonial powers codifying laws, like those of the Hindus and Muslims in South Asia, are enlightened by a revised taxonomy. It would not, by our formulations, simply be the case that codification was inapposite given the types of systems involved. Rather, seeing Hindu law as a reciprocity-based system and Islamic law as a common law variant we can focus on how these codes created, rather than redacted, legal orders and thus did not replace village panchayats or Islamic muftis but became indirect systems of state control set alongside those systems. Had they been variants of the same classificatory type they may more readily have replaced the indigenous legal regimes instead of attempting to subsume them wholesale. And we have also seen, in the West itself, the example that Allison gives of the failed attempts to apply the civil law's public law/private law distinctions to British practice. Examples could be multiplied many times. In each instance, greater attention to the criteria of power and culture may allow us to trace the lines of success and failure of influence more exactly than in the past. Similarly, taxonomic rethinking may help us to focus on the structure of power in Arab societies themselves—to use the law as a vehicle for understanding more about the ways in which power is dispersed, the distinctive nature of political institutions in the Arab world, and the subtle forms of counterbalancing of powers that may operate through such institutions.

Indeed, by concentrating on the larger issues of power distribution and attendance to unstable cultural concepts the study of legal institutions is removed from being a bounded subject of institutional configuration and history and brought back into the larger domain of political and cultural studies. Not only can the example of how legal institutions create and reflect cultural propositions and assumptions about

---

[72] The lack of enthusiasm Moroccans have shown for the alternative courts discussed in Ch. 7 may constitute another such example. There have also been suggestions of direct borrowings from Islamic law by the English system of law: See, e.g., Makdisi (1990).

the nature of power be attached to what we know from other domains of society, but our theories of social and cultural processes can be enlarged to cover a more unified set of features. To look, for example, at the ways in which concepts of intentionality or the development of a concept of probability occur in different legal domains, in conjunction with their elaboration in other realms, helps us understand how replication in different spheres gives to a new cultural paradigm that ingredient of appearing immanent which is so crucial to a concept's successful implantation.[73] To ask if the members of a university, corporation, or residential area share enough cultural orientations to share in a legal forum is to ask the deeper theoretical question whether and to what extent cultural concepts must indeed be shared for people to coexist within the same institutional form.[74] If culture is humanity's way of grasping experience it is foolish to treat the law, in any society, as a totally separable domain populated by strange terms and stranger practices. If we see it *among* the many domains of life, as one of the domains through which cultural and political patterns are reinforced by replication, and if we see law as part of the common sense of the society and not some contradiction to it, our theories can only be enriched by being enlarged to the scope and scale of those who live their lives by its terms.

And finally, a reconsideration of legal taxa helps us to focus on the importance of variation, as opposed to essence in our social theories. When, for example, one reviews other legal taxonomic systems which are internally contradictory and confused, it is apparent that much of the problem stems from a continuing desire to get at something that is of the essence of any given category. The same problem still infects some social theories, oddly enough most notably some that purport to be evolutionary in nature. If, to drive home the point one last time, one concentrates on ranges of variation, then at least one gets away from the claims of having discovered *the* feature that defines a system and begins to examine the reasons that might account for certain similarities. Theories are only as good as their assumptions, of course, but clearly the assumption of essentialism has long since seen its day in all of the social sciences and should have been eliminated from legal analysis as well.

There is, ultimately, a certain inherent contradiction in the formulation of any taxonomy. When, for example, one asks biologists about their taxonomies the response I commonly get is that the categories are more than the mere naming of things. If that were so one could simply give each thing a separate number.[75] But, of

---

[73] On intentionality, see Rosen (1995e).

[74] One is reminded here of Margaret Thatcher's famous remarks that 'there is no such thing as society,' as clear an assertion as any politician is likely to make that people could live together even though they share in no overarching primary set of attachments.

[75] See the discussion by Ritvo (1997: 24) on this point. In comparative law some people have suggested, by contrast, the elimination of any categorization. Tamanaha (1993: 214, n. 50) writes: 'A number of legal pluralists have concluded that a non-taxonomic identification of law is the only solution to the difficulties with locating law as a type. Accordingly, several have suggested that law can be identified on a continuum based upon the degree of differentiation of institutionalized norm-enforcement. . . . This "solution" does not escape the taxonomic enquiry of what law is, it presupposes the answer. Continuums that purport to represent the entire range of a particular phenomenon, excluding all else which does not fall within its category, are implicitly taxonomic. Use of the institutionalized enforcement

course, showing relatedness of things is unavoidable, since one would still have to decide if two things were the same or different in order to assign them different numbers in the first place. And the moment some sort of grouping begins some theory is at work as to why things go with other things—whether that reason be structural, historical, or ecological. At the same time there is a certain disingenuous charm to the biologists' assertions that they believe their categories to be entirely human constructs, rather than direct representations of some positivistic fact of nature, since, at the same time, each of them clearly believes that his own formulation does indeed get at truths that other systems have missed. This particular form of hypocrisy is not unlike that which is found in the social sciences and humanities, and which I would call 'the hypocrisy of the interpretive turn': All interpretations have value, say many scholars, but *mine* of course is right! What saves both the biologist and his humanist colleague from the worst charges that can be brought against hypocrites is that each system of classification is subject to revision in light of the data and questions that it is responsible for generating. And it is also a recognition that we analysts are indeed human beings—category-creating creatures—and that only by watching ourselves involved in this very process, whether applied to the biological world, the social, or the legal world, will we be able to monitor our own tendencies and their implications.

The result for our purposes may be that, from this perspective, systems that might once have seemed to have little in common might now be seen as versions of the same 'solution' to the role of law in society, and thus to be less like hairy-legged things than like vertebrates or arachnids. It may make less sense, therefore, to categorize particular instances under the rubric of religious law systems than to group them according to the ways in which they use local knowledge to cope with state power. Common law, like any taxonomic category, emerges from an understanding of its variation rather than its essence, and with it emerges, perhaps, a new set of issues that focus attention on the relation of common sense and common culture to common law and common approaches to the distribution of power.

In sum, the point is not, of course, for biology or for legal scholarship, simply to reconfigure our way of categorizing resultant forms when we look for the distinctive ways in which the common culture is filtered into and through the institutions of the courts. Whether it is in understanding how persons are constructed in Islamic societies or how time is thought to reveal the truth of persons in the West, what unites various instances of common law legal reasoning may be their emphasis on

of norms as the criterion for placement on the continuum means this characteristic defines law's "type".' The more serious question is that implied by asking whether all legal systems, like all species, are really situated at the lowest level of useful differentiation, and any division into sub-species—given the ability of all systems, like all members of species, to interact with one another—is not vitiated, as by distinguishing human sub-species, by further subdivision. Cf. Gould (1978: 231–6). This is, I think, one of those places where the biological analogy of interbreeding populations as the defining feature of a taxonomic level could lead to error: Human cultural systems, as ways of addressing experience, are more akin to the level of genus and order than species, inasmuch as they tend to retain their distinctive qualities even as they alter internally over time.

deriving those truths through the direct inclusion in the law of common-sense cultural categories. Both Islamic and Western common law systems are possessed of a kind of legal relativity, a sense that the categories of the law must fix decisions at any given moment while remaining alive to the fact that the cultural categories on which their techniques and legitimacy reside may be subject to variation.

More to the point, these cultural categories do not themselves possess absolute certainty: They are by nature indeterminate, ambiguous, malleable, and essentially negotiable. Thus the style of cultural reasoning and the style of legal reasoning, while potentially at odds given their different styles of clarity, nevertheless are forced into an alliance that creates a constant tension between the momentarily determinate and the inevitably contested. By paying very careful attention, as we tack back and forth from the legal to the non-legal domains, to the ways in which Islam and the West have linked their fates to the sources of their respective common cultures we can deepen our sense of the similarities among apparently diverse legal forms. In doing so we will not only find typological similarities we may have missed, but we will be able to consider the broader consonance among legal and cultural domains. There is, in short, still a good deal of truth to Holmes' assertion that if your path leads to law the way to anthropology is clear before you.

4

Responsibility and compensatory justice in Arab culture and law

The attribution of responsibility is one of the most problematic and revealing aspects of any culture. Whether it is in Cain's audacious challenge to his creator or in the Quran's assertion that 'no man bears the burden of another,' the allocation of responsibility taps into a host of assumptions about what human beings are really like and against what expectations their relations to others may be viewed and appraised. To address the issue of responsibility is, therefore, to consider a broad range of attendant concepts—justice, causation, identity, will—whose particular manifestations partake of both the regularizing structures and the deepest uncertainties to which each culture falls heir.

The anthropological study of responsibility has been largely restricted to discussions of witchcraft accusations, itself a domain deeply influenced by the structural-functional questions of who is to be held accountable for the unforeseen and what social purposes are served by the allocation of responsibility. So, we have been told, accusations follow the lines of social tension and serve as a kind of social insurance scheme, distributing the burdens of misfortune around the community. Such studies were crucial for showing that accusations were neither irrational nor without systematic repercussions. However, the inner states of individuals and the complexities of large-scale, literate societies were mostly ignored. Moreover, the theory could not account for change, and since nothing was ever seen as 'dysfunctional,' all seemed to be for the best.

Islamic law, by comparison to the examples used by most anthropologists, is more formalized but no less connected to the larger set of concerns about social order. The attributions of responsibility, like the other topics we have been discussing, are deeply embedded in the larger concept of the person and commonsense views of human nature and human society. Instead of focusing on the realm of formal law alone, therefore, the following chapter seeks to place the nature of compensatory justice in the broader realm of cultural assumptions and thus to use liability law to understand how, in life as well as in law, people attend to the accidents and injuries that occur.

Throughout these chapters I have suggested that in thinking about cultural life in North Africa and the Middle East an analogy that may prove useful to keep in mind is that of the marketplace, the bazaar.[1] It is a domain in which hawking and haggling are rampant, where prices are not fixed and considerable uncertainty may exist over the quantity and quality of goods, where attachments of a patron–client nature often prove most effective as economic strategies, and the overall well-being of a merchant

---

[1] For an analysis of the Arab marketplace proper, see Geertz (1979).

or consumer can change with striking rapidity. A similar image also applies to the realm of social relations. For just as the free play of individuals in the marketplace seems barely containable by the precincts of their endeavors or the limits of human audacity, so, too, in the formation of social relationships an intense process of inter-personal negotiation, framed by the conventions of language, etiquette, and social constraint, informs virtually every act. It is an image of contract and negotiation that is replicated in numerous domains: In the Quran, where mankind is envisioned as free to enter relationships of any sort so long as they do not overstep that limited number of substantive rules known as 'the bounds of God'; in popular discourse, where the vision of each person as the center of a network of obligations becomes the impetus for a constant quest for knowledge about others' ties and the ways they are most used to forming them; in literature and popular culture, where stories center on the ways others have maneuvered their social ties as they seek to carve out a safe haven in a world of premonitory chaos; and in law, where the image of humanity as proprietary creatures gives point to a host of procedures, presumptions, and prescrip-tions that seek to order this defining quality. Whether it is in the relations among total strangers looking for a basis of mutual comprehension and engagement or in the heart of the family itself, the sense of the negotiable relatedness of all persons runs as a constant theme in Arab cultural life. The implications of this orientation for moral and legal approaches to the ideas of responsibility and justice are, of course, profound.

Franz Rosenthal accurately captured a central feature of Islam when he said that since its earliest times it has been a religion in which 'man was seen . . . as the center of action in this world.'[2] In religious doctrine and popular views alike human beings are seen as so endowed with the capacity for reason (*'aqel*) that they may acquire control over their passions (*nafs*) and thus avoid the chaos (*fitna*) that their own forgetfulness and urges might otherwise engender. For reason to develop, however, it is important to place oneself in association with those teachers or leaders who, by the development of their own reason, can provide the context for the enlargement of one's own self-control. Thus knowledge of Holy Writ and of worldly affairs both serve to develop the capacity to act wisely and responsibly. And since, as the Prophet himself said, there is no distinction among believers except as to knowledge, there is even strong support in religion for the legal proposition that the more knowledge-able a person is, the higher the standard of responsibility to which he should be held.

The image of mankind as reasoning creatures is further supported in a number of other domains of social and cultural life. Consider, for example, the concept of time. In the West time has, at least since the period of ancient Greece, been envisioned, in no small part, in terms of such metaphors as growth, development, and unilinear direction. We say that time flies like an arrow, and we think of the person as possess-ing a life history that accords with such an image. In the Arab world, however, time does not reveal the truth of persons: It is not by tracing the course of a person's life

---

[2] Rosenthal (1983: 36).

over chronological time that one can most thoroughly apprehend a person's distinctive qualities. Rather, for the Arabs time is envisioned as a series of discrete packets of relationship, moments that encapsulate particular networks of obligation individuals have personally negotiated. To know a person, what one needs to know is not some distinctive self that perdures across time and is made evident in the course of growth and development. Instead, one wants to know the variety of relationships in which another has participated, for it is such relations that show the most essential feature about a person, his ties to others and his ways of establishing them.

The same image is manifest in narrative style. In the West stories are generally told in chronological order—again, because time reveals certain truths about persons. But Westerners who approach the Quran or listen to Arabs relating popular stories or accounts often find the recitation confusing and disjointed. Instead of moving in a fairly clear chronological order the story often jumps about in time: Instead of a clear picture of events being given by referring to the sequence of their occurrence, central characters are referred to in numerous situations whose precise chronological order is not necessarily given. Yet if it is not time but contexts of relationship that are central to this vision of the person the relative avoidance of strict chronology becomes more comprehensible. Thus the Quran shows us the figure of the Prophet by showing the various contexts of his utterances and acts, while popular stories show us individual lives, like the facets of a gem, by turning them round in the light of a series of relationships whose precise sequencing is comparatively unimportant.

The overall image of the person, then, is of a proprietary creature whose exercise of reason plays a significant role in the exploitation of negotiated bonds and whose totality is knowable to others to the extent that they can gain information about the variety of his ties to others. That each person has a high degree of freedom of choice is sustained in religion and lore: It is directly assured in Quranic statements emphasizing the contractual and covenantal quality of the ties between God and man and among men themselves; it is demonstrated in ordinary narratives, for example, where repetition is used as a device to demonstrate that at each moment in time a reasoning man can choose what to do and that no two moments are ever precisely the same, the multiplicity of relationships that form their surround being forever in a state of flux. Men do not fashion their own selves, in the sense of creating moral visions of their own, nor do they possess an internal psychological structure separate and distinct from their overt acts. Instead, men fabricate the contexts of their relationships, their webs of indebtedness, and in doing so create islands of relative certainty in a world of potential chaos. A constant quest for information about others' networks animates everyday life. It is a vision of the world that is well expressed by a Muslim trader in one of Joseph Conrad's novels when he says: 'In the variety of knowledge lies safety.'[3]

The presentation of one's freedom to negotiate relationships wherever they may

---

[3] Conrad (1976: 113).

prove most advantageous is also reflected in the Arabs' idea of truth. In the West we tend to regard assertions about relationship as capable of being tested for their truth value. To say that someone is your friend or has certain obligations to you may be true or false but is at least susceptible to evaluation in terms of its veracity. By contrast, for Arabs it is well understood that an assertion of relationship, standing as a bare utterance, is not necessarily subject to evaluation in truth terms at all. It is like a price mentioned in the marketplace which does not take on the capacity for truth assessment until something more happens, until it is validated. This validation itself may occur by the use of a holy oath, by agreement among the parties, by the formation of additional ties created in reliance on another's utterance, or by having someone who is himself regarded as a reliable witness acknowledge the statement. Once an utterance has been validated truth and lying become extremely important. Thus even in the conceptualization of truth the image of a marketplace of possible arrangements which men must be free to attempt without being marked as liars should the attempt fail reinforces the image of negotiation that runs through so many domains of Arab cultural life.

If it is the contexts of bargained-for relationships that is central to the definition of the person in Arab culture then it also makes sense that for the Arabs the idea of intentionality should also look somewhat different than that found in the West. The Arabic word for intent, *nīya*, not only means 'purpose,' 'design,' and 'will,' but inasmuch as these features manifest themselves in direct faith niya also means 'simple,' 'naive,' and 'sincere.' It suggests in its semantic range what informants readily acknowledge in actual use, that a person constantly displays what lies inside him when he speaks or acts. Indeed, most Arabs do not recognize the idea of a distinct inner self that could exist apart from action, only a realm of overt expressions that must of necessity conform to what a person must carry inside himself. To the extent that a person can be conduced to speak or act, or to the extent that one can learn of the variety of another's past utterances and deeds by careful investigation, one acquires direct access to that person's intentions. In ordinary social life this means that people readily presume to know others' states of mind and do not hesitate to elicit behavior or exert pressure by characterizing words and deeds in such a way that their attendant motivations may also be adduced.[4] In law, as we shall see, this means that judges usually presume they can discern intent simply from what a person has said or done, and that intent can, therefore, remain a distinct element of legal consideration even when, in terms of formal doctrine, it does not necessarily appear as a constituent feature.

For the Arabs it also follows that what matters most in evaluating actions is not their connection to a series of abstract propositions that lie behind them but to the consequences that actions have in the world, their impact on those networks of relationships, those webs of obligation, that are constitutive of reality itself. Thus in ordinary life one constantly encounters reference to the effect that words and deeds have

---

[4]   See Mills (1940), and Burke (1962).

in the world as the means for assessing what they really mean. And in law it is the consequences of an act, rather than its antecedent precepts, in terms of which a logic of remedy will be fashioned. Indeed, because the harm that people can do varies with their knowledge and hence their connections to others the evaluation of harm itself turns in no small part on the assessment of a person's situated ties.

When, therefore, we turn directly to the realm of Islamic law as it is actually practiced in contemporary courts the proceedings become far more comprehensible for being placed in their larger cultural context. Western scholars have often said of Islamic law that it lacks the rigorous logic of doctrinal development found in a number of the other great systems of law. No general concept of contract exists in Islamic law, it is said, only specific forms of permissible or impermissible contracts; no idea of good faith is present, only concrete practices that are or are not enforceable.[5] But such an analysis misses a key aspect of Islamic law. Although it is true that the legal scholar often appears in Islamic history to have played a more prestigious role than the court personnel themselves, and even the scholars did not strive for logical consistency as the preeminent goal of their work, Islamic law displays in its practice features that, by completing an otherwise truncated view, demonstrate the particular logic that informs its overall shape. This order is most evident when one looks at the ways in which facts are shaped for decision and evaluated for their believability.

In its modes of proof Islamic law gives effect to the underlying cultural assumptions of the society at large. For just as Arabs assess events and persons by concentrating on the individual person as a situated actor in a variety of particular encounters, so, too, in court it is by focusing on the socially constituted person that the judge can shape and weigh the facts. Thus, as we have seen, all evidence is regarded as essentially oral in nature. Witness testimony is the predominant form of proof: The greater the number of witnesses, the more consistent their story, and the greater their direct contact with the parties in question the more their version will appear to be credible. As we have seen, too, even documents are regarded as the reduction to writing of oral testimony, and the techniques for assessing their believability are not mainly those one thinks of for documentary proof—the correctness of form or the indication of forgery—but those associated with determining oral believability. Thus the main questions asked are: Who is this person who is testifying or whose words are inscribed here? What is his social background and to whom is he attached? In the past, each witness actually had to be certified as credible by the judge and notaries of the court before being allowed to testify, credibility itself being a function of a course of dealings with people in the community suggestive of sufficient contact that a person would not readily lie lest it affect his network of obligations and the willingness of others to form ties with him. Although at present this type of certification process no longer exists, the criteria for assessing believability remain those based on the face-to-face assessment of oral testimony.

[5] Schacht (1964).

Similarly, it will be recalled, the court continues to have attached to it certain personnel who are, in a sense, institutionalized reliable witnesses. For any document to be valid it must first be witnessed by two of the court notaries (*'adul*) who by inscribing their names lend their voice to that of the party in certifying a given transaction. When necessary, the court will also turn to one or more of the experts who are attached to the court and who are regarded by virtue of their experience to possess vital knowledge about such subjects as building practices, costs of living, or the nature of medical issues.

When a matter remains in doubt notwithstanding the use of witnesses, the court may also turn to the use of a decisory oath. This practice allows the court to assign one party the opportunity to take a holy oath and thereby win his claim. If the party who is offered this opportunity refuses, he may, however, require his opponent to take the oath and if the latter does so it will be the latter who wins. What makes the system highly distinctive is that it is for the judge to assign the oath first to one or another party not on the basis of who is the plaintiff or defendant in the case—this structural feature being present in the version of the decisory oath still found in some European jurisdictions—but on the basis of who it is, in the court's opinion, who is most likely to know what is true about the particular matter at hand. Thus what comes to play a great role in the oath is actually the same feature one finds present in the use of witness evaluation, judicial questioning, and the use of reliable witnesses attached to the court—namely, a constant reference back to local custom, local conventions, and local people who are familiar with local contexts of relatedness.

And it is here, too, that the consistency that appears lost at the doctrinal level shows itself most clearly. For Islamic law is, as it were, organized vertically, not horizontally: Its referent is not other doctrinal propositions logically related to one another to form a coherent body but the relation of general propositions to the local circumstances that give them content. Seen in this light, Islamic law is highly organized and developed. Custom need not be a formal ingredient of the law: It is the baseline to which each issue ultimately has reference and hence the support for a system that finds in localized persons, practices, and presumptions the content for its overall form. It is a system which can be highly effective in big cities or in rural locales if what we understand by effectiveness embraces two vital aspects: first, that the predominant goal of the law is not simply to resolve differences but to put people back into a position where they can, with the least adverse implications for the social order, continue to negotiate their own arrangements with one another; and, second, that even though the specific content of a court's knowledge about particular individuals may be both limited and stereotypical, the terms by which the courts proceed, the concepts they employ, the styles of speech by which testimony is shaped, and the forms of remedy they apply are broadly similar to those that people use in their everyday lives and possess little of the strange formality or professionalized distortions found in some other systems of law.

The result, then, is a legal system that remains relatively close to the terms and perceptions found in a host of other domains of social life. To many Muslims, courts can no more be expected to preserve individual rights than might be expected in life at large—nor be any less corrupt or any more wise. For them courts are familiar realms that gain in legitimacy from the very familiarity of their style and underlying assumptions; they are part of life and not some extraordinarily refined version of it. And it is in these terms—of seeking out the manifold connections between cultural conceptualizations and their legal articulation—that we can approach the particular issues of responsibility and compensatory justice.

COMPENSATORY JUSTICE

In many legal systems of the world the conceptualization of wrongful actions tends to be organized around such categories as private versus public, or criminal versus civil. Classical Islamic law begins from a slightly different base. It distinguishes those acts for which punishment is prescribed (*ḥadd,* pl. *ḥudūd*) from those in which judicial discretion may be exercised (*taʿzīr*). The former includes unlawful intercourse, drinking alcoholic beverages, theft, highway robbery, and the false accusation of fornication. Because these offenses are regarded as acts that violate the bounds, rights, and claims of God it is not for human beings to interpose their own judgment as to appropriate remedies. By contrast, discretionary remedies apply to all those unlawful acts for which mankind may set the appropriate level since they infringe on those 'claims of man' that the Quran specifically leaves men free to negotiate among themselves. Thus killing—to choose only the most notable example—is a matter to be composed by human judgment rather than prescribed punishment. Although, as we shall see, discretionary remedies are themselves shaped by a variety of conventions, their assessment and resolution are within the realm of human control.

The logic of the hadd/taʿzir distinction, however, goes well beyond a simple division of religious versus secular. It implies a set of cultural expectations and assumptions that are deeply intertwined with those we have already discussed. Acts that are subject to discretionary remedies have in common that they break the continuity of a relationship forged by human beings as proprietary creatures, but the break occurs in such a way that it is still possible to reconstitute ongoing relationships without having to consider their impact on society at large. The harm these acts cause is, in a sense, limited by the break in continuity of relationship which a properly chosen remedy could help to reconstruct. Hadd-type wrongs go beyond this boundary inasmuch as, in the Islamic concept, they not only intrude on a domain marked out by God but because that domain is perceived as fraught with vast potential for social chaos. It is a class of actions in which the reconnecting of bonds is regarded as particularly difficult and in which the systemic repercussions for many other networks of obligation are difficult to foresee and control.

Both types of action possess significant procedural safeguards that help to determine when an act is of one type or another, safeguards that are aimed, in part, at preventing mankind from mistaking one category for the other. Yet even these safeguards turn on the question of consequence and harm. Thus, in the case of unlawful intercourse classical Islamic law requires four eyewitnesses to the act itself, an evidentiary requirement that is not only difficult to achieve but which, when it is, demonstrates that the act must have been so open and notorious that its social repercussions are vast indeed.[6] Once established, hadd wrongs also take the offender out of the ordinary mode of assessing acts: Where normally Islamic law, like Arab culture generally, stresses the person in all his situated obligations and characteristic modes of interaction, the establishment of a hadd wrong removes the individual from further consideration as a person (in the Arab sense of that social construct) since reintegration is not possible. By contrast, ta'zir wrongs retain the full panoply of personalistic considerations found in all domains of Arab social life. Similarly, justice is rendered in the former case by the very act of depersonalization where in the latter it can only be rendered by the fullest possible consideration of the person. Or, put somewhat differently, justice for a hadd wrong consists in the withdrawal of sociality through depersonalization while ta'zir wrongs stress reintegration through retention of the normal modes of person perception. This pattern may also help to account for the seemingly inconsistent way in which intentionality and causality enter Islamic law.

It is generally said of Islamic law that it is a system that pays no attention to an actor's state of mind when a hadd-type wrong is involved. Here, the harm is regarded as so great, and the infraction so deeply involved with religious proscription, that a principle of strict liability may apply. When, however, one turns to the realm of ta'zir injuries the matter appears to become more complex. Thus in classical Islamic law the remedy for the killing of another varies, in part, with the intent of the perpetrator. But this intent is imputed predominantly from the weapon employed: If the weapon is the sort that is normally used for killing the intent to kill will be assumed; if something normally less lethal was employed it will not. Moreover, the recourse—retaliation by the deceased's kinsmen or the payment of bloodmoney—turns on the characterization of the intent of the actor.[7] However, when non-lethal injury to a person or damage to property occurs, Islamic law has traditionally focused on two distinct elements—the unlawfulness of the act itself and the range of damage caused. Thus it is predominantly the fact that an act is illegal that makes liability attach—hence even an infant may be held personally liable for the harm he does if his act was itself unlawful.[8] Nor can the victim's own consent ever justify the wrong. Liability exists only for those damages which the facts show were directly related to the act, the mental state of the actor being relevant only if it assists in establishing the causal connection rather than as a vehicle for introducing fault.[9]

Thus in classical Islamic law if an act is deemed wrongful no separate inquiry of

---

[6] Yamani (1968). See also the discussion of private versus public actions in Ch. 11.

[7] On the Islamic law of homicide, see Schacht (1964: 178–87); Kennett (1968); Tyan (1965); and El-Hakim (1971).

[8] American law, too, allows an action for liability against a child. See Garatt v. Dailey, *Washington Reporter*, vol. 46 (1955), pp. 197 ff.

[9] Chehata (1970: 140); and Limpens et al. (1983).

mental state is necessary, although a showing of mental state may be sufficient to draw the causal connection to direct damage which an assessment of the ordinary course of events could as well reveal. This apparent interchangeability of strict liability with certain considerations of intent—what to some appears an inconsistent use, or poor logical development of, the concept of intentionality—makes sense, however, when seen against the cultural conceptualization of others' minds to which we referred earlier. For if it is believed that a man's acts are necessarily connected to his state of mind and that such a set of acts can be deciphered in terms of social background, connections, and modes of negotiating obligations, then it follows that for the Arabs another's intentions are regarded as readily available to discernment and do not constitute a separate domain hidden from human view. This attitude is clearly articulated by judges who say that they can always tell what is in a person's mind— by reviewing the course of his utterances and actions. A Saudi judge put the matter in the following way: 'The judge has to have an acute sense of observation; for example, just by looking at a suspect he should be able to tell what the man had concealed in his testimony.'[10] Or as a Moroccan judge put it: 'If I question people, if I find out who they are and what they have done, I can always tell if they are lying, I can always tell their intent (niya).'

Similarly, one sees in the legal ideas associated with liability the constant stress on consequence so common in other domains of Arab cultural life. Direct damages are compensable in law, including the costs that relatives of an injured party may have to incur in visiting and caring for the person. The way in which the chain of damages is itself constructed has certain distinct features. First, the damage must be concrete: What European lawyers call 'moral damages' and Americans 'compensation for pain and suffering' are not included. Secondly, the chain of causation does not extend to everything that might be foreseeable but only to those injuries that disrupt the injured party's capacity to operate within his web of obligations. Thus, thirdly, even involuntary injury possesses the same quality as voluntary acts since it is the harm it does, not the meaning that lay behind the deed, that is central. Moreover, the category of wrongs includes not only acts that are clearly unlawful but those undertaken in disregard of a person's security (*shart as-salāma*)—a category that allows a significant degree of discretion within the general framework of focusing on the impact on the injured person's obligational network. It is the rupture to what is most distinctive to human beings—their proprietary associations with persons, directly or through things—that shapes what the law seeks most to protect, whether it be the killing of a kinsman or the usurpation (*ghasb*) of another's property. It is this emphasis, too, that is central to the remedies that Islamic law has fashioned.

From this perspective we can now recapture and elaborate the Islamic ideas of responsibility and justice. We have already seen that, in a sense, responsibility is

---

[10]   Sheikh Abdulla Qadir Shaybat al-Hamd, a Saudi legal scholar, is here being quoted with approval by Sheikh Saleh Ibn Mohammad al-Laheidan (1976: 162), a member of the council of the Supreme Court of Saudi Arabia.

connected not to the question of what lies behind a deed so much as to what it leads
to. To this day in Saudi Arabia, where the system of compensation for unlawful
killing still applies, it matters less why a killing has occurred than that compensation
must be paid for its repercussions. What one is responsible for—who one is responsible to—is the schema of social obligations by which any individual may possess
identity and by which society as a whole may stave off the threat of chaos.
Responsibility is a personal matter even though compensation may have to be
acquired by utilizing one's collective attachments.

Indeed the cultural conceptualization of responsibility is closely linked to ideas
about the nature of causality itself.[11] Briefly, Arab social and legal thought has tended
to draw causal chains quite narrowly: A person or other living entity is said to have
caused something if no other sentient being intervenes to displace the commonly
expected results. Two distinct lines of analysis have followed from this orientation in
the course of Islamic legal thought.

On the one hand is the line of direct causation. This is exemplified by such
instances as the following: If a man opens the door to a bird's cage and the bird flies
away, it is the bird and not the man who, by the exercise of its natural propensity,
has caused the escape; if X unlawfully places a stone on a public path and Y, in stum-
bling over it, injures Z, only Y is said to be the cause of Z's injury. Such examples,
which appear not only in classical texts of an earlier age but in some modern jurisdictions, suggest that causation, and with it responsibility, are to be limited to only
the most direct and 'natural' consequences of an act. By thus limiting causality the
system reinforces the cultural emphasis on direct and personal contacts, and places a
significant limitation on arbitrary judicial action and the potential for socially and
politically disruptive retaliation.

A second line of analysis, however, looks to the idea of fault, in the sense of over-
stepping the permissible limits of action. It holds that if one acts in a way that is not
normally regarded as appropriate to a given endeavor, the consequences of this negligence may be attributed to oneself despite intervening factors. Thus a man who loads
a pack animal improperly is liable if the pack later falls and injures another, and a
man who lets too much water run out on the road to settle the dust is regarded as
the cause of a horse slipping and falling on a passerby.

Although these two approaches have had a long and varied relationship in different periods and jurisdictions they share certain distinctive cultural emphases. For
both imply that there are culturally recognizable propensities possessed by all creatures and things, and that the normal course of causality is a function of their innate
natures. Humans are not responsible if some other entity, with a nature of its own,
displaces theirs unless, by failing to recognize the nature of the artifacts and creatures
that fall under their control, they allow them to do harm to others. It is a way of
thought that can, therefore, hold children strictly liable for their injurious acts or

---

[11] The following discussion draws on examples found in Tyan (1926). See also Pacha (1944) and
Ruxton (1916).

blame an animal for doing what comes natural to it because human beings must simultaneously take responsibility for what comes within their proprietorship and be free from responsibility for that which gives expression to its own intrinsic nature.

It is here, too, that the ideas of excuse and accountability enter. For most Westerners, responsibility incorporates elements of mental state and morality. One need hardly subscribe to the moral imagination of a Richard Nixon who, caught in the tightening web of Watergate, said (as did Ronald Reagan during the Iran–Contra affair) that he was prepared to accept the responsibility but not the blame in order to understand that in the West the line between self and society may sometimes be made to coincide with the line between the moral and the legal. By contrast, for Arabs the extent of actual liability has very little if anything to do with the willfulness of one's acts; fault is largely displaced by repercussion, itself an amalgam of one's own situation and that of the injured party. And since one is responsible for the network one creates, one is necessarily responsible for the harm one might engender. Blame, in the sense of fault, is seldom an issue in moral or legal discourse; responsibility, in the sense of repercussions for the network of others' obligations, carries its own moral imperative inasmuch as it renders worldly position and social order vulnerable.

As responsibility focuses on the situated person so, too, does the idea of justice. For justice in Islamic life resides not simply in each event but in the distribution of events over the range of obligational ties.[12] Asked whether they would subscribe to a principle like that of American law which says that similar cases ought to be decided similarly, Islamic judges consistently respond by saying that since no two individuals are the same no two cases are really the same, and that even the same person in a later situation has accumulated a changed set of relationships. Regularity, they say, lies in using the same modes of reasoning to a conclusion, but two judges might reasonably come to different results even though they use similar forms of reasoning. Justice lies not in the similarity of result but in the regularized assessment of the totality of one's personhood. That is why it makes perfect sense in such a system to say, in the words of the Moroccan saying: 'When the times are just, one day is for me and one day is against me.'[13]

Justice and responsibility are also, no doubt, connected to views about the nature of power. Briefly, it can be argued that in the Arab view power stems from an extremely wide range of sources. Whereas one man may use wealth as a vehicle for acquiring power, another may rely (in a way that is favorable to his own ambitions) on his masterful rhetorical abilities to capture the terms that define a given situation. Power, being diverse, is very difficult to hold on to, and others may rapidly challenge existing pretensions from highly diverse bases. Arabs frequently use the word that is often translated as 'rights' (*ḥaqq*, pl. *ḥuquq*), but its implications are not the same as the Western idea of a right. Haqq, it will be recalled, means 'obligation,' and thus the

---

[12] Islamic concepts of justice will be discussed more fully in Ch. 9.
[13] Scelles-Millie and Khelifa (1966).

distribution of bonds of indebtedness among sentient beings. It does not convey the Western sense of an indubitably supportable claim. One only has rights, the Arabs say, to the extent that one can enforce them. To be away from your 'rights'—that is, to be away from your land, the people who support your claims to that land—is to have no right. One does not, therefore, look to the law or to political figures to enforce an entitlement but to add themselves to your network of interlocked associates whose particular resources can then be brought to bear on your behalf. And it is in this context, finally, that we may be able to consider some of the features of compensatory justice as it exists in the contemporary Arab world.

Modern commentators frequently say that in many new nations, where formal tort law was never elaborately developed, one is often confronted with either the breakdown of traditional approaches or their replacement by colonial models, and that the quest for an authentic, indigenous way of handling injury is, as in so many other domains of these nations' lives, a quest to recapture something that never really existed. Thus it will be said, for example, that collective liability, or at least collective support for individual liability, has broken down along with family solidarity and that, given so fundamental a shift in social arrangements, earlier remedies have little present effect. Similarly, it is said, the nature of wrongs has changed: Where once there may have been individual injuries, now the harm done may extend to hundreds or thousands of people, and if the wrongdoer is not of such stature as to be untouchable by ordinary litigants, he may, by the scope of his injurious act, be essentially insolvent.[14]

As they apply to the Arab world these points have quite mixed applicability. It is not, I think, true that individual litigants can rely less on familial ties than previously for support in their legal claims. Indeed, there is reason to believe that as the use of lawyers has increased and as litigation has expanded many people find themselves having to renew and rework their kin-based obligational bonds as they seek to use them for purposes of legal disputes. Just as partisan politics has had the effect, in many areas, of reinforcing the modes of interpersonal negotiation, so, too, legal disputes have come to constitute an additional forum within which similar intensification of obligations becomes necessary.

At the same time, the impact of the colonial experience on the legal systems of Arab countries has been profound. In many instances substantive Islamic law has now been restricted to matters of personal status, and even here many countries have sharply modified traditional Islamic rules, procedures, and judicial organization. In the realm of tort law, for example, the two major influences have been the Ottoman Civil Code, the *majalla*, and French law. The Turkish Code, which dates from the mid-nineteenth century, was clearly intended to be a modernist break with traditional law, and although it does not constitute a simple adoption of European models it moved sharply away from certain Islamic practices. The majalla remained close to Islamic practice in its de-emphasis on formal considerations of fault or intent,

---

[14] Tunc (1983). For an anthropological approach to issues of strict liability, see Moore (1972).

concentrating instead on the distinction between direct and indirect damage.[15] The majalla remains the basis for the law only in Jordan, but its effect in opening the way for systems of codification in the Middle East was extremely important.

A far wider range of Arab countries has been influenced by French law. French tort law is often said to use the single-rule technique: The basic proposition, taken from article 1382 of the Napoleonic Code, says that every act that causes damage makes the person by whose fault the damage occurred liable for compensation. Some countries (Egypt, Syria) have retained the unlawfulness of the act as the only condition for liability; others (Tunisia) have gone further in introducing the concepts of negligence and moral damage which were quite absent from classical Islamic law. Indeed, under the influence of French law a significant number of Middle Eastern countries now use fault along with illegality as a test for liability. In some instances these changes reflect attempts at the amalgamation of Islamic and Western ideas. Iraq and Kuwait, in particular, are countries in which the codes, drawn up after the Second World War by the Egyptian jurist Abd al-Razzaq al-Sanhuri, reflected extensions of Islamic categories to previously unaffected domains. Thus the categories of usurpation (ghasb) and destruction of property came to include injuries that had previously been dealt with by bloodmoney payments. This was particularly significant because bloodmoney payments depended for their operation in no small part on the willingness of the injured party or his survivors to accept the compensation, whereas inclusion of these wrongs under the category of disruption to continuity of possession places far more control in the hands of the state.

And it is this latter element—state control—which has, of course, become increasingly important. Not only have newly independent nations, like their colonial predecessors, seen fit to assert power through jurisdiction but they have sought to do so through the promulgation of codes and compensatory schemes that include a much more elaborate list of specific torts than was previously susceptible to judicial consideration. Moreover, the vast scale of potential injury, brought about by the use of modern technology and marketing, has necessitated greater state involvement. Although there have been few cases of massive injury in the Middle East to compare with the Bhopal disaster in India, the Chernobyl disaster in the fomer Soviet Union, or the various environmental cases in Japan, Europe, and the United States, it is clear that in many less noted cases Arab governments have had no other choice than to compensate victims in the certain knowledge that little chance for recovery against the actual perpetrator would be possible.[16] Indeed, in some countries, like Algeria, no-fault compensation schemes have been introduced to handle road accident cases in such a way that damages for personal injury are entirely eliminated from tort actions and it is possible to sue only for property damage.[17]

[15] For a selection of majalla principles as they relate to tort law, see Liebesny (1975: 218–20).

[16] Soon after independence in Morocco in 1956 there was, however, a major case precipitated by the wide-scale sale of adulterated cooking oil, a scandal that resulted in criminal penalties for the perpetrators but which was so vast that personal compensation could not address the harm done.

[17] Tunc (1974).

And yet the question remains whether, notwithstanding foreign influence, the actual course of adjudication for injuries will retain a distinctively Arab design in those countries that have not thoroughly abandoned the use of Islamic law. From what little we know of those countries that have attempted to reinstate Islamic law—Pakistan, Sudan, and Iran—it is primarily in the realms of criminal and family law that reform efforts have been directed. However, one could imagine that the course of tort law, too, could be affected by broader cultural changes that may be under way. These changes take us right back to the fundamental cultural aspects of Arab life with which we began.

The possibility exists that we are seeing for the first time in the Arab world a shift in such basic ideas as probability, causality, and intentionality.[18] For example, in the past people spoke of events as either occurring or not occurring: There was no real discussion in terms of whether one could increase the likelihood of one result or another. Now, in agriculture, social arrangements, and political events one hears from time to time a language of probability, of events being assessed for the features that will affect the frequency of their occurrence. Just as in the West where, until the seventeenth century, probability referred to authority rather than evidence, so, too, in the Arab world it may be that these apparently probabilistic statements still have as their referent the opinion of reliable authorities rather than the existence of data which everyone could perceive equally. If so, the personalistic element will have remained strong and the evidentiary element weak notwithstanding some change in the terms of discussion. If, however, a real conceptual shift is occurring, it is possible that a wide range of matters—the legal implications of compensatory justice not least among them—could be swept up in a reorientation of basic assumptions. Similarly, there are linguistic hints that causality is coming to be spoken of not just as strings of events made comprehensible because some reasoning creature intercedes at virtually every point in the chain but as sets of occurrences that possess ordering principles that are not dependent on human agency. Indeed, both intentionality and responsibility as fundamental cultural concepts could also be undergoing change, as the ability to discern intent from overt connections is disrupted by increased mobility and responsibility moves inexorably toward strict liability in the face of uncertain networks of obligation.

Thus far, perhaps, the emphasis on personalism in Arab cultures remains and 'the game' of negotiating relationships at all possible points remain very strong. For just as chess became the consummately correct Muslim game (whereby mankind demonstrates its capacity for reasoning its way toward safety) and games of chance became theologically incorrect (because they suggest that man is subject to God's will but without the reasoning ability to make the best of the realm that has been assigned to his control),[19] so, too, in life and law Arab culture demonstrates a highly personalistic vision of responsibility and justice which may, for a long time to come, affect the procedures, and even the substantive law, by which compensation for injury takes place.

---

[18] For a detailed discussion of this point, see Rosen (1995a).
[19] Rosenthal (1975: 167).

Part 2

In and out of court

5

From courtroom to courtyard: Law and custom in popular legal culture

The study of legal systems by Western scholars is replete with analytic dichotomies. Among the most common are the polarities formed by civil/criminal, substantive/procedural, public/private, fact/law, and formal/informal. These differentiations, purportedly observed as self-evident phenomena in the West and further 'naturalized' by legislation and connection to the discourses of religion and politics, have also been projected onto other legal systems through the accepted terms of comparative legal scholarship. The results, however, have often served to validate Western assumptions more than they have furthered scholarly understanding.

The distinction between law and custom is precisely one of these dichotomies that has become so ingrained in much of Western thought that it seems merely to reflect reality. Anglo-American lawyers are used to persuading courts that the 'custom and usage in the trade' should be used to understand what parties meant, say, by the terms of a contract, while continental lawyers, following in the wake of distinctions drawn in Roman law and more recent codifications, maintain that custom becomes law only when formally brought into the ambit of the latter by legal personnel. Orientalists, almost all of whom have grown up in this continental perspective, have projected this naturalized view onto Islamic law. In doing so, they may have obscured the way in which custom is envisioned in the courts and among ordinary people, at present as well as at various moments of Islamic socio-legal history.

The criticism I wish to raise about an unquestioning reliance on the law/custom distinction revolves around several ethnographic findings and theoretical arguments. Specifically, I will try to show that it is quite common for North Africans (and, from reports of colleagues, among Arabs throughout the Middle East) to believe that local practices not clearly forbidden by the Quran do not stand apart from the formal religion but are, in the strictest sense, themselves Islamic; that custom and non-judicial modes of addressing conflicts are, therefore, not regarded as separate sources of law because they serve, both legally and culturally, as residual categories for all local practice not forbidden by the Quran; and that if law is seen as part of culture, and culture as part of law, we can expect to find an irreducible continuum running between law and custom, courtroom and courtyard.

Culture, by its very definition, implies the process of dividing up experience, largely by means of language and other symbols, into a number of categories and arranging these categories into a comprehensible system. This is no less true of the domain we call law than of any other. As we learn about other cultures' ways of organizing experience we must, of course, take care that we neither reify the categories of our own analysis nor attribute to all parts of another culture the categories generated in our own, or a particular segment of their, society. If, for example, we rely uncritically on the distinctions between law and custom, or between formal and informal means of adjudication, we may fail to see that the lines separating each pair are not only blurred in actual practice but that they do not fully represent the conceptual distinctions drawn in other societies. The research task, therefore, becomes, in part, one of capturing the participants' own system of categorization and considering how such a system affects a wide range of social and cultural activities.

Specifically, I will try to show in the context of North Africa that the categories of law and custom, rather than being discreet and conceptually divided, overlap, and even merge, in ways that are very well recognized by petitioners and court personnel alike. Islamic law is thus seen as an overlapping juncture of custom (*qā'ida*) and religion (*dīn*), a conceptually distinct domain, albeit one that intersects with both the customary and the religious. Customary principles and procedures are, therefore, not regarded as separate from Islamic law but as Islamically legitimated categories for all local practice that is not clearly forbidden by the shari'a. Moreover, it is because law and custom, in this conceptual order, are so intertwined that ordinary people and those charged with official application of the shari'a can envision themselves and one another as practitioners of a simultaneously localized and universalized shari'a. My main examples will be drawn from both Morocco and Tunisia.

THE CASE OF THE AVARICIOUS HUSBAND

While reading the records of the qadi's court in Sefrou, Morocco, in the late 1960s I came across a case (no. 1959/444) involving litigants from the nearby village of I'awen, a settlement of Berbers (all fluent in Arabic) that I had been studying for some time. According to the record, in October 1959 a man by the name of Bel Lahsen filed suit against his wife Kanza, claiming that she had received into her own hands the bridewealth payment (*ṣdaq*) of 37,500 francs, but had subsequently refused to come before the court notaries (*'adul*) to have a legal marriage contract registered. The plaintiff further stated that he and Kanza had been living as man and wife until nine days earlier, when his wife ran away. He was petitioning for a court order for her return and the registration of their marriage.

After numerous delays a document (called a *lafíf*) was presented by the plaintiff in which twelve neighbors of the parties swore before notaries that the plaintiff (described as aged sixty and unemployed) had been married to the defendant (aged forty-five) for seven months, and had never divorced her. A second pair of notaries had heard the separate (though unsworn) testimony of each of the twelve and certified (in a document called a *stifsar*) that each had reiterated the testimony contained in the lafíf.[1] The attorney for the defendant offered no counter-proof, at which point

---

[1] The *stifsar* (also called *latíf al-mustasfar*) is also discussed in Mir-Hosseini (1993: 101). The procedure bears similarities to the *rasm istir'a'* analyzed in Powers (1990a: 245, n. 97).

the court summarily ruled that the defendant must return to her husband's home and live with him in peace.[2]

Since I had been working intensively with one of the most important and knowledgeable men in the litigants' village I asked him what he knew of the case. He told me that the plaintiff was indeed an elderly man, someone he would characterize as 'shady' (*'awer*). The plaintiff used to be well-off but in recent years had wasted a lot of his money. He had also gone through a series of wives, including the defendant in this case, keeping each for a short while and then divorcing her. When Kanza decided to get out of the marriage she went to the public prosecutor, a distant relative, who tried to convince Bel Lahsen to divorce her. When the husband refused to do so Kanza ran away. After the court ruled against her, Kanza chose to go to jail rather than obey the order to return to her husband. At that point people from the village began to tell Bel Lahsen that it was shameful for him to remain married to the woman and, in an attempt to get him to divorce her, suggested that Kanza might have been unfaithful to him anyway. Bel Lahsen eventually agreed to a *ṭalaq khul'*, the parties agreeing that Kanza would keep her original sdaq but renounce all claims to marital support. My informant was clear that everyone thought Bel Lahsen engaged in these marriages in order to extort favorable terms in the ensuing divorce. Indeed, by the time I had learned of the matter Bel Lahsen had already married and divorced yet another woman in the same fashion.

A reading of the record alone—or, for that matter, observation of the entire courtroom proceeding—would not have revealed the complexities of the case. Villagers knew that Bel Lahsen married one woman after another and made life sufficiently difficult for them that they were willing to pay (or forgive legal obligations) in order to extricate themselves from the union. They knew, too, that the women involved were not at fault but that it was not uncommon for women to go to jail in order to mobilize public pressure against a husband from whom they could not get a judicial divorce. Even more to the point, both parties knew that the statutory and judicial aspects of their case formed both a context for and a backdrop to the overall shape and course of the dispute: Each used the law to bolster relationships and positions aimed at achieving a given end, and each used the extrajudicial aspects of the dispute to bolster the legal shape with which their relationship would conclude. To them, what happened outside of the court was law as much as what occurred within its precincts: The boundaries of legitimacy did not stop at the courthouse door any more than the bounds of the legally permissible ended with the code books or judicial pronouncements. Interviews with court officials revealed that they, too, were not only aware of such practices but invited them as part of the dispute process: They expected local practice and pressures to offer at least partial solutions to problems they could not themselves completely resolve.

---

[2] The court also ruled that the witnesses' documented testimony could serve in place of, and was indeed stronger than, a marriage certificate notarized by the 'adul. The ruling of the Sefrou court was upheld in each particular by the Court of Appeals in April of the following year.

Even the seemingly formal procedures of the court cannot be limited to matters under its direct control. The stifsar—the 'verification' of the witnesses' testimony before two notaries other than those who took the initial lafif testimony—constitutes a juncture of law and custom, one of those practices that some court officials say is not part of traditional Islamic law but which they are willing to include within the category of the shari'a for several reasons: (*a*) because it does not contradict the shari'a, and (*b*) because it partakes of a process for determining truth that pervades, and indeed unites, religious and social convention at a common point.[3] Again, it is not that the law has adopted the custom of the stifsar. Rather it is that the two domains merge through commonly shared approaches, each permitting demonstrations of its vitality through its ability to affect relationships regardless of where that relationship is presently enacted or momentarily resolved. And the fact that all parties referred to these procedures and maneuvers as shari'a further underscored the common conceptual domain they occupied.

THE LAW OF THE CLERKS

Legal anthropologists have found that it is quite common in the United States, as well as in a number of developing nations, for the clerks associated with courts to play an extremely important role in the development and outcome of a case.[4] Frequently, it is they who tell potential litigants what their chances are of success and how best to go about making their case, or discourage litigants through particular characterizations of the evidence, the law, or the judge. Clerks may even mediate disputes in their offices or play out the role of judge to those who are willing to accept their opinion.

As I have worked in the clerks' offices in the qadis' courts of Morocco, I have repeatedly witnessed this process. Typically, someone—man or woman—comes in with a scrolled document tightly clutched in one hand and a look of mixed pride and trepidation on his or her face. Potential litigants understand perfectly the Moroccan style of bureaucratic procedure. They begin by speaking to whoever addresses them but take care that others present hear their argument. Sometimes there may even be another person in the room who sits quietly along the wall. At a certain moment in the litigants' discussion, the uniformed aide (*mukhazni*) who has been standing by intercedes to impress a point on the clerk, the potential litigant, or both. Eventually, another clerk (or the other man who has been present but silent throughout) says a few words to the clerk, who pronounces the awaited advice. The litigants have all along suspected that the other man might well be the public prosecutor or the administrator of the court (who can actually sit in for the judge to accept documentary

[3] The customary nature of the stifsar is supported by the opinion of the court in Case No. 1965/65, Qadi's Court of Sefrou, Morocco.
[4] See, for the American case, Yngvesson (1993).

evidence) and are aware that it is common practice in the Moroccan bureaucracy for just such a figure to be the one who has the final decision. There is even a Moroccan saying that translates well into the English, 'the words to the pillar, but the meaning to the post,' so that with strangers present one often acts as if the questioner is not the one you may really be addressing.

The substance of this process extends from outright dismissal based on anything from the officials' approach to the law to assumptions about the honesty, probity, and importance of the claimant or the claim. Remarks made after people leave the office indicate that attitudes about gender, ethnicity, and cleanliness are by no means irrelevant to the clerks' advice. Yet more to the point, it is these clerks, mukhaznis, and attendant court personnel who directly shape the flow of information and substantive results between courtroom and courtyard: It is they who often shape the assessment of 'facts' and channel the judicial process. Their subsequent remarks clearly demonstrate that they understand the out-of-court elements at work in cases, and either bring those factors into play or defer to them as their own perceptions suggest.

Once again, it would be analytically misleading to think of the clerks and the litigants as occupying separate domains that occasionally interact, or even as persons who take on distinct roles as the situation varies. Rather, it is their common understanding—clearly demonstrated in their shared and untechnical language, their assumptions about human nature and modes of determining truth, and their personal involvement in similar situations in which relationships are not defined or bounded by institutions—that renders the threshold of the court the most artificial and permeable of boundaries. It would make no sense for them to tell the story of a case from the perspective of only one domain because litigants and court personnel do not perceive either law or life as so contained. Indeed, much of the court officials' legitimacy as intermediaries lies in the fact that they express, with greater speed and lower cost, the same willingness as the qadi to keep wide the bounds of relevance, thus merging both local and institutional knowledge.

Of equal importance, perhaps, is that court personnel, more than the judges themselves, mediate and link law and custom as shared aspects of the shari'a. Or it is these personnel who join the terms of the institutionalized shari'a as textual support and the popular conception of shari'a as compatible custom. The clerks, experts, mukhaznis, scribes, and secretaries thus play a critical role in the process by which a common set of overlapping conceptualizations, created and sustained from different sources of legitimacy, is forged into a unified domain.

LEAR IN MOROCCO

Everyone knows the Tradition that has the Prophet saying that knowledge of the laws of inheritance constitutes half of all useful knowledge in the world. And everyone in Morocco, however well or poorly educated, has a firm grasp of the essentials of inheritance law, particularly as it relates to women receiving one-half the share granted men of similar genealogical distance from the deceased. What is also commonly known, and not uncommonly practiced, is a variety of ways to avoid even this degree of inheritance for one's female heirs. Consider the example of a man named Hamou, from a village in the Middle Atlas mountains.

An elderly man who was among the wealthiest of the hard-working sheep entrepreneurs from his settlement, Hamou preferred that his choicest properties be divided exclusively among his sons, to the detriment of his daughters and their husbands. So he went before the notaries and signed over most of his property to his sons. He then entered into separate, but unnotarized, agreements with each son for the return to Hamou of one-half of the profits of each parcel during Hamou's lifetime.[5]

People I spoke with in the village initially appeared to be of two minds about what Hamou had done. Asked directly if Hamou's actions were consistent with the shari'a, a number of informants said that what Hamou had done contradicts the religious law, which specifically leaves half-shares to daughters, and that by effectively disinheriting them Hamou was acting contrary to the spirit of the law. On the other hand, as even many of the same people said, Hamou's tactic—which, they insisted, is hardly limited to him—is perfectly legal, not explicitly forbidden by Islam, and may be justifiable given the relationships involved and the old man's need to depend on his sons for support. Many repeated the phrase 'a contract rules over the shari'a,' thus indicating that, so long as the contracts with his sons were independently valid, those agreements govern formal shari'a requirements. Indeed, as they added, what Hamou did *is* shari'a, local practice thus being conceptually merged for them within that overarching category. They appreciated that Hamou did not have his agreements with his sons notarized, but insisted that subsequent oral testimony may force greater social recognition of the arrangement than is accomplished by using the 'adul. They noted that it mattered little that several of Hamou's daughters were married to Hamou's nephews, though Hamou was risking disputes with his own brothers by his tactic. They also feared that unless informal divisions of the remaining property could be effected at the time of Hamou's death intrafamilial disputes, which village leaders would try to mediate, might exacerbate the situation. They were, therefore, more concerned by the repercussions of his acts than by any sense that what he did was not well within the conceptual domain of the shari'a.

Hamou's method of dealing with the exigencies of inheritance law highlight a number of points for us. The expressed ambivalence about the Islamic nature of Hamou's arrangement is particularly intriguing. The very same people who recognized that it diverged from the basic Quranic concept of inheritance were quick to characterize it as an acceptable practice which, not being clearly forbidden by Islam,

---

[5] Hamou's arrangement bears some similarity to the classical *'umrā*. Indeed, as Powers points out, one must think of Islamic inheritance law not simply as a set of Quranic prescriptions but as an entire system, one that includes a number of features that place emphasis on the social process of property devolution. See Powers (1990b).

may be seen as included within the sharīʿa. This is not a case of the 'double-mind-edness' that Sir Hamilton Gibb attributed to Arabs—the retention of mutually exclusive ideas made compatible only by self-serving rationalization or blatant fiction—but a demonstration of how the boundaries remain open among propositions that, fully segregated, would fail to reflect the conceptual universe of these Muslims.

Hamou's practice also highlights the intertwining of familial politics and law. All of the elements to which anthropologists of law have addressed themselves are present here: the bargaining that goes on in the shadow of the law; the manipulation of symbols and relationships within and beyond the domain of formal law; the interaction of kinship, law, and property as Hamou tries to insure that his sons will not do to him what King Lear's daughters and their husbands did to Lear. To view the court documents drawn up for Hamou or to read the innumerable cases of inheritance disputes that result from similar arrangements is to touch only part of the law, part of the relationship. Since Islamic law and practice form a complex singularity in which the features Westerners think of as 'legal' may be worked out in the domain Westerners think of as the 'extralegal,' and vice versa, no picture of either domain makes full sense without considering how both are in theory and in practice thoroughly united.

ADOPTING WESTERN MEDICAL KNOWLEDGE

The legal recognition of Western medical ideas has been at once an easy and a difficult matter for Moroccan jurists and legislators. On the one hand the actual practice of Islamic law in Morocco is heavily dependent on experts. Notaries, experts on local levels of marital and child support, female experts on women's bodies, and the extensive use of reliable witnesses all bespeak this emphasis. At the same time, Western medicine contradicted many indigenous ideas—from the length of pregnancy, to the capacity of infants to nurse, to the probabilities of various injuries resulting from particular causes. Just as in the West, where new techniques for fertility, life support, and transsexual surgery pose vexing questions about law and common sense, so too in Muslim countries the legal approaches to foreign medical concepts shed light on the permeability of the border between law and society.

To take only a few examples from the records of the qadi's court of Sefrou:

In 1959, a man sued his former wife, from whom he had been divorced six months earlier, for custody of their young child. He said that his former wife had remarried ten days before he filed his suit, that he wanted their child turned over to him, and that he wanted his former wife to be tested by a doctor to see if she was pregnant.[6]

---

[6] Case No. 1959/187, Qadi's Court of Sefrou, Morocco. A similar case involving the use of tests made by a medical doctor is found in Case No. 1958/212, Qadi's Court of Sefrou, Morocco. On Islam and the judicial applications of medical knowledge generally, see Ghanem (1982) and Rispler-Chaim (1993).

Normally, the expiration of a three-month waiting period (*'idda*) would decide the issue of any pregnancy that could be attributed to a woman's former husband. But the Moroccan Code of Personal Status (Mudawwana, ¶¶ 76 and 84),[7] in an attempt to harmonize past practice with modern medicine, builds on the earlier notion of the 'sleeping fetus' to allow a woman's pregnancy to last for as long as one year from the date of repudiation by, or death of, the husband. But if, says ¶ 76, at the end of a year there remains a doubt about whether the woman is pregnant, the court can appoint 'medical experts' to determine the woman's condition, and on the basis of their advice declare an end to her waiting period or its prolongation by the time necessary to determine her condition. The Code does not specify if such experts must be licensed physicians (who could not possibly support the proposition that a human pregnancy can last twelve months) or, as in the past, a woman knowledge-able in matters relating to females, an *'arifa*. The case in question did not resolve these issues.[8] However, only a few years later in a case in which a wife accused of abandonment of the marital home defended herself by presenting a medical certifi-cate in support of the claim that her husband had abused her by engaging in anal intercourse, the court ruled that the doctor's testimony proved nothing of how the woman sustained her injuries and that only the female experts attached to the court could determine such matters.[9]

Here, as in numerous other cases and interviews that could be cited, one encoun-ters the courts trying to make a place for modern medical science in the traditional system of knowledge and its institutionalization that had applied for preceding generations. For present purposes the point I want to make in relation to these cases is this: Both courts and legislators were able to make the transition to increased use of medical science to the extent that they were able to fit it into a system of proof and procedure that gave emphasis to knowledge wherever gained. They found legit-imacy for this approach to knowledge itself not within the narrow confines of legal culture but within the context of the law's own larger legitimacy being entwined with conceptions of knowledge that span every domain of social life. The courts could, therefore, allow results to be produced outside of the formal realm of the law and subsequently drawn into it precisely because this is part of the understanding of how the law has worked in society notwithstanding the appearance of a law focused on scholars rather than practitioners and participants. The relative absence of disloca-tion occasioned by these alterations is thus incomprehensible if seen only as an instance of law and custom, formal and informal, having to contend with one

---

[7] Royaume du Maroc (1993).

[8] Similarly, ¶ 84 states that the minimum period for a pregnancy is six months, when, of course, a woman might be delivered of a child sooner, the term 'pregnancy' not being defined in the light of modern technology. See also al-Habbal and Haqqi (1997). Indigenous beliefs, like that of the sleeping fetus, also were raised in a 1989 Egyptian case, in which the court held that a man may indeed have taken a genie as a second wife, and since he had not first acquired the requisite consent to do so from his first wife the latter was entitled to a judicial divorce. Edge (1989).

[9] Case No. 1963/397, Qadi's Court of Sefrou, Morocco. The dossier also identifies this as Case No. 150, notebook 4B.

another: It makes sense when seen as part of an ongoing process in which those boundary lines were never sharply defined. The shari'a is not just a body of substantive laws but a number of procedures which derive and reciprocate legitimacy from being shared with modes of thought that cross-cut numerous domains of social life. Here, then, custom and religion become merged at the level of the shari'a, less as a body of substantive law than as a set of procedures that gathers within its legitimating arms practices that gain and share their power by their common categorization.

THE CASE OF THE CLANDESTINE BUILDERS

One of the most common practices in Morocco, as in much of the developing world, is for people to build houses illegally, both in terms of the site on which they have squatted and the standards by which the house has been constructed.[10] In Morocco, this practice takes several unusual turns. The initial process of construction is not itself the unusual element though it is, perhaps, relevant to the overall picture. Squatters usually put up an enclosure of thorny branches (like those used to corral animals), construct their houses within the enclosure at night, and by the time officials must decide whether to pull down the temporary enclosure they would be forced to destroy an entire structure, if not an entire settlement. Indeed, the first structure to be put up in such an area is often a mosque—and one named for a daughter of the King at that—which few officials would want to be remembered for destroying. It is the legal elements of these squatters' tactics, however, that concern me here.

Squatters commonly construct their houses in full accordance with local building codes. Moreover, they go to the people who work as notaries or as court-appointed experts on land and have documents drawn up detailing their construction agreement. These agreements usually stipulate that someone other than the builder/resident is paying money to be used for the construction, in exchange for a possessory right in an upper floor. Because the land has not been obtained legally these contracts are themselves not legal. Even when land is obtained with government permission, joint ownership of the property is not permitted: The terms set by the government for legal construction on public lands require the builder to be the sole owner of the structure. The fact that the construction is illegal, even clandestine, would seem to render these documents both worthless and unnecessary.

But the squatters know that it is very common for practices that were once outside the formal bounds of the law to be brought inside—or, to put the matter as many informants do, since contract governs shari'a (*shart kats-hakem 'al shra'a*) the two realms do one another's work and are thus practically indistinguishable. Indeed, when I interviewed the head of the notaries for the Fez courts—a man who previously

---

[10] For a general discussion of this situation, see Agoumy (1994). For a comparative example, see Karst (1971).

served at every level of the Moroccan judiciary, including a period as a justice of the Moroccan High Court—he told me he was instructing the notaries under him to register these documents. When I suggested that such documents were illegal—that they could not be introduced as evidence in court and could not be used to assert any claim whatsoever—he said to me: 'We cannot leave them [these people] outside of the shari'a' (*ma-imken-l-nash n-khelihum 'al berra sh-shra'*). In time, he added, just as their building in accordance with local codes will lead to these settlements being 'regular-ized' within the ambit of local administrative structures, so too their legal arrange-ments will get regularized and they will not have lost their involvement in the shari'a and its processes.

Clearly such an attitude and such a practice cannot be accounted for as the mere meshing of the formal and the informal, as though the very context that binds them into a single whole were irrelevant. The head of the Fez notaries is, after all, neither authorized on his own nor awaiting judicial or legislative recognition of the custom-ary before denominating it shari'a. The belief that stipulation *is* Islamic, that inclu-sion is the norm and exclusion must be explicit, and that the work of each domain can be carried out in any other makes comprehensible a process that might otherwise be dismissed as legal fiction, logical error, or piecemeal convenience.

RECONCEPTUALIZING TUNISIAN MARRIAGE

Marriage in contemporary Tunisia, according to that country's Code of Personal Status—and consistent with the main line of Islamic law practiced in Tunisia—is said to occur when an exchange of bridewealth (*sdaq, mahr*) is made and registered with the proper officials. In recent years, however, Tunisians have reconfigured the defining moment of marriage to be when lawful consummation occurs—and they have done this not by a change in the law but by wholly 'informal' means.[11] To understand why and how this has occurred one must place the formal law of marriage in the context of several other legal and social factors that apply in Tunisia.

In keeping with the Tunisian approach to the 'modernization' of Islamic law—reforms that include the abolition of polygamy and the reservation of the power of divorce to the courts alone—the Tunisian legislators, building on a traditional Islamic legal practice, instituted the use of a payment of marital compensation (*muta'a*) to be set by the court at the time of divorce. Young Tunisians, particu-larly the more educated ones, began to find this payment inconvenient and burdensome. Moreover, they found that quite often in the months following a marriage the partners proved incompatible: Women complain that their new husbands go out with their male friends and ignore them; men complain that

---

[11] See, Hermassi and Hmed (1983). Several examples from Morocco, in which litigants manipulate the demand for consummation as a means of altering the terms of the marital contract, are cited in Mir-Hosseini (1993: 175–6).

their wives are constantly dominating their attention and pressuring them to separate themselves from their families of origin. Divorce means payment of the compensatory gift. But if the 'marriage' were not yet a legal marriage when the split occurs, the financial and legal burdens of a divorce could be avoided. For this reason people began to separate marriage into two parts. They would enter into a marriage contract and have the contract, including the bridewealth payment, properly registered by 'adul or civil officials. They would, however, continue to live apart in a kind of extended engagement period to see if they really could get along. They would consummate the union only later—treating the consummation as the defining moment of the marriage. If they chose to separate before the union was consummated, they would present themselves to the court claiming theirs was an engagement requiring no muta'a. The Tunisian courts have come to accept this practice and enforce it.

Now it is true that in at least one school of Islamic law consummation is indeed an acceptable basis for defining the moment of marriage, and even though that was not the dominant school of thought in Tunisia the increasing eclecticism of Islamic legal systems is not unknown in the country. But this is not the basis for the change that has occurred, not least because all Islamic law is superseded in Tunisia by the Code. The change can only be understood as a vehicle by which people have come to adapt to a legal regime with which their social practice is out of step. And even though Tunisia is deeply committed to the use of modern codes and to a greater measure of equality in family life for women, the change, desired as much by women as by men, has managed to receive effective implementation. Thus notwithstanding the rhetoric, and indeed in large part the reality, of modernist reform, Tunisians have allowed the line between law and practice to remain blurred, permeable, and responsive to changed viewpoints. The result is additional confirmation for the need to examine law and social practice as indissolubly linked and not as analytically compartmentalized domains.

LAW, CUSTOM, AND POPULAR CONCEPTUALIZATIONS

The cases and practices cited above could be multiplied many times over. If one looks at the way in which assumptions about human nature are implemented in both courtroom and courtyard, if one considers the modes by which utterances are tested for their believability, or if one considers the processes by which intention, causality, and probability are displayed in life and in law, the theme that is central to this chapter keeps recurring: In the conceptual universe of North African culture shari'a lies at the overlap of custom and religion. Laymen can thus interpret many of their local practices and assumptions as truly Islamic, while legal personnel, sharing in the same conceptual order, can incorporate and utilize the local in the application of the shari'a. Custom and law are not completely discreet categories—institutionalized entities that compete for identity and legitimacy—but are, in many instances, conceptually merged.[12] Taken from the perspective of these indigenous ways of categorizing Islamic law and custom some very intriguing interpretations, historical as well as contemporary, begin to present themselves. Let me close by suggesting several.

Students of the history of Islamic law may want to reconsider some of their interpretations in the light of a revised view of the relation of law and custom. Increasingly, scholars have found support for the role that custom played in the early years of Islamic legal development.[13] Others have shown that during the medieval period custom still had to be accounted for in some fashion.[14] But where such infusion of custom has been regarded as an occasional trickle or an idiosyncratic intrusion promoted by a rare commentator, the possibility exists, as in so many other instances of the study of Islamic legal history, that by reading the past in the light of anthropological and contemporary studies of law we can see that custom is indeed, and always has been, a source of Islamic law—but not in the European sense of source which has been projected onto Islamic law, but as an integral aspect of the shari'a itself. The internal contradictions in some historical accounts of Islamic law may be resolved if one sees custom not as something attended to occasionally by certain thinkers but as a constant factor in the life of a legal system that from the outset integrated it into the legal rather than seeing it as a separate entity.

An emphasis on custom also has a leveling effect, which may have been as important in the past as in more recent times. If the customs of Muslims are envisioned by them as integral to law then practices that are not in the control of either political authorities or particular elites may remain open to alteration, automatically receive legitimization *as* Islamic, and thus reinforce, by replication, the constant emphasis on maintaining multiple bases upon which power may be built.[15] Viewed in connection with the nature of power in the Arabo-Islamic world the dispersal of power through the legitimation as religious of local custom coincides with many other cultural factors, thus further prompting the need for viewing law as part of culture and not a domain that can be understood solely in terms of its doctrinal artifacts.

Kenneth Cragg has written of Islam: 'What does not contravene is permitted. Short of its arbitrary, religious and legal obligations Islam admits what the generality do.'[16] His point was that, if not strictly forbidden, local practices may be regarded as more than consistent with Islam: They may be denominated Islamic. This attitude may well account for the continuing spread of Islam among divergent local traditions, for to accept the faith is to be able to bring along non-contradictory local practices

---

[12] Max Gluckman describes some of the problems associated with drawing too fine a line between law and custom: '[C]ertain false problems had crept into the analysis of primitive law because of a tendency to regard it as something quite different from developed law. One of these false problems is the attempt to find a distinction between law and custom, as if they are in some sense antithetical concepts. Law can only be posed in antithesis to non-law. Custom has the regularity of law but is a different kind of social fact . . . [T]he jurisprudential conception of custom as one source of law, in the sense of judicial decision, and also as a part of the whole *corpus juris*, can be applied without distortion to the Lozi data' (Gluckman (1955: 261–2)).   [13] Libson (1997).   [14] Hallaq (1999).
[15] See also the discussion in Ch. 8, pp. 133–50.   [16] Cragg (1965: 186).

and have them included within the ambit of the Islamic. The historical power of this amalgamative mentality goes beyond the missionizing appeal of Islam. In the 1930s, for example, when the French tried to divide Moroccans by placing Arabs under Islamic law and Berbers under customary Berber law the Berbers were deeply offended: They insisted that since their practices were permissible within Islamic law they *were* Islamic law, a viewpoint that contributed markedly to the Berbers' involvement in efforts to achieve national independence from the French. To this day, not only in North African countries but as far away as Malaysia and Indonesia, one hears the same assertion, and the same connections and debates that mark the positions of those who favor one or another side of the institutional and ideological coin.[17]

Indeed, it is this last point that may lead us to yet another explanation of the dynamic tension that characterizes the relationships that have been dichotomized along the axes of the formal and informal, the customary and the legal. Studies of ritual, myth, and religious conceptualization suggest certain alternatives. For example, in his study of the re-enactment of Abraham's sacrifice by the people of southern Morocco, Abdellah Hammoudi argues that the ritual of the animal sacrifice, as practiced by Muslims worldwide, and the concurrent ribald masquerade, as practiced by these local mountain people, are connected in a subtle and easily missed dynamic. Hammoudi's description of the 'formal' ritual of sacrifice and 'informal' ritual of the masquerade is one that, in his own words:

considers as a single, nondivisible ritual process the masquerade that parodies and contests central values and institutions which sacrifice purports to sanctify and legitimize. . . . [E]ach part of the ceremony produces discourses that censor rival ones, but to no avail, because there is always an 'other scene' in which occulted discourses strike back. All of the scenes in this theater of regulated improvisation articulate contradictory sets of statements and witness to their irreconcilable character. They attest to both the necessity of ideals and norms, and the impossibility, even the danger, of abiding by rules governing cherished values in religion, community, marriage, and so on.[18]

Similarly, the particular form of symbiosis that links the formal and informal sectors of the law may well be one in which each contains the terms of its own limitation: For the law on the books or in the court to fully assert that local practice not only completes Islam but covers most of its domain is too threatening to be acknowledged directly; yet to fail to contain the local is to risk undermining one of the law's own sources of legitimacy, its power of inclusion. For local practice to lay claim on its own to Islamic legitimacy risks its detachment from the mainstream of the community of believers; to accept its implementation through court personnel and a shared language of evidence is to yield its own momentary completion to agents it cannot fully replace. At each step the Siamese-twin quality of the local and the universal, the customary and the institutionalized comes to the fore. The 'gates of independent reasoning' can never be fully shut when the side door of local inter-

[17] See, e.g., Bowen (1993).   [18] Hammoudi (1993: vii).

dependence is left ajar, the key left conveniently under the mat. Whether it is in the amalgamation of clandestine building with established law or in the reconfiguration of the defining moment of marriage, a critical process of mutual incorporation seems to be central to much of the way that ordinary people and officials alike conceptualize the shari'a in modern North Africa. It is a matter of no small import to our understanding of the history and course of Islamic law that the faithful's attachment to Islamic law can remain all the more firm when laymen and professionals alike enact a concept of shari'a that embraces the local and the cosmological under a single conceptual heading.

6

On the docket: Changing conventions in a Muslim court, 1965–1995

A legal record is a peculiar artifact. It purports to contain as full an account of a case as may be necessary to identify the parties, the issues, and the nature of the proceedings, and to incorporate such data as may be necessary for a subsequent court—particularly a court of appeals—to understand the work of the original forum. At the same time a legal record is a highly edited, often stylized, body of information: The form of the documents it contains shapes the issues, the 'facts,' and the image of the participants; the manner in which a local clerk chooses—or has the interest, skill, or time—to elaborate on the proceedings affects subsequent uses of the record; and the unstated assumptions that affect what is included may vary among judges or change over time, thus rendering it difficult for officials and scholars alike to capture the full meaning of the case. Such problems, though common to any historical record, call for a special effort if the fuller significance of a legal docket is to be grasped.

We have already seen that legal documents may have a different quality in the Arab world than they do in the West: They may be treated as the reductions to writing of oral statements, and will be approached for what they say about the person involved rather than as ends in themselves. At other times and places in the Middle East they may be treated as symbolic figurations of the relations of persons to things, as the backbone for regularizing a colonial regime, or as the common denominator for encouraging transactions across a far-flung empire.[1] The records of a court system will also reveal a good deal about the points of tension in a community and how they may change over time. And they may even show how a host of everyday relationships, within and beyond the confines of the law, develop in response to changing political and historical circumstances.

Prior to the beginning of the French Protectorate in Morocco in 1912 notaries kept copies of the documents they witnessed, the original remaining with the party seeking its recordation. These 'pocket notebooks,' as they were called, were not kept in the court, and their contents were often only discoverable by references made to them in later cases. The French regularized record-keeping—including records of Berber law proceedings—and in the years following national independence records have continued to be carefully maintained. Since judicial decisions are often rather cryptic much of the interest in the records lies in their reflection of types of disputes and the supporting documentation. As the courts also reflect broader changes going on in the political and social organization of the country one can also see, by studying the court's overall docket, how the legal system itself is undergoing change, and how these changes get embodied in documentation. It is to an

---

[1] See, e.g., Messick (1993) and Wakin (1972).

understanding of how these records relate to the activities of the court and community of
Sefrou, Morocco, that the following chapter is, therefore, addressed.

I had already been working in the Moroccan city of Sefrou for nearly a year when,
in 1967, I began my study of the courts. Sefrou, which has since grown to about
70,000 residents, was at that time a city of about 25,000 that also served as the
central market and administrative center for a region of some 200,000 rural people.
Several mornings a week, for many months, my assistant, Yaghnik Driss, and I would
sit in the clerks' office reading through the records. Yaghnik was at that time a
schoolteacher, the holder of an advanced degree in Islamic studies from the
Qarawiyin University in Fez, and had been one of my language teachers for the
preceding year. Together we would read and translate the records. As our work
progressed, and my grasp of the law developed, a specific research plan began to take
shape. Having studied the docket statistics for a number of years and having spent
some time sampling various kinds of cases from a range of recent years, I chose to
use 1965 as a base year and to read through every single case—a little over four
hundred of them—for that year.

My choice was based on several factors. First, I thought that because the cases
were quite recent I would have a reasonable chance of getting additional information
from people in and out of the court who would still recall the proceedings. Court
personnel changed with some frequency, but I had learned that there were a number
of people who had been around for the last few years, so I would have a good chance
of getting the views of several of them should a particularly interesting case come to
our attention. Secondly, I had learned that most appeals were acted on within one or
two years, and while we did indeed encounter records that were unavailable because
they had been sent to the appellate court as part of the original or a related case we
were able to see how many cases that were the subject of appeal were ultimately
decided. And finally, my overall knowledge of the area and its recent history,
combined with an initial survey of cases from a number of recent years, led me to
believe that 1965 was not a particularly unusual year—in terms of national events or
the local economy—such that I could be dealing with a 'typical' year without first
establishing its statistical representativeness.

So Yaghnik and I began to read. We had several distinct advantages going for us
in our work. We were seated at a small table in the little room shared by the two
clerks of the court, both of whom were extremely pleasant and generous men. We
constantly discussed the cases we were reading with them and as a result got a great
deal of additional information about how various qadis tended to approach their
cases, background comments about the litigants and their reputations, and clear
explanations of some of the more arcane aspects of record-keeping and Islamic law.
We even discussed which of the earlier scribes had the most beautiful handwriting
and which cases different qadis had said they found most interesting and challenging. Because the clerks were keeping records of current cases that I was also following in court, I was able to compare what they placed in the records with what I had

seen in court or heard discussed by various officials. Thus the records became for us living documents, whose current fashioning imbued predecessor documents with an enormous sense of continuing relevance.

But there was one other clear advantage to our working situation. The clerks' room was located inside the courthouse, just beside a little courtyard but before the entrance to the main part of the building. Litigants and potential litigants wandered in and out of the small office with great regularity: The uniformed aide only prevented their entrance to the courtyard on the days when court was in session, thus leaving people who routinely passed by the courtyard to enter the clerks' room uninhibited. We therefore had the opportunity to see how people used the clerks as informal advisors, as interpreters of the documents they often carried scrolled in their hands, or as informal arbiters when they wanted to test the legal waters or avoid the trouble or expense of a formal proceeding. As a result, we not only saw what makes it into the records but what does not—and therefore what additional features remain vital to an understanding of the law as a complete and living system.

The record of an average case in the 1960s was not very elaborate. It began with the complaint (*mqal*), which was usually drawn up by a scribe in the marketplace but on occasion by the parties themselves. Only rarely at that time was a lawyer involved. Indeed, there were no lawyers residing in Sefrou when I began my work there, and it was, therefore, necessary to bring one up from Fez if any was to be used. (This, as we shall see, was perhaps the biggest change that was to occur in the court system over succeeding years.) In addition to the complaint the dossier consisted of copies of any documents relevant to the proceeding, with authorized translations if the original was in French. Litigants often arrived at court with several documents, which the clerks had to sort through for relevance. Often this was the source of some embarrassment and tension. A great many of the litigants were not literate and they treated the documents as near-sacred objects to be protected at all costs and as powerful artifacts that made them feel uncomfortably dependent. Moreover, when the clerks told them that a certain piece of paper was irrelevant they clearly felt at the mercy of the court not only for the shaping of their complaint but because they had such a clear attachment to these artifacts as the keys to a successful dispute that when they were rendered irrelevant parties were quick to express confusion and disappointment.

In truth, the clerks did not narrow issues as they developed a dossier so much as they indicated to potential litigants the materials they would need in order to have a chance of a successful outcome. These might include documents from the head of one's quarter certifying impoverishment or the written expression by the government-appointed head of one's tribal faction of a party's absence or default. In any case, the encounter became at once instruction in the bureaucracy of the modern state and an opportunity to try out on the clerks the likely results of one's suit. The patience of the clerks in this regard varied a good deal, and their appreciation of illiterate and uninformed countrymen was not always unreserved.

Several points about the way in which legal norms were shaped thus reveal themselves at this initial stage of contact with the courts. First, the 'bounds of relevance' (to borrow the phrase of Llewelyn and Hoebel) were not sharply demarcated by the complaint process or personnel. The complaint did have to include a precise remedy requested and name the parties with specificity. But unlike, for example, the English writ system, it was not a mechanism for reducing the scope of the judge's consideration. Secondly, the norms of the legal process were being communicated to litigants in no small part by the clerks even though they were not formally involved in the decision-making process. As informers, more than as gatekeepers, their role in the system was very important. And third, the norms that were being articulated, at the initiation stage and throughout, were as much of the process by which one would be heard as of substantive law that might be applied.

The actual caseload of the court in 1965 was not, as it turns out, all that different from the early 1990s. The number of decisions involving matters of personal status has remained relatively constant at around 400 per year. This is not, however, because of any lack of growth, but as a result of it. That is to say, in 1965 the court in Sefrou operated for the surrounding district and people had to come into town in order to have a case heard. As the population has grown the district has been administratively subdivided several times and courts have been established at several areas in the countryside. This has kept the Sefrou court's caseload relatively constant—a level which the clerks in the early 1990s described as not at all burdensome.[2]

---

[2] The following figures show the caseload of all types of civil cases for the courts of first instance in the entire region (*circonscription*) of Sefrou, which includes courts in outlying areas as well as in the city:

Year	new complaints	cases decided	cases pending
1989	2,326	2,114	847
1991	1,992	2,018	1,088

Source: Royaume du Maroc (1990: 390), and Royaume du Maroc (1992: 388) respectively.

As of 29 July 1991, according to the clerk, 205 cases involving matters of personal status had been decided in the city court so far that year. This was the basis for his estimate that the number would continue at about 400 per year as it had for some years past. I do not yet have statistics on the Sefrou court's personal status caseload beyond that date. For comparable statistics, see Mir-Hosseini (1993). The caseload figures for all types of cases addressed by courts of first instance throughout the country are as follows:

Year	new complaints	cases decided
1983	766,356	786,848
1984	722,744	775,717
1985	692,121	729,676
1987	781,742	770,222
1988	759,571	705,866
1989	876,289	780,531
1990	810,256	772,880
1991	824,713	806,539

Sources: 1983 to 1985: Ministère du Plan (1986); 1987 to 1991 Royaume du Maroc (1990) and Royaume du Maroc (1992)

The types of cases have, however, varied somewhat over the years. The vast majority of cases involving personal status fall into several categories: maintenance (*nafaqa*)
(129 cases in 1965; 329 in 1990); abandonment of marital duties (*nushūz*) (121 in
1965; 62 in 1990); custody (*ḥadana*) (13 in 1965; 55 in 1990); inheritance (*tarika*)
(8 in 1965; 40 in 1990); judicial divorce (*taṭliq*) (6 in 1965; 25 in 1990); and suit
to force a husband's return (*ḥusen l-muʿashara*) (22 in 1965; 2 in 1990). The remaining cases involved a few each on such disparate issues as the return of a spouse's
belongings, suits by wives who want the couple to live in separate housing from that
of her in-laws, permission to raise another's child, support for foster care, visitation
rights, repayment of a portion of the bridewealth, annulment, and payment of the
consolation fee due at divorce.

Although no major patterns of change are discernible certain trends do appear. In
particular, custody cases are clearly on the rise. This stems in part from increased
awareness on the part of many women that the law that grants them custody of small
children but favors the husband and his maternal relatives when the child reaches
puberty does not often suit the best interests of the child. Although there have been
pressures to change the Code of Personal Status to reflect this latter standard no
formal alteration has yet occurred. However, judges have been using their discretionary powers along these very lines and have increasingly altered the situation to
reflect the child's needs rather than mechanically apply formulaic provisions of the
Code. Indeed, judges consistently told me that they regard custody matters as the
most difficult to decide, in part because they often feel the tug between what is best
for the child and the kin-based requirements of the past.

Claims for maintenance may also have increased over the years as movement of
rural people into the city, a series of difficult drought years, and increasing willingness to bring personal matters into the limelight of a court have led many women to
seek support from recalcitrant or absent husbands. Similarly, there has been a rise in
women seeking judicial divorces rather than buying their way out of a marriage by
forgiving the husband various debts. Indeed, in 1993 the King oversaw a change in
the Code of Personal Status to provide that husbands who fail to convince the judge
that they have an acceptable reason for exercising their unilateral right of divorce may
be subjected to a higher 'consolation payment' to the wife as a result (¶ 52b). The
King's assertion that half of the population must increasingly share equal rights on
family matters has thus far resulted in only incremental alterations in the Code, but
such changes are by no means insignificant in a country whose personal status laws
have remained so close to traditional Maliki rules for nearly four decades of independent government.[3]

---

[3] Among the changes made to the Code in 1993 are a clear requirement of the woman's consent to
marriage (¶ 5), a requirement that a wife must be notified when her husband proposes to take an additional wife (¶ 30), and a requirement that both parents be responsible for a child's support during the
course of their marriage (¶ 99). Other changes made in 1993, such as the formation of a group of
members from both families who will help the court reach a settlement between the parties (¶ 156b), are
widely regarded as pro-forma and of no real consequence. Precisely the same reaction was given to me

Divorce rates—computed as the number of divorces divided by the number of marriages in a given year—have declined in Sefrou from the 35–40 per cent range of the 1950s–1970s to a rate of just under 25 per cent in 1991. Fully 30 per cent of the divorces still are of the type called *khul'*, in which a woman pays her husband a sum of money or forgives him a debt in order to get him to divorce her—sometimes because she has no grounds for a judicial divorce, sometimes in order to keep custody of her children.[4] There is no indication that judges are more or less willing than in the past to investigate the potential abuses associated with this form of divorce, but activists have succeeded in casting light on the problem and the late King's interest in incremental change may lead qadis to respond more readily to the claims made in this regard by women and their lawyers.

And indeed it is the role of the women and of the lawyers that probably constitutes the most intriguing aspect of changing judicial norms in Morocco. Western images of Islamic law assume that the courts are primarily places where men find reinforcement for their more powerful position *vis-à-vis* women. In fact, the situation is rather different. Courts are primarily places where women bring their claims—and where they succeed three times out of four. Data from my research, as well as from studies done by Mir-Hosseini, coincide in showing that women use the courts far more than men and that if they see their cases through to judgment women usually win. Given the fact that most cases involve support and the recalcitrancy of husbands, that women are often backed in these claims by male relatives who do not want to bear their support, and that documentation is rather easy to obtain from local officials to support claims of non-support, the success rate of women may not be altogether surprising. When combined with the willingness of many women to go to court and to speak with great effect when they get there the matter is even less surprising.

Similarly, the rise of lawyers is, if not surprising to the Western eye, a particularly important development for Moroccans. By the early 1990s there were more than a dozen lawyers in Sefrou, almost half of them women; in 1999 there were sixty lawyers, of whom three were women, practicing before the ten judges. Families that have their own internal disputes increasingly find it worthwhile to resolve differences with their lineal kin long enough to raise the money necessary for their own personal legal suits. And the courts, once so eager to listen to parties and decide issues as part of an attempt at re-establishing ties on some workable basis, now seem more concerned with having the lawyers bring issues to them with a clarity and relevance parties often ignore. Courts now use a special assistant to the judge, called a *musa'id*, who is university-trained in both modern and traditional law, and to whom one first relates one's case. The musa'id in turn may offer advice, convene a group of relatives

about similar provisions in the laws when I was doing research in the courts of Tunisia and Malaysia in the early 1990s. For the Moroccan provisions, see Royaume du Maroc (1993). See also Khachani (1998).

[4] Mir-Hosseini (1993: 87) gives figures for Rabat and Sale in 1987 of 35% and 37% respectively for khul' as a proportion of all divorce types granted. For Sefrou divorce statistics at various periods in its history, see Rosen (1968b: 184).

to help make a settlement, and will present the outline of the case to the qadi and submit recommendations as to its disposition. The notaries and experts previously occupied a crucial role in the filtration of matters to the court, but the musa'id is a more court-directed, bureaucratic agency than were these other institutions.

In addition a number of cases are being handled by the submission of documents to the court with only the lawyers expected to speak. Indeed, a request must be made for a session in which witnesses and the parties themselves speak to the court. Among the results of these changes are: parties are less able to raise issues of each other's over-all character and reliability if they must speak through attorneys; techniques for assessing 'facts' have been developing at the expense of well-established modes of assessing persons and their individual believability; and the presentation of novel situations encourages the judges to consider cases like those involving child custody as matters of legal policy-making as well as individuated judgment. These changes are more significant in large urban areas; in smaller towns and rural areas people still speak very much for themselves.

All of these changes do not, however, mean that what occurs in court has been rendered irrelevant or that parties are being silenced by the intervention of lawyers. It is still the case that in most instances lawyers are not present and people speak for themselves. Even when lawyers are used and no hearing for the parties has been scheduled it is not uncommon to see the qadi call the parties up to the bench to clar-ify a point and for that to develop into a direct inquiry by the judge and an oppor-tunity for each party to argue his claims. Whether in these situations, in scheduled hearings, or when lawyers are absent the style of judicial inquiry has changed rather little in a generation, qadis are still interested in determining the relationships among parties, the nature of past dealings they have had with one another, and the intensity of their attachment to the dispute involved. Judges say they are well aware that a single decision seldom ends a dispute, and they remain quite comfortable listening to the parties' own ways of trying to argue their interests. Where lawyers are present for a scheduled hearing it is still very difficult to keep any Moroccan client from putting in his or her own arguments, and not infrequently the lawyer must effec-tively stand to the side while the judge and litigants go at it.

This is especially important as it concerns women. If it is true, as I have argued elsewhere,[5] that the courts have developed techniques, similar to those used in the culture at large, for assessing persons and their believability, and women are the courts' primary clients, then the attitudes toward women becomes especially impor-tant. Women continue to speak without hesitation in court, often interrupting the judge and clerks, and frequently expressing their willingness to go to jail rather than submit to their husbands' tactics. While I suspect that the courts are increasingly moving away from older styles of person assessment and toward greater reliance on professional experts, circumstantial evidence, and bureaucratic documentation, it does bear emphasis that little seems to have changed in regard to the forcefulness

---

[5] See Rosen (1989a).

with which Moroccan women present themselves in court and the willingness of judges to listen to their personal circumstances.[6]

The court used to make a great deal of use of experts attached to it for purposes of determining such things as the appropriate level of support for a person of a given socio-economic standing or matters that would intrude on a woman's bodily privacy. These experts were also very important because they pushed the determination of facts down and away from the qadi and rendered judgments both more local and less a matter of overt judicial discretion. Increasingly, these experts have been replaced by the local administrator of an urban quarter or tribal locale (*muqaddem*), while medical doctors have increasingly displaced the old women who served as experts on matters concerning females. Other experts, particularly those dealing with land, remain extremely important. This deference to expertise and to the norms of the social welfare system have removed personnel from direct attachment and dependence on the courts, something that may, as we shall see, affect issues of corruption but more significantly affects the inclusiveness of the court in the establishment of its own standards.

Similarly, the notaries used to be physically housed in the courthouse and people who needed to have a document signed by these official witnesses clearly saw them as linked to the court. There has now been a return to what was in fact an earlier pattern, namely, the notaries have their own offices—or operate out of their homes—and are not housed with the court. Whatever its effects on privacy of dealings and aspects of corruption it is clear that the image of the notaries as separate from rather than attendant upon the court is reinforced by this physical separation.

Indeed, the issue of corruption cannot be avoided in any assessment of the norms of judicial practice in Morocco. Obviously my information is anecdotal rather than systematic and I can speak only from impressions, casual conversations over many years, and general rumor rather than from direct and systematic knowledge. My impression remains that payment to judges, directly or indirectly, is rare and that it has a relatively limited place in the workings of the legal system. The notaries are another matter. It is not uncommon to pay them more than the standard fee to draw up a document that contains false information that may serve, for example, to avoid taxes on the sale of land or affect the implications of a later marital dispute over property ownership. I have even had people come to me while I was in the field asking that I draw up a perfectly honest document for them because they did not want to have to pay a notary who was threatening to refuse the job unless they added something to his standard fee. What has developed, particularly in places where the caseload of the court is great or where the lawyers need to make the best use of their time, is the offering of 'gifts' to court personnel to obtain a favorable time on the docket, to be certain of getting a needed document in the proper form or at the earliest date, or even to get a delay in a hearing so that the clock continues to run on a husband's support obligation. That everything in court must be serviced personally by lawyer

---

[6]   On changing evidentiary standards, see Rosen (1995a).

and client, rather than by phone or mail, just as in other forms of negotiating relationships, reinforces the opportunities for corrupt officials to use this personalistic cultural style to their personal advantage.[7] Courts exist in a larger environment now in which Moroccans feel that civility and the opportunity to advance oneself have been undermined by an overall emphasis on wealth as the primary vehicle for success. Still the image of the courts is one of corruptible functionaries but relatively honest judges. A personal anecdote may help to underscore this point.

Some years ago I heard of a local court official who was removed for using court personnel for his private errands. At the time I accepted the story as true. I later learned that the notaries had made up this story to get him removed because he was trying to stop their illegal activities. The man was later brought back to a higher post in another jurisdiction where the same thing happened again. By the time his career reached its acme he had risen to a very high position indeed—including one in which he oversaw a great many notaries—precisely because his honesty could never be shaken. It is a story at once of the style of bureaucratic management in Morocco—send a person down one step and then raise him up two in order to make him more grateful to and dependent on the hierarchy—and of the nature of corruption in the courts.

All of these matters have an effect on the shape of the documents that represent the case for a court of appeal and for posterity. Since decisions are not reported and judges do not, therefore, build on one another's decisions, and since judges invariably insist that no two cases are alike because no two persons or situations are exactly alike, it is no surprise that the records themselves are rather limited. Besides the complaint and an occasional document little more is found than the briefly stated judgment. Reasons will only be given when an issue raises unusual factual problems, or when a judge is concerned about being overruled on appeal. Moreover, because of all that may be going on outside of the court, even information hinted at during the hearing may never find its way into the record, or may be fraught with error when it is included. The following record of a case I collected from my baseline year may help to exemplify this point:[8]

16 January 1965: The plaintiff, Hussein, complains that his wife, Itu bent Hamou, deserted him four days ago and will not return despite the requests of a group sent to her by the plaintiff for that purpose. The plaintiff wants the court to order her to return to him and be a good wife.

1 March 1965: The defendant had not showed up for the first hearing. Now her maternal uncle comes with a document giving him the right to represent her. This document also says that at the time it was made out the notary also saw the defendant's marriage certificate and its registration number is recorded. The court now rules that, having heard testimony from both sides, it is the opinion of the court that

---

[7] On the contexts and style of corruption in Morocco, see 'The Circle of Beneficence: Narrating Cohesion and Corruption in Morocco' in Rosen (forthcoming).

[8] Case No. 65/10, Qadi's Court of Sefrou, Morocco.

a woman has no right to leave her husband's home even when a legal dispute is in process. The defendant is therefore ordered to pay the court costs of 5 dirhams and to return to her husband's house temporarily during any court proceedings.

I happened to be working in the area the litigants came from and knew one of their distant relatives very well. He told me that soon after the defendant's father married her mother she left and returned to live with the brother, the same man who later came to represent the defendant in court. Indeed, the mother gave birth to the defendant while living at her brother's house. When the girl grew up her father gave her in marriage to the plaintiff, and though originally she was agreeable to the marriage she, like her mother before her, soon left and returned to her uncle's house. Since being ordered to return to her husband, my informant said, the couple have been getting along pretty well. But, he implied, there is a long history of familial strife here and the uncle, who supported both mother and daughter, feels he has a far greater stake in the outcome than is represented in any of the recorded proceedings. Indeed, the hearing apparently went off on a series of long-running disputes, none of which comes through in the record.[9] Thus what one has, whether at the appellate level or for local perusal in a later dispute, will by no means represent either the range of issue heard by the court or the concerns that may have prompted the dispute in the first place.

What happens outside of a court of law is, therefore, no less important to the course of development of legal norms themselves than are the more formal elements involved. One fact is particularly striking in the Moroccan example: In a significant number of instances cases are dropped by the petitioner before ever reaching judgment. In 1965, 71 out of the 410 cases (17.3 per cent) involving matters of personal status filed in the Sefrou court were dropped before reaching judgment. I do not have exact figures for the 1990s but all indications are that the rate has increased significantly. Mir-Hosseini reports that in 1987 in the Casablanca court women withdrew their cases 21 per cent of the time (and men 38 per cent), abandoned their cases 22 per cent of the time (as compared to male petitioners who did so 21 per cent of the time), and had their cases dismissed before judgment by the court 15 per cent of the time (as opposed to men whose claims were dismissed 20.7 per cent of the time). Thus in 58 per cent of the cases filed by women their claims never reached decision, while in the case of men the number reached a staggering 80 per cent.[10] All of this suggests several things.

First, the courts are often stages for a dispute rather than fora for their settlement: Litigants use a court filing as a threat, a tactic, and an element of the overall context of disputing rather than as the preferred or final arbiter of their problem. Once a case is filed other social pressures may begin to have effect. Indeed men often realize that the court is likely to rule against them, so they drop their cases or find other means

[9] The record also contains various mistakes about the parties' places of residence and some minor errors in their names.
[10] Mir-Hosseini (1993: 48, Table 1.4).

to conduce their wives to accede to their demands. Where qadis may once have played the role of mediator—and may still do so for wealthier litigants who do not wish to expose their situations so publicly—they are (and perhaps always have been) more likely to find themselves part of the overall dispute and not simply the preferred instrument of resolution.

Secondly, over one-fifth of Moroccan households are headed by women and a legal suit may be one of the devices by which women gain attention for their needs and rally familial support. Judges are also well aware that a case may really be about some long-term dispute between families, and that the issue actually before them is secondary to these broader considerations. Once other social actors and pressures come to bear, or once a familial dispute takes on another shape, women's suits may be withdrawn or abandoned—not always, of course, to their individual advantage.

And thirdly, the standards used in the larger dispute—a dispute that may incorporate property, long-standing difficulties, or parties not directly involved in the present case—will draw upon an array of factors in whose shadow some tentative arrangement may finally be made. Judges are not unaware of these factors and may allow their questioning to establish a context in which such extrajudicial considerations may do their work for them. As in social life generally, the judges seem to understand full well that relationships—and their attendant disputes—rarely come to a complete end, and they are perfectly willing to let the interstices of the law be filled in by the content of changing—or at least fluctuating—social arrangements.

Morocco is noteworthy for the very moderate changes that have come to modify traditional Islamic law over the course of the last forty years. Since the passage of the Code of Personal Status in 1958 only the modest changes noted above have taken place, and these at a pace that has been glacial at best. Stability may have flowed from this pattern and the legitimacy of the law reinforced. But it is perhaps no less important to appreciate that where legal norms have changed this may have occurred more as a result of changes in the ways in which persons and events are comprehended in society at large than through any formal changes in the law itself. As people move around more and as social ties become less certain, indices of character and constraint that the courts relied upon in the past may be less compelling. The judicial process may become more concerned with the testimony of professionalized experts, the role of circumstantial evidence, and the statistics of national support levels than the opinions of local experts knowledgeable only in local standards. On occasion judges will take the lead in such matters as altering the criteria of child custody or assessing the burden placed on a wife by her absent husband. But for the most part qadis appear more disposed to allow the norms to change from outside of the court rather than from within. The Moroccan courts do appear to be in a transitional phase: The increasing use of lawyers, the decreasing reliance on experts, and the changing ways in which issues are presented by court personnel to the judges may, in time, affect the way that information is brought to the court and even the way the court comes to view the people who appear before it.

In and out of court

Legal systems like those one encounters in much of the Arab world thus simultaneously engender and reflect the larger social contexts of which they are a part. Since
legal norms may only appear to gather formal effect when embodied in a substantive
or procedural code it is easy, without detailed work in and out of the courts, to miss
just how much social conventions nurture juridical precepts. A court docket thus
becomes an entry point to a series of changes that must themselves be understood by
placing that docket in a larger context. Certainly Morocco cannot stand for the
whole of the Arab experience or the last four decades for the whole of Islamic legal
history. But as we begin to gather a clearer sense of the actual workings of these local
courts and see how they relate to the societies in which they are embedded we can
begin to see in greater detail how the particulars of cultural norms intersect with
those of the courts and mutually reinforce the image that participants gain from
each.

7

Local justice: A day in an alternative court

State-run courts often come in various types and may, notwithstanding common rules of procedure and appellate oversight, operate in quite varied ways. Litigants may also have some choice in the forum employed or the avenues available for the consideration of their cases. A suit may even be brought before different jurisdictions, with the rules governing conflicts of laws themselves being open to variant interpretation. Alternatively, an out-of-court settlement may be sought by one or both parties, with the court—which may have encouraged the settlement—itself playing a rather different role than that of simple adjudication. People may even seek help with their disputes through the intervention of friends, relatives, and workmates, or turn to the more regularized roles of religious intermediaries, accepted modes of eliciting public sentiment, or interpersonal alliances formed for other purposes than addressing the issue at hand.

Anthropologists and legal scholars alike have tried to understand the interrelation of various modes of addressing disputes under a variety of conceptual headings: They have described an array of 'legal levels' or the structure of 'alternative dispute resolution mechanisms,' specified the 'secondary rules' by which state-run courts alter their own dynamics or noted the forms of 'legal pluralism' through which extrajudicial mechanisms interact with those controlled by the state.[1] Although the present chapter will critically address some of the broader concerns raised by many of these approaches, the fundamental orientation employed here remains consistent with the overall thrust of this book: I am, therefore, less concerned with institutional forms alone—the rules or principles they employ, or the fact that they emanate from the state or from beyond its direct control, much less whether what is involved is entitled to be called 'law.' Important as some of these questions may be, the approach preferred here seeks to relate institutions to cultural forms, to see how conceptualizations that cross-cut a variety of domains of ordinary life express themselves in the range of options afforded potential litigants and affect their attitudes toward and use of these various alternatives. Toward that end I want first to consider a set of formal courts established alongside the regular court system in Morocco some years ago, and then to place developments of this sort within the context of various forms of mediation and support that affect and express the elements that actual or potential disputes bring to the fore.

A DAY IN AN ALTERNATIVE COURT

In the summer of 1978 I returned to Sefrou, Morocco, for additional fieldwork. I had heard from several people that since my previous visit a law had been passed

---

[1] Among the better-known approaches and terminologies are Pospisil (1967) ('legal levels'); Petersen and Zahle (1995) ('legal polycentrism'); Bohannon (1957) ('legal realms'); and Moore (1978) ('semi-autonomous fields').

instituting a new set of courts. These courts, I was told, were to operate in rural areas, to employ local custom, to involve relatively small sums in contention, and to offer no opportunity for appeals. Because their predominant purpose was to give speedy consideration to matters that need not go before the regular courts, and they were, in whatever sense, meant to represent local sentiments and standards, I was especially curious to see such a court in operation.

I inquired about the rural courts from several of the officials in the regular court system, and although no one said anything directly, the persistent claim that they knew little about these courts sounded a note more of purposeful avoidance than of genuine lack of knowledge. When I worked in the courts more than a decade earlier there had been a uniformed aide who kept order in the qadi's court and performed various minor tasks. He was a man whose capacity to retain his equilibrium when dealing with the contentious people appearing before the court never failed to impress me. He had also taken me under his wing, treating me with a combination of respect and curiosity. In the intervening years he had worked his way up to the post of chief administrative clerk of the court, a change marked by the replacement of his mufti uniform with an elegant djellaba, bright red fez, and white leather slippers, and he still possessed all the dignity and good humor for which I remembered him. In the course of one of our conversations I mentioned that I had heard of the new courts and mused about how interesting it might be to visit one. He said nothing and I knew enough not to push the matter. I was, however, only modestly surprised when, a week or so later, he said, rather casually, that it was all set, I was due up in the nearby village of Bhalil tomorrow to spend the day in an alternative court.

Bhalil lies only a few miles away from Sefrou, over the last hill before the start of the great Sais plain that runs down toward Fez. In the late 1970s the village still contained only a few thousand inhabitants, and though it felt more developed than most rural agglomerations it nevertheless qualified for the establishment of one of the new courts. The administrative level into which the courts were implanted was that of the *jema'a l-qarawiya*, or *commune rurale*, a region overseen by a local administrator (*qaid*) and often coinciding with groups of tribal factions bearing some common identification. The court itself is referred to as the *maḥkama* of that administrative unit and its judge as a *ḥakem*, the same terms used at that time for the courts of general jurisdiction. In the case of Bhalil the jurisdiction of the court was restricted to the village itself and its most immediate environs and I knew that it was common for people from the rural hinterland stretching to the west and south—some of whom spoke Berber as well as Arabic—to move in and out of the village with some regularity.

The court was located adjacent to the post office in the central part of the village, in a large room entered by way of a covered porch. Several sizable, low windows opened onto the porch and throughout the session people leaned in through the windows to watch and listen to the proceedings. At the front of the room was a long counter. To one side, against the wall, stood a small cabinet in which I noticed a number of dossiers and a copy of the printed guide handed out to all of the rural court officials. A table set in the middle of the room served both as a place at which disputants and litigants could stand while facing the court and as a repository for a number of current case files.

The judge himself was a rotund man in his early forties who wore a clean white djellaba, a hat of the sort favored by many traditional men of his generation who work in the civil service, and yellow slippers. He did not speak French, though he did drop a few French words into his remarks to me, as for example when he explained to me that he was allowed to fine people anywhere from 10 to 800 dirhams ($2–160) and then translated the numbers into French for me. Though a touch pompous and sometimes confused (when he tried to cite the provisions in the judges' guide covering fines he got them all mixed up), he treated me most courteously and was concerned to explain to me the operations of the court. Besides the judge the court included a second-in-command (*nayeb*)—a more decidedly rural-looking man in his forties, Arabic-speaking, with a son at university in Fez—who came in near the end of the day's proceedings and actually heard the last case of the day. There was also a young male clerk and a uniformed aide seconded from the office of the qaid. In overall appearance, then, the court mirrored the regular courts in almost all respects.

Before the proceedings began the judge explained to me that he was authorized only to hear cases in which the value of items in contention did not exceed 1,000 dirhams (about $110 dollars in those days), unless both parties agreed to allow him to hear a case involving up to 2,000 dirhams. The whole point of his court, he said, was to give speedier judgment than was possible in the regular courts: A judgment can be entered the same day as the hearing, he said, the local administrator being informed within three days should enforcement be required. He pointed out the ledger listing the names of the parties, any witnesses, the decision reached, and any additional remarks. I could not help but notice that, for the pages I could see, nothing was written in the column headed 'remarks.' The judge went on to explain that two experts were attached to the court, one of whom had lived all his life in Bhalil and knew the local property situation extremely well, and that an expert was often sent out to determine the facts in cases involving land. The court, he said, may hear cases involving rent, credit, boundary incursions by individuals or animals, and other minor disputes involving property, but may not decide cases that would result in changing any property lines, or any disputes that touch on matters covered by the Moroccan Code of Personal Status (Mudawwana). He remarked that he had been elected to a three-year term by the members of the commune rurale, and I learned from the statute that he received reimbursement for his expenses but no salary. He mentioned that about 6,000 people were eligible as electors. He concluded by pointing out that if a case involves disputants from two different communes the case must go to the regular court in Sefrou, and that while cases cannot be appealed, parties can challenge his jurisdiction before the Sefrou court. This might happen if, for example, the parties are concerned that the judge (or one of his close relatives) is related to or has had legal dealings with one of the parties, or if one of the litigants has failed to get proper notice for appearance.

Shortly after nine o'clock the uniformed aide cried out 'The Court' and the judge, who had gone into the back room so that he would have a place to come out from, entered the courtroom and, with the clerk at his side, seated himself at the front counter. He pronounced 'in the name of the Almighty' and (glancing over at the portrait on the wall) 'the King,' and stated that this was a hearing of the jema'a l-qarawiya of the Bhalil region. The court meets formally only once a week and the docket for this day consisted of about a dozen cases, several of which were put over to a later session because of the failure of one or another party to appear. The entire session lasted a little over an hour. What follows are my notes on some of the cases heard that day.

The first case involved a fight over olives, worth about 350 dirhams ($72), that the plaintiff claimed had been improperly taken from his trees by the defendant. Each of the parties explained—or more accurately shouted out—his version of the matter: that the trees were his and the other had come over and taken the olives from them; that the trees were in fact *his* and he had every right to take the olives. The judge asked if either had any proof as to his claim but none was produced. The judge made no further inquiry into the circumstances of the dispute and rather precipitately ruled that the defendant should pay the plaintiff one-third of the amount sued for. This clearly displeased both parties: The plaintiff kept shouting that he was owed for all of the olives, the defendant that he owed nothing since they were his in the first place. Both could be heard still shouting after they had been escorted from the courtroom.

An old man, poorly dressed, and a woman dressed in the Bhalil style—a white cloth of tufted cotton wrapped around her head and draped down over her body, colorful but ragged clothes peeking out from underneath, plastic booties on her feet—now came before the court. The man claimed that the woman had not been paying him her rent of 1,200 rials (about $24) per month. She told the court that the sum agreed on was actually a lesser figure and that she would not pay the plaintiff the amount he was demanding. A witness was called. He swore to tell the truth and only the truth, and then testified that he rented a place similar to the woman's in the same building from the same man for the sum of 1,200 rials per month. The judge told the woman that if she wanted the terms of the rental agreement changed she would have to go to the Sefrou court to do so, but that it was his judgment that she must pay the 1,200 rials. The woman complained loudly against the judgment and continued to do so as she was conducted out of the court.

The plaintiff who now came before the court said that the defendant took some produce from his garden, mainly some grain that had been cut and was waiting to be threshed. The defendant answered that he and the plaintiff owned adjacent fields of grain and that the plaintiff had actually intruded on *his* land and harvested some of his crop. A witness was called and sworn. The judge asked him if he had ever been in jail. The witness reluctantly said yes. For what, asked the judge. The witness tried to evade answering, but under some pressure finally said it had to do with a girl. He then proceeded to testify that he saw two people, one of them the defendant, in the plaintiff's garden at the time the plaintiff claimed the pilfering occurred. The judge quickly ruled that the court-appointed expert would be sent to look at the properties and see if one or another of the parties had overstepped his boundary lines.

The next plaintiff said that the defendant's cow crossed into his garden and ate some of his produce; the defendant said it never happened, that it was not his cow that did it. The judge asked the plaintiff if he had any witnesses. The plaintiff mentioned some names and the judge put the case over by a week in order to allow time for the witnesses to be presented. But the plaintiff was clearly incensed and all the way out kept shouting that the defendant was a thief and that the whole proceeding was ridiculous.

Two men, one older and obviously well-off, the younger dressed in good-quality Western clothes, were the next to be called. The older man presented several documents to the judge which the latter, using somewhat exaggerated intonation on the literary Arabic, read out loud. The paper was a formal request for the case, initially brought by the younger man, to be removed to the Sefrou court. The dispute involved land and the older man claimed that since a boundary incursion was involved and this court was not authorized to hear cases that may affect boundaries the case must be transferred. The judge agreed and ordered the case removed to Sefrou.

Near the end of the hour a group of half a dozen people, obviously known to the judge from previous hearings, came forward. The judge asked if they had been able to reach a settlement (*sulḥ*); they all answered no. A number of written documents were handed around, the judge looking somewhat out of his depth as he tried to keep them straight. He brought the hearing to a conclusion by ordering the expert to go out and take a look at the land in question.

If the day's proceedings were relatively brief and the judge's initial explanation of his powers necessarily abbreviated, subsequent inquiry was to show that the day's proceedings were indeed highly characteristic of the overall process and attitudes associated with these alternative courts. I spoke with the judge for some time after court was adjourned. I also obtained a copy of the manual I had seen in his cabinet as well as the published proceedings of a panel sponsored by the League of Moroccan Attorneys held in 1976 to discuss the newly established rural courts. Over the course of many years I have asked other people in the countryside around Sefrou and other parts of Morocco about the rural courts operating in their regions. Themes that were clearly present that day in Bhalil have been repeated many times as a result of these inquiries.

The commune courts were modeled on a similar set of courts instituted in both the cities and countryside of Iran during the reign of the Shah. The 1974 Moroccan legislation[2] is at once quite specific about some matters and extremely vague about

---

[2] Royaume du Maroc (1975a).

others. Article 5 clearly stipulates that the judge must be a Moroccan national, at least 40 years old, having no police record, and presently residing in the commune he serves. In addition to specifying the issues and sums over which the court may exercise jurisdiction the statute states that litigants shall pay no fees to have their cases heard but may be subject to a range of fines or penalties. One section of the law encourages speedy judgment rather than overly careful examination of the files, while another provides that immediate judgment excuses the court from announcing its decision within three days, it being up to the discretion of the judge to allow a decent interval before the judgment is actually enforced.

The enabling statute also contains a lengthy section concerning the criminal penalties which a judge, on his own, may apply. These are divided into three categories, each carrying an increasing range of fines that may even be applied to juveniles aged twelve to sixteen. Nearly seventy-five highly specific misdemeanors are listed, among them throwing rocks, taking still-productive stubble from a field, and claiming to be an official tour guide or travel agent. The list is, in a sense, an indication both of the infractions that might lead to further disputes or violence and an indication of the government's image of protectible public interests. Although very wide-ranging indeed, this portion of the court's jurisdiction appears to be little used, and neither lawyers nor political parties have commented on it.

Much of the concern—and perhaps the intended strength—of the law lies in its very vagueness. Comments by the participants at the League of Moroccan Attorneys' symposium held in 1976 to analyze the new courts reflect a variety of concerns about this vagueness, as well as with the overall design of the courts. Since this is one of the few published discussions of the system it is worth describing in some detail.[3]

In his remarks, Professor Ahmed al-Idris Al-'Ilmi noted that nowhere does the enabling statute indicate whether the 'people's judge' (*qadi sh'abi*)—as he refers to him—should have any judicial experience (*khibra qānūnīya*), as compared to 'professional judges' (*al-quḍāt al-mihnīyīn*), who must have both theoretical and practical experience. He complains that judges are not even required to possess the qualities of 'knowledge and piety,' the implied reference, perhaps, being to those characteristics contained in the Caliph Omar's foundational remarks about judicial qualifications. A supplementary statute[4] does specify the process for selecting judges: the convening of a nominating committee that includes the president of the Court of First Instance (*al-maḥkama al-ibtidā'īya*) of the region involved, two representatives from the General Prosecutor's office (*al-niyāba al-'āmma*) chosen by the Ministry of Justice, the presidents of the commune rurale and the local Chamber of Agriculture, and the administrator (qaid) or assistant administrator (*khalīfa*) of the district. However, as the author rather circumspectly suggests, given the usual problems of committee decision-making, the best candidate may not emerge from this process of selection. He notes, too, that if a 'people's judge' is thought to be incompetent he may be temporarily suspended by the Ministry of Justice or permanently dismissed

---

[3]   al-Maghrebiya (1976).   [4]   Royaume du Maroc (1975b).

by the Supreme Council of Judges (*al-majlis al-a'la lil-qudāt*), a procedure the author regards as inappropriate since the 'people's judge' is by nature different from the 'professional judge' (*qadi mihnī*) and therefore the standards of competence should be different. He indicates that the 'people's judge' is not a government official (*muwazzaf*) and that by statute may only serve one term. Nevertheless, he concludes that, since the statute only says that the judge should operate according to 'basic principles' (*al-qawā'ād al-'āmma*), the judge should be expected to have some training and give some indication that he is aware of the great social responsibility he bears.

Other speakers at the lawyers' roundtable discussion pointed out related problems. 'Abbas al-Fasi noted that someone who has the standing to bring a case before the new courts is simply described by the term 'person' (*shakhs*), thus failing to indicate whether all legally responsible people (*dhātin* and *it'ibārīn*) are qualified to file suit, or only the clearly delimited range of individuals specified in other legal statutes. He noted that, since all litigants are exempt from paying any court fees, people with limited incomes will be able to bring cases. However, he worried that, notwithstanding the ability of those they sue to bring a countersuit, the system will simply encourage people who are uncertain of the justice of their claims to file cases. And although litigants must file a claim in writing, the failure of the statute to indicate what, if any, role attorneys may play in the preparation of such pleadings may undermine the informality of the proceedings.

The remaining speakers were more concerned with the type of law to be applied by the courts and with issues of political entanglement. Professor Rashid 'Abd al-Razzaq suggested that the silence of the statute on what law is to be applied at the judge's discretion—whether Islamic law (*shari'a*), secular law (*wad'ī*), or custom (*'urf*)—is nothing less than a threat to the 'rights of the people' and a danger to society as a whole. Such uncertainty, he said, serves only to protect the interests of the upper classes at the expense of the weaker classes. While praising the new courts for emphasizing arbitration (*tahkīm*) over imposed adjudication (*'adāla*) in civil cases, and for bringing relief from the burden that such cases pose for the state, he asked whether the new system is not merely a return to the arbitrary justice of village and tribal leaders (*qiyād*) and urban elites (*bashawāt*) that obtained prior to independence. The 1,000-dirham limit represents an entire year's income for many rural people, he said, implying that such individuals may find that virtually all claims they might have will be channeled to courts that lack the clear laws and procedures of the ordinary courts.

His colleague, 'Abd ar-Rahman b. 'Amru, was just as concerned about the method of selecting judges. He argued that there is no provision for freedom of the courts from government interference. The term 'qualifications' (*mu'ahallāt*) as applied to the judges is vague, the procedures for selecting a nominating committee (*hay'at al-intikhāb*) are unclear, and such uncertainty assures the interference of the government in the process of judicial appointment. He was especially concerned that, since the nominating committee includes local political leaders and that the Ministry of

Justice can suspend a sitting judge, an unhealthy link will exist between local political elites and the courts. Substituting transfer to the regular courts (*ihala*) for appeal
(*ta'n*) is an inadequate safeguard for litigants for whom 1,000 dirhams may figure so
large as to warrant the option of an appeal.

Mr Ben 'Amru supported his skepticism with figures showing that in the existing
civil courts cases are actually dealt with fairly quickly. He found that many districts
do not have one of the new courts yet and that those already in place do not represent local distinctiveness inasmuch as litigants may come from widely separated
areas. The absence of such guarantees as the right of appeal, he argued, has not
achieved simplification (*tabsīt*). He suggested that the experience of the new courts
thus far indicated that users were not particularly poor, which in turn suggests that
the exemption from fees not only encourages repeated litigation but actually serves
the interests of those who are quite well-to-do. He concluded that trust in judges was
not increased by this new system which, as a whole, he characterized as a failure.

Many of the concerns raised by the lawyers attending the symposium have been
supported by comments made by people in various parts of Morocco over the years,
as well as by my conversation with the judge of the Bhalil court after that day's
session in 1978. When, for example, I asked the judge about the law he applied he
said, rather self-importantly, that he judged according to custom ('*urf*) and the
Quran, though neither was evident in his procedures or in his judgments. When we
talked about the practices of the people who come before him he said that there are
no special customs of the Bhalil people, but added that when he does need help he
talks to the head of the individual's village quarter (*muqaddem*) or to some of the
people who really know the area. He indicated that he relied a good deal on his
experts, and (in response to a leading question on my part) admitted that he would
talk over some cases with the local administrator.

The judge went on to say that you can always tell who good people are, and
himself claimed to know everyone in town and to be able to draw on that knowledge
in deciding cases. When I suggested that it might be difficult to know if a person's
intentions (sing. *niya*) are good or bad he made the same argument one encounters
throughout so much of the Arab world: All you have to do is look at what a person
does, he said, in order to determine what is in a person's head. If someone is bad it
will show up in the way he acts toward other people, and you cannot hide what you
do. This shows up very quickly, he continued, and people know if you do things
'straight' or 'crooked.' With the other members of the court nodding agreement, the
judge expressed his own certainty on this matter: From past actions you can tell quite
well what a person has done in the case now before the court.

Both in the limits of his knowledge and in the limits of his independence the rural
court judge of Bhalil represented some of the reservations one hears about these
courts. The judge was, I believe, not one of those whom the Bhalil people, given a
wholly free decision, would have chosen. A man of no particular local importance,
he was, however, one of those the local administrator would most likely want in the
position. Bureaucratic and not too independent of mind, the Bhalil judge was hardly

a 'big man' or respected elder of the region. Notwithstanding his initial claim, his own responses, and my later inquiries, confirmed that he was not especially knowledgeable about the area. Many of the litigants, including older men who had lived all of their lives in the village, showed him a mild if not marked disdain. Speaking with a very well-informed man from a nearby district about their own rural court, I asked how the judge was chosen and was told he was picked by the men of the commune rurale. When I asked if the qaid, the local administrator, was involved, my informant gave me a knowing smile and replied that the qaid is *always* involved. He went on to describe how, in their area, the qaid had called him in and told him, as he had told others, that he would really appreciate it if so-and-so were picked as the local judge. Naturally, said my informant, that is the man they picked. Indeed, he added, the man is not particularly well known to people in their area either.

The way in which the judge is selected may not be wholly divorced from the way in which he reaches his decisions. Under the statute the judge is selected by an electoral college composed of 100 people from the commune, and overseen by a committee of judges and administrators, including, perhaps most notably, the qaid himself. In court, cases not infrequently occur in which the judge, who could decide the matter at hand very quickly, chooses to put matters off. Informants suggested that in such instances the judge, or his assistant, may then touch base with someone from the qaid's office. Indeed, it was only very late in the day, when everyone else had left and I was still chatting with the judge and his assistants, that I noticed a man who had been there the whole time and who now came up and stood by us. When I acknowledged him he was introduced to me as being from the qaid's office.

Critics of the rural courts say that they perpetuate the rural elite. A high-ranking member of the Socialist Party placed this factor, along with the judges' lack of training and use of any formal body of law, at the forefront of his criticisms, as did several of the lawyers in the symposium we mentioned earlier. This criticism may, however, be somewhat misplaced. It is, perhaps, more likely that the qaid handpicks his man and, though some of the qaid's concerns (e.g., landlord–tenant relations, local practices affecting the rights of property owners, poor people pilfering from the rich) may coincide with the interests of local elites, these are dependent variables in the overall equation of power. Rather, it is the perpetuation of centralized control over the rural areas, not simply the maintenance of a rural elite, that is being served here. The judge in Bhalil himself said that important families would be ashamed to bring their disputes to any court and that it is not the elite who account for the cases before him. He joked that in three years someone else would take his place, following another election, and the suspicion is rife that judges, being unpaid, have some understanding that the qaid will help them in other ways after their term of office. Nor is the judge using local custom in any systematic way.[5] Instead, the rapidity of his decisions

---

[5] There is very little known about what, if any, local custom is being applied by these courts in rural areas, but my own informants suggest that in the Middle Atlas region it is all but non-existent. The only hint to the contrary is a brief remark by David Hart: 'There are signs today, since 1986, that bits and

and his reliance on local experts and consultation with the qaid's office for stickier situations suggest that the common goal is to keep potentially disruptive disputes from developing into major incidents.

The courts do not, in fact, operate as part of a heavy-handed governmental apparatus. Indeed, it has long been a hallmark of the Moroccan polity that it is not a closely watched state, and the lively use of all sorts of forums serves as a testament to the relative independence of all the courts. In the years since their founding, questions of the rural courts' independence have not exercised even the opposition parties, nor has the potential afforded by the statute for extensive criminal jurisdiction been implemented. Rather, the primary dissatisfaction that one hears is the same as that which was evident that first day in the Bhalil court, a form of dissatisfaction that says a good deal both about the type of legal system that accords with ordinary legal sensibilities and about the popular, if not always articulated, sense of justice.

Recall the day in the Bhalil court. With the exception of those whose cases were being transferred, virtually every litigant was upset by the judge's decision. Shouting is not unusual in the regular courts, and judges often want to see the intensity of feeling in order to gauge an appropriate response. But as much as one hears people expressing dissatisfaction with the outcome, litigants before the ordinary courts seldom express overt contempt for the proceedings as a whole. In the rural courts, by comparison, people have no hesitancy in expressing their outrage. The judge, as we have seen, may put matters over or send out experts as he gets some sense of how to manage cases consistent with the interests of the qaid's office. But in the majority of instances the primary consideration seems to be speed. Where no proof is immediately forthcoming or likely to be produced the judge usually just splits the difference. (The resulting outrage may have accounted for the judge's joking reference to someone else having his job in a few years.) Two factors influence the parties' reactions.

The first concerns the type of legal process these courts represent. In Chapter 3, I argued that the Islamic courts may be seen to represent a variant of the common law system of adjudication. I suggested that when one organizes a typology based on the distribution of power and the incorporation of inherently unstable cultural conceptualizations one sees that Islamic legal systems emphasize indirect control and the localized articulation of cultural concepts. But the rural courts do not fit this pattern. They are really a state-organized reciprocity-based type of apparatus inserted into a common law system. They do not, in fact, utilize local custom or any body of recognized law and for that reason seem to my informants to have no recognizable process, nothing they can get a grip on, no point of attachment through which they

pieces of customary law are gradually coming back to the rural (and formerly tribal) Berber-speaking regions of Morocco, through the appointment of a series of local specialists, qadis in customary law, in all the relevant market sites in the countryside, but it is doing so slowly and in a very "low-key" manner, with the reinstatement of selected and only minor items of custom' (Hart (1996: 367)). Hart is presumably referring to the commune rurale courts here, though his reference to qadis may either be a local, if curious, usage or a minor oversight on the author's part. Neither he nor any other person I know of has done a full-scale study of these courts.

can formulate their arguments or draw on their connections and experience to configure a set of supporting ideas and associations. Just as the attempt to introduce lay jurors who would assist judges in the trial of a case failed because it was a civil law device applied to a common law tradition, so too the introduction of rural courts has failed to garner popular support because it is a reciprocity-based device in common law clothing, a system that appears to be supporting direct social relationships but which, by splitting the difference in the interest of speed, fails to speak to ordinary people's sense about how such institutions are supposed to fit in to the larger realm of negotiable social relations.

There is also a second discrepancy, one that goes to the related sense of justice. As we shall see in Chapter 9, justice for Moroccans, as in the Arabo-Islamic context generally, implies the rational evaluation of the persons before the court and the weighing of various aspects of their situations so as to determine appropriate equivalencies. It is not equality that matters, but equivalence; not so much rights, as conducible obligations; not determinate rules of law, but respect for the rules of the game. The rural courts fail by cutting short the inquiry and issuing decisions that merely split the difference so that both parties feel that they have not had 'their day in court.' They do not believe that their felt sense of injury has been attended to in a way that is recognizable: There is no inquiry into *who* they are, no recognizable appraisal of how burdens should be apportioned, and no appreciation that the dispute, which may go on in various ways for a very long time, needs the markers of occasional judicial intervention as part of the overall process of the parties' ordinary engagement. The intensity of the shouting by most of the departing litigants speaks loudly to their sense that the court is not acting in a way they can recognize as admirably legitimate, notwithstanding their willingness to use such courts, like any other instrument, as they try to find their way in a contentious and labyrinthine world. To further understand the discordant nature of these proceedings it may be valuable to compare them to several other styles of dispute-processing available to those who might otherwise (or in addition) bring their difficulties to the 'people's court.'

ALTERNATIVE DISPUTE-PROCESSING MECHANISMS

There being so many ways to build one's networks of affiliation, and so intense an emphasis on the constant configuring of the bonds of obligation, it should come as no surprise that Arabs have a highly elaborated set of mechanisms available to attend to their actual or potential differences. This is not the place to give an exhaustive description or appraisal of all of these mechanisms: Many of them—from structured bloodmoney debts to the 'peace of the market,' from the role of saints as arbiters to the ritual-like conduct of the 'song duel'—have received extensive treatment in the literature. Instead I want to concentrate on several practices that constitute part of the context within which people choose whether or how to make use of the regular and rural courts at all. I also want to suggest why being cut off from these mechanisms as part of the larger context of social relations is so striking an aspect of the rural court environment.

One characteristic of formal legal proceedings in Morocco is the presence in the proceedings themselves of a number of the litigants' relatives or supporters. From the people who wander into the clerk's office of the qadi's court with a relative in tow to the cluster of allies who strategize and hover close at hand, the presence of others is felt both directly and indirectly. This is far less true in the rural courts. There, with no need for the financial support required for a regular court case and little need for experience in the filing or arguing of one's case, litigants tend to stand alone. Few witnesses are presented, and none who speaks for a person's general reliability; no lawyers are present, so interested supporters who might otherwise have helped raise money for the case are not noticeably involved; no appeal is possible, so continuing concern with the formal proceedings is summarily cut off. The whole network of people within whose reach one is embedded and from whom one draws both identity and expectation is largely irrelevant, and their absence, so striking by comparison to the regular legal process, may have a bearing on the distressed reactions individuals display before the 'people's court.' Put somewhat differently, the mutual effect of proceeding before an alternative court and the uses made of other 'dispute-processing mechanisms' may be quite different than if an action before the regular courts is part of the overall backdrop. To understand why this may be so it is valuable to gain a brief overview of the roles of various types of intermediaries.

The term translated as 'go-between' in Arabic is *wasīta*, from a root that means 'middle.' Wasitas come in many forms and may be drawn upon for a wide range of purposes. They may be sought out by parties themselves or effectively imposed on them by others who fear disruption to their own lives. A distinction some people make, in regard to various forms of intercession, is that between permissible interactions that produce ends either favored by religion and morality or treated as morally neutral—the term for such actions being *khair* ('virtuous,' 'good,' 'benign')—and those actions that are bad, or impermissible (called *sharr*—'malicious,' 'harmful,' 'damaging,' 'iniquitous'), and for which the use of intermediaries may either be useful for the avoidance or repair of an undesirable act or relationship, or constitute a perversion of the use of such go-betweens. Thus an intermediary may be used to smooth over a dispute or to get an introduction to a business client; alternatively the practice may be perverted by using him to arrange an illicit association or a bribe. In either case, it is one of the characteristics of the role of a wasita that he goes alone, rather than with the petitioner, to see the other party and that to refuse the imprecations of such a go-between casts no shame on the person who has been approached. Their use is so widespread and generalized that, as one man put it, they are to the proper functioning of society what food is to the proper functioning of the body. The contrast between the broadly interstitial role of the wasita and some other forms of mediation is, however, quite marked.

The *'ar* refers to a group of people who have been sent with or on behalf of an individual to request some forgiveness or consideration from the one petitioned. It shares with more personalistic forms of the 'ar—such as the ritual constraint through a sacrifice or the ingratiating act toward a religious figure—the notion that the one upon whom the 'ar is thrust will feel some sense of shame in the presence of the supplicant if he fails to respond favorably. He may even encounter some supernatural sanction. The group itself may consist of one of four main categories of people: descendants of the Prophet or a saint (*shurfa*), persons who are knowledgeable in the sacred law ('*ulamā*'), important men of the region, or small children.[6] In the past an 'ar might be used to get the family of a deceased to accept bloodmoney in order to ward off a feud, but it is more commonly used nowadays, for example, as a pressure group to get a father to agree to marry his daughter to the petitioner or to arrange compensation for a civil injury. The combination of social pressure and generalized supernatural support contributes to the shape and effectiveness of the 'ar.

Two other types of groups may be employed. The *meshikha* is a respected group of people known to both parties and used primarily for 'good' things. It differs from the 'ar both in its treatment of relatively minor matters and insofar as refusal to accede to its request is not shameful and carries no external sanction. The group represents the good faith of one party to another without taking any joint responsibility for the petitioner's good conduct. It may be employed, for example, when a wife runs back to her parents after an argument with her husband, and the latter sends a meshikha to apologize and request her return. Often it is the recipient of the meshikha's attentions who has requested that such a group be sent to obtain the attestation of these people as to the good faith of the petitioner and their influence on his future behavior. Since no supernatural sense of shame applies, it is only the respect in which the group is held that will affect its success. By contrast, the *sulh* is usually employed where more disruptive (*sharr*) relationships are involved. The term itself means 'to arbitrate' or 'reconcile,' and it is a process much commended by the Quran.[7] There is never a sacrifice or use of children associated with a sulh, and it may be used to stave off trouble before it can begin, as for example when heirs cannot agree on the division of an estate and their potential dispute could affect many others adversely.

Now the interesting thing about the rural courts is how little these mechanisms fit in with their own proceedings. One would not necessarily expect external devices to play any formal role—for the court to turn to them for assistance or for the parties to employ the same techniques for conducing help from the court that one uses in other contexts. But when one looks at proceedings before the regular courts, and

---

[6] An example in which children might be sent as an 'ar was described by one informant in the following way: A man makes a rude remark to a woman in the street. She tells her husband who proceeds to the spot but mistakenly beats up the wrong man. The injured party has the husband thrown in jail, but before he has formally pressed charges the wife sends her children to the injured man as her 'ar. In the face of an 'ar composed of small children, who are so clearly dependent on their father, it would be shameful for the injured man not to be forgiving.

[7] 'If two parties of the believers fight, put things right between them; then, if one of them is insolent against the other, fight the insolent one, till it reverts to God's commandment' (Sura XLIX: 9).

when one follows litigants in and out of the court, one realizes very quickly that the extrajudicial institutions of mediation form an important part of the array of options that may be at work in any formal legal proceeding. Such institutions form not simply the shadow within which legal negotiation occurs but are an integral part of the array of legal options of which the courts are but one. The specific concatenation of devices employed will vary as much as any person's obligational network, but the repertoire of possibilities—their availability in the tempo of a dispute in which a dizzying array of interests may be in play—will all be potentially available if a lawsuit is in question. The rural courts are simply not part of this predominant apparatus of Moroccan interpersonal maneuvering; they cut off rather than form part of the over-all design of such relationships, and the absence of such maneuvers bespeaks the relative lack of involvement, as well, perhaps, as the more agonized sense of isolation, that litigants bring to the proceedings.

Much the same can be said of other mechanisms that come into play in Moroccan disputing. Guarantors (sing. *damen*) play a vital role in the marketplace and in those relationships where one can tap into another's network as support for one's own. But when a court pays no heed to those who can vouch for an individual, when documents that contain the notary-validated testimony of reliable witnesses are of no use, and when evidence of a person's general reputation counts for nothing in a court that summarily splits the difference, one's entire legal sensibility is seriously undermined.[8] Even the styles of argument so often seen in and around the regular courts resonate with the styles seen in ordinary relationships—the posture, the rhetoric, the invocation of the opinion of those standing around.[9] It is, again, as if litigants in the rural courts are unable to draw upon their normal sources of cultural support—the reverberations and resources available from the other domains of life in which they operate, and to which the rural courts lack any real attachment.

The choice of legal mechanism, broadly defined, is, for Moroccans, less an exclusive decision than a portion of an ongoing strategy. As we have seen, cases frequently go on for very long periods of time and often involve matters that are not part of the formal proceeding. But that very array—of lawsuit and shaming group, supernatural imprecation and mundane finagling—that gives disputing its place in a larger sociocultural world of ordinary relationships and comprehension fits less well when it is the rural court that is involved. It may be part of one's strategy to go to these courts, but such litigation is less easily assimilated with the ongoing use of multiple sources of disputing than is true for other domains. That Moroccans find the usual courts unsatisfying reinforces the importance of understanding alternatives to formal court proceedings in cultural, rather than exclusively structural, terms, and it is to the criticism and replacement of theories that pose such an emphasis that we must now turn our attention.

---

[8] On his use of the phrase 'legal sensibility,' see Geertz (1983: 185–234).
[9] For an example of such argumentative style, see Rosen (1984: 128–9).

LEGAL PLURALISM AND CULTURAL UNITY

The range of alternatives available for dispute-processing by Moroccans raises many of the same questions addressed by numerous scholars under the general rubric of legal pluralism. Although its phrasing and meaning vary widely, the concept of legal pluralism has done a great deal to shake comparative law out of its emphasis on using state-based and state-sanctioned legal norms as the baseline for analyzing diverse legal systems. Whether by stressing the multicentric nature of lawlike propositions and conducements, by pointing to the social institutions through which multifarious aspects of people's lives may be structured according to rule-like orientations, or by demonstrating that common pressures may exist to work out relationships notwithstanding the structural independence of legal domains, the studies of legal pluralists have helped to wean comparative law from its statist emphasis.

At the same time such advances have left us with several dilemmas, dilemmas which, not surprisingly, animate many other domains of social and cultural theory. How, one is forced to ask, is it possible for people to maintain a sense of ordered social relationships if the domains within which their disputes are addressed are so disparate as to lack any overarching appeal to people's loyalty or sense of how things ought to be done? Can we be sure that we have not replaced our statist-ethnocentrism with a kind of locality-ethnocentrism if there remains at least the logical possibility that multiple localized disputing mechanisms are as confusing and unpredictable as any state-run court? Indeed, to borrow Elizabeth Colson's way of putting the matter, if disputes do not usually lead to harmonious settlement but to the public clarification of the nature and implications of contentiousness itself, are state-sponsored courts and local disputing mechanisms not better tested for the similar reactions people have to them than for their structural differences?[10] And if 'law,' however characterized, is to be seen as part of life and not some exquisitely separable element of it, to which larger theories shall we attach ourselves to account for the similarities and differences between law and religion, family life, economic ties, and other domains of a people's existence?

Addressing these questions as part of a larger anthropological approach to law opens up the issues surrounding legal pluralism and helps us move away from narrow concerns about what law is and who has it. In the process of taking up such an approach several aspects of cultural theory come into play. First, it may be suggested that if one views law as part of culture and culture as a set of orientations which gains its very life by reverberating through numerous analytically separable domains so as to appear immanent in all of them, we may be able to account for some of the commonalities that pluralism might seem to undercut. Such a focus can lead us, secondly, to ask not only how the process of rule-generation occurs but in what ways common-sense assumptions about features that cross-cut virtually all domains of law

---

[10]　Colson (1995).

and life—assumptions about human nature, particular kinds of relationships, the 'meaning' of given acts—are themselves intertwined with and integral to the process by which one tests the scope and validity of assessments of fact and person in a variety of cultural domains.

Focusing on process as a mechanism for generating not just rules but connections of common sense among cultural domains can also lead us to consider how the individuals in particular cultures may retain as non-contradictory those propositions that may appear to others as incapable of simultaneously occupying the same space. By considering the implications of Weber's recognition that psychological as much as physical coercion may underlie a legal order and by exploring Santos' stress on the phenomenology of diverse legal orders converging in the mind of the individual, we may be able to advance our consideration of how parallel orders of law may exist in Morocco.[11] Indeed, we may also be able to ask how the cultural structuring of such convergences affects the presence or absence of a sense of alienation when religious and secular, state-sponsored and non-state mechanisms appear logically unable to occupy the same terrain.

Let us begin with the question of cultural orientations. Central to this approach is the argument that cultures are held together when common orientations and assumptions are present in a number of domains of social and intellectual life, such that their replication gives the appearance to adherents that these beliefs and relationships arise not from their own initiative alone but possess an aspect of reality so deep as to seem obvious. Examples range from those of classical sociology (Durkheim's analysis of effervescent images that run through elementary religious life, kinship, and economic exchange, or Weber's argument that the Protestant ethic ties together the belief in the salvation of one's soul in a non-sacramental environment with the secular sainthood confirmed by working successfully in one's calling) to those evident in our own societies (where, for example, medical science approaches illness through the same metaphors of competition that inform our approach to the marketplace, the battlefield, and the personal struggle for meaning in one's own life).[12]

When law is looked at in these terms the emphasis falls not on the distinctiveness of law as a domain (the role of professionals, specialized language, and peculiar institutional history) but on the ways in which legal questions do (perhaps in very many instances *must*) partake of the same or recognizably similar assumptions prevalent in other domains of the culture. Thus, as we have seen, in the case of Morocco assumptions about human nature (the play of passion and reason, differentially distributed in men versus women, children versus adults) make comprehensible the law of personal injury or the process of determining the facts in a land dispute, precisely

---

[11] Weber wrote: 'A "legal order" shall rather be said to exist wherever coercive means, of a physical or psychological kind, are available; i.e., wherever they are at the disposal of one or more persons who hold themselves ready to use them for this purpose in the case of certain events' (Weber (1954: 17)). For Santos, see text accompanying n. 21 below.

[12] On the metaphors of reproduction and illness, see Martin (1991) and Sontag (1990).

because without partaking of the reverberations of these orientations in religion, social thought, family life—in short, commonsense—it would not be possible to render meaningful consideration of the situations with which the law is presented.

Seen from this perspective some of the classic questions of legal pluralism take on a somewhat different cast. John Griffiths[13] has rightly criticized both M. G. Smith[14] and Sally Falk Moore[15] for suggesting that, for the former, the legal order is congruent with a nested set of corporate-like social institutions bound together by an overarching structure, or that Moore's emphasis on 'semi-autonomous legal fields' wrongly assumes that each such field gains much of its form and content from its interaction with, even its repugnance of, state-centered law. Tamanaha has gone further and charged that those who employ the idea of legal pluralism mistakenly equate the norms of social interaction with those of state law. The result of such conceptual confusion, he argues, is to assume, quite incorrectly, that law has the power on its own to produce patterns of social relationship and to obscure the quite different way that state law affects relationships as compared with any other kind of institution.[16] Notwithstanding his criticism of those who continue to pursue a distinctive definition of law,[17] Tamanaha may be faulted for continuing to focus on structural forms rather than on the conceptualizations that affect the ties among diverse realms of social interaction, such that courts may, at one moment, generate new social patterns by capturing the terms by which people understand their relationships or, at another, fail to service their own professed goals precisely because they are inconsistent with the orientations that suffuse other domains of life.[18] By contrast, a cultural emphasis finds among different domains a process by which commonsense orientations are adopted, rejected, transformed, or reversed—but in every way gaining legitimacy and justification for their powers and their results by virtue of their engagement with these resonant orientations.

We shall see an extended example of the value of such an approach when, in Chapter 8, we look at the issue of trust in Islamic law and Moroccan society. There it will be argued that Moroccan social relations rest on the negotiation of bonds of indebtedness among persons who have gained control of their passions by the development of their reasoning powers through religious education, dependence on people who are themselves attached to others, and by demonstrating how reliable they are once they have given their word. To address the question of when is a bargain made solely by emphasizing the use of a technical form promulgated by the courts would run counter to ordinary sense about what makes a person trustworthy. Instead the

---

[13] Griffiths (1986).   [14] Smith (1969).   [15] Moore (1978).

[16] '[W]hen legal pluralists refer to "law" they have identified and run together two very different phenomena: institutionalized identification and enforcement of norms, and concrete patterns of social ordering' (Tamanaha (1993: 211)). See also the essays in the special issue on legal pluralism in Belley (1997).

[17] Tamanaha (1993: 201). See also Ch. 3 on Islamic law as a common law system.

[18] Other criticisms of Tamanaha's position include the argument that legal pluralism has pointed to the fragmentation in many instances of state law and the rise of extralegal processes of legitimation. See Olgiati (1997).

referential use of reliable witnesses—defined as people themselves so embedded in ties of obligation that they will not lie lest they lose their dependants—coupled with the religiously sanctioned use of oaths or the public indication of a bond that others may now rely upon, all give coherence and comprehensibility to the legal emphasis on persons over forms and contractual obligation as present interrelation rather than speculative consequence.

Clearly rules do emerge from any institution addressing issues such as when does trust convert to binding agreement or when is a kinship tie implying generalized support worthy of concerted pressure aimed at achieving behavioral conformity? But at a deeper level what may knit together different domains and generate common approaches is a cultural process by which assumptions of human nature or human relations are rendered applicable, where the reasoning process itself partakes of the mode of fact creation and causal connection that is regarded as adequate for explaining events and actions in various domains. If, then, we see, as is the case in Morocco, that courts apply commercial statutes drawn from European models or criminal statutes almost identical to those of former colonizers, we must also ask whether the process by which facts are determined or persons are assessed are those not of the European style but distinctive to Moroccan ways of conducting these inquiries in other domains of cultural life. And when we do approach matters in this way we can see at once where the consonance and strain may occur, where the very challenge by one domain to another focuses attention on reconciling competing cultural orientations, where a challenge to existing assumptions forces many issues to be reconsidered—as has occurred with many fatwas in Islamic cultural/legal history—and where the power of leaders intercedes to move matters to the next stage of consideration or cover them over as largely unresolvable.

These features are particularly highlighted when more than one style of law is present in a single regime. Legal pluralism has usually been characterized as 'a situation in which two or more legal systems coexist in the same social field.'[19] Such joint occupancy may, of course, take a variety of forms: It may be a contentious struggle for the same space with each regarding the presence of an alternative as violative of some sociological version of the natural principle that two bodies cannot occupy the same space simultaneously; it may take the form of mutual disregard, where each acts as if the other is not really there or is tolerated only as long as some superordinate interest is not seen to be threatened; or it may constitute a kind of concurrent jurisdiction, in which either may be operative depending on context, personalities, or costs. The first often characterizes the position of strict Islamic fundamentalism (e.g., the Taliban of Afghanistan), the second that of traditional Islamic deference to confessional laws of other 'people of the book,' and the third that of the semi-formal operation of those national legal systems where jurisdiction may be held simultaneously by religious and 'secular' courts.[20] Whichever is the case, some accommodation

---

[19] Merry (1988: 870).

[20] For an example of how one might be able to choose between two Moroccan courts that have jurisdiction over land matters, see Rosen (1989a: 29–30).

must be made in the mentality of the participants to account for the simultaneous presence of these multiple orders.

Santos has characterized this aspect of legal pluralism as one in which 'the conception of different legal spaces [is] superimposed, interpenetrated, and mixed in our minds as much as in our actions. . . . Our legal life is constituted by an intersection of different legal orders, that is, by interlegality[,] . . . the phenomenological counterpart of legal pluralism.'[21] His position is not altogether unlike that of Jacques Vanderlinden, who argues that it is the individual alone who finds himself in a position of legal pluralism, 'the condition of the person who, in his daily life, is confronted in his behavior with various, possibly conflicting, regulatory orders, be they legal or non-legal, emanating from the various social networks of which he is, voluntarily or not, a member.'[22] I have already suggested that these different domains may be linked not so much by structural forms as by cultural orientations. But that issue to the side, the question in any specific context is how these diverse phenomenological realms cohere within the cultural and psychological domains. For this purpose let me return to the Moroccan case, as I see it.

Morocco has been described by one scholar as 'a land of compromise.'[23] In many respects this is a fair characterization. Certainly one of the distinctive cultural features of the country is the existence side by side of various institutions that could appear as incompatible. In law this shows itself in a variety of ways. Maliki Islamic law, Berber and Arab customary practices, former colonial law, confessional laws, and contemporary Moroccan codes exist simultaneously.[24] For the moment it is the way these orders appear to exist in the mentality of Moroccans, rather than in institutional structure, that concerns me. In this regard it is noteworthy that informants express relatively few objections or sense of contradiction among these diverse elements. Litigants think nothing of looking to the choice of forums occasioned by the overlap of jurisdictions, each of which stems from a different legal background. They treat this choice as they do others in their social life—as strategic decisions to be made among the array of relational possibilities that life does, and commonsensically would, afford them. Just as ties to others are negotiated in an environment in which cultural postulates are not regarded as mutually contradictory but capable of being amalgamated into variant designs by different persons, so, too, legal propositions and institutions are treated as resources to be added to the process by which interpersonal relations are formed and transformed.

The result appears to be a very diminished sense of contradiction among identifiably distinct legal orders: However much preference may be expressed for one or

---

[21] Santos (1987: 297–8).

[22] Vanderlinden (1989: 153–4); see also Vanderlinden (1971). [23] Gallagher (1963).

[24] Berber law was frequently highly formalized, with written codes and elaborate institutions ranging from tribal factions that served as specialists to elaborate fact-finding techniques involving co-swearers and ordeals. Most of the formal aspects of Berber law have fallen into disuse, but only further study will tell if elements persist in less visible form.

another regime individuals think nothing of using alternatives when it is pragmati-
cally desirable. The colonial period largely withdrew commercial and criminal
matters from Islamic jurisdiction in its promulgation of codes and its institutionalization of courts quite distinct from those of previous times. This pattern has been
continued into the independence period. Yet it is remarkable to see the extent to
which elites and ordinary people accept this jurisdictional/code differentiation. This
may be, in part, due to the Moroccan habit of political accommodation, but it is also
part of the overall cultural style that treats institutions as resources while maintaining a common cultural emphasis on person perception and fact determination that
runs through all of the different legal orders. Thus in a criminal court one finds
much the same modes of and emphasis on the assessment of persons as situated in
networks of obligation that one finds in customary or Islamic domains; in commercial courts one finds the same assumptions about causality one finds in ordinary
event analysis and historic explanation.[25] It is these cultural features that make
domains that might otherwise appear mutually incompatible so similar and hence
mutually available.

Recall now the case of the rural (or 'people's') courts. There is the sense that the
court's style does not accord with common-sense understandings of what constitutes
a proper consideration of one's complaint, that it does not mesh with the alternative
forms of mediation that may be integrated into the overall strategy of a dispute, and
that it does not accord with a resultant sense of justice through a process of weighing and evaluating equivalencies. These feelings frequently leave both parties angry
and alienated. In the absence of a felt sense that the techniques of assessment are
consonant with those experienced in other domains, people feel cut off from the
resources of disputing and the larger implications most disputes have for interlocking networks of affiliation. For them, proceedings in the rural courts seem less the
addition of another basis on which 'the game' can be played than an example of the
imposed power that they are unable to engage with in their own form of give-and-
take based on shared assumptions about people, events, and consequences.

Similarly, as we have seen, Moroccans have long treated 'customary' law as part of
Islamic law, not as something set alongside it. We saw, too, that when the French, in
1934, attempted to split Arabs from Berbers by placing the former under their own
customary law and the latter under Islamic law, the Berbers revolted, arguing that
Berber law *is* Islamic law, in the sense that Islam allows what is not clearly forbidden.
The sense among Moroccans that custom continues to occupy a place in the law that
is not apart from Islam but integral to it goes a long way toward retaining a sense of
psychic unity, a common legal sensibility, among the diverse legal orders with which
they live.

---

[25] The comparison to Malaysia, as analyzed by Horowitz (1994), is particularly striking in this
regard. Horowitz argues that 'to be authentic a legal system does not need to be indigenous' (p. 570), and
that in the Malaysian case, notwithstanding the indications that 'dualism creates discomfort and incon-
venience among the participants' (p. 574), the resulting dual system of Malay law and common law is
sufficiently capacious that a clear sense of authenticity is possible.

All of this is not to suggest that the culturally unifying aspects of Moroccan law exist without countervailing strains. Elites who at independence found themselves unable to go back to pre-Protectorate legal patterns or forward to wholly Europeanized codes tended to naturalize the divisions of legal realms, as if family law were 'properly' dealt with by Islam and commercial law by European-style codes. Their 'as if' attitude contributed to the codification, along very traditional lines, of much of Moroccan family law, but it was still done—as it largely continues to be done—at the expense of greater equality between the sexes. Just as Moroccans have little difficulty wearing Western clothes at one moment and traditional garb at another, or moving back and forth among languages, so too they may have accommodated these legal alterations in form only insofar as they also continue to embrace cultural commonalities in procedure and assumption.

The legitimacy of various legal domains may also rest on their utilization of these cultural commonalities such that alienation from the law is less severe than in some other parts of the world. Relatively few Moroccans feel that fundamentalism speaks to their needs since alienation from the law, where it exists, stems not from a contradiction with religion but from that degree of bureaucratization and incivility which makes people feel they are not able to use the various legal possibilities as vehicles for the formation and restructuring of their interpersonal ties. For all the discussion about revising women's rights there is little sense that Moroccans are encountering a moment of searching for new moral guidelines and hence rather little propulsion for rethinking the legitimacy of contending forums or sources of psychological constraint.

Marc Galanter (1981: 22) has argued that as a sense of all-encompassing community has declined, it has largely been replaced by 'a world of loosely joined and partly overlapping partial or fragmentary communities.' Although this may be true for many countries, including Morocco, such a social structural emphasis may fail to give adequate consideration to the ways in which common orientations—about such ordinary matters as person perception, causality, the nature of human nature, and the criteria for determining truth—affect the unity or diversity of legal orders within a pluralistic context. Other countries of the Middle East, more seriously affected by colonialism or economic disruption, may display quite different patterns on a continuum of cultural unity than does Morocco, and each case needs to be considered in its own right from this cultural perspective. Only then will the contradictions of the one be seen as identities in another. Moreover, the theoretical challenges to cultural analysis—how much must people share common orientations in order to live together within a single social system; when divergence of orientation does occur through what mechanisms does it most readily express itself—will be best addressed if comparative legal data is brought into consideration.

Legal pluralism can then be seen as an analytic tool rather than as a theory or an explanation. Just as a microscope does not explain anything about microbes, legal pluralism does not explain the subject of its concern. Rather, it lets us see what is there, in this case a living, seething field in which law shows itself to be a process of regularizing relationships—a process that involves competing approaches which may be bound together by their reliance on common cultural orientations. Moreover, such an orientation suggests where we may look for incipient strains among emerging legal alternatives, namely in those very cultural domains—of person perception and event analysis, of fact determination and differentiating ideas of causality, time, and consequence—that set one society apart from others. Whether it is 'people's courts' or those of the state, the use of intermediaries or the constant maneuvering among available types of association, the nature and degree of consonance between cultural orientations and their attendant organizational forms yields a fuller picture of legal sensibilities than does a restricted emphasis on the structural levels, fields, rules, or 'laws' of disparate domains. In the end, the case of legal pluralities in North Africa and the Middle East affords an especially rich opportunity for rethinking the relation of legal alternatives at the same time that it challenges some of the most fundamental issues in social and cultural conjunction posed in the modern world.

8

Whom do you trust? Structuring confidence in Arab law and society

How does one go about trusting another person? At what point does trust occur and what are its preconditions? Where does the image of a larger set of persons and circumstances fit in, and what are the external constraints brought to bear on the creation or perpetuation of trust? As social relations change do the conditions or the requirements for trust also change, and if so, to what extent do the changes in one domain of social life affect those in cognate areas?

'The problem of trust,' to borrow a common phrasing of the entire cluster of issues and concepts related to these concerns, has exercised the imagination of philosophers in the Arab world no less than in the West. Ibn Khaldun's famous formulation of 'asabiya, the solidarity of closely related persons, tracks many of the same issues that exercised Condorcet, Locke, Hume, and Rousseau, all of whom, in their own ways, sought in the foundations of trust the foundations of human society itself.[1] To many thinkers, in both Europe and the Muslim world, a significant part of the issue of trust lay not only in its moral and religious aspects but in the roles played by law and political organization. In this chapter I, too, want to consider 'the problem of trust' in the regions of the Arab world with which I am familiar. But as an anthropologist and comparative lawyer I want to give particular emphasis to the ways in which using this focal point can help us to understand how broader cultural conceptualizations and the particular kinds of relationships they help to inform operate in the everyday experiences of the people involved.

THE CULTURAL CONFIGURATION OF TRUST

A useful entrée to this topic is provided by Adam B. Seligman in his book *The Problem of Trust*. Seligman argues that trust is engendered when people occupy numerous social roles, themselves fraught with indeterminacy. Rather than simply granting unconditional trust or confidence through a strict system of social roles that cannot cope with the new level of role complexity, people increasingly recognize the autonomy and freedom of choice of other persons and engage them in a form of generalized exchange. As confidence in the ability of the system of social roles to

---

[1] On Ibn Khaldun's theory of society and history, see Khaldun (1958) (especially vol. i on 'group feeling' among tribesmen, and vol. iii, pp. 302–4 on the existence of 'group feeling' among urban people), and Mahdi (1957). For his elaboration of the bearing of Ibn Khaldun's ideas on the problem of trust in North Africa see Gellner (1988). For a recent analysis of the philosophical issues affecting trust, see Hollis (1998).

insure predictable relationships declines, those interstitial points where contact with another is made (but where some degree of uncertainty persists) become points for the recognition that people can experience themselves and attribute to others similar qualities of choice and freedom.[2]

There is much in Seligman's account, like those of many other philosophers and religious scholars, that is both vague and lacking in universal application. Few anthropologists would argue nowadays that strict role behavior characterizes any human society or that the quantity of available social roles is simply a matter of the size of the society involved; few social scientists regard the idea of the 'modern' or even that of the 'market' as unqualifiedly self-evident. The very construction of each of Seligman's criteria is highly distinctive to different cultures, such that certain elements are combined in quite different patterns than the one he posits as universal. At the same time, Seligman's orientation does help to highlight some of the specific issues that need to be addressed in a description of trust in Arab society.

Seligman writes: 'The looser the fit between the person and the role, the more every aspect of role behavior and mutuality is negotiable. But as Durkheim taught us long ago, there must be a limit to negotiation for society to exist.'[3] There is, however, a great deal of difference between saying that there is some bedrock foundation upon which society is built (some *conscience collective*, deep structure, or fundamental material base) and arguing that, in particular societies, the structure is precisely one in which all relationships are indeed conceived as negotiable within a set of standards about how recognized negotiation itself may go forward. If, as I have argued at length elsewhere,[4] relationships among Arabs are indeed 'essentially negotiable,' then even if greater role differentiation does occur the deeper question is whether and how it affects this process of negotiating relationships. In Morocco, for example, I have no doubt that people appreciate, as Seligman phrases it, that 'it is in the very "otherness" of the alter that one puts one's "faith." '[5] But the distinctiveness of others—the recognition of their freedom to choose among whom they will form ties of dependence—is not a precipitate of increased role complexity: It is a recognition of a reality that is at the core of every relationship. The result, in this particular cultural context, is that trust must be serviced, renewed, reasserted by each person at virtually all moments: It comes not from new uncertainties of complexity but from the constantly perceived complexity of uncertain, ambivalent social life. To see how some of these elements evince themselves in the Arabo-Islamic worldview it is, as is so often the case when dealing with this part of the world, essential to grasp some of the terms involved in Arabic itself.

There are several words in Arabic that convey the general meaning of trust. *Amān* (and related derivatives from the root *a-m-n*) is usually translated as 'safety,' 'protection,' 'security,' and 'fealty.' The Quran repeatedly uses the term, admonishing believers to live in a condition of aman and to infuse the land in which they live with

---

[2] See, e.g., Seligman (1997: 39–43, 129, 160).   [3] Seligman (1997: 168).
[4] Rosen (1984: 185–92).   [5] Seligman (1997: 45).

this attribute. Aman, however, tends to convey a sense of personal attachment between those who trust one another rather than confidence in institutions, office-holders, or even one's own knowledge or abilities. Aman is not the unconditional giving over of oneself that is implied by 'submission' (the meaning of the word *islam* itself), nor is it an act that lacks a substantial exercise of reason and choice. Indeed, as Izutsu suggests, someone who is worthy of trust is, in the Quranic worldview, someone whose own words do not simply conform to reality; 'they should also conform to the idea of reality in the mind of the speaker.'[6] It is this embodied 'intention to be true to reality,' this attachment through another's intended apprehension of the true, that is sought by the relationship of trust. That such trust can be removed, revised, or replaced—that it goes to the willed grasp of the real by another—is, therefore, central to the cultural and semantic import of aman.

Another term, *wathiqa*, means 'to rely on,' 'to depend upon,' 'to place confidence in,' 'to trust.' Interestingly, the second-form verb created from the same root yields 'to make firm,' 'to make solid,' and 'to consolidate.' The fourth form, which adds the element of causation to the second form—making intransitive verbs transitive (e.g., 'to sit,' as a Form II verb, becomes 'to seat' in Form IV)—now yields the verbs 'to tie,' 'fetter,' or 'bind up.'[7] Thus the semantic overtone is clearly that 'confidence' and 'trust' consolidate or solidify attachments, but also that the act of placing one's trust in another produces a situation of being bound or fettered. This is not an uncommon pairing in Arabic cultural concepts: To attach oneself to a leader or saint also carries the implication of being fettered, while the term for close kinsmen also yields a verb meaning 'to bind,' 'fetter,' or 'captivate.'[8] Westermarck cites a proverb using a derivative of this term to suggest that one should be aware of the dual implications of trusting even the *imam* behind whom people pray: 'Trust him—and pray behind him!'[9] Thus the image of trust and confidence conveyed is not simply one of turning oneself over to another: To the contrary, trust, in this sense, is a creative act of mutual limitation.

Similarly, *wakala* and its cognates mean 'to entrust' or 'to put someone in charge.' But in one verb form, the sixth, it not only means 'to trust each other' but also 'to react with indifference,' 'to be non-committal.' The semantic connection here is intriguing. Form VI of the verb is actually the reflexive of the Form III verb, which itself constitutes the application of the act implied by the root of the verb to another person. So, for example, if various Form III verbs mean 'ignorant,' 'busy,' and 'appear,' their Form VI variations mean, respectively, 'to affect ignorance,' 'to pretend

---

[6] Izutsu (1966: 90). On the concept of sidq ('truthfulness'), see the discussion and references in Rosen (1984: 121–5).

[7] On Form II and Form IV verbs, see Haywood and Nahmad (1993: 164–5).

[8] In both Arabic language and literature the inherent ambivalence of terms is of great and pervasive importance. Rosenthal (1997: 42), speaking about the role of double meanings in certain Arabic literature, says '[in] the Muslim view . . . all matters human have a positive as well as a negative side.' See generally, Berque and Charnay (1967). See also Rosen (1984: 21–4) and 'Memory in Morocco' in Rosen (forthcoming).   [9] Westermarck (1930: 265).

to be busy,' and 'to feign something.'[10] In the case of wakala, as we have seen, the Form VI verb means 'to trust each other,' but other permutations yield 'indifference' and being 'non-committal.' The clear implication is of holding oneself apart, even when turning over one's trust to another, as if, having actually made the decision, one remains somewhat detached from the action, subject to it. It is a feeling many Westerners can, perhaps, understand, whether it be when you hand yourself over to a doctor and feel that sense of unconcern that flows from no longer having to decide what to do about yourself or when, in the face of power, you lose interest in your own situation as control has either seeped away or been diverted to a realm where the powerful are imagined unable to get at you.[11] In their utterances, their bodily expressions, and their accounts of past events one can detect numerous incidents in which, for the people of North Africa, trust hovers on that line of committal and its recognized concomitant, non-committal. The inherent ambivalence is integral to the concept itself. In a world in which people are known by those to whom they are attached in a variety of settings, the joinder of trust and indifference underscores the connection to another person, the addition of another context, the definition of another circumstance by which people are transformed from who they were into who they now become.

Philosophers have argued that trust cannot be willed: It has even been described as an emotional state, an attitude of optimism about the competence of others.[12] The Arab 'solution' to this problematic, however, is to try to place oneself and others in contexts where such confidence can be heightened by virtue of the total surround.[13] For Arabs, who believe that it is contexts of relationship, not invariant capabilities, that most fully define a person, actively entangling them in webs of indebtedness constitutes the greatest predictability and security that one can have for their actions towards oneself. But 'willing' the contexts of relationship carries with it those very ambivalences that Arabs would recognize in many Western philosophical accounts as well. Trust, of course, may not always be welcome; indeed it may be seen as coercive. And Arabs, sensing that double edge of security and being fettered, are quick to note the problem—whether it be in the play of words that suggests close kin are like scorpions who hook themselves into you, or in the attitudes towards living saints as simultaneously responding to one's needs and demanding unremitting attention.[14]

---

[10] On Form VI verbs and their meaning, see Haywood and Nahmad (1993: 170–1).

[11] I have given a more extended example of this sentiment in American legal proceedings in Rosen (1989a: 1–2).

[12] Baier (1986: 244) and Jones (1996: 15–16). See also Becker (1996).

[13] The Arab 'solution' recalls the general statement of Prichard (1949: 16): 'Suppose we come genuinely to doubt whether we ought to pay our debts, owing to a genuine doubt whether our previous conviction that we ought to do so is true, a doubt which can, in fact, only arise if we fail to remember the real nature of what we now call our past conviction. The only remedy lies in actually getting into a situation which occasions the obligation, or if our imagination be strong enough in imagining ourselves in that situation, and then letting our moral capacities of thinking do their work.' The Arab order of moral self-governance, in a sense, is to place oneself in just such situations and indeed follow the possibilities it entails.

[14] See 'Ambivalence Towards Power' in Rosen (forthcoming). The ambivalence toward saints is also noted in Gellner (1988: 148).

If trust is itself often resistant to the evidence of its misplacement, the game of creating ties of dependence keeps options open so that, from the Arab perspective, alternatives, fostered by the inherent ambivalence of the key concepts and relationships, minimize the possibility of being bound by only one set of options alone.

It is here that the etiquette that surrounds the formation of ties of trust comes into its own. Seligman, using the example of anti-smoking regulations instead of trusting that others would be considerate of its impact in certain settings, says:

> By voluntarily refraining from smoking and circumscribing my will in favor of the interests of a stranger, I was establishing in however passing, fleeting, and inconsequential a manner, a social bond. I, in fact, both of us, were granting one another a measure (however infinitesimal) of symbolic credit to be redeemed at an unspecified time by a third unspecified party. ... [T]he increasing inability of people to engage in such negotiation and trust (itself the outcome of the loss of familiarity, which in turn is rooted in greater role segmentation) leaves more and more realms of interaction defined solely by system constraints which are, in their very nature, inimical to the development of trust.[15]

Etiquette for Arabs, by comparison, does not imply a generalized benefit to an unspecified third party. Relationships are about those present, those with whom one has direct interaction, or those who, through a specifiable chain of consociation, can be seen as directly linked to the consequences of one's acts. In a sense, 'the public' is not a unit that exists in the conceptual realm. There is certainly the community of believers (*umma*) for whom disruption (*fitna*) seriously threatens the capacity to enact those requirements of proper faith and peaceful existence. But there is essentially no concept of public 'property,' in either a spatial or metaphoric sense. All things are 'owned,' whether it be land or objects or the universe over which God alone sits as owner (*mul*). One does not speak of public space as owned by the public: It is really space over which someone has no ownership relation and therefore it is space through which one has no interdependence with others.[16] The criteria of civic virtue and civil society to which Seligman's thesis leads him are, in the Arab context, better seen not as a set of institutions separate from interpersonal bonds but as the mapping of interpersonal bonds as they are known to others at any given moment. Thus, what one focuses on is a set of obligations that have been fashioned between and among people who have contracted such worldly consequent ties as can be traced to one another's actions.

Etiquette sets the baseline for being able to establish such bonds. To receive

---

[15] Seligman (1997: 173). For his discussion of etiquette and its cultural distinctiveness, see his remarks at pp. 64–5.

[16] See, generally, Kahera and Benmira (1998), where the authors give a number of examples (e.g., the passage by a 17th-cent. jurist quoted on p. 148) consistent with this interpretation. I question, however, their assertion that '*the street was a public space owned collectively* ... whereas a lane, alley, or cul-de-sac was considered a private road which may be shared by adjacent properties' (Kahera and Benmira (1998: 150); italics added). See also the discussion on the absence of a legal definition of the public sphere in Ruthven (1984: 176–9). 'Ownership' is a concept that must be unpacked culturally, the idea of a mul not being simply reducible to 'ownership' in the present Western sense. On the concept of mul in Morocco, see Rosen (1984: 23–4).

another, to ingratiate oneself to another, to mark out who has created such bonds with whom, is to establish the baseline for one's own negotiated network. At present people often remark on the loss of just this complex of etiquette, and with it the possibility of forging those bonds upon which one's success and security in an unpredictable world rest. Indeed, among people who are engaged in business dealings this loss of etiquette is particularly poignant. Often they express regret at the limitations of being able to start from a base of not knowing another, imagining the inherent possibilities of interconnectedness for mutual advantage that 'the game' previously allowed. Their references to the Prophet as a businessman recall the same sense of a moral community formed by mutual dealings; their suspicion of politics as lacking in the long-term fabrication of bonds of indebtedness and their vision of the state as lacking in any reciprocity whatsoever are keenly felt. As in those historic business coalitions to which we shall refer in a moment, the expectation is not, as Seligman's general account would suggest, one of role segmentation producing greater need for trust relations. Almost the reverse is true: The complexity of all roles has become increasingly simplified as multiple connections to the same person are reduced to single-stranded ties of position or profession. The accompanying loss of trust in others is itself engendered by a loss of confidence in the ability to play the complicated game of interpersonal negotiation that used to operate.

Indeed, it is central to Niklas Luhmann's argument that trust reduces complexity.[17] But as we have noted, not only may trust be coercive—as, for example in the Arab context, where one ingratiates oneself to another in an attempt to conduce later assistance—but as one tries to protect one's trust in another by investing all the more heavily in it, additional complexities are generated.[18] This may be seen, again in the Arab context, when efforts are made to publicize one's relationship with another in order to demonstrate overall importance and reliability, while still trying to keep many details unknown so as to be relieved of the entanglements and pressures of other people. Complexity, then, exists at the level of these interpersonal bonds, and a significant part of any person's efforts will be devoted to the use of personal and social resources to make one's way under conditions of conceptual ambiguity and interpersonal uncertainty. Both of these features come out with particular clarity as one looks at some of the institutions and relationships used to manage the risk and ambivalence entailed in this context.

Increasingly women have taken on important roles in the Moroccan marketplace. Deborah Kapchan notes that they not only account for over half of the vendors in the marketplace at Beni Mellal, but that the market as rough equalizer is seen as a place of admixture, of hybridity, in which all of the ambivalence felt toward women combines with the morality of outright competition.[19] Women now maneuver males in public as they have more commonly done in private. Whether it is in the process of bargaining or in their use of oaths and lies, the women vendors appear at once no different than the men active in the same setting and particularly 'modern' inasmuch

---

[17] Luhmann (1979).   [18] Shapiro (1987).   [19] Kapchan (1996).

as men do not—or do not yet—expect to form with them the kinds of clientele relationships they have had with men, in which a 'favor' done in the marketplace might
be grounds for pressured reciprocity in an election or marital negotiation. Women
both reduce complexity by their presence in the market and add new complexities,
and it remains to be seen whether they will move into shops as well as remain in the
open-air markets, and if so whether their roles will begin to change.[20]

In several articles concerning the trading relationships among North African
Jewish traders in the medieval period, Avner Greif offers a model of the relations of
trust for that period which also has great currency for contemporary relationships
involving Muslims as well.[21] Greif argues that traders formed 'coalitions,' economic
networks in which the reputations of traders, often dealing at vast distances and with
significant time delays, were crucial to their own future endeavors. These reputations
were themselves supported by sufficiently high rewards given for past dealings,
combined with a system of information in which such dealings became well-known
to other dealers, such that it was to each trader's advantage for the next deal that he
should be regarded as one with a history of reputable dealings. 'The [resultant]
"trust" did not reflect a social control system or the internalization of norms of
behavior. . . . Rather, the Maghribi traders established a relationship between past
conduct and future economic reward.'[22] Punishment, if necessary, could be meted
out from multiple sources since the fundamental unit was the coalition as a whole,
not a single trader with whom one dealt.[23] Short-term, repeated contracts had the
advantage that information about a recent dealing could be quickly communicated
within the network, and thus family firms did not need to develop to perform the
work of reliability.[24] Coalitions were, of course, limited by the extent of their information transmission, and though a premium had to be paid to a coalition member
as compared to an outsider, the diminution in risk warranted the expense.[25] Indeed,
the bounds of information transmission also limited the ability of coalitions to
respond to new opportunities, so that while negotiating costs may have been kept
low, overall profits were not maximized by such a system.[26]

There are several features about this system that have particular relevance to our
understanding of trust among contemporary Muslims. Greif notes that, in theory,
culture could perform the work that coalitions perform as systems of information

[20] Women also now figure very prominently in the bureaucracy of Morocco as well. Having done
better than most male students in their exams and having, for a generation now, availed themselves of the
seniority attaching to the bureaucracy—as well as leave policies during pregnancy and assured jobs if their
husbands are transferred—women occupy numerous posts in the hierarchy. Interestingly, people say that
women are no less corrupt than men in similar posts.

[21] Greif (1989) and Greif (1993).   [22] Greif (1989: 881).

[23] Greif (1993: 539).

[24] Greif (1989: 885–6). Greif explains the relation of law to the value of frequent contracting with
the same coalition members: 'According to the theory of repeated games, by paying an agent a wage "high"
enough during each period he is known to be honest and by making future employment conditional on
past conduct, a merchant can insure that the present value of the lifetime expected utility of an honest
agent is larger than what the agent can obtain by cheating and facing the prospect of being unemployed'
(Greif (1993: 530)).   [25] Greif (1989: 878–9).   [26] Greif (1993: 544–5).

transmission. That is, a series of prior rules of acceptable behavior could be employed to sort out uncertain situations in advance of their occurrence, with hierarchical structures reinforcing the application of these rules. Greif, however, notes: 'While culture requires *ex ante* learning of the rules but no *ex post* communication, hierarchy does not require *ex ante* learning but requires *ex post* information transmission between the parties.'[27] Greif attributes to the problems of communication and transportation technology in the medieval period the absence of hierarchy and the emphasis on cultural norms, embodied in the customs of the merchants. But many of these same patterns hold among Muslims of the present day, where technology is not a problem. Instead, the emphasis on consociational ties fits together with a host of cultural orientations that conduce to a pattern of directly serviceable and interchangeable forms of reciprocity. The leveling forces of constant renegotiation may undermine long-term coalitions, but they do reinforce the emphasis on the transmission of information about others' actions, so that as any person encounters another he may have some degree of predictability about his behavior. Once again, the tension here is between getting as much information as possible and preserving it for one's own uses, a pattern that produces some, but not all, of the results of the medieval coalitions.

A second feature concerns the frequent use of what Greif calls incomplete contracts, in which merchants told their agents to do whatever they thought best if circumstances did not fit prior expectations. Such instructions may have undermined coalitions inasmuch as agents might act for their own benefit, but it is noteworthy that similar sentiments are expressed by contemporary Muslim businessmen both as a test of another's reliability and as an aspect of the reputation they expect others to respect. The result is to reinforce the ambivalence obtaining in relations of trust, to reinforce the very role differentiation that lies at the heart of all interpersonal contacts. Closely related to this cultural orientation is the emphasis placed on the customs of the merchants. In modern Muslim relations, as in the medieval Jewish forms, specific legal requirements were often trumped by local customary practice.[28] We will see later how this plays out within the context of Islamic contract law, but it is worth noting at this stage that such an emphasis fits with the idea that if one is to form a bond of trust with another neither a rigid set of prior cultural rules nor a hierarchy of enforcement procedures will be thought to fit with the need to constantly maneuver within changing circumstances where 'solidifying' carries implications not just of securing but of being bound. Custom has the quality of maintaining local options, local variation, local control over the very rules of the game which might otherwise become the rules of the dominant alone.[29]

---

[27] Greif (1993: 543).

[28] Greif (1993: 543). The contractual forms Greif discusses were also present among Muslims as well; see Udovitch (1970).

[29] One reason Muslims express hostility toward the United States in many instances is connected with this point. They often feel that America's idea of the 'new world order' (as President Bush put it at the time of the Gulf War) meant that the rules chosen would be those that favored the West from the outset. The maintenance of local custom has long been a way by which the institutions of Islamic law place a counterweight to those who would so capture the terms of the game in ways that, while appearing neutral, are in fact advantageous to themselves.

Trust may also be engendered by being regularized in the relations of particular sectors of the population. Saints are carved out by the Muslims of North Africa as interstitial figures, their very status 'betwixt and between' underscoring both their reliability as interlocutors and their potential danger as marginal to a series of normative categories.[30] But commercial dealings with saints or their descendants were not particularly favored; the deep-seated ambivalence, the fact that in so many other respects they occupied the same categories as non-saintly Muslims, and the significant degree of movement in and out of the category of the saintly as opinion and circumstance altered, all contributed to their occupying a category that was separate only for certain restricted purposes.

The Jews, by contrast, long occupied a unique position in this regard. It was, I believe, precisely the fact that they were not part of the interchangeable set of reciprocal obligations attendant on the negotiated ties Muslims forged with one another that allowed the Jews to be regarded by the Muslims as figures of considerable trust.[31] Commercial relations—extending even to the joint ownership of property—were facilitated by the limited range of convertible obligations Muslims and Jews could have toward one another. Genuine friendship was common as a Muslim could say things to a Jew that 'did not count' (in the sense that there could be no expected obligation of intermarriage or political support) and hence a 'purely' economic relationship favored the possibility of trust. Clearly there was greater power in many forms on the side of the Muslim in this relation, but the matter was not always clear-cut and simple: Factors of reputation for protection, joint investments protected by Islamic law, and the personal emotional bonds that often developed rendered the pattern of power itself anything but unilateral in design.[32] For the Arabs of the west the departure of the Jews—and for the Arabs of the east the 'arrival' of the Jews—has challenged the trust placed in them as resident strangers and has challenged the very attributes of person-to-person trust that played a distinct role in North African lives through at least the first half of the twentieth century.

An implicit contract could be said to have existed between the Muslims and Jews of North Africa that entailed a substantial degree of trust. Often, however, contracts—whether within or across religious/ethnic lines—partake of the explicit provisions of Islamic law. Islamic contract law thus provides an excellent vehicle through which we can see many of the assumptions about persons and relationship that inform the broader construct of trust. It will be helpful in this regard to consider such matters as the role that promises play in the creation of bonds of obligation, the ways in which the focus on the consequences of contractual ties relates back to the structure of the obligations themselves, the ways in which customary practices and stipulations agreed upon by the parties may actually take precedence over a legal requirement, and how the idea of risk is handled in transactions that require future performance.

---

[30] See generally Geertz (1968); Gellner (1988); and Hammoudi (1997).
[31] See Rosen (1968a) and Rosen (1972).
[32] See the example given in Geertz (1973: 7–9).

CREATING A LEGAL FRAMEWORK FOR TRUST

Western scholars usually point to several features regarded as distinctive to Islamic
contract law: that contracts are of certain types, that there appears to be no general
theory of contracts; that contracts for future performance are impermissible because
they are inherently speculative; that considerations of public policy, though permissible in some schools of thought, are formally marginalized; and that if value is not
added a transaction is tantamount to unjust enrichment, and is therefore both
morally reprehensible and legally unenforceable. As Western scholars have begun to
look at a wider range of sources and have made the first tentative moves away from
a comparative law perspective that takes continental forms as the baseline for defining and assessing transactions, each of these propositions has begun to be called into
question. If to this one adds a cultural perspective to the understanding of legal
systems, not only is the Eurocentric model further eroded but some consistency may
be found at the socio-legal level for aspects of Islamic contract law that have seemed
unsystematic to previous investigators.

   In his excellent study of the history of Western contracts, James Gordley demonstrates that although many European philosophers and lawyers have imagined that a
coherent theory suffuses their approach to contract law in fact no such theory has
actually been at work in Western legal history. Both Aristotelian concepts of contract
and the subsequent theory of contract as the meeting of independent wills have
consistently failed to reconcile specific issues—such as those relating to fraud, duress,
extravagant gifts adversely affecting others, mistake, and implied terms—with their
own professedly unified theories. Western scholarship on Islamic law, as we shall see,
has also been heir to this misplaced belief in the existence of such coherent theorizing, with the result that Islamic law is often found wanting when measured against
the proffered standard. But if, once again, we use these philosophical discussions to
see how Islamic cultures have addressed similar questions, some intriguing comparisons present themselves.

   Gordley argues, quite sensibly, that it is rather circular for modern legal philosophers, such as Charles Fried and John Rawls, to argue that one has a moral duty to
adhere to the conventions by which promises are made simply because fairness
requires that one follow the rules of a game from which one also benefits: By not
giving reasons why one should, in fact, keep to one's commitments, or why the failure to do so is not a permissible matter of exercising one's own will, the analyst is
'packing his conclusions into the definition of contract.'[33] And yet, as is so often the
case, what may not pass muster as a matter of formal logic may very well suffice as a
matter of socio-logic. Gordley's own argument implies such a possibility when he
goes on to say that we are ultimately forced, as some of the medieval and scholastic
scholars had noted, to explain the essence of a contract, like other human actions, by

---

[33] Gordley (1991: 234).

its end.[34] In the case of contracts in the Arab world such an approach means, I believe, looking at the consequences for human relationships, as seen in the broader context of the set of informing social and cultural orientations, to understand how a system may, notwithstanding its seeming illogic, define contractual obligations in terms of valued relationships. Put somewhat differently, we may be able to see that the Arabs operate through a social and contractual system which is radically relativized, one in which permissible relationships are those one can manage to construct within operational parameters that are themselves subject to modification as one marshals one's capabilities to make them hold sway. The result is neither chaos nor stasis but a kind of ordered anarchy in which what the market will bear in relationships is what the market will bear in one's ability to maneuver among multiple linked elements that, by virtue of their linkage, are amenable to constant variation in their perceived consequences. To make all this rather more concrete let us turn to several aspects of contract law and see how they are embedded in the larger context of relationship.

It is commonly said of Islamic contract law that there are a relatively limited number of specific types of permissible contract but no general concept of contract. The Quran merely admonishes people to keep to their agreements, but it offers no guidance for a theory of covenanting.[35] Scholars have disagreed as to whether a contract incorporates the expressed will of the parties or whether the implications of a particular type of contract are made to apply when the forms of its initiation have been properly met.[36] Although many of the scholars of the Hanafi school may be read as indicating that the will of the parties is irrelevant, the weight of opinion is that for the other schools (and perhaps for the Hanafi as well) the parties' will is not irrelevant. What may create some confusion is that the issue is largely put in terms of two other features which are more crucial to an understanding of Islamic contract law, the role of knowledge and the role of intent.

Islamic contract law, like Muslim culture at large, places a great premium on knowledge, and a great burden on those who produce significant consequences in the world to develop their knowledge. Thus it is assumed that parties have the capacity to

[34] Gordley (1991: 240).
[35] See, e.g., Quran, Suras V: 1; IV: 33; and XVI: 91 on contracts.
[36] Chehata (1968). See also Makdisi (1985b: 334–7), indicating that Chehata himself has revised his view to note that both intelligence ('aql) and intent (qasd) do play a role in contracting, such that the 'psychological element' of contracting (rida)—which Comair-Obeid (1996: 6) defines as 'the state of mental assurance of the declarant favourable to the contract'—is indispensable to a valid contract. Makdisi tries to reconcile Chehata's two positions—that intent is 'a phenomenon extrinsic to the will' and that it is a psychological phenomenon—by arguing that Chehata is saying that intent is presumed to exist within a person unless it can be shown objectively to have been absent. As I have argued elsewhere, I believe these two elements—of the subjective and the objective—are reconciled in the concept of intent (niya) inasmuch as external indicators of attachments in the world are believed to give direct insight into inner lives, such that a judge can say he always knows another's intent simply by learning of his worldly consequent connections. See Rosen (1984) and Rosen (1989a). This broader cultural notion appears to be at work both in contract law and in issues of strict liability, where interiority is believed to be so coupled to externalities that only incapacity could account for their divergence.

acquire the knowledge necessary for their agreements unless clear evidence to the contrary can be shown. Many features of the law conduce to the maximization of people's access to knowledge, notwithstanding the constant struggle to glean information for oneself alone. One of the traditions of the Prophet purports to say that he forbade sales contracts which had any additional stipulations in them. Although, as we shall see, this proposition was, at the least, more honored in the breach and, at the most, drained of all import if social harm resulted from the stipulation,[37] an argument could be made that limiting the forms of contract contributed to the distribution of knowledge. Limited forms may ameliorate the potentially disruptive aspects of information that is very unevenly distributed. The Prophet, an intelligent and experienced businessman himself, may well have implied that permitting anything the parties willed—so long as it did not contravene Quranic prescription—may have an adverse effect on social stability and political solidarity: Without ever explicitly addressing the issue, the Prophet's implicit jurisprudential theory, which will be discussed in Chapter 11, may well have favored the maximization of common knowledge through the limitations on contractual forms.

Whether this speculation has merit, it does coincide with other ways in which knowledge comes into play in what may be thought of as the implicit jurisprudence of Islamic contract law. Consider, in this regard, the role of risk (to which we will return momentarily) and knowledge as they concern unlawful gain. Islam forbids the practice of *riba*, which is usually associated with (or even translated as) usury, but which more accurately accords with the broader concept of unjust enrichment. But the evil of accepting something when no value is seen to have been added lies, perhaps, not in some theory of the relation of work to value but in its relationship to knowledge. Nabil Saleh, for example, has said: 'Once more it is worth stressing that it is not *business risk* which is disallowed but the risk generated by a want of knowledge which materially obscures any of the constitutive elements of a given transaction.'[38] And those material elements are the adverse impact on society if knowledge is so skewed as to result in harm to the community of believers, and, closely connected to this, the need for contracting parties to express their fundamental humanness by being held only to the commitments which they actually intended. Unjust enrichment, then, is an affront to the distribution of knowledge and to the forms of intent which should be encouraged in a society free from disruption.

Some schools of Islamic law, particularly the Maliki in North Africa, were far more explicit than others in stressing the element of intent (*niya*). But it may be plausibly argued that once intent enters into consideration it is very hard to cast it out again. Because niya is so central to everything from the legitimate act of prayer to the image of a mature person, because, in short, it suffuses so many other domains of social and cultural life, its importance in contract law should come as no surprise. Moreover, it has been one of the analytic tools which legal scholars and judges found

---

[37]   See Arabi (1998: 33).   [38]   Saleh (1986: 116).

they could employ when determining whether an unfair or socially harmful effect may result from a particular act.[39] Thus even those analysts who see intent as an accessory element to a contract agree that, in the words of Comair-Obeid, it remains 'a necessary condition for its validity,' a factor whose absence would vitiate the agreement.[40] Indeed, by retaining intent as an objectively determinable aspect of consent jurisconsults and judges may have ameliorated the limitations of specifically allowable forms of contract in a way that accorded very well with moral and cultural concepts about the relation of intent and consequence in relations affecting the social order.[41]

Thus we can see that, as in the West, even if one did rely on a will theory of contract for an analysis of Islamic contract law, it would neither be logically sufficient nor, as a matter of fact, has it been treated as sufficient by Muslim scholars, lawyers, or businessmen. From will alone one cannot get answers to questions of fraud, duress, or the like. But if parties can agree on the modalities of their agreements—on the time, place, and circumstance that inform their bargains[42]—and if they can conceive of their agreements as binding, in part, because they are the expressions of qualities associated with a man of circumstance operating to effect in the world, then it becomes possible to measure defects in agreements against these cultural standards rather than against formal structures of agreement alone.

Some of these factors become evident when one considers, for example, the problem of mistake in contracts. John Makdisi has noted that Islamic law requires that the contractual object be such that it does not lead to controversy: 'The knowledge of the object of sale and the price—a knowledge barring controversy—is a condition of the validity of the sale.'[43] Although standards have varied with different schools of Islamic thought, this element of knowledge appears as a common concern. Ignorance as to the quality or specifics of the object which is the subject of the contract affects the validity of the agreement not, I think, because the true risk of uncertainty is the social disruption that may flow from interpersonal controversy, but because of the broader fear that inappropriate private contracts may lead to social chaos (fitna). Better, then, to err on the side of allowing a perceived change of circumstances to relieve one of commitment to an agreement than to risk adverse social consequences.

This latter point may connect with the classical requirement that contracts be

---

[39] See generally Toledano (1974) and Hallaq (1994).

[40] Comair-Obeid (1996: 6).

[41] 'To preserve a proper balance in any contract, to avoid jahallat [ignorance, unbelief] and keep out riba [unlawful advantage through excess or deferment], and in order to follow divine precept imposing strict justice, the Muslim jurisconsults have greatly reduced freedom in drawing up agreements. . . . The classical authors of the first centuries of Islam elaborated precise rules concerning the effect, the structure and the drawing up of contracts, and put strict limitations on the profit to be gained. These brakes on contractual freedom have allowed the fuqaha' [Islamic legal experts] to overprotect the will of the parties by offering the possibility of opting out of contracts and by adopting the objectivist position concerning defects of consent' (Comair-Obeid (1996: 206)).

[42] See Comair-Obeid (1996: 7) on the question of contractual modalities.

[43] Makdisi (1985b: 339). The internal quote is from the the 12th-cent. Hanafi legal scholar Kasani.

formulated in words of the past tense. 'Sale is concluded by offer and acceptance expressed by two verbs in the past tense, such as "I have sold" and "I have bought," ' wrote the sixteenth-century Hanafi scholar Ibrahim al-Halibi.[44] Using the past tense, I would suggest, is a way of publicly demonstrating not just the conclusion of the agreement but that the consequences of that agreement should now be capable of assessment by anyone who is using his knowledge as he should in the world. It is a statement that such and such has occurred affecting our ties and that the consequences are not those of some vague future but those which will now affect many others. It is a conceptual joinder of knowledge and worldly consequence which is central to the whole structure of agreements of trust and the shaping of a world whose reality lies in the distribution of ties among the sentient.[45]

It is here, too, that the element of harm can be carved out for separate consideration. The well-known Tradition in which the Prophet says 'no harm to another nor any done back to him' (*la darar wa-la dirar*) conveys at least a clear sense that harm is a central criterion of concern in social relationships. As we saw in the discussion of compensatory justice (Chapter 4), Islamic tort law also focuses mainly on questions of harm. In their discussion of medieval property and nuisance law, Kahera and Benmira discuss examples ranging from whether an adjacent neighbor could produce noxious smells in the pursuit of his trade or whether there was harm in someone urinating in a mosque.[46] More importantly, they demonstrate not only the ongoing creative casuistry of the jurisconsults and judges asked to address these matters, but that the meaning of harm derived mainly from local practice. Even when the choice among alternatives was the work of a creative expert, his view might become part of accepted local custom if he was himself sufficiently respected. As we will see, this approach relied on the concept of the public good among other devices. Here it is worth noting that harm is generally a calculus of the social consequences of an individual act and that the limitations on such acts derive less from a logic of antecedents than from an appraisal of consequences.[47]

In the context of contract law we can see from a number of examples some of the criteria for determining when harm has occurred. For example, a contract can be revoked altogether if the circumstances of a party change in ways that, in Western law, would have no such effect or would prompt some form of compensation. Thus leases can be terminated due to a change in the lessor's finances, because of travel plans or a shift in employment, or if special costs are encountered during performance.[48] Similarly, the amount of compensation due even in modern Arabia is a function of the harm that the loss is thought to do to different categories of persons.[49] To take another example, the dispute over whether one may permissibly

---

[44] Quoted in Liebesny (1975: 210).

[45] See the discussion on the validation of utterances in Rosen (1984: 117–33).

[46] Kahera and Benmira (1998).

[47] This distinction, as articulated by John Dewey, was also central to our earlier discussion of Islamic case law in Ch. 2.   [48] Sloane (1988: 747), citing Coulson (1984).

[49] Sloane (1988: 750).

sell the debt of one person to another, or whether repurchases for a higher price constitute unlawful gain, has been seen by some commentators—especially those who favor futures contracts as permissible under Islamic law—as inconsistently decided by classical thinkers.[50] But one might, alternatively, see the common denominator in many of these instances not as unlawful gain as such but as part of the calculus of social harm: It is very difficult to determine what the social consequences might be—and what harm may result—if one set of people or one kind of agreement/relationship is converted into something else. The criteria for running the usual calculus of consequence—who are these people, what is the relationship, what is the specific nature of the social chaos that could result from allowing them to make such a deal—are clearly undermined when the very parameters of the social bond are themselves rendered unclear. In the absence of a concept of harm that is not dependent on the perception of persons/relationships/consequences it is not surprising that economic bonds, such as futures contracts, that might appear to be quite precise and predictable to modern market-makers should appear to Islamic law officials to be dangerously unpredictable.

Contemporary thinking about insurance law provides another area for insight into both the idea of harm and the Islamic notion of risk. In his discussion of this topic Skovgaard-Petersen shows that the debates in modern times have raised questions as to whether insurance is a form of engagement in uncertain contracting and even whether it implies that Providence does not wreak harm by reason but only as a result of frequencies accounted for by large numbers. Risk has traditionally been seen at the level of the individual instance—whether it be in finding too speculative an agreement about the sale of a wild bird or the return to the hive someone owns of a swarm of bees. Insurance poses a challenge to this individuated, casuistic stance precisely because it calls forth questions about the assessment of individual acts when larger patterns appear to be at work.[51]

In each of these instances the role of the public interest and customary practice play a significant role. For a long time many Western scholars insisted that considerations of public interest (*istislah, maslaha*) were of no real importance to Islamic law, either because it had no need for such considerations given other modes of analysis or because public policy could not triumph over the idealism of formal Islamic doctrine.[52] But in certain respects these scholars did not find instances of public interest analysis precisely because they assumed that the law lay in the doctrine, not in the practice. As others have looked at the opinions of jurisconsults and the decisions of judges, however, they have indeed found such considerations to be both plentiful and legally significant.[53]

Similarly, the same bias against the role of custom has had to await recent

---

[50] Kamali (1996: 211–14).   [51] Skovgaard-Petersen (1997). See also Vogel and Hayes (1998).
[52] Schacht (1957: 141). See also Kerr (1966: 55).
[53] The list is growing rapidly, and includes, for very different areas, periods, and interpretations, Hallaq (1997); Masud (1977); Baghby (1985); Kamali (1991: 267–83); and Kahera and Benmira (1998: 138–9).

research: Since custom was not one of the four listed modes of analyzing law in classical thought, and since most Western scholars saw custom as a realm that is conceptually opposed to law, a deeper understanding of the role of custom has had to await scholars who look beyond doctrine to practice and opinion.[54] In his study of contract laws in the modern Arab world Saleh shows that present-day codes, following earlier practice, allow judges in Egypt, Iraq, Kuwait, and Qatar to look first to custom and only failing guidance there to look at the shariʿa, whereas first preference is given to shariʿa in the civil codes of Syria, Bahrain, Jordan, and North Yemen.[55] In many other countries, whether they do or do not have modern codes, the actual state of things often suggests that custom still fills up the actual content of legal approaches precisely because it is usually seen not as opposed to the shariʿa but as the locally permissible version of the shariʿa. In each instance, as we are now beginning to learn, custom does serve *de facto* as a source of law and does figure, often with priority over doctrinal embodiments of the shariʿa, in the decision of matters affecting interpersonal relationships.

One final point is worth noting in this regard. Frequently one hears the proposition in the Arab world that a contractual stipulation takes precedence over the shariʿa. What this generally means is that if a stipulation does not contradict a specific Quranic proposition it may take precedence even over the interpretations that at any given moment are regarded as the corpus of Islamic law. The rationale for granting precedence to such stipulations seems again to be that if the Quran is not contradicted what is permitted by local practice *is* Islamic law, and in that sense stipulations are not so much taking precedence over the shariʿa as redefining its boundaries.[56] Either way, it is a bold demonstration, whose parameters only further research into the actual practice of Islamic law can elucidate, of the extent to which Islamic law is indeed open to both variation and change.

'THE PROBLEM OF TRUST' REVISITED

A contract is not the reduction to writing of mutual mistrust. Leaving aside the reasons usually given in Western law schools for this proposition (that memory is fallible, that terms need to be clarified, or that the act of contracting focuses attention on the serious nature of the engagement) a contract is also an expression of underlying assumptions about relationship, an expression of the way important things (time, human nature, utterances) really are. But contracts can also show where some of the fault lines are in relations of trust, the points where people's fears and expectations are situated. We know that there are some societies

---

[54] Here, too, the list of recent work grows long and varied, including Libson (1997); Kahera and Benmira (1998); Dutton (1999); and Arabi (1998: 35) (referring to the Hanafi and the Ottoman Majalla: 'Such clauses as are part of local custom (ʿurf) are legally binding despite the fact that they are external to the basic terms of contract'). See also Hallaq (1999).

[55] Saleh (1989).   [56] Compare Arabi (1998: 42).

in which promises are not kept because listening to others' concerns and appearing to take them seriously is thought to be more important than risking distress by failing in even some small way to honor fully the terms of a specific promise.[57] But this is not the case in the Arab world, where, as I have argued, mere utterances, once validated by recognizable means, are taken very seriously and promises, as validated utterances, become vital to a person's reputation and consequences in the world.

Indeed, we may see the issue of trust generally in this part of the world as deeply connected to the particular form of personalism that informs social life at large. Maine, of course, argued that contract is opposed to status,[58] but in this case I think contract should be seen as an element of extended personalism. The people one trusts and the people with whom one enters into contractual relationships are not merely replaceable, fungible actors in the social and economic world: They are the people by whom you will be known, and thus one can never fully divorce the question of *who* they are from the question of who you are.[59] 'Live together like brothers, do business together like strangers,' says the Arab proverb.[60] But when brothers are often expected to be points of potential fission and when there is a trust and intimacy with the stranger that often exceeds that felt toward those who can make claims upon you, the subtle irony of the saying becomes evident.[61]

To some extent various Arab societies have attempted to regularize, indeed institutionalize, relations of trust. The extensive use of recognized market guarantors and official witnesses is one of the ways in which personalistic attachments became fictively extended to relationships that did not incorporate the expectations of reciprocity that gave shape and credibility to the models on which they were based. Trust is not for the Arabs, as Hart has suggested generally, situated 'in the no-man's land between status and contract.'[62] It is integral to the whole social world of essentially negotiable relationships. The notion that a society must have some point of structure beyond which matters cannot be reduced has often misled students of the Arab world to posit that structure—that point of trust where one simply has to rely on others—at the level of collective entities suffused by 'group feeling' or attachment to moral precepts that move them around like so many automata. For the Arabs, as I have been suggesting, the concept of trust and its manifestation in society and in law

---

[57] Korn and Korn (1983).

[58] Maine (1986), and my 'Foreword' to the reprint at pp. vii–xx.

[59] This is why I do not entirely agree with Jim Gordley in his unpublished paper when he says that markets do not develop where personal ties reign. Much of the Middle Eastern and Asian economies are a mix of the personal and the fungible, and the meaning of a trade partner cannot be reduced to a singular market model based on a Western idea of replaceability.

[60] Kapchan (1996: 42) quotes another version of this proverb: 'Settle your accounts with me as if I were your enemy, and entertain me as your brother.' A far more sardonic version says: 'Even out our accounts as if I were your enemy and afterwards you came at me as if I were your brother' (Scelles-Millie and Khelifa (1966: 121)).

[61] One is reminded of Hesse's phrase about 'the intimate disclosure to a stranger.' See also Rosenthal (1997).   [62] Quoted in Seligman (1997: 27).

are an exemplification of the far more complex and subtle proposition that structure lies in the process. It is here, fraught with all the ambivalences attendant upon it, that the Arabs have made their cultural home. It is here that they have reposed their trust. It is here that we must encounter them and see the connections that hold their own universe of meaning together.

Part 3

Justice past and present

Europe past and present

9

Islamic concepts of justice and injustice

What Socrates promises is a standard of justice; what we get is an elaborate metaphor. But so it has been ever since, with the great discussions of justice.[1]

Justice (to soften a borrowed phrase) is a veritable courtesan among words: Its connections are always subject to alteration, the consequences of its involvements always open to contention. 'Justice,' as Edmund Cahn has said, 'is unwilling to be captured in a formula' even though it remains 'a word of magic evocation.' Such uncertainties have been a magnet for Western philosophers for centuries. For Plato, justice was the harmonious order of an ideal community; for the ancient Greeks and Hebrews the enactment of retribution for unforgivable harm; for the Christian Fathers the divine gift of mercy for the ineluctably sinful. Modern philosophers have continued the quest for an ultimate grasp of justice through such terms as fair exchange, utility, the social contract, equality (at least within category), or personal deserts: They have (to cite several titles) equated justice with impartiality, fittingness, dialogue, efficiency, and rights.

On rare occasions philosophers have even noted that seeking universal attributes of justice may be a feckless pursuit. To place the discussion in terms of private property for those who believe that resources should be controlled by those who make beneficial use of them, or to emphasize individual liberty to those who see the collectivity as the irreducible unit of social life may be to cross the line from the universal to the mutually incomprehensible. Even the image of justice as the norm and injustice as insupportable deviation may controvert others' perception that injustice is indeed the standard against which other attributes should themselves be gauged. To point out such variations is, however, neither to engage in mindless relativism nor to subvert the uses of rigorous logical analysis. Rather it is to point out that the indeterminacies of metaphor, the vagaries of singular attributes (whether of desert or fairness or equality), and the open-endedness of ordinary terminologies nevertheless achieve a degree of workable specificity in any given culture and time. If cultures are 'the answer,' philosophy may tell us the question they address.

Characterizations of justice in other cultures often reveal more about the analyst than the society under consideration. Commonly, Westerners see in the Arabs' rhetorical emphasis on justice exaggerated or provocative assertions rather than situated meaning; even more thoughtful generalists may see in the Quran itself only an emphasis on justice as submission, debt, balanced fear, and retribution. As in any quest for the understanding of another culture relativism has never implied giving up one's own sense of values or relinquishing the quest for common elements of human dignity or worth. To understand what justice means in the context of Arab/Muslim culture and why it is seen in that context as

---

[1] Solomon and Murphy (1990: 4).

a crucial concept that embraces so much of their sense of placement in the world may take us further along the path both of understanding the particularities of justice as it is lived in this part of the world and toward a more enlightened sense of how to carry on the conversation about common concerns across the boundaries of culture and religion.

ELEMENTS OF ISLAMIC JUSTICE

A commentor on Islamic culture has written that:

[W]hereas Christianity is primarily the religion of love, Islam is above all the religion of justice. This does not, of course, mean that Christians are necessarily better at loving than Muslims, or that Muslim society lends itself more successfully to the realization of justice. . . . Nevertheless . . . the two watchwords, love and justice, can usefully act as signposts to a wide range of differences between the two religions in terms both of their acknowledged practices and dogmas and of the unconscious prejudices of their adherents.[2]

Comparisons with Christianity aside, it is indeed a striking feature of Arab popular culture and politics that the concepts of justice and injustice play such a central role in everyday life and thought: in discussions of history, where the times may be seen as just or unjust; in stories, where the qualities of the characters are assessed in terms of their just behavior; in social perception, where the appropriate response to another's behavior may be measured against the justice that flows from the relationship; in politics, where movements and demonstrations reverberate with claims of— or for—a justice that is often felt to be absent; and in law, where what people often seek is not merely to win but to have the justice of their claim given public recognition.

When we turn to the idea of justice in Islamic thought two features stand out immediately. The first is that the terms used to characterize justice in the Quran are not spelled out in philosophical detail yet pervade the text with enormous regularity and force. As one commentor has put it, 'neither in the Quran nor in the Traditions are there measures to indicate what are the constituent elements of justice or how justice can be realized on earth.'[3] Nevertheless, it is possible to see in the Quran and the Prophet's own actions an implicit theory of justice that informs both the reading of those texts and their later applications. The Quran—the exact and unaltered word of God—has frequent recourse to a vocabulary of justice which is grounded on the proposition that humankind is responsible for all those actions that lie within the exterior bounds set down by God. To pay one's moral and fiscal debts and to temper retribution with mercy are qualities to which mankind is enjoined. A person who is just therefore engages in acts that are framed by an awareness, born of the pursuit of reason over passion, of the harm that may be done to the community of believers by acting otherwise. The Quran (Sura VI: 152) actually enjoins the believer to 'be just,

---

[2] Ruthven (1984: 227–8).   [3] Khadduri (1984: 10–11).

even if it should be to a near kinsman,' and demonstrates practical application when, for example, it recommends that contracts be written down in order to avoid subsequent doubt.

The Quranic conception also suggests that ultimately justice is connected with the interior life (*bāṭin*) of the believer rather than with external appearances (*zāhir*),[4] and hence that true justice must be accompanied by the proper intentions. Repeatedly the Quran assures mankind that God is incapable of acting unjustly and that those whose well-intended acts accord with divine prescription will indeed receive divine reward. Since Islam is, to a very great extent, a religion and attendant set of cultures that, while acknowledging the distinction between the interior and the external, nevertheless presumes in everyday discourse that overt acts give evidence of internal states, it is not surprising to find that those features of justice to which people refer link act and concept in a host of ways. Indeed, to the Arabs among whom I have worked the belief is very strong that one can tell interior states by one's acts and that action itself formulates interiority.

It is against this almost Wittgensteinian view that the analyst is, therefore, able to factor out at least three distinct domains of meaning when trying to discern what is implied for many Muslims by the idea of justice: relationships among men and toward God are reciprocal in nature, and justice exists where this reciprocity guides all interactions; justice is both a process and a result of equating otherwise dissimilar entities; and, because relationships are highly contextual, justice is to be grasped through its multifarious enactments rather than as a single abstract principle. The just individual is one to whom power appropriately devolves because he has regulated his ties with others according to balanced, reciprocal obligations that reduce social chaos and facilitate ever greater networks of indebtedness among those who develop their God-given reason to understand the divine word and the mundane world alike. Justice as equating implies that reason and experience must be used to calculate similarities, a process that shows itself in analogic reasoning (*qiyas*) no less than in attending to the differences among men and women, Muslims and non-Muslims and assigning each category to its respective domain. The contextual quality of justice shows itself in the quest for an understanding of the spheres within which each person or historical moment exists and the ways in which fundamental qualities and kaleidoscopic changes must be scrutinized and balanced. These three aspects— justice as regulated reciprocity, justice as equivalence, and justice as relational/contextual—are clearly represented in holy scripture and in received cultural orientations.

When Arabs speak about justice they invariably connect it with the idea of the just person, the person who is characterized by *'adl*. The root of the term 'adl means 'to set straight,' 'to be balanced.' If a person is 'adl he possesses believability, reliability—and indeed witnesses traditionally had first to be certified as 'adl before being allowed to give testimony, this reliability itself being largely determined by the individual's reputation for being embedded in a host of socio-economic ties which he has

---

[4] Johansen (1990).

constantly to service. Thus, deeply connected to the idea of being 'reliable,' 'balanced,' 'just' was—and is—the idea that a mature person is one who engages in a variety of ties with others and that these ties are themselves the embodiment of ongoing reciprocity. Moreover, just as God endowed humans with the ability to contract their own relationships within the limits set down by the Quran, so too these relationships of reciprocity are of the essence of a true community of believers. Thus three forces converge around this aspect of justice as reciprocity: the idea of the individual as a freely contracting agent who best enacts the capacities with which God has imbued him by using his reason to create situations of permissible advantage; the idea of a community of believers, which derives its legitimacy from those very networks of embedded dependencies through which individual effort is given social utility; and the idea of the state as an entity which is not itself possessed of justice but which serves best when it seeks to regulate reciprocity in ways that do not contravene the scope accorded the individual and the community.[5]

One way of seeing how a society, and with it a period of time, may be either just or unjust is to focus on the related concepts of interpersonal linkage and balance to which the Quran and popular discourse pay great attention. To grasp the first of these two aspects of justice it is important to review what is meant by the concept of *ḥaqq*. This richly nuanced concept is commonly translated as 'right' or 'duty,' but its implications are far more diverse and subtle than those translations alone convey. Basically, haqq is the distribution of rights and duties, the interconnected set of obligations and associations by which man and God, and man and man, are linked to one another.[6] Indeed, it is precisely the distribution of obligations which constitutes the fundamental reality of human existence, which is why haqq also means 'reality' and 'truth.' Moreover, as may be suggested from a reading of Smirnov's analysis, haqq carries the sense of 'due possession': It is not that things are fixed in time and space to a correct position from which they ought not to be displaced but, rather, that in a system of interpersonal linkages people will possess obligations that simultaneously describe both their place in the network that holds society together and constitute the basis on which others will accord them prestige and respected authority.[7] Here we can see why the antonym to haqq, *zulm* (from the root z-l-m), implies inapposite placement: As Izutsu notes:

[5] Compare this orientation to that of Brian Barry, who says that justice as reciprocity is itself composed of (1) requital (returning good for good received); (2) fidelity to agreements voluntarily entered into; and (3) mutual aid (particularly helping the needy). Barry does not see how these qualities can be made duties between nations or generations, and doubts that any general principle exists for justifying the need to give return for benefits received or that human beings ever have had a clear interest in looking after the needs of the next generation (Barry (1980)).

[6] See Rosen (1984: 60–70) and Smith (1971).

[7] Smirnov (1996: 344). Smirnov here emphasizes that 'each of the rights due has its own "place" (makan). By the overall "correct" distribution of such "places" and the allocation of the "rights" in their due "places," "harmony" (i'tidal) is achieved. "The obligatory" is "the truth" and "the due possession." ' This formulation is rather too static to fit my understanding of Islamic culture, at least in the present day, hence my own formulation departs somewhat from this particular part of Smirnov's formulation.

The primary meaning of ZLM is, in the opinion of many of the authoritative lexicographers, that of 'putting in a wrong place'. In the sphere of ethics it seems to mean primarily 'to act in such a way as to transgress the proper limit and encroach upon the right of some other person.' Briefly and generally speaking, *zulm* is to do injustice in the sense of going beyond one's own bounds and doing what one has no right to do.[8]

That the linkage of persons in essentially dyadic relationships should form one of the key points around which justice and injustice turns is further developed by Smirnov, who writes:

The rights-obligation set (*huquq* [plural of *haqq*]) is at the same time an ontologically necessary assemblage of traits that characterize the given existing thing, the given link of the power-and-rule structure. 'Giving what is due' in order to 'guarantee' (*istifa'*) this *huquq* set is not only and not just an act of moral righteousness; it is first and foremost done to secure the ontological *stability* of the thing in question, that is to say, its being truly established in the flow of changes.

This justice, or 'giving what is due' and 'establishing the true' (*haqq*), turns out to be the 'preservation' and 'maintenance' of this needed-in-order-to-exist assemblage of *huquq*. . . . Consequently, justice is deviated from when the exactness of 'preserving the middle' is lost, through a twist this way or that. . . . [The] maxim, usually attributed to Muhammad, was a commonplace among medieval intellectuals: 'the middle of things is the best.' It is the middle in which the *two*, separated from each other and opposed (*muqabala*) to each other, merge and come to harmony, producing a unity that makes genuine sense.[9]

This emphasis on linkage and reciprocity—which, as we shall see, is possible between persons but not between individuals and the state—is represented both in the mundane and in the supernatural realm. On the level of the world there are those who connect the existence of civilization and a number of individuals who possess the qualities of 'adl to the very existence of justice. The sixteenth-century poet Madjdoub was not, I think, true to his sobriquet 'The Sarcastic' when he wrote: 'No kingdom if there are no citizens, No citizens without the exchange of goods, No exchange of goods if there is no city, No city without 'adl.'[10] On the supernatural level, it is said, for example, that on Judgment Day each person will appear before God, his or her good and bad deeds having been assiduously recorded throughout life by the angels resting on each shoulder. All the members of each religion will, however, be arrayed behind their prophet—the Jews with Moses, the Christians with Jesus, the Muslims with Muhammad—and each of the prophets will vouch for those who followed them. At this ultimate moment of justice God will thus not only have

---

[8] Izutsu (1966: 164–5).

[9] Smirnov (1996: 345–6) (original italics). See also Kassem (1972).

[10] Scelles-Millie and Khelifa (1966: 123). Scelles-Millie and Khelifa translate 'adl as 'justice d'élites.' This curious gloss does, however, make a certain sense. Although, as we have been arguing, 'adl is a feature that inheres in persons rather than in groups, it may be thought of as a quality which, if enough people possess it, characterizes both their time and their place. In the sense of a number of persons possessing this quality to make a city both viable and just—indeed as an attribution which, like public opinion, relates to one person yet constitutes a collective assessment—it does not seem entirely inconsistent with the fundamental idea of 'adl as a personal attribute to posit its larger communal aspect.

the record of each individual's ties to others but will see the linkage each possesses to one of His prophets, and His assessment, inherently just, will be framed in no small part by this linkage.

If one aspect of justice found in both sacred text and common culture concerns the intertwining of duties and obligations, a second concerns the concept of balance. Ibn Khaldun put the matter with characteristic clarity: 'Justice is a balance set up among mankind.'[11] The term 'adl, as we saw, has as part of its root meaning the idea of being in balance. As Ayoub has phrased it: "Adl in Islam means a balanced approach to all things, including life. Therefore 'Adl or 'Adil also is a reference to a person who is morally, behaviorally, and spiritually balanced.'[12] Smirnov draws a contrast between balance in a Western sense and that implied by the Arabic when he says: 'Alluding to the archetype of the scales, one may say that Western thinking is concerned with the pans of the scales and their contents, while for classical Islamic thought the stress lies on the central balancing pivot.'[13] Although one hears contemporary Muslims conceptualize justice in terms of scales no less than of a pivot point, the overall contrast drawn by Smirnov has considerable importance for the way in which disparate entities are equated in order to achieve justice. Indeed, maintaining a balance on a point is an impossibly difficult task for all but the most adept, thus reinforcing both the sense of ambivalence inherent in virtually any relationship and stance in Arab culture and the constant emphasis on finding linkages to keep yet other relationships in balance.[14]

Justice, then, incorporates a sense of reciprocity, a series of largely dyadic exchanges through which balance is made manifest. Reciprocity—both as commercial exchange and as 'gift-giving'—figures significantly in the popular image of justice as well as in political organization. In a study of Arab comic strips, for example, it has been said of one famous cartoonist that '[t]he system of values expressed revolves around two linked concepts: generosity and exchange, the latter figuring a kind of immanent justice.'[15] Each 'gift' provokes a still more generous recompense, thus mimicking the image, common in the Quranic view of divine judgment and integral to the process of sociological ingratiation, that each gift will result in a generous recompense. A constant search is required for the appropriate level of exchange among the comic strip characters, less generous types serving as foils for those who

---

[11]   Khaldun (1958: ii. 2, 105).

[12]   Ayoub (1996: 19). There is also a related term, *qist*. Whereas 'adl refers to qualities in the person, says Ayoub, qist 'refers to the way in which Muslims deal with one another and God deals with us. . . . Qist means acting fairly with others. . . . Qist, then, is social justice in its broadest sense—first in our relationship to God and second in our relationship to society' (Ayoub (1996: 19 and 22)). Izutsu interprets qist, as it is used in the Quran, as a synonym of 'adl, though he also notes that it stresses fair dealings: Qist, he says, is 'used chiefly as a forensic term for justice, or impartiality in dealing with others. As such, the word is most often applied to the verdict in a trial. . . . The word is also used in reference to the standards and obligations in commerce. In the Qur'an there are frequent exhortations to "give full measure and full weight, in justice" ' (Izutsu (1966: 209–10)).

[13]   Smirnov (1996: 346).

[14]   On ambivalence, see 'Ambivalence Towards Power' in Rosen (forthcoming).

[15]   Douglas and Malti-Douglas (1994: 94).

act properly. The cartoons thus reinforce what the authors call 'the notion of justice as appropriate exchange.'[16] Moreover, they argue, '[b]y being directed to reciprocal relations, justice is severed from overall social organization,' in the sense that exchange serves not the goals of individuals alone but a just order that transcends particular sets of relationships.[17] Similarly, in the political realm, Hammoudi argues that the monarch must constantly dispense gifts which, at the same time, create bonds and antipathies, the just ruler being one who maintains the inherently un-stable balance against the chaos and injustice that arises with one person—even a king—perpetually getting a disproportionate share.[18]

Justice as regulated reciprocity reveals itself in a host of concrete ways. In situa-tions of contract it incorporates a series of precise types of contracts none of which, however, protects the foolish or ignorant from the repercussions of their own bad bargains.[19] It shows itself in the domain of compensatory justice, where each person is expected to be responsible for the exercise of his or her reasoning powers to avoid doing harm to others. And justice as regulated reciprocity reveals itself in the way that people characterize periods of time as just or unjust depending on the extent to which this free expression of reciprocal advantage and its inherent limitation on the arbitrary acts of others has given the community as a whole a sense of proximity to divine organization. The point is made most forcefully in the Quran when the reper-cussions of unreciprocated action are underscored by the warning that 'the unjust have no patron and no helper' (Sura XLII: 6).

To some commentors this emphasis on reciprocity has been viewed in quite nega-tive terms. Santillana, for example, wrote:

the Arabs have immoderately exaggerated the fundamental basis of their system. The idea that justice consists in reciprocity has been pushed to its extremist consequences by them. . . . [T]he prohibition of interest in every form, the dislike of every kind of risk, the exclusion of any uncertainty in contracts . . . depend from the same general idea, which is that in all cases the rule of equality is infringed, and with it justice; and the lawyer has only in view the read-justment of the balance.[20]

Santillana's criticism is, however, based on his belief that Islamic and canon law share an exaggerated emphasis on the strict application of rules. He not only misses

---

[16] Douglas and Malti-Douglas (1994: 98).
[17] Douglas and Malti-Douglas (1994: 99).
[18] Hammoudi (1997: 48–53).
[19] Ralph Newman has written: 'Among the other legal systems of the world there is only one in which relief is denied as a general principle in cases of overreaching. In Islamic law, "maghbun" is one who has suffered something to his great disadvantage, but for whom the law provides no relief. Minor misrep-resentation does not give rise to any remedy, nor passive misrepresentations, as where a person, knowing the true value of his property, allows it to be thought that it is of far greater value than it is in fact, or fails to disclose the true facts, and sells the same at a price far in excess of its true value.' Newman goes on to quote another commentator, Hooper, to the effect that 'Muhammadan jurists, while not expressly laying it down in terms, seem to consider it to be the duty of the contracting parties to be prudent men of busi-ness, and if one person allows another to get the better of him he must abide by the results of his own lack of prudence' (Newman (1961: 95–6)).
[20] Santillana (1931: 309).

the distinction, to which we shall have recourse shortly, between equality and equivalence, but the social emphasis the Islamic idea of reciprocity incorporates—its
emphasis on orderly and predictable behavior in a society characterized by the full
play of personality and the ability of the law to limit the potential chaos such individual effort might engender.

HISTORICAL ASPECTS OF ISLAMIC CONCEPTS OF JUSTICE

The pattern that emerges, then, is one in which it is predominantly the 'just' individual who is both the standard for inclusion in the community and the entity
toward which power properly devolves from the community in order that he may
serve to regulate the negotiations among contending individuals. When the Prophet
was alive there was no question as to how this quality of embodied justice was represented in the administration of world affairs. But the elements of Islamic justice
became a source for contention among moral and political theorists from the
moment when, following his death, Prophetic governance in direct accord with
divine precept was no longer supportable. The elements of Islamic justice were the
source of contention among moral and political theorists from the outset of Islam.
During his lifetime the Prophet governed in direct accord with divine precept. After
his death disagreement centered on which line possessed the capacity to rule justly
and which procedures for rule should hold sway. For Sunnis political justice lay in
acknowledging legitimate authority through community consensus (*ijma'*); for the
Shi'i it lay in the strict perpetuation of the line of legitimate succession. For the Sunni
the ruler's legitimacy was in theory hedged by the need for consultation (*shura*). The
Sunni Umayyad dynasty, however, combined the doctrine of an elected caliph with
the idea that the responsible believer is the one who does not fail to obey the legitimate successor to the Prophet. Others, known collectively as Qadiriyah, believed
that each man is responsible for his own acts and that political justice lies not in
compulsory obedience but in holding even the caliph responsible for his unjust acts.

Notwithstanding its claims for continuity, the model of the caliphate failed to
provide specific guidance for a theory of the just sovereign. During the brief period
in the eighth century when the 'Abbasid dynasty favored them, the Mu'tazila argued
that divine justice is beyond human grasp but that human reason can best approxi-
mate divine justice through the exercise of reason and free will. Indeed, they argued,
it is by such acts that one gains unity with that inner sense of justice toward which
all men are naturally directed. Although the Mu'tazili emphasis on reason and unity
brought them into conflict with more powerful opponents, the terms of the debate
were set: To the legalists (including the later systematizer al-Shafi'i (767–820) men
choose to do justice or injustice through their adherence to the law; to al-Ash'ari (d.
935 or 936) men could do justice but could not create its very terms; to al-Tahawi
(d. 933) and al-Baqillani (d. 1012) the very uses to which God's created justice is put
are themselves creative acts. By contrast, the Shi'i theorists of the Buyid and Fatimid

dynasties of the tenth and eleventh centuries argued that, in the absence of an infal-libly sinless spiritual leader (*imam*), men may even defend themselves through dissimulation (*taqiyah*) against an unjust caliph—a practice that Sunnis regarded as little more than personal convenience. To both of these positions Sufi theorists, like Ibn al-'Arabi (1165–1240), countered that justice can be made manifest in this world not by creative acts of reason but only by engagement in ecstatic devotion.

As Islam spread into new territories and as contact with classical Western thought increased, Islamic thinkers had to consider the practical applications of justice in law and politics. The Virtuous City of al-Farabi (*c.*878–*c.*950) was to be assured 'first in the division of the good things shared by the people of the city among them all, and then in the preservation of what is divided among them';[21] the Just City of Ibn-Sina (980–1037) was constituted by a social contract among administrators, artisans, and guardians, the welfare of all being secured by a common fund of resources. As the demands of actual administration increased, specific content for these propositions developed. The concept of public interest (*maslaha*), as elaborated by al-Ghazali (1058–1111) and al-Tawfi (d. 1316), received legal force by calculating social conse-quence against individual interest; procedural justice lay in the qualities of the judge's character, in the use of a council of advisor/assessors, in the use of advisory opinions by outside scholars, and in the increasing use of elaborate procedures for ascertaining the credibility of witnesses. The traditional absence of appellate struc-tures reduced dependence on any fallible judge, although the accepted legitimacy of different schools of Islamic law and resident experts allowed local custom to inform the practice of daily justice.

Because justice was seen to pervade all domains of life, Islamic thinkers sought to unify political, legal, and social justice. In the face of Mongol invaders and Western Crusaders, Ibn Taymiyah (1263–1328) sought to stem the decline of Islam by urging that despotic rulers must give way to a politicized shari'a in which, for example, precedence would be given to family unity over emotion-laden repudiation, and just wars would be limited to defensive actions. From his initial emphasis on society as a fluctuating balance of religion and social solidarity (*'asabīyah*), Ibn Khaldun (1332–1408), observing the decadence of fourteenth-century Egypt, increasingly stressed procedural regularities and discretionary penalties (*ta'zir*) as a check on polit-ical injustice. Although he and others believed men were inherently unjust,[22] their more secular political approach to issues of justice had to wait until later ages to achieve a more activist orientation.

The commentors of the classical and medieval periods were no different from their successors, then, in one key respect: They suspected that a ruler could not be truly just. One way of accounting for this attitude, then as now, is to hark back to the issue of justice as reciprocity. It can be argued that the state itself cannot be just—though certain

---

[21] Quoted from al-Farabi in Khadduri (1984: 86).

[22] 'The poet [al-Mutanabbi] thus said, Injustice is a human characteristic. If you find a moral man, there is some reason why he is not unjust' (Khaldun (1958: i. 262)).

leaders for a time may be so—precisely because the state is unreciprocity incarnate. Early jurists said that the caliph can be justified but not just. They were, in a sense, recognizing that the state has legitimacy inasmuch as it manages tasks that are necessarily hierarchically arrayed, such as leadership in war and oversight of various criminal laws. The state also has the ability to support the vertically arrayed layers of society in such a way as to keep alive the capacity of individuals to form ties to others that may yield important networks of their own and socially desirable networks that hold all of society together. But the jurists were also, I would suggest, saying that without being able to claim the powers of the Prophet no representative of the state could be allowed to convert prestige to power—that either he remains a person, like others, embroiled in the process (more or less justly conducted) of forging linkages and hence dependent on others, or he becomes a figure apart, an institution rather than a person, unable to engage in genuine give-and-take and hence incapable of acquiring the attributes of the just. Ibn Khaldun even restricted the concept of injustice to acts that bring about utter ruin: 'It should be known that this is what the Lawgiver (Muḥammad) actually had in mind when he forbade injustice. He meant the resulting destruction and ruin of civilization, which ultimately permits the eradication of the human species.' He argued, therefore, that only the acts of God or a king could result in injustice, not those, for example, of a robber: '[I]njustice can be committed only by persons who cannot be touched, only by persons who have power and authority.'[23] His analysis thus shows a clear connection between the state, whose power is unrestrained by reciprocity, ordinary mortals who are capable of justice only through interrelationship, and God who alone reconciles opposites and is thus capable of total power and total justice.

The jurists themselves could claim to be able to avoid the fate of becoming unjust not only by refusing salaries but by professing to fulfill a duty that someone must perform on behalf of the community of believers as a whole. That a number of scholars actually refused, even on pain of torture, to take positions in the state apparatus suggests not only their moral purity—as the tellers of these stories are wont to say— but a recognition that accepting such a position involves a kind of social death, a denial of their embeddedness in the system of reciprocity by which others attribute to them the qualities of personhood and justice. For a judge or legal scholar to be implanted in a multiplicity of roles involving others in his community is not to be prone to favoritism but to be subject to the forces of opinion and entanglement that bind men together and limit their adverse acts; to be separated institutionally is to be removed from these constraints and hence the attributions of justice.

JUSTICE AS RECIPROCITY AND EQUATING

Coming at justice in this way perhaps we can also understand something of what Arabs mean by corruption. A brief story may help set the scene here. A few years ago

---

[23] Khaldun (1958: ii. 107). See also pp. 107–10 on those who are capable of injustice.

I was in the home of a Berber friend in the mountains of the Middle Atlas for the Friday afternoon lunch, a time when the men of the village congregate from their dispersed tasks following the weekly prayer. At one point in the conversation about Moroccan politics my host turned to me and asked if there was corruption in America. When I allowed as to how indeed there was he asked me for an example. I proceeded to describe Watergate. 'Ah, no,' he said, 'that's just politics (*siyasa*).' So I described a kick-back arrangement. 'No, no,' he responded, that's just business (*biy'a ou shra'*).' I thought a moment longer and finally came up with an example of nepotism. 'Oh, no, no, no,' he said dismissively, 'that's just family solidarity (*'a'ila*).' As I sat trying to think up something that would pass muster, my host turned to the assembled men and, with a nod of the head suggestive of clear understanding and admiration, said: 'Now you see why America is such a strong country; they have no corruption.'

Needless to say I did not let the opportunity pass, if not to save the honor of my nation as being every bit as corrupt as anyone else's, at least to figure out what they regarded as corrupt. And the answer I got was one I and others have heard repeated throughout the Arab world and much of Southwest Asia: To be corrupt is to fail to share in whatever comes one's way with those with whom you have forged bonds of interdependence. This may be broad enough to cover vast public harm—as when people die because a selfish entrepreneur has sold adulterated cooking oil. But it usually focuses on the narrower range of direct connections. To 'eat' things yourself is not merely self-serving but is itself corrupting of the whole body of believers. To bribe an official or favor a relative is not corrupt if it actually acts as a check on their power—indeed on the power of the state, which needs you as part of this system to work. Indeed, a distinct politesse that makes actions predictable and manipulable accompanies such affairs. It is when officials do not need to rely on a host of people engaged in such conduct, when they receive large amounts from a few people and summarily dismiss all the others, that they begin to 'eat' the largesse without sharing it and true corruption, with all its attendant incivility, spreads. It is this to which people point when suggesting how corrupt, how unjust present times have become. It is, therefore, as a deep expression of the centrality of justice as regulated reciprocity that corruption can be defined as the failure to share with one's network of co-dependants.

The aspect of justice as reciprocity is closely allied to that second aspect I want to discuss, namely the idea of justice as equating. The term 'equating' is more appropriate than 'equality' or 'equalizing' because Islam and contemporary Arab culture stress the notion of balancing things by finding something of equivalent weight or import, not something identical in nature or overall worth. Among the many terms for justice are *mizan* and *qistas* which mean 'scales,' and it was in this sense that the caliph 'Abd al-Malik reputedly wrote in the first century of Islam that 'justice means the rating of a thing as equal to a thing of another kind so as to make it like the latter.'[24] This element shows itself in various ways. In legal thought the process of

[24] Khadduri (1984: 8).

analogic reasoning (qiyas) is certainly central to Islamic jurisprudence, and the search for equivalencies, though undoubtedly a discretionary art that depends as much on the perspicacity and reputation of a given judge or scholar as on settled traditions within a given school of law, is itself a quest for ever-changing visions of the comparable. An excellent example and analysis drawn from the comics of the Egyptian Firdawsi shows not only the aspect of justice as finding equivalence but the intertwining of this aspect with justice as reciprocity and as judicial action:

[E]ven in the relatively simple society of the Firdawsian [comic] strips, the search for the appropriate level of exchange, that is, the harmonization of generosity with reciprocal justice, is not always easy. A man sells his house for the agreed price: a normal exchange. The son of the new owner finds a pot of gold in the new house and exclaims: 'Look, my father, here is a treasure that God has sent us!' But the father will not accept it and insists that the money belongs to the previous owner of the house. The latter refuses it in turn, since he had not known of its existence. The wise judge finds a solution: the son of the one man will marry the daughter of the other and the couple will accept the gold as dowry. The generosity of the two men provokes the search for a principle of exchange, effectively found by the *qadi*. By offering the money to the young couple, each man gives and receives at the same time.

But why such a complicated solution based on the narrative pretext of marriageable children of the opposite sex? A simple division of the money would have eliminated generosity, crucial in the transformation of mere exchange into justice. Equally striking is the fact that the *qadi*, faced with a legal problem, never answers the question and at no time invokes Islamic law. The generosity-as-immanent-justice system effectively precludes positive law, even Islamic law.[25]

Justice as equating also appears in the very subtle and complex relation of knowledge to order and risk in Islamic thought. Since knowledge, and the human obligation to employ it, is of the essence of the responsible and aware believer it is intriguing to see that an orderly, and hence a just, world is one in which knowledge becomes fixed in individuals who can then employ it to direct relationships in accord with the highest sense of personal freedom and social utility. But whereas in the West, as Fedwa Malti-Douglas points out, a sense of order is achieved when knowledge is achieved, in the Arab world order must go one step further; it must bring about justice in the sense of establishing relations of equivalence among the various components of society in a way that meets the needs of various contexts and purposes.[26] It is only when action to equate renders the world of ordered relationships incarnate that justice is done. There is a saying among investors on Wall Street—'to know but not to act is not to know.' The Arabs, I suspect, would agree with this insight but would go one step further and say that to know but not to act is not to be just. And what one must know in this world in order to act and to be just is precisely how things can be calibrated to one another, weighed in one another's terms, equated for the multifarious purposes to which all things and persons may be put.

---

[25] Douglas and Malti-Douglas (1994: 96–7).   [26] Malti-Douglas (1988: 85).

The problem of equating arises prominently, of course, in those matters of personal status affecting the legal position of women. One could, of course, point to various statutes and practices in Muslim countries, and any number of textual assertions and customary assumptions, that portray women as essentially different and inferior to men and hence, from the point of view of those who have invariably exercised public power, justifiably subjected to differential and clearly inferior legal rights. But this is not the feature I want to concentrate on for the moment. Rather I want to suggest two things in regard to the role of women and—to the limit of my own understanding—women's own orientations toward ideas of justice: first, that an emphasis on justice as equating rather than equality is shared by both men and women; and, second, that when male judges must choose between treating women as less than men and larger issues of equivalence they not uncommonly opt for the latter at the expense of the former. Let me explain what I mean.

There can be no doubt that to most Arab men—and to a great many women as well—men and women are seen as fundamentally different, and the religious distinctions that attend this belief have profound legitimacy. Yet a larger, almost Aristotelian, notion is also at work here, namely, that entities which are different should be treated differently, that justice lies precisely in recognizing and validating these differences, and that injustice would flow from a contrary position.[27] At the same time the idea of justice as equating—as putting on a scale that reflects difference, as sticking to the straight course by balancing things that are different through the calibration of proper place and weight—has deep religious roots and wide contemporary appeal. The Quran (Sura IV: 128–9), for example, says: 'You will not be able to act equitably (*ta'dilu*) to all your wives, however eagerly you may wish to do so. But yet do not be altogether partial (*la tamilu kull al-mayl*) so as to leave one as in suspense.'[28] Even though 'equitably' here, I think, implies equivalence, the implication is that it is very difficult to work out such equivalence among several wives, a simple division of goods not being true to the differences involved. One will have to search around for a basis of equivalence and persuade others that the division is indeed equitable. Because of this difficulty still greater harm can arise to a woman's reputation, to the relations between the spouses' respective kin groups, and to the woman's own emotions by leaving her, both temporally and socially, in suspense.

[27] In the Arab case it would not, in this regard, be accurate to characterize justice, as Cupit (1996) does generally, as acting in accordance with another's status, and injustice as misclassifying another's status. For while the Arab idea of justice involves the idea of relating to others in a way that does not necessarily incorporate an emphasis on distribution, it is not status that matters but the processes by which interpersonal networks are under constant revision.

[28] The translation used here is that of Izutsu (1966: 211). Izutsu cites this passage to show the contrast between 'adl and mayl, which means 'partiality' or 'favoritism.' Arberry translates this passage as: 'You will not be able to be equitable between your wives, be you ever so eager; yet not be altogether partial so that you leave her as it were suspended.' The difference between 'suspense' and 'suspended' is an interesting one, but both readings taken together may actually capture the full import of this passage better than either alone.

The same underlying assumptions inform contemporary situations where men and women often seek their own analogies, their own equivalencies in ways that undoubtedly treat each other's positions as fundamentally different even though both employ a common procedure for ascertaining balance and share a common discourse of equation-building regardless of 'objectively' distinguishable results. The emphasis on reciprocity is a shared orientation; the emphasis on finding equivalencies is part of both groups' approach to the just. And failure to appreciate how, for better or for worse, this broadly shared orientation informs daily acts and future hopes distorts our understanding of both men and women in the Arab world.

It is also true, I think, that in some instances we can see that even male judges are prepared to place greater emphasis on finding equivalencies than on simply confirming female inferiority—instances that show the superordinate emphasis that commonsense and socio-religious sentiment put on orderliness as equated difference. What I have in mind here are cases I have recorded where a judge is specifically confronted with a situation in which a woman's inferior rights under the law are ignored because it is believed by the judge that only by avoiding the strict letter of the law can he equate matters whose imbalance is, in this particular situation, unfairly exaggerated by a refusal to do otherwise. I have in mind cases where a judge grants a woman the sort of definitive divorce from an abusive husband that is contrary to the legal requirement that the divorce be revocable at the husband's will because the judge sees the threat of continuing harm to the woman as too great. There are also instances in which custody is given to the mother even though the law awards it to the husband, because the calculus of interest expressed by the judge equilibrates emotions, education, or familial support differently than would result from focusing on the assumptions connected with treating the sexes differently in custody matters. My point, of course, is not to argue that Islamic law is thus egalitarian: If anything, it is the contrary—that equality is simply not a central aspect of Islamic conceptions of justice, but finding the right things to weigh against one another is, and those equated entities may change over time and be far more subtly shared and arranged than concentration on statutory law or Holy Writ alone may adequately reveal.

Justice as a process of determining equivalencies obviously presents certain overall difficulties, in particular that of choosing some common basis for assessment. The Western emphasis on equality is itself certainly fraught with analytic difficulties: Does equality require compensation for past wrongs or present affirmative action; does equal pay for equal work devalue individual accomplishment; can separate but equal education meet the criteria of equality just because monetary expenditures are identical? Equality can, in theory, be solved in a number of cases with identical treatment, however difficult it may be to determine that one has held 'all other things equal.' But a standard of equivalence may be more radically relativizing: Both the standards and the results are highly dependent on the multiplicity of attachments people have rather than on some externality. A calculus of social consequence rather than a calculation of identical recompense must be employed.[29] Infinite regress is, however, arrested by the very modes of attributing to persons and situations the repercussions they may have; the criteria for measurement of equivalence turn back in on the criteria of social interaction, such that, in law as in the culture at large, the focus constantly returns to the particular instance and its implications. Along the way the felt sense of justice can vary from one moment to another, one situation to another, never achieving repose in some universal medium of evaluation yet never escaping the religious and commonsense perceptions about the nature of people and their effects on each other's social ties.

JUSTICE, COLONIALISM, AND MODERN ARAB THOUGHT

As colonial powers moved into the Middle East and as the Ottoman empire began to fragment, each of the criteria for justice began to encounter new and challenging implications. The intrusion of Western colonialists, particularly in the nineteenth century, prompted two major strands of thought on the question of justice. Modernists sought to include institutions modeled after those of the West into their political systems, although traditionalists found Western approaches inconsistent with Islam. Jamal al-Din al-Afghani (1838–97) believed that the injustices of Muslim despots could be rectified by renewing the principle of consultation in the form of elective assemblies and by the political unity of all Muslims against Western powers. Like his predecessors he combined moral renewal through revitalized virtues with a political program that would insure fuller community participation. But when al-Afghani's proposals failed to move Muslim tyrants or the populace at large, some, like his student, Muhammad 'Abduh (1849–1905), looked to Western procedural standards, which they did not regard as incompatible with Islam, for guidance. As a

---

[29] Smirnov writes: 'It is making one equal to the other (equality between two necessarily *separate* entities) that is important in the [Western] case, and theoretical discussion tries to determine the accuracy of this equalizing and to find the *only* true (always the *one*) decision. In the [Islamic] case it is the fact of balancing the opposites that is important, this balance being reached by means of the centering and mediating pivot; the theoretical task is to find out how the two might be linked to form a balanced unity and what the conditions are for such a linkage' (Smirnov (1996: 346–7); original italics). While I do not share Smirnov's positivistic approach to Western law and question whether the ideas of 'unity' and 'harmony' represent the terms of ordinary Muslims at present (who seem more disposed to a view in which a kind of running imbalance is inherent in the nature of social relations), I do agree with his view that the metaphor of calculation is prominent in Western approaches to justice whereas the assessments of Arabs tend to be far more relativistic. An intriguing approach has been taken by Mohammad Sidi Ahmad, a reporter for the Egyptian newspaper *Al-Ahram*, who uses the phrase 'subjective parity' to refer to the Arabs' sense of the balanced justice necessary to go forward with any relationship. He thus points to the example of Sadat crossing Suez, by which it becomes possible for him to deal with his enemy even though he loses territory, or the need for Israel to withdraw a few miles from the Golan so that Syria, even though withdrawing some 30 miles, would be able to enter talks with them. Again, I see this less as an example of a kind of static balancing than of establishing contact by showing that the other is affected by you—is literally moved—so that the subjective nature of the running imbalance of negotiated relationships can go forward.

judge and grand mufti 'Abduh issued fatwas allowing, for example, the use of inter-est through postal bank accounts. He often spoke in terms of revelation and natural law as well as in terms of the compatibility of revelation with evolution and social reformation, but his equivocation and his deep concern with the moral transforma-tion of society signaled precisely the dilemma faced by many of his era who were forced to consider the implications of both Western and indigenous forms of injus-tice.[30]

Many of the conflicts between modernists and traditionalists centered on the adoption of new legal codes. The very idea of a code was largely a Western one, but the process of codification forced many Muslims to consider which propositions they regarded as essential to Islam and which as dispensable accretions. Moreover, the process of adopting codes offered the opportunity for establishing a system for legal changes. Of central importance was the formulation of the Majallah, or civil code, which was applied throughout Ottoman territories in the 1870s. Together with the short-lived Ottoman constitution of 1876, it marked the trend that culminated in Turkey's unilateral disestablishment of Islam and its wholesale adoption of European codes. By contrast, French colonial territories adopted many features of French commercial and criminal law, but these countries retained relatively intact their Islamic family law practices until they achieved national independence.

Owing largely to the efforts in the late 1940s of the Egyptian jurist 'Abd al-Razzaq al-Sanhuri (1895–1971), civil codes were drawn up for Egypt, Iraq, and Kuwait, with other countries drawing upon elements of his work.[31] In each instance it was left to shari'a principles to fill in where the codes were silent. In fact, more often than not, Western substantive law filled in the whole of the civil law, and the sense of distinctive Islamic principles—of fault and liability, of intentionality in contracts or unconscionable agreements—was largely replaced by non-Muslim concepts.

By contrast, the strain between Western and Islamic standards of justice has been most significantly tested in family law. Following independence in 1956, Tunisia took the more extreme position, formally abolishing polygamy and requiring all divorces to be pronounced by the judge. At the other extreme, Pakistan and the Gulf States continued highly traditional forms of Muslim family law, largely turning aside outside forces. In between lay a vast array of compromises: from Morocco, where the code remains very close to Maliki principles but places increased discretion in the hands of the qadi, to Malaysia, where local custom (*adat*) grants wives a share of all marital assets at the time of divorce.

The struggles over appropriate laws of personal status have profoundly affected views of the nature of Islamic justice: As women became more educated and occu-pied a greater role in the economy justice was conceived by many as greater equal-ization, though not full equality, of men and women. At the same time the very forces that led to liberalization contributed to the backlash against it. Fundamentalists, from Ayatollah Ruhollah Khomeini in Iran to the Muslim Brothers

---

[30] See generally Kerr (1966).   [31] See Hill (1987).

in Egypt, find the relations of men and women one of the domains where Western influence has distorted justice by rendering an imbalance among what they see as natural differences.

Similarly, in the criminal law the precepts of divine revelation have been read to imply invariant punishments (*ḥudūd*) for listed offenses and discretionary punishments (*ta'zir*) for a broader range of infractions. Some of these penalties, though rarely applied, conflict with international human rights conventions, while others bespeak localized standards of justice—as when, for example, a learned man may be held to a higher standard of behavior than an unlettered one, because his acts are thought to have greater consequences for society. Recent attempts by the ministers of justice of Islamic nations to compose a uniform penal law have yielded a document no country is likely to adopt, because each nation adheres to quite different standards of punishment. The very process of drawing up such a document reveals both the commonalities and the discrepancies wrought by different histories and attitudes.

Issues of social justice have also taken very different paths. Although the language of distributive justice is broadly shared, neither modernists nor traditionalists have succeeded in capturing its terms for any universally accepted program. The combination of Islam and socialism in Algeria and Libya, for example, has resulted in the greater use of the central government for the redistribution of resources; moderate states, such as Indonesia and Jordan, have used public funds to reconstruct the educational system and provide greater security against disaster. But again, what is seen to be just depends far more on the political and economic circumstances of each country than uniformly adopted beliefs about Islamic justice. In this respect the intellectual history of the concept of justice replicates much of earlier history, for it is the local amalgam, proffered as distinctly Islamic, that both unites and separates Muslim nations.

One common concern is the nature of economic justice, exemplified by the permissibility of charging interest. Riba, which is usually translated as 'usury,' but more accurately refers to any form of unjust enrichment, was historically avoided by various legal fictions. The rise of Islamic banking, however, has resulted in practices that are meant to conform simultaneously with modern economic institutions and the prohibition on interest. This development is particularly important because it is rare for Islamic conceptions of justice to be embraced in specific institutional enactments. Historically, unjust enrichment was avoided through a variety of legal fictions or outright disregard. Islam prohibited interest, though, not because of any unique economic or religious criteria but because it is an example of something obtained without adequate reciprocity.[32] This contrasts to mere misrepresentation, which is generally not prohibited: in the words of the Ottoman-inspired Code (article 356 of the Majallah): 'The existence of flagrant misrepresentation in a sale, but without actual deceit, does not enable the person who has been the victim of such misrepresentation to cancel the sale.' Unjust enrichment is unjust precisely because it involves the lack of reciprocity that goes with delayed and uncertain return. It is worth recalling Saleh's formulation: '[I]t is not

---

[32] For additional examples of unjust enrichment in this context, see Rosen (1989a: 61 and 66–7).

business risk which is disallowed but the risk generated by a want of knowledge which materially obscures any of the constitutive elements of a given transaction.'[33] And indeed it is the absence of face-to-face interlocking ties constantly serviced that is seen as truly material to any economic tie: It is the social element of the bargaining stance that must be ever-present for society to remain tied together, to be balanced, to be orderly, to be just.

Many of these issues have taken on renewed importance, as we have noted, as a result of the movement in several parts of the Muslim world to incorporate a prohibition on interest into modern banking practice. The highest court in Pakistan ruled that all forms of interest are repugnant to Islam, and though the ruling is opposed even by a government that rode to power in part on its claim to bring Islam to all facets of Pakistani life, there is pronounced opposition to this total ban. Other countries have, however, found that interest is not necessary to all forms of modern banking practice. One of the more successful banks in Egypt now is the Islamic bank, and a similar one that has begun operations in Malaysia is proving highly successful. That depositors may become shareholders and receive a return on their investment rather than interest on an account may, of course, be little more than a new legal fiction. But the fact that fictions are needed is not unimportant. It remains to be seen just where this issue will go in various Muslim countries, but one thing is indisputable: The sentiments surrounding this matter are propelled and informed in large part by that larger sense of justice and injustice which senses unevenness, unequated dealings, an absence of socially regulable reciprocity in dealings where advantage does not flow from face-to-face interaction.

As fundamentalist regimes have taken power in Iran, Sudan, and several Malaysian states—and as their influence expands in Pakistan, Algeria, and Jordan—the equation of shari'a with justice has been no more fully consummated than at other times in Muslim history. Although formally pre-eminent, Islamic law is not, in fact, given unalloyed application in any of the Islamic republics. Moreover, justice—in the sense of receiving a fair share of the wealth of the state—has led to demands for the delivery of actual services rather than the imposition of formal law alone. Thus the terms of justice have been put into play once again, and the quest for new equivalencies, new contexts, and new forms of reciprocal obligation has become embroiled in bureaucratic and party structures.[34]

JUSTICE AS CONTEXT

The umpire has regard to equity, the judge to law.

Aristotle

This brings us to the third aspect of Islamic justice that needs to be considered, namely, justice as a relational, a contextual concept. For the Arabs justice—as

---

[33]   Saleh (1986: 116).
[34]   See generally the discussions and proposals in Mannan (1986) and Iqbal (1988).

humans are capable of conceiving and enacting it—is not an absolute, a set of proposi-tions to which the insightful must penetrate and give expression in the world. To the contrary, this capacity not only lies beyond the grasp of humankind but is, in a very distinct sense, unnecessary to human existence. What matters for humans is to use their reason to create a set of relations within the community of believers and for those rela-tions to be evaluated in terms of their efficacy for social order rather than as the embod-iment of absolutes. As contexts change the different facets of people and their relationships change. To know a person is to know how he or she acts in a variety of contexts; to know truth is to know the range of possible ties people form with one another; to know justice is to exercise reason through common modes of analysis—anal-ogy, equating, assessing reciprocal influence—that yield equally valid if divergent results.

This feature shows itself in a host of ways in Arab culture: in the judge's discre-tion to open the 'bounds of relevance' to include aspects of an entire relationship; in the insistence by men and women, rich and poor, Muslim and Arab non-Muslim that the context of their place in society must be considered if justice is to be done; and in the meting out of punishments, where those who 'should know better' because of their knowledge and connections should, in theory, be punished more severely than those whose worldly consequent ties do not affect the community's well-being so markedly.

This relational/contextual aspect of justice also means that the same act can have very different meanings according to the consequences for relationship that flow from it. Muslim judges always say that a principle like deciding similar cases simi-larly would be unjust because people are different and even the same individual's situations vary from moment to moment. The same man whom the judge finds embedded in a set of negotiated ties of one sort at a given moment may have to be held to a different standard when the kaleidoscope shifts and his relationships vary. To judge without considering context would be to violate all sense of justice. It is an approach that reminds one of the story, as retold by Steven Gould, of the moment in the 1956 baseball season when Don Larsen was one batter away from pitching the first perfect game in World Series history. With a count of one ball and two strikes on him the twenty-seventh batter, Dale Mitchell, let a high and outside pitch pass. But the umpire, Babe Pinelli, understood better: He instantly assured a perfect game by calling strike three. As Gould puts it: 'A batter may not take a close pitch with so much on the line. Context matters. Truth is a circumstance, not a spot. . . . By long and recognized custom, by any concept of justice, Dale Mitchell had to swing at anything close. It was a strike—a strike high and outside. Babe Pinelli, umpiring his last game, ended with his finest, his most perceptive, his most truthful moment. Babe Pinelli, arbiter of history, walked into the locker room and cried.'[35] I have never followed a Muslim judge into chambers to see him (or nowadays sometimes her) cry, but I have seen them find, in one case after another, that context is truth, even if the parameters of truth are themselves portrayed as inviolate.

---

[35]   Gould (1985: 227).

If justice is central to the way that Muslims think of themselves it must also be noted that injustice plays no less central a role. Injustice (*jawr*) is often felt rather than articulated, and Arabs tend to believe, like Montaigne, that institutions, far from eradicating injustice, often provide a forum for its elaboration.[36] Justice, for most Arabs, can only be expected where face-to-face constraints allow reciprocity to work, whereas the state, as we have noted, is seen as *un*reciprocity incarnate. It is not necessary that 'injustice' be specified with as much precision as the concept of justice for it to have an enormous cultural and emotional effect. Veena Das has said that 'it is sufficient for societies to have an idea of evil; they don't have to have a clear image of the good.'[37] In a similar vein, people do not have to be able to specify all the features of injustice in order to have a sense of when it is present. Where international actions or local corruption lead to a felt sense of imbalance the personal offense that is taken is profound. Justice, to Arabs, is not, as Adam Smith had it for the West, the least of the virtues because it merely entails the avoidance of harm. Nor do Arabs see injustice as incapable of being rectified. What gives even the felt, not fully articulated, concept of injustice concreteness is, I believe, the idea that, even if a life has been lost or property irretrievably destroyed, the indispensable element of social life can indeed be restored—the pursuit of the 'great game' of reciprocity and ingratiation, obligation and negotiation by which the very process of human interaction, as divinely ordained, can and should proceed.[38]

Arabs believe that social life is a running imbalance of obligations but that it is not the imbalance that applies at any given time that matters but whether the process by which the moving sets of relationships are themselves formed has become unhinged. Stability comes not through stasis but through motion: Just as walking is a kind of constantly controlled falling so too life is a process of controlled imbalances. Orderliness is maintained by insuring the system of rectifying one imbalance with another. That is why power, even if momentarily concentrated, must be subject

---

[36]   The term jawr and its semantic range is elaborated in the political context of tyranny by Lewis, who says: 'The terms used for "tyranny," their synonyms and their antonyms, give some indication of how tyranny was perceived and defined in Muslim lands. The commonest term is *ẓulm*, which occurs very frequently in the Qur'an. . . . There it seems to have the broad general meaning of "misdeed," "wrongdoing," and hence "injustice." In post-Qur'ānic usage it is increasingly specialized in the latter sense, and is sometimes coupled with *jawr*, a word the primary meaning of which is "deviation," "straying from the path," whence also the derivative meaning of "wrongful or unjust treatment." A common messianic tradition speaks of a *mahdi*, a "divinely guided one," who in God's good time will come and "fill the earth with *'adl* and *qisṭ* as it is now filled with *ẓulm* and *jawr*" ' (Lewis (1988: 155, n. 30)). Even Saddam Hussein has made use of these terms when he called on 'the Arab nation' to 'correct the deviations of those who have deviated' by rising up against those Arab regimes that did not come to his support after the allied bombing raids of late 1998: 'Revolt, sons of the great Arab nation, against injustice and let your voices be heard' (Jehl (1999)).

[37]   Comment at conference on human rights, published as Hammoudi (2000).

[38]   Elizabeth Wolgast (1987) has thus argued that injustice is not secondary to justice in that it seeks to right the imbalance that has resulted from some inappropriate action; the wrong committed can never really be expunged, the scales cannot be set back to a pre-existing balance. But as is so often the case, culture can traverse logic, in the Arab case by rendering 'the game' itself the central artifact to be kept in working balance rather than any particular and momentary outcome.

to cross-cutting dispersal, why boundaries must be capable of being traversed, why bets are always hedged, why one always needs to know about everyone else's ever-changing contexts of relationship. To act justly is to get 'the game' back on track when it has been disrupted by some factor, like the predominance of money as the indispensable means of forming obligations, or the intrusion of outsiders whose economic or military action is, rightly or wrongly, thought to disrupt the system of negotiated indebtedness. There are, of course, winners and losers in the game, but it is important to bear in mind Ibn Khaldun's admonition that injustice can occur only when power is so concentrated that another can wreak total ruin on an opponent. Otherwise, the game is constructed so that no one who knows even minimally how to play should be completely destroyed: charity aids the momentary loser, family attachment retains some degree of support, and even enemies should not be crushed since they may be allies in the future.[39] Justice is the most essential, if indeterminate, of virtues for Arabs because it keeps open the quest for advantage and equivalence, a quest seen as central to both human nature and revealed orderliness in the world of reason and passion.

And this, ultimately, may help us to understand both the commonalities and the marked differences between Occidental and Arab concepts of justice. Where Westerners speak a language of rights and entitlements, Arabs speak a language of context and relationship; where Westerners tend to expect knowledge to reveal the order of things, Arabs see knowledge as the vehicle through which ties are formed. Justice flows from the reciprocal and equated relationships that knowledgeable people produce. And where Westerners tend to expect justice to be achieved in any given situation and for justice to be, at least ideally, something natural, something emanating from the innocent, many Arabs would probably agree with the somewhat more skeptical, if balanced, Moroccan saying that 'if the times are just, one day is for me and one day is against me.'[40] Nowhere, perhaps, do these features of Islamic thought come through with greater clarity and poignancy than in a tale told among the Berbers of the High Atlas Mountains of Morocco about how Justice and Injustice came to be separated for all time.

At the beginning of time Justice and Injustice lived as neighbors. One day Injustice proposed that Justice join him in a pilgrimage to the shrine of a saint. 'Prepare your provisions well,' Injustice said, 'for the voyage is a long one.' On the assigned day the travelers set out. During the daylight hours they made their way and in the evening each prepared his own meal from his provisions. Every evening, however, Injustice refrained from taking more than a few dates and a mouthful of

[39] Friedman notes the relation to the enemy in this passage about the Ottomans: 'The most enduring example of the gentle authoritarian tradition was that of the Ottoman Turks. . . . The more popular support the Ottoman rulers garnered through the ages, the more they sought to sustain their authoritarianism without resort to force, but instead by building bridges to key sectors of the societies they ruled, by allowing others to share in the spoils and by never totally vanquishing their opponents, but instead leaving them a way out so that they might one day be turned into friends' (Friedman (1989: 92)).

[40] Cited in Scelles-Millie and Khelifa (1966: 86).

water, and when Justice asked why he was not eating, Injustice simply replied that he was not very hungry. So it was for the entire outward voyage.

On the return trip Justice found himself short of food. On the first evening Injustice ate greedily from his store of honey and bread, meat and butter, offering nothing to his companion. Justice reproached him for acting so badly but Injustice only laughed at the naiveté of his friend. After another day of long, hot travel, Justice again awaited some gesture on the part of his companion, but none was forthcoming. Noticing his friend's weakened condition Injustice said: 'If you want to eat you must pay me, because I cannot feed you for nothing.' 'But I have nothing to give you,' replied Justice; 'I'll pay you when we arrive home.' Injustice refused, saying, 'You must pay me now since you want to eat now.' Justice asked the price that he would have to pay in order to eat, and Injustice replied: 'You must give me one of your eyes.' Justice's heart sank, but ultimately he decided to comply, reasoning that it was better for Justice to exist with only one eye than not to exist at all. The terms of the agreement were immediately executed. All the next day Justice stoutly resisted hunger and thirst, but by nightfall he could hold out no longer and ceded to Injustice his other eye in return for a bit of food. So it was that Justice became blind and wandered alone out into the desert.

The themes in this painful allegory replicate those in other domains of Islamic thought. Justice is, like all others, responsible for his own actions and their consequences. His plight is deeply personalized in much the same way that justice is an attribute of personhood rather than an abstract proposition. The lack of generosity of Injustice gives sharp emphasis to the Prophetic Tradition that says 'you can give an unjust law to a just judge, but you cannot give a just law to an unjust judge.' It is ironic, too, that it should be Injustice who scrupulously adheres to the Islamic prohibition against contracts for future performance and regards as unjust enrichment the failure to pay for something at the time of its delivery. Perhaps Justice is punished for agreeing to an unbargainable contract; perhaps Injustice gains only worldly ends and will ultimately suffer because, as the Quran says, 'the unjust have no patron and no helper.'[41]

Love, then, may be central to the way that Christianity has come to speak of itself and to establish a relationship among seemingly disconnected elements of mundane and extraordinary experience. But it is a concept around which people in the West, as heirs to its implications, find a constant swirl of ambivalence and imprecision. So, too, I think, justice serves for the Arabs as a focus for connecting disparate occurrences with the attempt to conduce interaction along predictable lines. In the context of working toward peace in various parts of the Middle East it is important to note how the Arabs measure, equate, and contextualize various proposals in terms of their own sense of justice and injustice. The Arabo-Islamic felt sense of justice is, in the end, neither vague nor indeterminable, but powerful for partaking of textual opacity

---

[41]   The Berber allegory appears in French translation in Souag (1976). The paragraph that follows the story has previously appeared in similar form in my earlier work (Rosen (1989a: 75–6)).

and relational concreteness. If every religion must balance the transparent and the opaque, and some tend more to one pole than the other, Islam has undoubtedly created a balance that centers on its own conceptualization of the just. Whether social justice comes to imply a redistribution of resources or power, whether personal justice comes to mean greater equality or lesser intrusion by the state, it is against this tangled, ambivalent, refractory, and transcendent feeling of justice that so many Muslims will continue to situate their expectations and their hopes. If, following Aristotle, it is wise that we fashion theories that are no more precise than the subject matter allows, it behooves us, in our own quest for mutual cooperation and forbearance, to comprehend the Arabs' felt sense of justice and to render it the full measure of our sympathy and understanding.

10

Muhammad's sociological jurisprudence

In recent years the disciplines of anthropology and history have drawn increasingly close to one another. Maitland had long ago said that ultimately anthropology would become history or nothing at all, which one might have thought must be true because by the time anthropologists manage to write up most of their field notes they actually are discussing history! Certainly one of the most exciting exercises that can be conducted involving anthropology and history is to use the one to interpolate the other, to read between the lines of the historical data with the insights afforded by direct fieldwork among the heirs to such traditions in order to test for connections that had previously escaped notice. Like an archaeologist who must stitch together the last bits of an artifact using a baseline of examples that seem to lie to either side, or like a pathologist who must sort through an array of examples to reconstruct the instant case from its categorical surround, the keystone to such interpolation lies in thoughtful comparison.

Being neither expert in early Arabic texts nor eager to play the role of mullah manqué I can cheerfully move back and forth across time taking as guidance for my speculations the wise admonition of the White Queen to Alice that 'it's a poor sort of memory that only works backwards.' And as one who is immune to charges of being a poor historian for being no historian at all, I can shamelessly attempt to use my field experience in the courts and cultures of contemporary North Africa to suggest a different reading of the earliest days of Islamic jurisprudence.

My interpretation necessarily differs from that of some more specialized scholars. The Western Orientalists who have studied the early Islamic period have contributed enormously to our understanding of this critical moment in history. But they were not immune to the theoretical and political promptings of their day. Theories of evolutionism and diffusionism current in the German scholarship of the turn of the twentieth century, coupled with a view of law based on Roman and continental experience, colored their interpretations of the role played by the Prophet as the builder of a system of law. Indeed, the standard view Orientalists promulgated was that anything worthy of the name law did not develop until more than a century after the Prophet's death. My challenge to that view is based on several premises that differ markedly from those of the Orientalists: I do not accept the civilians' view that law is a form of command embodied in statutes and regulated by professionals. Nor do I think that a sharp distinction between procedural and substantive law serves an understanding of all types of legal systems. And finally, I do not think that either law or jurisprudence is separable from the larger culture within which each operates and to which each is linked by ties of everyday assumption and common orientation. The fact that few Orientalists have ever studied an operative court in the Middle East is especially sad in this regard. For were they to do so they too might be struck by the enormous similarities between the contemporary and the historic, and might be more willing to reconsider their views of the past in the light of what they see in the present. Such interpolation can, of course, be only suggestive, but if we are to take seriously the possibility that the Prophet did indeed possess a jurisprudential theory that was vital to the success and development of the movement he began, then reading between the lines may point out possibilities that earlier assessments have failed to consider. It is toward that end that we must, therefore, begin by understanding in some detail how earlier approaches to this problem may have blinded us to the Prophet's contribution to a social theory of law.

Students of Islamic law have a rather odd habit: They tend to leave the Prophet himself out of consideration when analyzing the development of Islamic law. To a certain extent this is understandable. Muhammad did not explicitly portray himself as a systematizer of a legal system nor is the voice of the Quran predominantly that of a lawgiver.[1] Indeed since the Prophet is regarded by believers as having been but the unlettered hand through whom Allah spoke to humankind, the suggestion that the Quran actually represents the voice or handiwork of any human being is tantamount to unbelief.[2] And though the practices of the Prophet during his lifetime were later to be taken up as a source of law itself, these authenticated acts and utterances have neither the status of Quranic prescription nor that of indisputable law.

While believers have, for reasons of faith, largely avoided consideration of Muhammad as the formulator of law, Western scholars have looked for the precipitation of an Islamic legal system in those artifacts—statutes, cases, courts, and commentaries—through which organized law is said to exist. The received wisdom of these Western scholars has been that Islamic law did not take shape until, nearly a century and a half after the Prophet's death, the sources of law were regularized by al-Shafi'i and various schools of legal thought were developed which gave both these sources and their methods of implementation an institutional structure. This view, largely associated with the work of Joseph Schacht, sometimes goes so far as to suggest that the stories concerning the words and habits of the Prophet in his lifetime were invented by a later age solely in order to serve as a source of political and

---

[1] Scholars disagree as to how much legislation the Quran actually contains. To some the count is about 10 percent of the 6,237 verses; to others the count is only 200 verses, 70 of which deal with family and civil law, 10 with constitutional law, 13 with jurisdiction and procedure, 10 with economic and financial matters, and 25 with international relations. Compare Lippman et al. (1988) with Khan (1983). Others argue that since the verses that deal with law are longer than most other verses in the Quran, the count should be based on length not number of verses. However one counts, it is broadly agreed among Orientalists that the tone of the Quran is not predominantly that of a legislative text and that, religious duties aside, a relatively small proportion of the text concerns law.

[2] To believing Muslims the Quran, as the word of God, is completely separable from the words and deeds of the Prophet himself. However, inasmuch as the Prophet continues the voice of the Quran and is seen by believers as acting consistently with the Quran, I shall speak of the jurisprudence of the Quran and that of the Prophet as continuous and consistent without in any way wishing to imply either that the latter was acting separately from the spirit of the Quran or that the Quran represents the voice of anyone but Allah.

legal unification.[3] Some writers maintain that the Prophet possessed no concern with formal law but only with the articulation of a moral and spiritual message.[4] Others have argued that the Prophet realized after his move from Mecca to Medina that he was often being called upon to serve in a legal role and could no longer fail to embrace law within the ambit of the religious without otherwise imperiling the fledgling religious/political community of Islam. Yet even this viewpoint, asserted with great force by S. D. Goitein, only credits the Prophet with concern for the religious implications of law and denies any distinctively legal vision to the Prophet's religious program.[5]

By contrast I would like to suggest that there is indeed a legal—indeed, a jurisprudential—vision present in the Quran and in what we know of the Prophet's own orientations. It is not simply derivative of other systems of law[6] nor does it depend on replacing the believer's acceptance of the Quran as the direct word of God with a predominantly secular view of that text. Rather I want to suggest that there runs through all those artifacts touched by the Prophet himself a view of society and its constitutive forces that is deeply concerned with law and which, taken as a whole, may be thought of as a kind of sociological jurisprudence. Its most essential ingredients may even be described by a set of juridical postulates that are, at every point, also statements about the nature of human nature and human social arrangements. Indeed, as I will try to indicate, this jurisprudential vision both served to consolidate the changes wrought by the advent of Islam and established an orientation which, in theme-and-variation ways, continues to inform much of Islamic life to the present day.

* * *

The vision of society represented in the Quran and in the Prophet's utterances and acts is essentially personalistic and relational. Morality and practice are conjoined inasmuch as the individual, as the momentary embodiment of a set of negotiated social attachments, is called upon to engage in reciprocal ties to others that do not overstep what the Quran repeatedly calls 'the bounds of God,' the limited set of obligations imposed by Allah. Thus in the early years of Islam, according to Wilfred Cantwell Smith, we do not find the term for law, *shari'a*, used in the sense of a code of laws but in its verbal form indicating a process, an activity, through which the immediacy of the moral is acknowledged and incorporated into one's own character through its involvement in the guidance of interpersonal relations.[7]

Everything conduces to this emphasis on the person as the fundamental unit of a

---

[3] See Schacht (1950); Schacht (1974). An extreme version even maintains that: 'The ancients have all had their particular laws, yet a science of law, abstract in nature, and distinct from laws and codes, does not seem ever to have been thought of before the renown [*sic*] Moslem jurist, Al-Shafi'i [born AD 767, AH 150]' (Dallal (1986: 2)).

[4] See, e.g., Hassan (1970: 12 ff.); Smith (1965: 593); and Savory (1976: 60).

[5] Goitein (1960).　　　　　　　　[6] See Crone (1987).　　　　　　　　[7] Smith (1965).

moral society—from the vision of morality as reason embodied, to the view of society as revelation enacted. Man is seen as a reasoning creature, one who must utilize his God-given powers to arrange his ties effectively in the world. As Fazlur Rahman put it: '[A]ll violation of morality for the Qur'an is equally a violation of reason.'[8] It is in that sense, as Walther Braune said, that God's law accords with human revelation: Society and community are merged in this vision, with the individual person thus serving as the best representative for the ideals of the community as a whole.[9] From the central Quranic idea that 'no man bears the burden of another' one sees that the obligations imposed by Allah leave great scope for the elaboration of one's own relationships with others. In one's direct dealings with Allah it is intention that matters: 'Deeds are judged according to intentions,' says a Tradition of the Prophet, 'each man's accounts are drawn up according to his intentions.'[10] Yet even intentions are discernible through one's situated ties. If you know a man's background, connections, and ways of dealing with others you can tell his intentions: God, knowing these features to the full, knows even those intentions that encroach on the bounds He has set forth. And these intentions receive both regularity and embodiment in the use of oaths, contracts, and the testimony of witnesses.

Throughout the Quran considerable attention is given to the taking of oaths. Often the reference is to oaths taken *vis-à-vis* God, but repeatedly the impact of oaths on God and man alike is blurred, the implication being that an oath affecting the one is not without impact on the other. 'Take not your oaths as mere mutual deceit,' says the Quran (Sura XVI: 96), 'lest any foot should slip after it has stood firm, and you should taste evil.'[11] Oaths take utterances out of the realm of ordinary discourse—the casual elicitation of a position from which bargaining might begin, the trial expression of a possible relation—and bring them into the realm of the true where they can be assessed as true. Covenant and contract are much more than metaphor in the Quran: They are fundamental relational bonds among reasoning beings which, provided they do not overstep divine ordinance, are within the responsibility of humankind to construct.

Neither the Quran nor the later accepted traditions of the Prophet are terribly detailed about which contractual arrangements are acceptable or forbidden.[12] Yet the absence of such a code should not be read to imply the absence of a jurisprudence of contract. As we have seen, not only is the maintenance of one's commitments central to moral stature, but since reliability inheres in the furtherance of one's word, moral duty and the preservation of social harmony find their juncture in the person who honors his undertakings. Moreover, the Quran incorporates certain propositions of contract law which, even if not in the form of legislation, clearly involve a set of

---

[8] Rahman (n.d.: 16).
[9] I am indebted to Babar Johansen for bringing this to my attention.
[10] See the elaboration of this and similar Traditions in Goldziher (1981: 42).
[11] On examples of oath procedures in Islamic law, see Wigmore (1941: 220–1).
[12] The Quran is, however, explicit about the need to write down contractual commitments and the need to use witnesses to verify them. See the important passage at Sura II: 282–4.

juridical postulates. Reciprocity is constantly evoked as a central idiom of relationship, an idiom which, when coupled with the emphasis on reason, leads to the idea
that one who suffers for not having sought the knowledge by which he could protect
himself may not later complain that someone took advantage of him. Thus, as we
have seen, it is unjust enrichment, not simply usury, of which Islam disapproves
because it is essential to Prophetic jurisprudence that social relations and the dispersal of power not be permanently skewed by disproportionate control of knowledge.
The emphasis on the reliable and knowledgeable man of social action becomes
particularly important where truth must be established by witnesses.

In Islam, from its earliest times, it is clear that proof depends far more on who it
is that says a thing is so than on what may be determined independent of who asserts
it. But where this could lead to considerable inequality based on the birth or rank of
the witness, the Quran makes clear that such standing is neither inherited nor fixed.
Rather, each person must show, through the continual servicing of his commitments,
that he is indeed true to his word. By emphasizing the relational legitimization of a
witness—his believability based on adherence to his social bonds—the Quran underscores social ties as the basis for a jurisprudential ethic. Indeed, having once established that it is the person who is to be assessed for the believable, Islam sustained a
discourse, already current in pre-Islamic times, from which an elaborate system of
person perception could be worked out. To this day one finds that Islamic judicial
practice is rich in techniques for determining a person's relationships and hence his
credibility while being rather poorly developed in terms of assessing facts independent of persons.

It is here, too, that the Prophet's emphasis on the concept of 'trust' also figures
prominently. Trust—*amana*—really means to demonstrate reliability, standing by
your commitments. It is intimately related to the idea of a person being, in no small
part, the embodiment of his word—of his utterance being so fraught with consequence to relationships that its very articulation becomes, indeed *is*, that most
concrete form of reality, the effect it has on the ties among reasoning creatures.[13]
God himself is trustworthy because His inimical word has, among other things,
created a context for human interaction: A man or woman is trustworthy for so
constructing his or her obligations that a mere utterance furthers those obligations
by raising confidence in the predictability of their social implications. There is law
in this, particularly in such institutionalized forms as the legal guarantor of a transaction (*damen*), or the role played by the leader of a group of craftsmen whose word
affects the repute of his trade (*amin*). There is also law in this Prophetic concept of
trust in that it knits together the concept of the person as configured relationship
with the community as elaborated personhood, and thus constitutes a critical
jurisprudential grounding for the leap of confidence for those who recognize in
themselves the tension that must always exist between the natural drive for advantage and the security of mutual benefit.

---

[13] This argument is elaborated in Meeker (1979).

Moreover, I strongly suspect that the Prophet himself knew perfectly well what Ibn Khaldun was to elaborate much later, that within tribes—and even more so within cities—not only must oaths bind men into publicly acknowledged bonds of trust but the treachery of violating obligations must be blunted by allowing religiously sanctioned mechanisms for escaping them. Ernest Gellner is right to say that 'treason . . . maintains equilibrium through realignment,' and that, by cloaking in piety and reverence the refusal to take or support an oath, dispersal of power itself may be reinforced.[14] The Prophet, I think, understood both the urban and tribal variants on such trust and encouraged both local practice and the legal articulation of such flexibility as an integral part of his own jurisprudence.

We can see this emphasis on the socially constructed person as the focus of a jurisprudential attitude when we look at some of the legal issues about which the Quran is actually quite explicit. Consider the all-important issue of inheritance. Along with marriage, inheritance is one of the few legal relationships the Quran and the Prophet address directly: There is even a saying that half of all the knowledge worth possessing is that which concerns inheritance. For a long time Western scholars believed that the emphasis given by Islamic law to the shares that different categories of relatives should receive represented the practice at the time of the Prophet, as well as the spirit of the passages concerning inheritance in the Quran itself. David Powers, however, has argued that this focus actually represents a shift by the Prophet's successors away from the intent and practice of the Prophet's own day, when the emphasis was actually on testamentary disposition and the classification of heirs without reference to fixed shares.[15] Such an argument makes considerable sense when we realize how consonant this personalistic emphasis is with other aspects of Quranic jurisprudence. For just as the use of contracts, witnesses, oaths, and intent all focus on the relational person who, in the expression of his reasoning powers, gives effect to the moral requirements of Islam, so, too, one would readily expect that the transmission of property might be within the control of individuals whose personal identity turns on the resources they use to establish a voice in the world. Moreover, as we shall see, by not allowing inheritance to be controlled by rules of partition dependent on social category, property—like power—can be dispersed across generations. The irony, however, is that this change in the original intent of Islamic inheritance law may well have been connected to another key feature of Muhammad's jurisprudence, namely the role of custom.

In the form set by al-Shafi'i, custom does not constitute a source of Islamic law. As a result, scholars have largely ignored custom or downgraded it to a very subservient place. But there is much in the Quran and the acts of the Prophet to suggest, to the contrary, that custom does not warrant great emphasis precisely because of its dominance, not its subservience, in the Islamic jurisprudential ethic. Not only does the Quran say that anything which does not violate the bounds of God is permissible, but it is precisely custom that fills up this opening with particular content. And that

[14] Gellner (1988: 146).　　[15] Powers (1986).

content, being the expression of those features of personal forms of relationship characteristic of a given region, acquires its legitimacy both as commonsense features of person perception and as juridically cognizable propositions. Thus by making local custom an integral part of Islamic jurisprudence, rather than a separable source of it, the Quran and the Prophet embrace the local in the religiously universal and add credence to both.

This emphasis on the local as integral to the universal is consonant with much of the history of Arab social life and law. Power is localized and dispersed, with each individual constituting a possible nodal point, through any of a number of mechanisms, for creating a constellation of dependants around him or her self. One does not expect, therefore, justice to be an integral feature of the state; rather it is particular reliable persons, whether laymen or jurists, who may embody the features of the just. Appellate structures have no necessary place in such a scheme because knowledge and piety do not have to lead to a specific result, provided they partake of a shared mode of using reason and assessing consequences to construct a socially useful approach.[16]

Indeed, the jurisprudence of the Quran supports just such diversity of opinion. There is a famous Arab saying that 'the person who does not understand divergence in doctrine has not caught the true scent of jurisprudence.' So, too, the saying that 'disagreement among my people is a mercy': Such an ethos underscores the non-centralization of power that each of these utterances supports. This tolerance for a variety of viewpoints on matters of substance is, moreover, consonant with the Prophet's emphasis on allowing a range of localized relationships to be regarded as Islamic rather than as separable from Islam. But it also emphasizes an equally positive commitment to pushing the resolution of differences down to the level of the local where broader guidelines of social relationship supported by Prophetic endorsement could take hold. Process became more important than substantive law but was no less definite or central to a jurisprudential vision for being diverse, local, and circumstantial in its articulation and impact.

Similarly, one can see quite clearly in the earliest sources of Islamic thought the styles of reasoning that would later receive institutionalized embodiment by the various schools of Islamic law. Reasoning by analogy, *qiyas*, already evident in the Quran, fits with other aspects of the sociological jurisprudence of the day inasmuch as it

---

[16] Different results, whether in cases or readings of text, are supportable if the process of reasoning is similar. Writing about how a believer is to contend with disagreement among those knowledgeable in the law, James White says: 'The traditional Muslim answer has been that all of the several readings of a text are valid, notwithstanding their inconsistency, if they are each reached by a mind diligently engaged, in good faith, in a search for its meaning. The judge, or the believer, can follow any of them and still follow the law: but his choice too must arise from a good-faith search for meaning, within his capacities. A world of difference is thus created; it is kept from the prison-house of "single meanings"—of thinking that meanings translate directly from text to text—by honest attention to language, to particularity of phrase and context; it is kept from the chaos of indifferent relativism—of thinking that nothing can be known or understood, no common values held—by a principle of humility and sincerity, or what I would call the ethic of the translator' (White (1990: 268)).

contributes to the assessment of the equivalence of two entities being compared and thus does not privilege the one without granting some legitimacy to the other. A commentator of the first century after the Prophet's death wrote: 'It is said that justice means the rating of a thing as equal to a thing of another kind so as to make it like the latter.'[17] By seeking to equate entities as a way of extending propositions from familiar to unfamiliar circumstances early Islamic jurisprudence acknowledged both the legitimacy of alternative approaches and the capacity of local practice to fill in the legally unknown with the socially recognizable. Analogic reasoning, among other devices, is particularly suited to this equivalizing ethos.

Indeed from earliest times adjudication—with its implication of winning and losing, the favoring of one party over another—was by no means the preferred model for the resolution of differences. The Quran speaks of the Believers as a people of the middle (Sura II: 137), and the image is constantly invoked of mediation and inter-stitial relationships as most appropriate to handling disputes.[18] The Prophet himself clearly preferred the role of mediator, though particularly after the move to Medina he found it necessary to offer authoritative opinions affecting an increasingly diverse group of followers. Yet the emphasis is quite definitely on the retention of social order—the preservation of society against chaos (*fitna*)—rather than the elaboration of a series of juridical propositions. In that social reinforcement, that process of placing people back into locally sanctioned relationships with one another, the Quran and the Prophet set a clear jurisprudential tone. Subsequent judges, relying on this ethos, can, therefore, try to rebalance the reciprocity of relationships that the state may break; they can right the balance for the community as a whole by drawing on custom and reason to place people back in a position of working out their permissible relations peaceably.

Mediation was also consonant with another value that may well take its lead from tribal organization. The politico-religious jurisprudence of the early Islamic period favored the dispersal of power. This may seem odd given the fact that the Prophet clearly wished to overcome local loyalties and his successors sought to establish a polity that would embrace very extensive territories. In fact these two elements are not incompatible in the Islamic conception of power. For the central state was to exercise only relatively limited authority, while much of the legal realm was dependent on the local. The equalizing forces of Islamic thought—the emphasis on learning as the only basis for admiration, the assertion that 'a difference is not a distinction,' the absence of hierarchy (whether of ruler or of appellate judge)—conduce to an ethos of dispersed power. Many of the institutions of tribal organization—and even, at times, of the towns—further insured that too much power would not remain in too few hands for too long without challengers being encouraged and legitimized. This may even connect to the inheritance system, as we saw, insofar as

---

[17] Quoted from an opinion solicited by the Caliph ʿAbd al-Malik by Saʿid Ibn Jubayr, in Khadduri (1984: 8).

[18] See, e.g., the passage in the Quran at Sura IV: 65, and the discussion in Serjeant (1978: 1–2).

the avoidance of exclusive reliance on fixed partible inheritance encourages the redistribution of wealth and property. In terms of jurisprudence we can see, then, that the silence of the Quran and the Prophet on detailed issues of law does not necessarily mean the absence of a legal system: Rather it may mean that all the supporting elements—of local custom, personalistic responsibility, bargained-for relationships—are part of a concrete emphasis on dispersed power within the community of believers and maintenance of common identity at the level of the religiously shared.

This interpretation of the Prophet's sociological jurisprudence—as intensely personalistic, relational, and concrete—is consistent with what is known about the history of this formative period. The Prophet had sought to persuade the people of Mecca to give priority to religious identity over that of kin-based groupings. Such an orientation was increasingly consistent with the changes occurring in their own society and economy. Like the Prophet himself, the leaders of Meccan society were merchants and their commercial relations had already begun to take precedence over their actual and fictive ties of kinship. The inhabitants of Mecca, most of them members of the Quraysh tribe, even appear to have given special status in the pre-Islamic period to that god, whom they called Allah, who was the guardian of non-kin social relationships.[19] Unable to convince the Meccans of his assertions about the supernatural, Muhammad accepted the invitation of the people of Yathrib (later called Medina), whose internal bickering cried out for a credible mediator, to move to their city. The message that the Prophet carried to them, and his quick victories against the Meccan merchants, reinforced the power of his emphasis on a religiously based polity that transcended kinship attachments.[20] When the final victory came over Mecca itself he was thus able to join two locales in both of which the message of strength through affiliation above the level of kinship was proved by worldly accomplishment.

In such a social, economic, and political environment the emphasis on a jurisprudence of personalism could thus find fertile support. Muhammad, it can be argued, had not formed a state in which ties of tribe or locality had been rendered subservient to a superordinate entity. Rather, the early Islamic polity was more like a super-tribe, in both the urban and desert regions, in one key respect: In both locations the form of kinship attachment had already become one of intense personalism. That is to say, it was the person as an increasingly separable entity, negotiating commercial arrangements and their attendant social ties, who was becoming the key unit of society, not the tribe or segments thereof. Personalism should not, of course, be confused with individualism; in many respects it is one of its contraries. For a personalistic orientation stresses the socially situated and contextually constructed embodiment of a set of traits and ties attributed to one by others: Each person is not the central moral unit capable of fashioning himself outside of such bonds. In an environment of such personalism it is imperative to garner the attachments and respect of others, rather

---

[19] Wolf (1951: 338–9).
[20] See generally for this period the account in Burton (1994: 1–16).

than to depend on kinship or a separable domain of interiority as the hallmark of one's identity. Just as the universalizing religion that nevertheless permitted many local practices to be incorporated as Islamic strengthened the appeal of Islam without threatening customary actions, so, too, a jurisprudence that emphasized the negotiating and contextualized person suited the developing political form Islam was taking. The Prophet's sociological jurisprudence, no less than other creative aspects of the religion he announced and enacted, did have to await later institutionalization to become a critical factor in Islamic life: There was no single birth hour of Islamic law, and it may have taken some time, following his death, for the Prophet's message to be converted into a form of law of the type that is recognizable to later European scholars. But for the people of his own times, and for the comparativist who is used to seeing legal systems that do not match Western models, the jurisprudence of the Prophet's own day has all the hallmarks of a distinct system of law. The forms were to be elaborated in the century or two following his death, and to be revised throughout Islamic times. But a definite style of sociological jurisprudence had already been exemplified by the Prophet in his own time. By reading back from its current manifestations and our comparative understanding of similar legal forms we can, perhaps, recapture some of the legal system to which later scholarship has been insufficiently attentive.

* * *

In sum, the vision of the Quran and of the Prophet is one that gives unusual stress to the role of the socially constructed person as the locus of moral and religious responsibility. That factor, as a number of scholars have argued, may have contributed to the failure of Islamic law to develop a notion of the legal personality, particular corporate forms, or a concept of the community as a legal entity.[21] But this ethic also had, perhaps, the purpose of maintaining both a moral emphasis on each person and of reinforcing a legal ethic—indeed a legal system—that was resolutely local, personalistic, and consonant with an image of the person that Islam sought to reinforce. What Marshall Hodgson has called 'shari'a mindedness'—the idealization of Prophetic practice by eighth-century legalists who wanted to extend the customs of Medina to Islam as a whole—has never succeeded in replacing a deeper jurisprudence that places the person in a definite scheme of practical ethics based on relationships and individual effort.[22] If, as the Tradition says, the Prophet was sent to further the principles of good character, and if such character was itself seen in terms of one's relationships with others, then the Prophet's jurisprudential vision was no less central to his mission than his broader message of the community of believers.[23]

The Islam of the Prophet's own day thus exemplifies not merely a social and moral tone that could later be given legal form, but is itself a legal system, a jurisprudence

---

[21] See, e.g., Ruthven (1984: 176–8). [22] See Hodgson (1974).
[23] On this tradition see Khadduri (1984: 141).

of social relationship based on assumptions about human reason and the proper dispersion of power. There is no 'epistemological black hole' in Islamic jurisprudence, but perhaps a linkage of a social and a jurisprudential vision, one in which the starting point is not rules but processes, not codifications but the articulation and enactment of acceptable guidelines, not antecedent precepts but the expression through concrete consequences of a vision of human nature and human relationships.[24] Islamic law is not a natural law, but a law naturalized—a concept of man as a juridical entity whose natural tendencies may be incorporated into a system that disperses power, localizes process, and personalizes events. It is a system that acknowledges that passing acquaintance may suffice for enduring relationships and that neither laws nor judgments will be true to the nature of humankind if they are more precise than the modes by which relationships themselves are formed and re-formed. Like an endless series of moves in chess—itself adjudged in the early years of Islam as more theologically correct than any game of chance—it is unnecessary to specify each possibility with a rule or to change the overall structure for the variety of possible moves to remain endlessly alluring.

Given this perspective the implications for present-day Islamic law and society are not without their own ironic twists. Fundamentalists, for example, find themselves in a particular bind: They cannot revise the shari'a even though, if the above argument is correct, the shari'a was never intended as a settled body of doctrine but as a socially oriented, chaos-reducing, locality-reinforcing means of producing morality and civility. If they focus on doctrinal consistency, fundamentalists would be changing the central thrust of the shari'a; if they focus on social consequence, they appear to be diluting the shari'a in the face of changeable custom. It is thus doubly ironic that change in the law of many Islamic countries may actually be in the hands of moderate regimes which can afford to maintain the resolutely local aspects of procedure and consequence while still propounding uniform codes that lay no claim to changing the holy law. Asian Muslims in particular have come to reify the shari'a as much as any Orientalist, converting the law into a symbol of ethnic identification. But even they, like their co-religionists in the Arab states, may well continue to regard Islamic law as a cosmological representation as much as a body of legal guidance. And when they do so they will actually be joining the highly localized and personalistic elements of their faith with the most rarefied and abstract ones—a process that the Prophet, as the masterful articulator of a theory of law and society, first announced over 1,300 years ago.

[24] The reference to 'an epistemological black hole' is attributed to Colin Imber in Asmal (1998: 255–6). See also Asmal's discussion, pp. 253–64, where he also cites the presumption that rules are the starting point of law in the work of Imber (1997: 33) and Schacht (1964). See also Calder (1993), and my review of his book in Rosen (1995f).

11

Private thoughts, public utterances: Law, privacy, and the consequences for community

Several years ago I was asked to give a talk at a panel of law school teachers on the regulation of speech and the concept of toleration in various cultures of the world. As I began to work through the ways in which Islamic law, in both classical and modern times, has come to handle blasphemy and heresy, slander and defamation, political and commercial speech, I began to grow increasingly uncomfortable. These categories, for which I could readily find analogs in the Muslim world, nevertheless did not seem to capture the central axes along which the people themselves appeared to be making distinctions. The more I spoke with people in the Middle East and the more I read back into the literature, the more it seemed that I was not really embarking on a study of particular forms of sanctioned speech, an isolated concept of toleration, or even the relation of the state to individual utterance. Instead, the categories that were being employed coalesced around the public and the private.

Just as Westerners know that Islam frowns on charging interest for loans, but do not necessarily know that usury is regarded by Muslims as only one instance of a larger category of unjust enrichment, so, too, the themes of the public and the private appear as the more inclusive categories along which are arrayed not only specific forms of speech but a broader conceptualization of the effect that utterances may have in the world. Since it is the degree of publicity of certain acts, rather than the acts themselves, that is crucial, the connections to the social consequences of inappropriate speech render certain legal and moral propositions, which appear internally contradictory, much more comprehensible. Through the example of slander one comes round to the role of speech in the construction of the person, and through both to the ways in which the public and the private are understood to interact in life and law.

The history of the private life, while increasingly well developed in studies of European history, remains to be fully explored for the societies of North Africa and the Middle East. S. D. Goitein's magisterial analysis of the Geniza documents, that rich archive of commercial and personal correspondence from the eleventh to the thirteenth centuries, has given us our most significant insight into aspects of life not otherwise captured in official documents.[1] Similarly, the archives of the Ottoman empire have contributed significantly to our understanding of everyday life in the history of the Middle East.[2] We can also further our understanding of both historical and contemporary materials that touch on the ways in which the private and the

---

[1]   See, e.g., Goitein (1967–83).   [2]   See, e.g., Gerber (1994); Tucker (1998).

public have intersected by reading the legal materials that are available in the light of our broader interpretation of the social life of the area.

From the outset it is necessary to be clear about what is meant, for the purposes of this chapter, by 'the private life' and to acknowledge the risks of transferring such categories across cultures and periods of time. My concern here is to take the idea of the socially constructed person in Moroccan society, as I have come to understand it, and to explore some of the different domains in which the world outside of such a person impinges, bounds, identifies, and even threatens him or her. How, one asks, does society offer protection, recompense, or moral support for the intrusion that has occurred? Whether it is in attitudes towards one's own body and the way others, including the state, affect it; in the arrangement of one's dwelling place so that the free play of the person may be given room to develop; or in the kinds of permissible or impermissible utterances that may be made about oneself or the groups with which one is identified, the law affords a useful entreé to an understanding of the bounds and qualities of a people's sense of the private and the public.

To the criticism that notions of 'private' and 'public' may be ethnocentric categories to employ in the first place there are, I believe, two main answers to be offered. The first is supplied by Georges Duby: In response to the question whether it is legitimate to apply the nineteenth-century notion of 'privacy' and 'the private life' to the life of the Middle Ages, Duby writes:

> All things considered, I believe the question can be answered in the affirmative. It was no more legitimate for historians to apply, say, the concept of class struggle to the feudal era, yet it has proved undeniably useful that they have done so. The exercise not only showed how the concept needed to be refined but, more important, clarified the nature of power relations in an archaic social system, in particular those relations that had nothing to do with class conflict. Hence we have not hesitated to use the concept of private life, anachronistic as it may be. We have attempted to identify the dividing line between what people in medieval society considered private and what they did not, and to isolate that sphere of social relations corresponding to what we nowadays call 'private life.'[3]

Secondly, in the case of Arab culture and law there is a very clearly developed concept of the private which makes comparison to the Western concept appropriate. It is, however, one whose qualities and implications carry quite different overtones as we move from one context of a person's social and religious involvement to another, but it is not as if we were applying a notion that was utterly foreign to the culture under study. Indeed, the legal aspects of regulating life in different zones of interpersonal relationship turn, in no small part, on a highly refined sense of what shall be regarded as 'public' or 'private' in the local context.

Thus the task that faces us is, in part, one of ferreting out the boundaries and the criteria by which the logic of the public and the private have come to be conceptualized in this part of the world. If, as I shall try to argue, there is no bright line that separates the private and the public, the person and the state, this does not mean that the

---

[3] Duby (1988: ix).

categories do not exist or that there are no organizing principles by which each domain takes on identifying aspects. Rather, as in other realms of Arab social and cultural life, a series of cross-cutting conceptualizations inform both domains and, by this very quality, give substance to both. The job of the analyst, in such a kaleidoscopic universe, thus becomes one of sorting out the principles by which available elements take on a limited array of recognizably Arab/Moroccan formulations, and to consider what these organizing principles can tell us about the implications that resultant forms have for the broader course of the private and public culture of the people whose lives they characterize. Toward this end I want to consider two main areas in which the private and the public intersect, namely, personal slander and group responsibility.

SLANDER AND DEFAMATION IN ISLAMIC LAW

From its very inception Islam has been deeply concerned about slander. In one of its most significant passages on the subject the Quran (XLIX: 11–12) states:

> O believers, let not any people
> scoff at another people who may be
> better than they; neither let women
> scoff at women who may be better
> than themselves. And find not fault
> with one another, neither revile one
> another by nicknames. An evil name
> is ungodliness after belief. And
> whoso repents not, those—they are
> the evildoers.

> O believers, eschew much suspicion;
> some suspicion is a sin. And do not
> spy, neither backbite one another;
> would any of you like to eat the
> flesh of his brother dead? You would
> abominate it. And fear you God;
> assuredly God turns, and He is
> All-compassionate.[4]

Two dangers thus attach to slander: First, the individual by his or her own utterance simultaneously acts against the will of God, thus giving evidence of unbelief, and, secondly, this kind of act undermines the unity and identity of the community of believers itself.[5] In this regard the Quranic passages cited above are striking for a

---

[4] See also the passages on fornication and slanderous charges of fornication at Quran XXIV: 2–19. In another important passage (XXXIII: 58) the Quran states: 'And those who hurt through slander the believing men and women undeservedly, they bear the guilt of slander and manifest sin' (translation used in Ally (1990: 28)).

[5] See Izutsu (1966: 161), as well as his overall discussion of the concept of *kufr* at pp. 119–77.

number of reasons. In the larger context of admonishing believers not to fight with one another the Quran equates one's own self with others: 'And find not fault with one another' is also translated as 'Do not slander yourselves,'[6] the implication being that what one does to another believer in this regard is adverse to oneself. Distinctions by social group or category are also not to be used slanderously. And in a characteristic style of argumentation this point is made to apply *even if* those mocked are better than one's own group.[7] Thus the practice of adverse comment is equated with personal sin, in the Islamic sense of being tantamount to unbelief rather than a state of individual iniquity, a state which, in turn, is inseparable from adverse social consequences.[8]

The specific terms used in the sources matter a good deal here. The Arabic term translated as 'backbiting' is *ghiba*. It comes from a root that means 'to be absent,' 'swallowed up,' 'concealed,' and hence 'to use someone's absence for maligning him,' 'to slander,' 'backbite,' or 'engage in calumny.' In the Quranic context it clearly means to call attention to one's own lack of attachment to the believing community by such an act; in the context of the determination of valid Traditions (*hadīth*) of the Prophet's own deeds and words it may imply a kind of character assassination of the transmitter himself.[9] Most intriguing, however, is the relation the term and its uses imply about the privacy and publicity of the utterance and its consequences.

Slander is, almost by definition, an adverse comment about another that is made public. Societies and legal systems vary in their perception of the seriousness of the utterance or writing and the extent to which it must be made 'public' in order to be sanctioned. In American law, for example, slander is the 'publication' (however communicated) in a non-privileged relationship (such as to a clergyman, doctor, or spouse) that calls into question the reputation or legality of another's conduct. In Islam 'publication' consists not of allowing any non-privileged third party to read or hear the remark but for it to be purveyed in such a way that virtually anyone could have access to it. Thus a wider public is imagined, a wider community of affected persons, indeed a wider collectivity taken as a single entity. For these reasons the relation of public and private take on a somewhat different configuration than in many other cultures.

In the Islamic conception slander crosses a subtle yet extremely important boundary between the private and the public, the realm of individual consequence and the realm of social consequence. As we have seen, the Islamic idea of sin already crosses these conceptual bounds drawn in Western thought by equating personal transgression with social harm. The connection is made quite explicit in a wide range of Prophetic Traditions and contemporary social and legal practices. In one such Tradition the Prophet reportedly says: 'If what you say of him is true it is backbiting

  [6] See Al-Qaradawi (1985).
  [7] On this style of argument, which he calls *trajetio ad absurdum*, see Lewis (1970: 19–20). For an application of this concept to Jews and women in Morocco, see Rosen (1984: 159 and 178).
  [8] See Izutsu (1966: 21).   [9] Ziadeh (1990: 88).

and if it is not true you have slandered him.'[10] We will see the legal distinction involved here in a moment: The sociological component appears to be that truth is not a defense against the adverse implications of the utterance—the harm that such a statement can do when made public. In a particularly famous saying we are told that 'God loves those who hide their sins.' This statement, which Westerners at times have misunderstood as a license for Muslim hypocrisy, in fact underscores the social harm that occurs when a person's immoral acts create adverse consequences for others. God will certainly punish sins—the Quran could not be more clear on the matter—but He would not have them punished in such a way as to further injure the community as a whole. The consequentialist thrust of backbiting and of slander thus takes a crucial, if not pre-eminent, place in Muslim culture because such utterances can readily lead to the blurring of personal sin and social needs, to unbelief in the tenets of the community of belief, and hence to social chaos.

Slander, as compared to generalized backbiting, has a more distinct place in Islamic jurisprudence: Slander is, in a sense, that form of backbiting which is so serious as to require legal sanction. Slander falls into several categories, but in general it constitutes an utterance which, whether true or not, calls into question the reputation of a respectable person essentially by accusing that person of an act which would be punishable under Islamic law. The archetypal instance is that given in the verses of the Quran that precede those cited above (Sura XXIV: 4–9), in which a woman is accused of adultery without four eyewitnesses being able to verify the accusation. Such a slander (*khadf*), unsupported by the necessary witnesses, is regarded by most schools of Islamic law as a private right carrying a non-discretionary punishment (*hadd*) which the slandered party, or his heir, may choose to enforce or ignore.[11] A hadith says that the Prophet condemned 'slander of chaste but indiscreet women,'[12] thus suggesting that both truth and publicity are requisite for a charge to escape characterization as slander. Yet if the act involved was so notorious as to be witnessed by four people it is clear that the element of social harm is a critical aspect of any such accusation. Thus notwithstanding the assertion by some thinkers of the consequences for one's own

---

[10] Cited in Al-Qaradawi (1985). This distinction is utilized in the following instruction from an Ibadi lawbook of the 12th cent.:

[Student:] What if a man addresses another man by his nickname which he doesn't like?
[Teacher:] He's punished.
[Student:] And what if he says 'You're no Arab, you're a non-Arab'?
[Teacher:] He's punished.
[Student:] And if he says to a man 'Son of a Zanji woman!' or 'Son of an Indian woman!'?
[Teacher:] He's punished unless the man's mother actually is Zanji or Indian.

(al-Kindi (1979–84: vol. 12, para. 160; vol. 14, para. 161.2; trans. Michael A. Cook, xeroxed classroom materials, Princeton University).

[11] Juynboll (1953: 201). Only the Hanafi school treats the offense as public, rather than private, in nature. See also Juynboll (1910: 293). In addition to suffering the Quranically imposed punishment of flogging, the slanderer will thereafter be regarded as an unreliable witness whose evidence will have no force in the future (Doi (1984).   [12] Cited in Doi (1984).

salvation of a false accusation,[13] it is the public element of such a charge that receives implicit emphasis.

The public aspect of private slander is evident in several other respects. Adverse comments are commonly made indirectly, so as to avoid the appearance of creating social disorder through direct confrontation. However, when such remarks or actions are made public the implications are clear. Thus honor becomes for a number of Arab cultures a related category, not subject to the strictures of Islamic prescribed punishment or evidentiary standards as such yet constituting a vehicle through which a sense of offense to one's reputation, and hence one's dependencies, may be strenuously asserted.[14] As in many other domains of Islamic culture intention is also important: To make an accusation in such a way that a number of others from outside one's immediate circle hear it, is regarded as clearly an intentional act, not merely one born of emotion or incompetency. Thus the ideology is maintained that the assertion, or the harm, was meant, and not accidental, though the logic and the proof lie not in investigating some barely accessible interior reaches of the individual mind but in the very fact that no competent person would engage in such a public assertion if he did not mean what he said.[15]

These same emphases are present when we turn to instances in which the harmful utterance is directed at a public figure or a central feature of Islamic concern. Here, in Quranic prescription and broader commentary, slander is equated with treason (*khayana*). Such an approach may seem the epitome of authoritarianism: If the king is the state or God is incarnate in the state then to slander the one is to undermine the other. In Islamic thought, however, it is the community of believers that is the unit adversely affected by the slander. Where treason in the West is an act against the state and thus against all its citizens, in Islam slander is a form of treason against the community of the faithful and hence against the capacity to maintain peace within that community. Thus the importance of publicity again remains crucial: An impious utterance kept largely to oneself or mentioned to one person at a time, a suggestion that the Prophet's actions may have lacked a certain decorousness or been of questionable emulation— these may be regarded as backbiting and hence immoral and unworthy. Roy Mottahedeh notes, for example, that 'Muslims also showed a fair degree of toleration toward heretics who did not publicly voice heretical views.'[16] Thus unless utterances become so public as to call into question the orderliness of society, they remain short of treason to the faithful. Two examples show something of the parameters of this concept.

---

[13] 'Ghazali gives special attention to the case where the offense committed is slander; unless the slanderer expiates and obtains forgiveness from his victim, some of his good deeds will be transferred to the credit of the latter, or some of the latter's misdeeds transferred to his account on the Day of Judgment' (Margoliouth (1910), citing Ghazali, *Revival of the Religious Sciences*, iii, 116 (AH 1306)).

[14] See generally Peristiany (1966); Gilmore (1987); and Stewart (1994). See also Slaughter (1993: 193–200).

[15] See Al-Qaradawi (1985: 319). On intentionality in this context, see Rosen (1985) and Rosen (1995a). The comparison to the Aristotelian notion of acting in anger as a way of acting virtuously on principles, rather than as the result of some loss of self-control, is especially striking in this context. See Horder (1992: 43–71).

[16] Mottahedeh (1993: 26) (original italics).

The Salman Rushdie affair, prompted in 1989 by the publication of *The Satanic Verses*, was, quite aside from the Iranian fatwa condemning Rushdie to death, seen by many more moderate Muslims as nothing less than an act of treason.[17] Like some believing Christians confronting the question of blasphemy and state power, they argued that if a text can belong to an individual a central religious text like the Quran can belong to an entire religious community, and infringement on its role in that community's self-respect and standing ought to yield state protection if not indeed state punishment.[18] The danger of leaving such utterances unsanctioned, many Muslims argued, is that of social disorder. This position is summarized by one commentator on the Rushdie affair when, in discussing both apostasy and treason to the Islamic community, he says:

a quiet desertion of personal Islamic duties is not a sufficient reason for inflicting death on a person. Only when the individual's desertion of Islam is used as a political tool for instigating state disorder, or revolting against the law of Islam, can the individual apostate then be put to death as a just punishment for his act of treason and betrayal of the Muslim community. . . . The individual apostasy which takes place quietly and without causing any public disorder should not be the concern of the Islamic authority.[19]

Social order—the preservation of society against chaos (fitna)—is itself seen as an amalgam of several component concerns.[20] One concern is with the truth of historical figures. If, it is argued, one can take any liberty with history, truth itself is undermined. Whether it is a film portrayal of the life of Muhammad or Christ, a denial of the Holocaust or a racially biased depiction of an historic figure, truth may be disserved and people incited to acts of aggression.[21] Just as in the West, where some countries protect against group defamation or 'incitement to racial hatred,' so, too,

[17] Both 'treason' and 'cultural treason' are terms applied to Rushdie's novel by Mazrui (1989), reprinted in part in Appignanesi and Maitland (1990: 202–10).

[18] See, e.g., Maitland (1990: 117). A characteristic position of Muslim critics is the following: 'If some writer uses my name and the names of some of my friends and also selects some situations and incidents of my life and distorts them and vilifies them do I not have the right to charge that person for slander and defamation? Should not the Muslim community have the right to condemn this man, for blasphemy because he is using a thin veil of fiction in order to vilify the Prophet and all that they hold dear to them? As the author [Rushdie] is not interested in presenting his own realisation of any truth, as he is preaching an anti-Islamic theory in the guise of a novel, his liberty as a writer ends and he should be treated as anyone producing blasphemous writing is treated.' Ashraf (1990: 19).

[19] Ally (1990: 26). For a general discussion of apostasy and Islamic law, see An-Naim (1986); Slaughter (1993: 177–82). See also Artz (1996).

[20] See generally, Kamali (1993) and Kamali (1997).

[21] A Muslim critic of Rushdie's book thus wrote: 'Controversial books can cause wars—not necessarily because they preach in its favour but because even divinely inspired doctrines, in frail human custody, are liable to be misunderstood' (Aktar (1990: 23)). This viewpoint also characterizes the position of a number of non-Muslim commentators on the Rushdie affair. Thus, Chief Rabbi Jakobovits of Great Britain wrote: 'What should concern us are not *religious* offences but *socially* intolerable conduct calculated or likely to incite revulsion or violence, by holding up religious beliefs to scurrilous contempt, or by encouraging murder' (*The Times*, London, 9 March 1989, reprinted in Appignanesi and Maitland (1990: 197–9, at 198); original italics). Another commentator wrote: 'While free speech is most desirable, it is not the only value. It therefore needs to be reconciled with such other values as avoidance of needless suffering, social harmony, protection of the weak, truthfulness in the public realm, and the self-respect and dignity of individuals and groups' (Parekh (1990: 90)).

many Muslims argue that the community of believers has a collective right to protection against slander of religious or historic figures when the slander is so public as to create the possibility of genuine social chaos.[22]

This aspect of publicity is also evident in some approaches to the issue of utterances concerning public officials. Talal Asad, for example, points to an acceptable form, called *nasiha*, in which one may criticize public officials:

Nasiha signifies advice that is given for someone's good, honestly and faithfully. It also has the meaning of sincerity, integrity, and doing justice to a situation . . . [s]ince in this context it carries the sense of offering moral advice to an erring fellow Muslim (*mansuh*), it is at once an obligation to be fulfilled and a virtue to be cultivated by all Muslims.[23]

Such advice may be given in public sermons or religious lectures. Although there are famous instances of Islamic scholars and jurists making public criticisms of officials, it is precisely in the public nature of such criticism that concern is often expressed. Unlike, say, American law, where communication to any third party may constitute 'publication' of a libel, the concept of nasiha implies not that it is done in front of another person but that it must be done so publicly as to constitute slander. Thus Asad points to the situation, probably not uncommon in Islamic political/religious history, of contemporary Saudi Arabia. Following the Gulf War, a group of several hundred religious scholars (*'ulama*) published an open letter to King Fahd demanding a number of political reforms. Answering through his Council of Senior 'Ulama, he reminded the critics that if one is seeking to correct another's moral behavior the relevant advice should be given privately and personally. Some of the King's supporters even claimed that to do otherwise was to convert morally corrective advice into ghiba, that very form of backbiting which the Quran and the Prophet so firmly condemn.[24] Thus whatever the tactical aspects of this affair—that a King subject to public criticism by moral arbiters may become a publicly accountable political figure, that nasiha deals with the moral regulation of the entire community of believers and therefore must be conducted publicly—it is clear that it is the issue of making such utterances in a public fashion that is the crux of the situation. This is equally important in the context of group defamation and group liability.

COLLECTIVE IDENTITY, BLOODMONEY, AND THE PUBLIC–PRIVATE RELATION

The coming of Islam brought with it a revision of the pre-Islamic customs of blood vengeance, and thus one of the earliest expressions of the reconfigured bounds of the public and private under the new religion. Prior to the advent of the Prophet the entire tribe was liable to blood vengeance or blood payments if any of its members had, intentionally or unintentionally, killed another. Under Islam the bounds of

---

[22] This may, in part, account for those attacks on the Jews that are sometimes couched in terms of slandering: For example, 'The Ayatollah Khomeini accused the Jews of defaming and maligning Islam and distorting its reputation' (Unterman (1990): 110).   [23] Asad (1993: 214).
[24] Asad (1993: 224).

group liability largely contracted to male agnates of the perpetrator, who was himself not required to contribute to the payment.[25] While the bounds of the responsible group and the distribution of contributions have varied a good deal from one region to another in the Arab world—and the practice has largely fallen into disuse under the modern state—the practice as a whole tests the concept of individual and group identity.[26] The payment of bloodmoney can be seen not as collective responsibility, in the sense that each person is replaceable by any other who might be killed in retaliation, but as collective liability, in the sense of payment being required from one's group. Thus the conceptual building blocks involved are not a series of collectivities as such but socially embedded persons whose religion opens up a conceptual distinction that did not exist before the Prophetic revolution. The sanctions that one's own group may bring to bear to keep an individual from asserting his own desires or emotions therefore play an important role in defining the private and the public.

Group identity has also been expressed in the pattern of confessional group association, particularly as it has related to both group defamation and collective responsibility. Although there is no formal category of group defamation in Islamic law, significant, if ambiguous, forms of protection were commonly accorded non-Muslims living within the Arab world, provided that various restrictions, ranging from taxation to deportment, were not violated. Jews and Christians, as 'people of the Book,' were usually accorded the right to practice their faiths even though their beliefs could be regarded as defamatory of Islam. Their protection came, in theory, from those passages in the Quran that acknowledge their capacity to practice these religions. As in all such sacred texts one can, of course, find contradictory verses which can be applied to different purposes.[27]And certainly the treatment of 'protected peoples' has been quite mixed in Arab history.[28] But the protection did

---

[25] Juynboll (1961b). See also Tyan (1965) and Schacht (1986).

[26] The practice has by no means been wholly eliminated. When a British nurse was found guilty in Saudi Arabia of murdering an Australian nurse, the brother of the murdered woman was allowed to decide if he would accept a bloodmoney payment in place of the murderess' execution. Similarly, following their conviction for killing several tourists in Yemen in December 1998, it was reported that the death sentences of the convicted could be commuted if the relatives of the deceased requested clemency, in return for which they would receive bloodmoney compensation from the convicted men's families (Gardner (1999).

[27] See, e.g., the passages in the Quran at Suras III: 110–14, CIX: 5, and VI: 108. See also the passages cited in Mottahedeh (1993), including the statement about others being either 'your brothers in religion or your equals in creation' at p. 35. Among the passages in the Quran that are very negative are Suras V: 51 and IX: 29. It is from a reading of these passages that Lewis is led to say that references to Jews in the Quran are 'mostly negative' (Lewis (1984: 10)). On the 'protected status' of the Jews, see Cahen (1965) and Chehata (1965). A hadith collected by Bukhari, however, says: 'A funeral passed and the Prophet stood up. When told it was that of a Jew, the Prophet replied: "Was he not a soul?".' Another Tradition states that 'Islam respects a human being only because he is human' (Al-Qaradawi (1985: 343)).

[28] See Cahen (1965) and Chehata (1965). The Quran (Sura II: 257) says that there is no compulsion in religion, although some scholars see the dhimmi relation as coerced submission: 'Since non-Muslims were given the choice between embracing Islam, becoming dhimmis and paying jizya if they qualified for that status, or fighting the Muslims, it cannot be said that there was no compulsion in religion' (An-Naim (1990: 149)). See also Artz (1996: 414–15). Another way of viewing the situation is to say that the system of confessional groups was a way of segregating each with an eye to having them police their own members against doing offense to the Muslim majority.

extend even to slander. There was not only the hadith that 'he who hurts a dhimmi [a protected 'person of the Book'] hurts me, and he who hurts me annoys Allah';[29] there was also the direct consideration of slander, as, for example, in the statement of one Maliki scholar: 'Whoever violates these obligations [to protect the dhimmi] against one of them by so much as an abusive word, by slandering his reputation, or by doing him some injury or assisting in it, has breached the guarantee of Allah, His messenger and the religion of Islam.'[30] The Ottoman version of this confessional group mosaic included the edict of 1840 which forbade the blood libel against Jews as a form of slander.

Once again, in the context of collective identity, we see the crucial element of a matter being made public for it to be threatening to social order and hence sanctioned. It was even the case that debates could take place in a public fashion between Jewish and Muslim scholars without implications of slander. The Quran (Sura XXIX: 46) states: 'And do not dispute with the People of the Book, except by (the way) which is best, unless it be with such of them as transgress.'[31] Such disputations were, in a sense, held within an interstitial zone—like so much of the relations with Jews—where public and private overlapped: Provided the key ingredient—avoidance of civil strife—was honored, no slander could attach. It is almost as if the Jews did not have to 'hide their sin' of unbelief in Islam because their belief in God and His other Prophets contributed to the existence of a separate space within the existing structure of the public and the private.

The same themes are replicated in a number of other instances, both historical and modern. For example, in the debate over whether Muslims should continue to live in lands that have fallen under non-Muslim domination, or whether they must return to the lands of Islam, one of the more important classical commentators, Al-Wansharisi, argued that if one quietly expressed a desire, after coming home for a time, to return to the non-Muslim land, or actually did so in a circumspect way, no punishment should follow. But if such expressions were pronounced openly and publicly they should be the subject of severe corporal punishment and imprisonment. As Asmal, discussing those who expressed such a desire to return to non-Muslim lands, puts it:

Al-Wansharisi seems to view this more seriously than the actual act of returning quietly (to *Dar al-Kufr* [non-Muslim controlled lands]) for it is proof of irreligiosity and possibly *kufr* [unbelief] leading to God's anger and chastisement. This seems to echo a juristic 'convention' in that other 'prohibitions' as well (e.g. wine-drinking), if they are transgressed privately, little or no action may be taken against the miscreant by the law or the ruler. But if it is done in public then the law and the ruler are called upon to act and punish the offender accordingly. However, if the prohibition is verbally denounced or rejected it is viewed as a capital offense because it amounts to a renunciation of Islam. It could be that dissent expressed openly might

[29] Al-Qaradawi (1985: 338).   [30] Al-Qaradawi (1985: 339).
[31] Cited in Al-Qaradawi (1985: 337). (This is not one of Arberry's translations.) Qaradawi suggests this means that a believer should avoid only those discussions with the People of the Book as might cause bitterness or arouse hostility.

also disenchant other Muslims and undermine the status of *Dar al-Islam* [lands under Muslim control] if not lead to wider civil unrest.[32]

Similarly, both apostasy and heresy are approached largely in terms of their public, rather than any private, implications. Renunciation of Islam in favor of another religion is, in the Middle Eastern cultural context, a necessarily public action: Religious identity is so significant a part of one's identity that it would be nearly impossible to change religion in some private or interior way. Some Islamic countries at present refuse to sign international conventions allowing freedom of religion precisely because they do not believe that one can leave Islam without it having systemic repercussions for the order of society, quite aside from any question of divine disfavor. In classical Islamic thought, heresy raises similar considerations. As Bernard Lewis has argued, it was 'innovation' (*bid'a*) that was regarded as a serious challenge to the order of things: 'The gravamen of the charge of *bid'a* levelled against a doctrine was not primarily that it was false or bad but that it was new—a breach of habit, custom, and tradition, respect for which is rooted deep in the pre-Islamic tribal past, and reinforced by the belief in the finality and perfection of the Muslim revelation.'[33] In each instance, as we have seen repeatedly in this cultural pattern, it is the quality of publicity and the fear that by becoming public a sensitive action may disrupt all of society that remains central in the Arab/Muslim conceptual order. We will see this aspect in one final set of examples, those relating to home, family, and the use of space.

GOING PUBLIC: PRIVATE LIVES AND PUBLIC CONSEQUENCES

The relation between the individual and the larger structures of the state and the community of believers has occasioned some understandable equation by commentators of the one with the other. Thus Farhat Ziadeh can say that 'Islamic law . . . does not separate the individual and the state,'[34] while Ali Mazrui notes: 'In Islam, there is no sharp distinction between church and state.'[35] These statements are understandable inasmuch as the ideal caliphal state fulfills the socio-religious needs of the individual or because, as we have seen, blasphemy is equated with treason. But it is also misleading to suggest that a strict identity of state/individual/believers exists in the modern Arab world, notwithstanding the propaganda of certain regimes. Indeed, in ordinary life the domains of the private and the public, both political and religious, are often quite sharply defined.

This is particularly noticeable in matters relating to home and family. Houses continue to be built in a way that makes direct observation of interiors difficult or impossible. Children are relatively free to move among dwellings and serve as informants for the adults about what takes place elsewhere. A constant tension exists

[32] Asmal (1998: 213).   [33] Lewis (1993: 284).   [34] Ziadeh (1990: 74).
[35] Mazrui (1989: 6).

between obtaining information from outside the house and letting a sufficient amount of information about one's own household be known to protect oneself in a variety of contingencies. If, for example, there is a legal component to a relationship much will depend on how public the private life has been rendered. A woman in Morocco has an absolute right, which is not infrequently employed, to be granted a place of residence away from her husband's kin and among 'righteous people,' people who could serve as witnesses in court to any impropriety on the part of her husband.[36] The meaning and importance of these boundaries may, of course, vary: In response to the question I had posed my students, 'Why does a woman ever need a husband?' a Saudi Arabian girl said, out loud but to herself, 'Because it is the only way to get any privacy.' She saw marriage, obviously, as a way of getting away from the intrusiveness of family within the precincts of the household. In most Arab countries one can get a court order to bar another from building a structure in such a way that it would be possible to see into one's own windows. Sometimes the concept of the private space of the family gets extended and reinterpreted. Men and women will now be seen dancing in one another's presence at Moroccan weddings, which was unthinkable a generation earlier. When I mentioned this to one man at a wedding, he said, 'We are all family (*a'ila*),' but his sheepish look showed that we both knew that many people present were not relatives and that this fiction maintained the appearance of the private. By contrast, when family arguments take place it is very common for the argument to spill out into public space so that others may participate in the determination of its outcome.[37]

Indeed, the very concept of public space is a highly ambiguous one, in keeping with the ambiguity that such space imparts to the relationships of power that may take place there. The concept of ownership is crucial to Arab culture. In a sense everything is owned by someone: There is a *mul* ('owner') of everything, even if it is ultimately *mul ana*, 'my Lord.' Private property (*mulk*) defines a person as much as his relationships. Public space is a concept that hardly exists: Individuals intrude onto sidewalks (such as they are), edge onto one another's land, press up against any unused area. It is as if public space were simply some space that had not yet taken on an identity with a particular person or group.

Similarly people keep knowledge of their assets close, often hiding property through dispersed relatives, allies, or friends. Speech is like property in this regard: It is a critical asset upon which one relies in the forging of attachments. The linkage between property and speech, for purposes of articulating the private and the public, lies, in considerable part in the concept of intent. For in hiding one's assets, as in hiding one's sins or hiding one's thoughts, one is avoiding a display of one's inner state, one's *niya*, or intent. Since it is at this level of intent that fault and sin lie, by not revealing them publicly through those words and deeds that are taken as direct

---

[36] For several legal cases from Morocco involving this and similar issues, see Rosen (1989a: 7–10). For the Egyptian situation, see Howard-Merriam (1988).

[37] For an example, see Rosen (1984: 128).

evidence of the state of mind that must necessarily accompany them, one avoids attributions of intent which might prove disruptive of social order. Thus speech, which has the power to reveal intent and disrupt society by disrupting the negotiation of interpersonal relationships, is kept within private bounds even as it must be openly asserted in many instances to make relationship possible. A delicate game thus ensues as each person seeks information about others' circumstances while strategically guarding his or her own store of information.

The state is not coincident with the individual in this regard, though it does provide some protection against intrusion of the sort described. Only if the individual makes his or her utterances or actions coincide with those that the state has come to preserve as its own does greater coincidence occur. In a sense, it could be argued, then, that it is the state that must most frequently guard itself against the private. This is not to imply that it does so through closely watching its citizens, though that is surely true in the more authoritarian regimes. Rather the state generally encourages individuals to keep their potentially disruptive thoughts hidden. As with religion, where God loves those who hide their sins, the individual is institutionally and culturally encouraged to keep his thoughts, his intent, hidden until and if they can be forged into publicly validated relationships with desirable social consequences.

In sum, the relation of the private to the public seems the more fruitful axis along which to grasp the conceptions used by Muslims in North Africa and the Middle East to address issues of toleration and the control of speech. For Westerners to say that there is no sense of tolerance in Islam, or that it existed only in some golden age in Spain, or that minorities have been tolerated only to the extent that they are politically weak and socially vulnerable, or that speech is allowable only so long as it is permitted by those in power, may miss the point. For if one is to grasp the conceptual scheme within which the experience of Muslims is cast, then, whatever else there is to say about these topics and whatever praise or criticism is to be assigned, only by appreciating how the public and private worlds are configured and how this conceptual order connects to a host of different domains of everyday life will the full set of meanings become available to us and the conversation across existing boundaries become more comprehensible.

12

Islam and Islamic culture in the courts of the United States

There are roughly 6 to 8 million Muslims living in the United States—more than the membership of the Presbyterian, Episcopalian, or Mormon Churches; more than all the Quakers, Unitarians, Jehovah's Witnesses, and Christian Scientists combined. Only one in eight of the American Muslims is of Arab descent, the two largest groups being comprised of immigrants from South Asia (24 per cent of the total) and native-born African-Americans (42 per cent). Although the Nation of Islam is the most widely known of the Black Muslim groups, its 20,000–50,000 members represent only a small fraction of that category.

Muslims and non-Muslims in the United States tend to go their separate ways, elements of race and the complexities of Middle Eastern politics contributing to a lack of direct engagement or wary antipathy more than outright conflict. The image of Arabs often found in the American press or films is, unfortunately, that of the terrorist rather than the family-oriented believer, the fanatic rather than the average person in the street. Non-Muslims may react adversely when a large mosque goes up in their neighborhood or view the speeches of a Louis Farakhan as representative of all Black Muslims, but for the most part contacts are limited and non-confrontational.

In the law, however, two characteristic orientations affecting American Muslims have come together. On the one hand, the practices of Muslims arriving from other countries have found legal expression as their native customs come into conflict with the practices of mainstream America; on the other, the themes of the American civil rights movement inform the ways in which Muslim religious life is asserted in the course of legal confrontations. Moreover, it is one of the more striking aspects of American law, especially American constitutional law, that it is from cases involving small, recently arrived, or (in the context of the United States) non-majoritarian religious groups that a great deal of legal development takes place. Much of the interpretation of the First Amendment right of free speech or the permissible extent of state involvement with religion has come about through cases involving minority concerns. To the long list of religious groups which, from the margin, have forced the law to be re-thought now are added the American Muslims.

In this chapter I am concerned to see in what ways legal cases involving Muslims have been affecting the development of American legal doctrine. I am also concerned, however, to show how American courts are comprehending Islam as a religion and Islamic law as an integral part of that religion. It is an exercise which is, no doubt, very much in its early days; however, it is at just such times that the terms of discussion are often set. This is, then, a developing story of Islam in a non-Muslim land, and the ways in which each is responding to the other through the context of American law.

HUMAN RIGHTS AND THE AMERICAN APPROACH TO RELIGIOUS AND CULTURAL DIFFERENCE

Universal rights require local implementation. Without such implementation they may have an important effect on international image-making, the development of new terms of discussion, and the formation of interest groups opposed to the status quo, but they may have no direct legal effect on everyday lives.

The United States has not adopted all of the international human rights conventions,[1] although increasingly United States courts have cited international conventions in their decisions.[2] Many international conventions, moreover, speak in very broad terms (e.g., The Universal Declaration of Human Rights Article 18 on freedom of religion) and, with the possible exception of the International Labor Organization Convention 169 on Indigenous and Tribal Peoples in Independent Countries, none speaks with specificity to the conflict of religion and/or culture within a given state.

In their place American courts rely on what is arguably the oldest extant human rights document in the world, the United States Constitution, whose two centuries of judicial interpretation have given specific, if changing, meaning to a variety of individual and collective rights and freedoms. To consider the recent history of such constitutional interpretation as it relates to the religious and social life of Muslims living in the United States is, therefore, more than to study the legal situation of this particular minority within American society. Rather it can be seen as a particular national implementation of those second- and third-order rights covered by various international conventions which must, of necessity, take on some local meaning to have concrete effect.

To look at the ways in which American courts have approached some of the issues raised by Islam and the cultures of the Muslim world is thus to gain insight into one of the most sensitive areas of encounter between these two traditions.[3] In what follows I will consider such issues as the judicial approach to the cultural defense plea, the legal challenges posed by the practices of Black Muslims, the recognition in American courts of practices associated with Islamic family law, and various claims of employment discrimination based on religious difference.[4] Throughout, I will try

---

[1] Among those that have been adopted are the Universal Declaration of Human Rights and the Covenant on Civil and Political Rights, although the latter is subject to a number of reservations and understandings that grant superiority to interpretations of the United States Constitution. The International Convention on Economic, Social and Cultural Rights has been signed but has not yet been ratified by the United States Senate.

[2] See the sources cited in Henkin, et al. (1993: 632).

[3] There are about 8 million Muslims in the United States, over half of whom are college graduates. Some 2 million African-Americans are converts to Islam, though fewer than 4% of them are affiliated with Louis Farakhan's Nation of Islam. On the experience of Muslims in the United States generally, see Bassiri (1997); Haddad and Smith (1994); Haddad (1991); and Haddad (1993).

[4] For a very valuable compendium of materials relating to these issues, see Moore (1995). I am not concerned in this chapter with the application of the commercial law of Muslim countries in cases heard by an American court. On that topic, see Forte (1993).

to consider how Islam has posed particular challenges to the shaping of American law itself and will, therefore, conclude by teasing out some of the general points which the analysis of the case law presents.

ISLAM, CULTURAL DEFENSE, AND IMMIGRATION

American law, unlike that of some European countries, makes no specific place for pleading one's cultural background as a defense to a criminal charge. Nevertheless, a host of cases—all but a few involving non-Muslims—have raised the question whether cultural background may serve as a basis for reducing the severity of the charge or the punishment. General approaches have developed out of cases such as the following: A reduced penalty for a Japanese woman who, relying on a custom from her native country, killed her two children and tried to kill herself upon learning of her husband's infidelity;[5] a Laotian man who was held to a lesser offense than rape and kidnapping for the traditional 'bride capture' of a reluctant fellow Laotian in California;[6] an Eskimo man who was completely exonerated of child abuse when grasping the genitals of a non-Eskimo child at the latter's birthday party;[7] a Haitian whose penalty was reduced when he pleaded that he killed another Haitian out of fear that the deceased was working deadly voodoo against him.[8] In each of these situations courts did permit information about the cultural background of the defendant to be heard as part of the proceeding.

Only a few cases incorporating a cultural defense have involved Muslims, and most of them relate to so-called 'honor killings.' In each instance a male relative—usually the father, but sometimes the husband or brother—has killed a woman believing that her sexual practices, real or imagined, had brought disgrace to her family, a disgrace that could only be eradicated, as it sometimes is in the home Muslim country, by her death.[9]

Throughout this chapter legal cases and law review articles will be referred to in the citation form used in legal publications: The first number refers to the volume in which the opinion or article appears, the number immediately following the citation refers to the first page on which the entry appears, and any following number refers to the page on which a quoted passage is found. The following abbreviations will be used: A. 2d (*Atlantic Reporter*, Second Series); Cal. Rptr. (*California Reporter*); F. 2d and F. 3d (*Federal Reporter*, Second Series and Third Series); F. Supp. (*Federal Supplement*); N.Y.S. 2d (*New York Supplement Reporter*, Second Series); P. 2d (*Pacific Reporter*, Second Series); S. 2d (*Southern Reporter*, Second Series); S.E. 2d (*Southeastern Reporter*, Second Series); and U.S. (*United States Supreme Court Reports*).

[5] People v. Kimura, No. A-091133 (Los Angeles Cty. Super Ct.), 24 April 1985.

[6] People v. Kong Moua, No. 315972-0 (Fresno Cty. Superior Ct.), 7 February 1985.

[7] Toomey (1985).

[8] I am indebted to Rosemarie Chierrici, who appeared as an expert witness, for bringing this upstate New York case to my attention.

[9] Though Islam does not formally permit such killings and sets extremely high standards for proving adultery, a number of Muslim countries, by statute or case law, effectively permit husbands to escape severe punishment for the killing of their allegedly adulterous wives. See Spatz (1991: 598–604). For anthropological accounts of honor killings, see Antoun (1972: 40–3); Cohen (1965: 71–94); Kressel (1981); and Stewart (1994: 139–43).

In one particularly notorious case that occurred in 1986 a Palestinian father, who had lived in the United States for a number of years, killed his sixteen-year-old daughter when she refused to stop dating a black boyfriend.[10] What made the case so unusual is that the father was a member of the Abu Nidal group of suspected terrorists and his home and business were the subject of FBI wiretaps at the time of the killing. Indeed, the act of murder, in which the girl's mother also cooperated, was recorded by the agents. Both parents were convicted of first-degree murder, and though the cultural background of the defendants was not formally at issue in the trial it played a role both by its presence and by its absence. The jury was well aware that the father was an Arab and that his wife, a Brazilian by birth, had lived with him in Palestine and was thoroughly immersed in an Arab family context. Jurors could see that the defendants and the relatives who came to court each day were in no way repentant about the killing, which the father insisted, in the face of the FBI tapes and all the physical evidence, was an act of self-defense. On the other hand, the jurors were never informed about the cultural context of 'honor killings' and possessed no understanding whatsoever of the forces working on the young girl.[11] As one of her brothers, who opposed the killing, said: 'I understand the law in America is the law. [But] I hope the intellectuals in the U.S. look at the cultural differences to defend these poor people. It's not [the father's] fault. It's the fault of the situation.'[12]

American jurors' knowledge of the cultural context of a crime is very much subject to the rulings of the presiding judge and the ability of the lawyers to marshal and gain acceptance for this type of information.[13] In many instances American

---

[10]   The case is described in detail in Harris (1995).

[11]   This may have included the father's desire to kill his daughter because she knew too much about his activities as a member of the Abu Nidal group combined with her desire to get away from her abusive father by the time of her next birthday.

[12]   Harris (1995: 257). Issues of a related nature were raised in the case of Mohammed Abequa, a naturalized American of Jordanian birth who killed his Turkish-born wife and fled to Jordan with the couple's children. Without any extradition treaty and in the context of Jordanian support for the Iraqis during the Gulf War the killing and kidnapping developed into an international incident. Abequa's brother, a brigadier general in the Jordanian army, sought to keep the children in Jordan; the deceased wife's sister sought help from Congressional supporters to have the children returned to the United States. Eventually, King Hussein took personal charge of the children, reputedly received an advisory opinion from the Jordanian religious court, and returned the children to the United States. Abequa was not extradited but was found guilty of second-degree murder and kidnapping and sentenced to fifteen years in jail. A New Jersey court later indicted him for the same charges and may seek his extradition and trial under the new treaty with Jordan after he serves his sentence there. Before Abequa's trial the Attorney General of Jordan had said of the killing: 'If he is defending his honor, it's like self-defense.' *New York Times*, 1 August 1994, 5. Abequa himself claimed that his wife was having an affair and that he strangled her as a result. Whether any subsequent trial in the United States would permit testimony on cultural background remains quite uncertain.

[13]   The same is clearly true in Great Britain where, as one author describes a similar case: 'Nothing in their own culture or experience equipped this jury of very ordinary-looking English people to comprehend that what had been described in court was an honor killing, one of the hundreds that every year claim Muslim women's lives' (Brooks (1995: 231)). See also her discussion of honor killings in the Near East at pp. 49–53. See generally Poulter (1986); Commission for Racial Equality (1990). In the case of the killing by a Turkish Muslim father of his sixteen-year-old daughter an Australian court held that if the characteristics that led to the accused's act were permanent rather than transitory, thus rendering him

judges will only permit testimony that bears on the mental state of the defendant, thus excluding expert testimony on cultural background unless used as part of psychiatric evidence[14]—an approach that has prompted more than one commentator to suggest that the insanity defense is the American version of the cultural defense plea. When cultural evidence is considered by the prosecutor it often affects the severity of the crime charged; if admitted at trial, it may have a dramatic effect on the level of punishment.

In either event, the fact that such evidence has found no formal place in American law, whether for Muslims or any others, means that most cases go formally unreported and do not join issue for purposes of determining law on the subject. A kind of legal fiction seems to apply in many cases: If counsel do not press for a formal place for such evidence they may get it in, but if they make too much of it the law's sense that it cannot make exceptions based on culture will tend to preclude it altogether. Formal exclusion of cultural information may have the advantage of not letting custom become frozen in time by judicial ruling and may also avoid the question of who speaks for the practices of a culture—especially one in which women are disadvantaged. This seeming hypocrisy may be based on the history of immigrant experience in the United States, where it has long been generally true that if a certain practice is disallowed by the courts but punishment is not initially great, the message gets out rather quickly to the immigrant community that such a practice will not be allowed in the United States as it may have been in one's native country.[15] Precisely this approach may be at work in cases involving cultural practices of Muslims in their adoptive country.

A related issue arises in deportation proceedings. Immigration laws in the United States are one of the few domains in which a court gets to address the moral stature of an individual: If a person is found to be characterized by 'moral turpitude' he or she may be deported.[16] Famous cases have decided whether homosexuality, euthanasia, or adultery evince such moral failing as to warrant deportation. No cases have been found in which deportation has been based on an acceptable Muslim practice, such as polygamy or child marriage. However, a related issue did arise in the case of *United States v. Al-Kurna*.[17] In that case the defendant, a native of Kuwait with Jordanian citizenship present in the United States on a non-immigrant student visa, disputed the charge that he had paid an American woman to engage in a sham marriage in order to remain in the United States. He argued that the payment was part of the Muslim custom of a bridewealth (sadaq, mahr) payment. The court

---

different from the ordinary man in the community, the jury could consider this fact—even though they would not be allowed to hear specific evidence about the man's cultural background in making that determination. R. v. Dincer, [1983] Victorian Reports 460–8 (Supreme Court of Victoria 1982).

[14] See, e.g., People v. Poddar, 103 Cal. Rptr. 84 (Cal. Ct. of Appeals 1972).

[15] This was found to be true even in the early part of the century, as reported in Claghorn (1923: 234–7).

[16] See generally Aleinikoff and Martin (1985: 377–400).

[17] 808 F. 2d 1072 (5th Circuit 1987).

permitted testimony by two witnesses about this practice and left it to the jury to determine the facts. The jury found against the defendant.

In other instances courts have had to consider the implications of deportation proceedings for individuals who would be returned to Islamic countries. In a number of cases Christians—often Copts—have asserted that they are entitled to asylum because they would suffer persecution in their native country where Islam is the official religion. In *Mikhael v. Immigration and Naturalization Service*, for example, the court found that the plaintiff admitted he had never been arrested, detained, or threatened in his native Egypt and had made extensive and repeated visits home while living in Saudi Arabia.[18] In another case I have learned about through a colleague, an Albanian Muslim woman from the former Yugoslavia pleaded guilty to the second-degree murder of her husband, who shared her ethnic background, after he beat and threatened her with a gun that went off during a struggle. She fears that if she is deported after her parole she will become the victim of a blood feud. Her brother, while living in the United States, has already disappeared and people from the husband's group keep showing up at hearings for her release. The court has yet to decide whether such cultural factors can be considered in forestalling deportation.[19]

BLACK MUSLIMS IN AMERICAN COURTS

Many African-Americans have joined the Nation of Islam and various other Black Muslim groups over the last couple of decades.[20] Although a few cases have arisen about such issues as the relation of zoning laws to the building of mosques, and Islamic dress standards,[21] most of the law relating to these groups has grown out of encounters with that small proportion of their membership incarcerated in American prisons.[22] Although these cases are unusual because prisoners may have certain of

[18] 1995 U.S. Ct. of Appeals LEXIS 5914 (9th Circuit 1995).

[19] I am indebted to Robert Hayden for information on this pending case. It may also be noted that similar issues arise when a girl who may be subject to circumcision is to be returned to her native country. A Canadian court has honored a Somali mother's request to bar her husband from taking their child home where she might be subjected to such a procedure. American courts have also granted asylum to a woman who left her native country to avoid female circumcision (Dugger (1997)). See generally Gregory (1994) and Kassindja (1998). It should be emphasized that female circumcision should not be thought of as a Muslim practice but as one engaged in by some cultures that are, among other things, adherents to the Islamic faith. Hammoudi and Rosen (1993).

[20] On Black Muslims in the United States generally see Turner (1997) and Kepel (1997: 7–78). On the founder of the Nation of Islam, see Clegg (1997) and Berg (1998).

[21] See especially the instances referred to in McCloud (1995–6); and Nimer (1997). On zoning issues, see Metcalf (1996). On the dispute about the building of a private Islamic school near Washington, D.C., see *Washington Post* (1998) and *New York Times* (1998). The Court of Appeals in Great Britain rejected the claim by a Muslim schoolteacher that his need to attend mosque services on Friday afternoons took precedence over the requirements of his employment. Ahmad v. Inner London Education Authority [1978], All England Reports 574.

[22] For an overview of cases involving Black Muslim prisoners' rights as affected by Supreme Court decisions in the 1988–9 term, see 78 *Georgia Law Journal* 1429 (1990).

their rights limited, they nevertheless present issues which might not arise in other contexts, and in doing so they force the courts to consider what sort of religion Islam is and what accommodations American institutions must make to it as compared to other faiths.

For many years the courts, under the leadership of the United States Supreme Court, were highly deferential to prison officials, finding few justifications for intruding on the latter's decisions. This approach, and the competing view being formulated against it, are particularly evident in the case of *O'Lone v. Shabazz*.[23] Writing for a bare majority Justice Rehnquist held that prison restrictions on the gathering of Muslim inmates for the Friday prayer met the standard of reasonableness required of all such prison regulations rather than the higher standard required when a non-inmate's constitutional rights are at issue. Justice Brennan, speaking for the four dissenters, argued that this ritual is a central feature of Muslim religious life and that prison officials should be held to a high standard when their action effectively deprives a person of his religious rights. It is interesting that, in both the majority and dissenting view, the question of the centrality of a religious practice remains important and that in both instances the importance of a Friday gathering is readily comprehended by the Court.[24] These two elements will, as we shall see, figure prominently in the way Islam is analogized to Christianity and Judaism by the Court and thus rendered comprehensible.

To understand the next shift in legal approach we must turn to a case involving American Indians and their religious practices. In *Oregon v. Smith*,[25] the Supreme Court held that Indians who belong to the Native American Church, in which the hallucinogenic drug peyote is used as part of the rituals, could be dismissed from their employment in the state's drug rehabilitation program under a state law banning all use of peyote. The majority argued that the proper standard to be used in such matters is whether a valid state statute of general applicability has been duly enacted and whether there is a reasonable relationship between what the legislature seeks to accomplish and the effects it has on a protected constitutional right. The result of the Smith decision was immediate and striking.

In short order a host of different religious groups coalesced to seek a Congressional reversal of the Court's approach. They all felt that if a majority-passed statute that could withstand scrutiny as 'reasonable' was all it took to affect a religious practice, no one's religion would be entirely safe from government intrusion.

---

[23] 482 U.S. 342 (1987). See also Turner v. Safley, 482 U.S. 78 (1987) (upholding prison regulations on the wearing of beards and attendance at religious services by Muslim inmates).

[24] The emphasis on the 'centrality' or 'indispensability' of a religious practice developed in large part in cases involving Native American religions. Sequoyah v. Tennessee Valley Authority, 620 F. 2d 1159, 1164 (6th Circuit), cert. denied 449 U.S. 953 (1980); Lyng v. Northwest Indian Cemetery Protective Association, 485 U.S. 439 (1988). On Native American religion and prisoners' rights, see Echo-Hawk (1996).

[25] Employment Division, Department of Human Resources of Oregon v. Smith, 494 U.S. 872 (1990).

For example, a state (or one of its subdivisions) could prohibit the sacramental use of wine if the law barred the use of alcohol by everyone. Or male circumcision could be legislatively characterized as child abuse and barred for religious Jews and Muslims if it was also denied to everyone else. Under pressure from an extremely wide range of religious organizations Congress passed the Religious Freedom Restoration Act of 1993,[26] which said that the government may burden the exercise of religion only by demonstrating that it is doing so in the least restrictive way possible and that there exists a 'compelling state interest' for doing so. This latter is a very high standard which the courts had themselves developed and case law clearly demonstrates that it is not an easy one for governmental entities to achieve.

It was in the light of this newly legislated standard that a number of cases involving Muslims, especially black Muslims, were subsequently decided. In *Malik Allah v. Menei*,[27] for example, the federal district court was faced with a claim by the members of Muhammad's Temple of Islam that they constitute a separate religion from the Nation of Islam and should be entitled to their own ministers to attend to their religious needs in jail. The court noted the professed differences between the two groups[28] and acknowledged that the government may not favor one religion over another. While pointing out that various Christian and Jewish prisoners must make do with chaplains who do not represent all of their sectarian differences, the court nevertheless ruled that separate ministers for the two Muslim groups is not mandated by the law. Soon after, in the case of *Muhammad v. City of New York, Department of Corrections*,[29] a similar issue arose. Members of the Nation of Islam sought separate religious ministration from that offered to other Muslim sects in the

---

[26] Public Law No. 103–141, 107 U.S. Statutes 1488. See also Steinfels (1993).

[27] 844 F. Supp. 1056 (Eastern District of Pennsylvania 1994). For an early decision analyzing whether the Nation of Islam constitutes a religion, see Delaware v. Cubbage, 210 A. 2d 555 (Superior Ct. of Delaware 1965).

[28] Among the differences noted (844 F. Supp. 1056, 1059, n. 9) were:.

Nation of Islam (Farakhan)	Temple of Islam
a. The messenger Elijah Muhammad is still alive	a. The messenger Elijah Muhammad. is dead
b. Ramadan in April (yearly)	b. Ramadan in December (yearly)
d. Pray with head in the direction of the ground	d. Pray standing up
e. Pray in Arabic	e. Pray in English
h. Believes Elijah Muhammad is on the mother plane (U.F.O.)	h. Believes Elijah Muhammad is dead in the earth
j. Participates in American politics	j. Never participates in American politics
p. We greet 'As Salaamu Allah'	p. They greet 'As Salaam Alaikum'

In an earlier opinion a federal court had accepted the significant difference between Sunni and Shi'a Islam but had also accepted the argument of prison officials that penological interests, including the fear of exacerbating factionalism, outweighed the need to supply multiple ministers. Matiyn v. Commissioner, Dept. of Corrections, 726 F. Supp. 42 (Western District of New York 1989). Whether this case would have been decided differently under the Religious Freedom Act remains uncertain.

[29] 904 F. Supp. 161 (Southern District of New York 1995).

Justice past and present

prison.[30] Relying on extensive testimony from experts on the Nation of Islam and from Muslim ministers working in the city prison system the court decided that there was no substantial burden to the plaintiffs' exercise of religion posed by denying them separate religious services or ministers from their own sect. From the court's lengthy review of Islam it is clear that they regarded Islam as possessing certain central features and that various manifestations of attachment to Islam— whether they involved style of dress or customary greetings—were not so central as to require state officials to treat each sect as a separate religion.

Many other Muslim prisoner cases have involved dietary practices,[31] the right to gather at certain times for prayer,[32] whether it violates Islam to compel a Muslim prisoner to handle manure and dead animals as part of his required work duties,[33] and the ability of Muslim prisoners to wear certain clothes[34] or change their names to Islamic ones.[35] Other criminal cases have concerned the effect on jurors of being told that a defendant is a Black Muslim[36] and the adverse consequences of barring expert testimony at trial on the positive effects of being a Muslim, the high moral standards of Muslims, and the expert's opinion that 'frequent references to Muslim names would inflame and alienate white southerners' on a jury.[37]

In 1997 the status of many of these cases changed when, in a case that did not involve Muslims, the United States Supreme Court struck down the Religious Freedom Restoration Act, arguing that it constituted an unconstitutional infringement by Congress on the powers of the judiciary.[38] Attorneys who work with minority group prisoners, especially Native Americans, claim that as a result of the statute's demise their clients are being subjected to significant cutbacks in their religious liberties.[39] The coalition that lobbied for passage of the law has not re-formed, and no legislation is poised to take its place. The implications of this legal development for Muslims, no less than for other groups, remains highly uncertain.

A rather different situation was posed by the professional basketball star Mahmoud Abdul-Rauf. For some sixty games Abdul-Rauf refused to stand during

---

[30]   There are reportedly at least fourteen different Black Muslim groups in America. Muhammad v. City of New York Dept. of Corrections, 904 F. Supp. 161 (1995), 167. One, called the National Republic of North America, Moorish American, which says that blacks should properly be called 'Moorish-Americans,' claims to be comprised of descendants of three Moroccan tribes, the Alis, the Beys, and the Els, each of which is symbolized by the use of these terms as prefixes to their names. United States v. Darden, 70 F. 3d 1507, n. 1 (8th Circuit 1995).

[31]   See Kahey v. Jones, 836 F. 2d 948 (5th Circuit 1988), Barnett v. Rodgers, 410 F. 2d 995 (D.C. Circuit 1969).

[32]   Bowe v. Smith, 465 N.Y.S. 2d 391 (Supreme Ct. of New York, Wyoming Cty. 1983).

[33]   Franklin v. Lockhart, 890 F. 2d 96 (8th Circuit 1989).

[34]   Wamel Islam Allah v. Irvin, 1995 U.S. LEXIS 39868 (2nd Circuit 1995) (bow tie is not part of Islamic religious garb).

[35]   Aziz v. Fairman, 795 F. 2d 1296 (7th Circuit 1986) (refusal by prison officials to accept Islamic names of new converts does not constitute grounds for suit for damages against prison officials).

[36]   See Faulkner (1994: 16).

[37]   Mills v. Singletary, 63 F. 3d 999 (11th Circuit 1995), at n. 42.

[38]   City of Boerne v. Flores, 521 U.S. 507 (1997).

[39]   For an argument that the law was having a very limited effect on prisoners' rights anyway, see Solove (1996).

the playing of the national anthem, claiming that the nationalism of the song ran counter to his belief that 'Islam is the only way.' The National Basketball Association saw his refusal as a violation of its rule that requires players and coaches to stand 'in a dignified posture' during the playing of the anthem, and the association suspended him for one game. Under threats of a fine and further suspension the player finally agreed to stand during the anthem, during which he said, 'I'll offer a prayer, my own prayer, for all those who are suffering.'[40] Because no fine has ensued and no legal suit contesting the Association's putative violation of his religious rights has been filed, no law has been established on this matter. However, this encounter clearly indicates another instance in which an evaluation of Islam, similar to evaluations of the beliefs of Jehovah's Witnesses or other non-mainstream religious groups, could play an important role in the development of American law.

Similarly, an incident involving the head of the Nation of Islam, Louis Farakhan, could result in legal action. In 1996 Farakhan visited a number of African and Middle Eastern countries, during which he held meetings with Saddam Hussein and Muammar el-Qaddafi, reportedly receiving a pledge of 1 billion dollars from the latter.[41] Some members of Congress have proposed calling him before hearings to question why he traveled to countries to which travel is not permitted and whether he should have to register as an agent of a foreign country. Farakhan's answer is that he is 'an agent of Allah.' Politics aside, a question could be raised whether religion may serve as a justification for acts like those of Minister Farakhan and how Islam would be approached in such a circumstance.[42]

Finally, an earlier case of a name change shows how at least one judge approached the question of Muslim identity in America. *In the Matter of Earl Green* involved a convert to Islam who wished to change his name to Merwon Abdul Salaam. While acknowledging his right to do so without court permission, the court refused to make the change itself, arguing that while

[t]he proudest patronymic in the land is available to the lowliest individual . . . [p]etitioner should realize that he bears an honored name and should not hide his original identity by the

---

[40] *New York Times*, 15 March 1996, 7B. See also the *New York Times* articles on 14 March 1996, 13B; 17 March 1996, p. 2, Sec. 4; 21 March 1996, p. 9B; and the editorial in support of the player's right to religious dissent, 15 March 1996, A28.

[41] *New York Times*, 22 February 1996, A1; and 27 February 1996, A20.

[42] Similar issues can arise when religious sermons contain language, such as that relating to a 'holy war,' that may seem to imply potential violence. See Grinstein (1996). A number of other issues raised by Black Muslim and other African-American cultural groups have important legal implications. Speeches by Louis Farakhan and his associates on college campuses have raised serious issues of hate speech and the legal aspects of such acts. Similarly, the teaching by a handful of African-American historians of a revisionist view of the past for which other academics find no support has raised issues of academic freedom and the determination of appropriate standards for appointment and advancement within the academy. See *New York Times* (1994); and Gates (1992). It should be noted that, unlike some European countries, the United States does not have any laws barring the denial of the Holocaust or other acts of genocide, any such enactments being almost certain to fail constitutional scrutiny. On the role of Farakhan and his followers in crime prevention and community development see the discussion and references in Butler (1996: 717, n. 214).

assumption of another name totally and strangely different from the one he has borne since birth. . . . Green is a name that possesses an American echo. . . . This birthright should not conceal itself behind such an alien shield. It has sufficient buoyancy to float upon the sea of time and in years to come the petitioner may hopefully add luster to the name of Green.[43]

As an example of one judge's inability to comprehend Islam within the ambit of his own experience this could not speak more loudly.

THE MUSLIM FAMILY IN AMERICAN COURTS

Unlike those in the United Kingdom, courts in the United States are reluctant to honor marital and familial arrangements made abroad that do not accord with the practice of the states in which the parties presently reside.[44] Already in the nineteenth century, in a series of cases involving Mormons, the Supreme Court had ruled that polygamy violates public policy,[45] and subsequent developments in constitutional interpretation, though not replacing state law as the sole legislative base in the United States for matters concerning the family, have done little to change this deference to the public welfare as interpreted by individual states. Thus when we come to more recent cases involving Muslim family ties, we operate in a context of state laws measured against public policy considerations no less than a desire to maintain familial ties that were legal in the place where they were established.

For example, in *The People of the State of New York v. Ibrahim Ben Benu*[46] a thirteen-year-old girl's father who had arranged her marriage to a seventeen-year-old boy was found guilty of endangering a child's welfare. The court acknowledged that the marriage may have been conducted according to Muslim law and custom and that the girl may have consented to the union. However, they found both of these arguments irrelevant since the public policy of the state renders underage persons incapable of consenting to such unions.[47] Similarly, courts have refused to recognize a temporary

---

[43] In the Matter of Earl Green, 283 N.Y.S. 2d 242 (Civil Court of the City of New York, New York County 1967).

[44] On the British approach, see Pearl (1985–6); Poulter (1986); and Poulter (1990). For comparable issues in the Canadian context, see Khan (1993).

[45] Reynolds v. United States, 98 U.S. 145 (1879).

[46] 385 N.Y.S. 2d 222 (Criminal Court of the City of New York, Kings County 1976).

[47] In 1997 two Iraqi men were also found guilty in Nebraska of sexual assault of a child when they brought thirteen- and fourteen-year-old girls into the country as brides. Their claim that this was permissible under Islamic law and custom did not succeed (*Chicago Tribune* (1997)). Given the desire not to penalize people who entered a marriage in the belief that it was valid even though a court later finds it not to have been, a number of American jurisdictions continue to distinguish between void and voidable marriages, the former being invalid from their inception, the latter from the date of judgment forward. The effect can be to avoid a question of illicit sexual behavior in this case by denominating the union as only voidable or, in instances like those referred to below, depriving a spouse of any property settlement when her marriage is found invalid. Much of this distinction used to surround the question of illegitimacy, but in Levy v. Louisiana, 391 U.S. 68 (1968) the Supreme Court found unconstitutional laws that discriminate between legitimate and illegitimate children, thus vitiating one of the main grounds for maintaining the distinction between void and voidable marriages themselves.

marriage contracted in Iran, notwithstanding the parties' good-faith belief in the validity of the union;[48] a proxy marriage between an Algerian and a Pakistani which failed to fulfill the legal requirements of a marriage in Great Britain, where it was entered into, or Pakistan, where it was merely celebrated;[49] and a dowry agreement which deprived the wife of any payment if she were to initiate proceedings for a divorce.[50]

In some instances the courts have upheld Islamic marital arrangements not out of deference to religious law but because the arrangements constitute private contracts or acceptable foreign proceedings that do not violate state policy.[51] So, for example, in the case of *Asma Akileh v. Safwan Elchahal*[52] the couple had signed a bridewealth agreement in which 1 dollar was paid immediately while the remainder was to be paid in the event of divorce. Subsequently the wife filed for divorce when she developed the genital warts for which her husband had received treatment before their marriage but which he had never revealed to her. The husband claimed it was his understanding that the bridewealth agreement did not apply if the wife was the one to file for divorce; the wife claimed her right to receive the money was absolute. The trial court had found the prenuptial agreement invalid for lack of consideration, but the appellate court, acknowledging that this was the first instance of such a case in Florida, reversed the verdict, finding the deferred payment of $50,000 binding because the wife had performed on the agreement by entering into the marriage. Neither the husband's subjective intent nor the purported indefiniteness of the agreement was held to invalidate the bridewealth arrangement.[53]

In another case a New Jersey court held that an Iranian wife who had transferred to her husband over $400,000 in securities was not making a gift to him, which must be included as an asset of his estate, but was partaking of that Iranian custom by which a husband traditionally takes responsibility for administering a wife's assets. Arguing that '[t]he facts in this case are sufficiently unique to require a disposition

---

[48] In Re Marriage of Fereshteh, 248 Cal. Rptr. 807 (Cal. Ct. of Appeals 1988). On such marriages generally see Haeri (1989).

[49] Farah v. Farah, 429 S.E. 2d 626 (Virginia Ct. of Appeals 1993).

[50] In Re the Marriage of Awatef and Nabil A. Dajani, 251 Cal. Rptr. 871 (Cal. Ct. of Appeals, 4th District 1988). The court took testimony from experts on Islamic marriage law and did not dispute the validity of the marriage under that regime. However, they found the arrangement contrary to California public policy not for the reasons offered by the wife—that having initiated the divorce she would be denied her dowry—but because such agreements encourage 'profiteering by divorce' in contravention of the state's public policy concerns.

[51] As concerns foreign judgments, the court in Shikoh v. Murff, 257 F. 2d 306 (2nd Circuit 1958) refused to recognize as a judicial proceeding the divorce that took place before the Islamic Mission of America, Inc., notice of which was then sent to the Consulate General of Pakistan in New York. By contrast, the New Jersey court in Chaudry v. Chaudry, 388 A. 2d 1000 (Superior Ct. of N.J., Appellate Division 1978) recognized as valid a *talaq* divorce pronounced in New York but challenged and ruled upon by two high court judges in Karachi.

[52] 666 So. 2d 246 (Florida Ct. of Appeals, 2nd District 1996).

[53] Other cases involve whether a Muslim mother's favoring of her son at the expense of her daughter constitutes neglect of the latter, In Matter of Fred S., 385 N.Y.S. 2d 222 (Criminal Court of the City of New York, Kings County 1976); and whether a Syrian Christian couple who were married in Morocco are governed by the law of Morocco for liability for each other's debts, Nationwide Resources Corp. v. Massabni, 694 P. 2d 290 (Arizona Ct. of Appeals 1984).

which is not bridled by standard presumptions or fixed rules,' the court chose not to rely on American doctrines of resulting or constructive trusts but to recognize that under Iranian custom the parties meant their assets to remain separate notwith-standing the appearance of a gift under some interpretations of American law.[54]

Thus we see that American courts have not deferred to Islamic law any more than any other religious or foreign law but have acceded to the arrangements of the parties when the clear public policy concerns of the state are not violated. Unlike those of some other countries, however, American courts are not willing to allow this degree of accommodation to go so far as to constitute different standards for different groups. In this regard, as in the case of the cultural defense plea, the assimilationist thrust of American law remains strong even as equitable principles seem to permit some degree of flexibility.

EMPLOYMENT AND RELIGIOUS DISCRIMINATION

Proving racial or religious discrimination in American courts requires a demonstra-tion not only that harassment has occurred but that it was intentional, and so severe and pervasive as to create a hostile work environment.[55] The Supreme Court has held that the main federal statute protecting against discrimination by a state insti-tution or employer was not solely intended to cover non-Caucasians, and that a person of Arab ancestry qualifies for protection under the statute.[56] But proving intent and the other elements of discrimination is a difficult level to achieve and the case law is clear that such suits succeed only in the most egregious of instances. A review of cases involving Muslims appears to support this general pattern.[57]

A case from New Jersey that received a good deal of local press attention will illus-trate the matter.[58] A professor at Trenton State College, himself a native of Somalia

[54] Shayegan v. Baldwin, 566 A. 2d 1164, 1166 (N.J. Superior Ct., Appellate Division 1989).

[55] The most commonly applied definition of sexual harassment, derived from the Guidelines of the Equal Employment Opportunity Commission, speaks of 'verbal or physical conduct of a sexual nature [that] has the purpose or effect of unreasonably interfering with an individual's work performance or creating an intimidating, hostile, or offensive work environment.' 29 Code of Federal Regulations ¶1604.11(a)(3). Although not binding on courts the Guidelines have been relied upon in fashioning the statutes and regulations of a number of states, as well as in a number of sexual and racial harassment cases. See Meritor Savings Bank, F.S.B. v. Vinson, 477 U.S. 57, 65 (1986). See also Harris v. Forklift Systems, Inc., 510 U.S. 17 (1993) (comments did not create abusive environment because they were not 'so severe as to . . . seriously affect [Harris'] psychological well-being' or lead her to 'suffer injury').

[56] Saint Francis College v. Al-Khazraji, 481 U.S. 604 (1986).

[57] Indeed, I have yet to locate a successful case involving a Muslim and a complaint of employment discrimination based on ancestry or religion. Among the unsuccessful cases are Barkat v. Excelsior Mfg., 1995 LEXIS 1572 (District Ct., Eastern Illinois 1995) (Muslim woman denied relief for a claim of reli-gious discrimination brought against her Hindu employer), and Schbley v. Gould, 1994 U.S. District Ct. LEXIS 17200 (District Ct. of Kansas 1994) (plaintiff fails to show employment discrimination on basis of religious harassment by employer who, among other comments, called plaintiff a 'camel jockey').

[58] The case was reported almost daily in *The Times* (Trenton), Hamilton-Metro Section from early November 1995 until the jury verdict on 6 December 1995. Testimony about Islam was offered during the trial by Professor Richard Bulliet of Columbia University, but I have found no published report of that testimony.

who was black and Muslim, accused two other members of his department of racial and religious harassment. Specifically, his accusation concerned the posting of racist cartoons and being taunted with food during the month-long fast of Ramadan.[59] Plaintiff's expert testified as to the psychological and physiological harm he had suffered as a result, while defense experts testified that the plaintiff was probably suffering from extreme anxiety and depression before he encountered difficulties with his colleagues.[60] Weighing heavily was the uncontradicted testimony that both defendants had successfully worked to overturn an administration decision denying the plaintiff tenure.[61] After deliberating for two and a half hours an all-white jury of eight women and one man unanimously rejected the plaintiff's claims.[62]

There are, however, instances in which the courts will support distinctions based on religion as well as those in which they will move sharply to bar them. In *Kern v. Dynalectron Corp.* a federal court upheld as permissible an employment contract that stipulated that only Muslims could be hired to fly helicopters over the holy cities of Saudi Arabia.[63] And when an airline stopped passengers from boarding its airplanes solely because they were dressed in the clothes associated with Muslims of the Middle East the court did not hesitate to find the practice discriminatory.[64]

PATTERNS AND PERSPECTIVES

Certain patterns emerge from the review of these cases, patterns that cannot be understood only as the approach by American courts to Islam and Muslim cultures in particular but as part of the legal approach to questions of religious freedom, employment discrimination, and criminal justice more generally. When both of these elements are taken together the interaction of cultures within the particular domain of the law can be seen as part of a larger political-legal-cultural pattern.

It is clear that American courts tend to approach Islam from their understanding of Christianity and Judaism. This is hardly surprising, but it has had some results that the courts themselves have had to self-consciously modify over time. On the one hand, Islam is rendered familiar by being seen as textually based, by having one day

---

[59] The plaintiff asserted that one of the defendants had interrupted one of the plaintiff's classes and tossed him a paper bag that contained a ham sandwich (*The Times* (Trenton), 10 November 1995, A2). The plaintiff also alleged that this same defendant had brought him a puppet with exaggerated black features and holding a slice of watermelon and said that the doll was for his 'little nigger,' referring to the plaintiff's two-year-old son (*The Times* (Trenton), 23 November 1995, A2).

[60] *The Times* (Trenton), 29 November 1995, A2.

[61] *The Times* (Trenton), 23 November 1995, A2.

[62] Although the plaintiff had, in no small part because of the efforts of the defendants, obtained tenure in 1988, he failed on four occasions to achieve further promotion because he had no publications. The defense argued that his reason for bringing the suit against the College was primarily to get more money. Before the case went to the jury the judge accepted a motion for a directed verdict in favor of one of the two defendants (*The Times* (Trenton), 6 December 1995, p. A1).

[63] 577 F. Supp. 1196 (Northern District of Texas 1983).

[64] Bilal v. Northwest Airlines, 1994 Minnesota Appeals LEXIS 1052 (1994).

that can be analogized to the Judeo-Christian Sabbath, by having dietary laws like those of familiar faiths, and by having houses of worship and times of prayer that do not look all that different from those of mainstream American religions. This has no doubt contributed to Muslim employees and prisoners gaining recognition for the treatment of Muslims that is similar to the treatment of Christians and Jews. And even where Muslim 'sectarian' differences are at issue the courts have applied the criteria developed in thinking about the fractionation of more familiar religions.

Given the jurisprudence of attending to non-majoritarian religions, however, the courts developed concepts which, when applied to all religions, have begun to show certain strains. From the encounters with the religions of Native Americans, who unlike Christians did not have site-specific practices or used substances that were not part of Western religious traditions, the courts developed such criteria as the 'centrality and indispensability' of a practice to a given faith. The result has occasionally been applied to Muslims as the courts have sought to determine what is important to a given Black Muslim sect or Muslim marital arrangement. As in the case of Native Americans this put the courts in the position of deciding what is central to another's faith, a position with which some judges have become increasingly uncomfortable. As this standard has largely been set aside in American Indian matters, so, too, it is likely to become outmoded in dealing with Muslims. And just as unfamiliar practices may not be barred by ordinances specifically aimed against them,[65] so the present move toward greater accommodation of religion will almost certainly affect Muslims as much as other American religious groups.

Certain stereotypes nevertheless persist, but they are stereotypes that Americans possess of their own society and polity and not only of Islam. In the cultural defense plea, for example, it is clear that images of a melting-pot society and of a necessary period of encounter with the standards of the new host society contend with one another to produce a certain legal hypocrisy—no formal cultural defense, but we still want to hear about a person's cultural background—that affects Muslims as well as many others. It is true, too, that Americans tend to see culture as an aspect of personality rather than as something collective, a view that fits with Judeo-Christian-American views of individualism, free will, and the ability to assimilate wherever one chooses. Just as Americans have trouble conceiving of choice as limited by culture, so, too, Americans are not prepared to give up a self-image that is coupled to that of the nation as a whole by deferring in any formal way to the constraints of separate attachments.

The United States is in the midst of an important period in what might be called its jurisprudence of culture. Two intertwined questions are being addressed simultaneously: How much difference, and of what sorts, are Americans prepared to accept? And, at what level—federal, state, or local—will the determinations of acceptable difference be decided? The United States Supreme Court has, in recent years, sought

---

[65] See Church of the Lukumi Babalu Aye v. City of Hialeah, 508 U.S. 520 (1993) (invalidating municipal ordinance barring animal sacrifice by members of the Santeria faith).

to propel far more considerations down to the state level than had been true for several generations.[66] At the same time debates rage on such topics as whether homosexual marriage will be permissible in some states, thus perhaps forcing other states to acknowledge such unions under the full faith and credit clause, or whether the provisions of the Constitution on religious freedom require an absolute wall of separation or a more nuanced form of accommodation. If history suggests anything in this domain it is, once again, that the cases brought from the margin will be those that set the terms of discussion for the mainstream approaches.

Assimilation and accommodation are thus often at odds with one another in American politics and law—whether it be in school prayer and public support for religious education, or in the appropriation of unflattering ethnic references in the promotion of sports or commercial products.[67] The Islamic religion and Muslim residents in the United States will continue to have to contend with these superordinate themes in American life and law as they pursue their own ways of seeking accommodation and distinction in this multicentric socio-legal environment. In doing so they may, as so many other groups before them have done, force Americans, through the legal system, to attend to the different beliefs and practices of those who reside in the country and to question fundamental concepts of law and civil society in the process.

If, as Professor Bennouna has suggested, universal rights must be subject to local implementation, and if, as Richard Falk has noted, every people must have an existential sense of such rights rather than a sense of them having been imposed upon them under the guise of what is the universally valid, then the American experience becomes an example of human rights coming from below (to borrow the characterization of Professor Afshari)—an example of what Saad Ibrahim has called 'the historicity of human rights.' Whatever its value for those whose lives are shaped by it and whatever its merits as a model for others, the continuing story of the legal position of Muslims and Islamic culture in the United States will offer a valuable subject for consideration in the patterns of local implementation of the human rights Muslims and non-Muslims alike are striving to achieve in each of the nation-states to whose life they contribute.

---

[66] See, e.g., the decision in Seminole Tribe of Florida v. Florida, 116 S. Ct. 1114 (1996).
[67] See, e.g., Newton (1995) and Coombe (1998).

References

AGMON, I. (1999), Gender and Welfare: The Discourse of the Family and the State in Late Ottoman Shari'a Court Records (unpublished conference paper).

AGOUMY, T. A. (1994), 'Housing the Urban Poor of Taza, Morocco, and the Impact of the Relocation Process', Ph.D. thesis, Near East Studies Dept. (Princeton: Princeton University).

AJANI, G. (1995), 'By Chance and Prestige: Legal Transplants in Russia and Eastern Europe', *The American Journal of Comparative Law*, 43: 93–117.

AKTAR, S. (1990), 'Art or Literary Terrorism?', in D. Cohn-Sherbok (ed.), *The Salman Rushdie Controversy in Interreligious Perspective* (Lewiston: The Edwin Mellen Press), 1–23.

ALEINIKOFF, T. A. and MARTIN, D. A. (1985), *Immigration: Process and Policy* (St. Paul: West Publishing Co.).

AL-HABBAL, M. J. and HAQQI, R. I. (1997), 'The Certainty of an Empty Uterus ('istibrā' al-raḥim) in Divorced and Widowed Women: A Qur'ānic-Medical Study of 'iddah and the Reasons for Variation in its Duration', *Journal of IMA*, 29/4: 182–5.

AL-KINDI, A. b. A. (1979–84), *Musannaf* (Cairo and Matrah: Wizarat al-Tutath al-Qawmi).

AL-LAHEIDAN, S. S. I. M. (1976), 'Means of Evidence in Islamic Law', in *The Effects of Islamic Legislation on Crime Prevention in Saudi Arabia* (Rome: United Nations Social Defense Research Institute), 149–92.

ALLISON, J. W. F. (1996), *A Continental Distinction in Common Law* (Oxford: Clarendon Press).

ALLY, M. I. (1990), 'Second Introductory Paper', in *Law, Blasphemy and the Multi-Faith Society* (London: Commission for Racial Equality and the Inter Faith Network of the United Kingdom), 21–9.

AL-QARADAWI, Y. (1985), *The Lawful and the Prohibited in Islam* (London: Shorouk International).

ANDERSON, J. N. D. (1958), 'Reforms in Family Law in Morocco', *Journal of African Law*, 2: 146–59.

AN-NAIM, A. (1986), 'The Islamic Law of Apostasy and its Modern Applicability: A Case from the Sudan', *Religion*, 16: 197–224.

—— (1990), *Toward an Islamic Reformation: Civil Liberties, Human Rights, and International Law* (Syracuse, NY: Syracuse University Press).

ANTOUN, R. T. (1972), *Arab Village: A Social Structural Study of a Trans-Jordanian Peasant Community* (Bloomington: Indiana University Press).

APPIGNANESI, L. and MAITLAND, S. (eds.) (1990), *The Rushdie File* (Syracuse, NY: Syracuse University Press).

ARABI, O. (1998), 'Contract Stipulations (Shurut) in Islamic Law: The Ottoman Majalla and Ibn Taymiyya', *International Journal of Middle East Studies*, 30/1: 29–50.

ARTZ, D. E. (1996), 'The Treatment of Religious Dissidents under Classical and Contemporary Islamic Law', in J. J. Wittle and J. D. Vyver (eds.), *Religious Human Rights in Global Perspective, Vol 1: Religious Perspectives* (The Hague: Kluwer International), 387–453.

ASAD, T. (1993), *Genealogies of Religion: Discipline and Reasons of Power in Christianity and Islam* (Baltimore: Johns Hopkins Press).

ASHRAF, A. (1990), 'Nihilistic, Negative, Satanic', in L. Appiganesi and S. Maitland (eds.), *The Rushdie File* (Syracuse, NY: Syracuse University Press), 24–7.

ASMAL, A. M. (1998), 'Muslims under Non-Muslim Rule: The *Fiqhi* (legal) Views of Ibn Nujaym and al-Wansharisi', unpublished Ph.D. dissertation, Faculty of Arts, University of Manchester.

AYOUB, M. (1996), 'The Islamic Concept of Justice', in N. H. Barazangi, M. R. Zaman, and O. Afzal (eds.), *Islamic Identity and the Struggle for Justice* (Gainesville: University of Florida Press), 19–26.

BAGHBY, I. A. (1985), 'The Issue of Maslaha in Classical Islamic Legal Theory', *International Journal of Islamic and Arabic Studies*, 2/2: 1–11.

BAIER, A. (1986), 'Trust and Antitrust', *Ethics*, 96: 231–60.

BARRY, B. (1980), 'Justice as Reciprocity', in E. Kamanka and A. Erh-Soon (eds.), *Justice* (New York: St. Martins Press), 50–78.

BASSIRI, K. G. (1997), *Competing Visions of Islam in the United States: A Study of Los Angeles* (Westport, Conn.: Greenwood Press).

BECKER, L. C. (1996), 'Trust as Noncognitive Security about Motives', *Ethics*, 107/1: 43–61.

BELLEY, J.-G. (1997), *Le Pluralisme, juridique/Legal Pluralism*, Special Issue of *Canadian Journal of Law and Society*, 12/2.

BERG, H. (1998), 'Elijah Muhammad: An African American Muslim Mufassir?', *Arabica*, 45/4: 320–46.

BERQUE, J. (1944), *Essai sur la méthode juridique maghrébine* (Rabat: n.p.).

—— (1960), ''Amal', in B. Lewis, C. Pellat, and J. Schacht (eds.), *The Encyclopaedia of Islam*, (London: Luzac & Co.), 427–8.

—— and Charnay, J.-P. (eds.) (1967), *L'Ambivalence dans la culture arabe* (Paris: Editions Anthropos).

BOHANNON, P. (1957), *Justice and Judgement among the Tiv* (Oxford: Oxford University Press).

BORRMANS, M. (1977), *Statut personnel et famille au Maghreb de 1940 à nos jours* (Paris: Mouton).

BOURGEOISE, P. (1959–60), *L'Universe de l'écolier marocain, fascicules no. 1–5* (Rabat: Faculté des Lettres et des Sciences Sociales).

BOWEN, J. R. (1993), *Muslims through Discourse: Religion and Ritual in Gayo Society* (Princeton: Princeton University Press).

BROOKS, G. (1995), *Nine Parts of Desire: The Hidden World of Islamic Women* (New York: Doubleday).

BRUNSCHVIG, R. (1960a), 'Aḳila', in H. A. R. Gibbs, J. H. Kramers, E. Lévi-Provençal, and J. Schacht (eds.), *Encyclopaedia of Islam*, i (Leiden: E. J. Brill), 337–40.

—— (1960b), 'Bayyina', in H. A. R. Gibbs, J. H. Kramers, E. Lévi-Provençal, and J. Schacht (eds.), *Encyclopaedia of Islam*, i (Leiden: E. J. Brill), 1150–1.

—— (1963), 'Le Systeme de la preuve en droit musulman', *Récueil de la Société Jean Bodin pour l'Histoire Comparative des Institutions*, 18: 169–86.

BURKE, K. (1962), *The Rhetoric of Motives* (Berkeley: University of California Press).

BURTON, J. (1994), *An Introduction to the Hadith* (Edinburgh: Edinburgh University Press).

BUTLER, P. (1996), 'Racially Based Jury Nullification: Black Power in the Criminal Justice System', *Yale Law Journal*, 105/3: 677–725.

CAHEN, C. (1965), 'Dhimma', in B. Lewis, C. Pellat, and J. Schacht (eds.), *The Encyclopaedia of Islam*, ii (London: Luzac & Co.), 227–31.

CAIN, A. J. (1993), *Animal Species and Their Evolution* (Princeton: Princeton University Press).

CALDER, N. (1993), *Studies in Early Muslim Jurisprudence* (Oxford: Clarendon Press).

CANTOR, N. F. (1997), *Imagining the Law: Common Law and the Foundations of the American Legal System* (New York: HarperCollins).

CHEHATA, C. (1965), 'Dhimma', in B. Lewis, C. Pellat, and J. Schacht (eds.), *The Encyclopaedia of Islam*, ii (London: Luzac & Co.), 231–2.

—— (1968), 'Le Concept de contrat en droit musulman', *Archives de Philosophie du Droit*, 13.

—— (1970), 'Islamic Law', in R. David (ed.), *International Encyclopedia of Comparative Law*, ii (Paris: Mouton), 138–42.

Chicago Tribune (1997), 'Two Sent to Prison for Underage Marriages', *The Chicago Tribune*, 24 September, 6.

CHLOROS, A. G. (1978), 'Common Law, Civil Law and Socialist Law: Three Leading Systems of the World, Three Kinds of Legal Thought', *The Cambrian Law Review*: 11–26.

CHRAA, T. (1956), 'Audience du 12 avril 1955', *Révue Marocaine de Droit*: 468.

CLAGHORN, K. H. (1923), *The Immigrant's Day in Court* (New York: Harper & Brothers).

CLEGG, C. A. (1997), *An Original Man: The Life and Times of Elijah Muhammad* (New York: St. Martin's Press).

COHEN, A. (1965), *Arab Border-Villages in Israel* (Manchester: Manchester University Press).

COLOMER, A. (1963), *Droit musulman, Tome Premier, Les Personnes—La Famille,* (Rabat: Éditions La Porte).

—— (1967), *Droit musulman, Tome Deuxième, Statut successoral* (Rabat: Éditions La Porte).

COLSON, E. (1995), 'The Contentiousness of Disputes', in P. Caplan (ed.), *Understanding Disputes: The Politics of Argument* (Oxford: Berg), 65–82.

COMAIR-OBEID, N. (1996), *The Law of Business Contracts in the Arab Middle East* (The Hague: Kluwer International).

COMMISSION FOR RACIAL EQUALITY (1990), *Britain: A Plural Society* (London: Commission for Racial Equality).

CONRAD, J. (1976; orig. pub. 1896), *An Outcast of the Islands* (London: Penguin).

COOMBE, R. J. (1998), *The Cultural Life of Intellectual Property* (Durham, NC: Duke University Press).

COULSON, N. (1956), 'Doctrine and Practice in Islamic Law', *Bulletin of the School of Oriental and African Studies*, 18/2: 211–26.

—— (1959), 'Muslim Custom and Case-Law', *Die Welt des Islams*, 6/1–2: 13–24.

—— (1964), *A History of Islamic Law* (Edinburgh: Edinburgh University Press).

—— (1984), *Commercial Law in the Gulf States: The Islamic Legal Tradition* (London: Graham & Trotman).

CRAGG, K. (1965), *Counsels In Contemporary Islam* (Edinburgh: Edinburgh University Press).

CRAPANZANO, V. (1980), *Tuhami: Portrait of a Moroccan* (Chicago: University of Chicago Press).

CRONE, P. (1987), *Roman, Provincial and Islamic Law: The Origins of the Islamic Patronate* (Cambridge: Cambridge University Press).

CRUZ, P. (1995), *Comparative Law in a Changing World* (London: Cavendish Publishing Limited).

CUPIT, G. (1996), *Justice as Fittingness* (Oxford: Oxford University Press).

DALLAL, S. J. (1986), 'The Judicial System of Islam', *The Search: Journal for Arab and Islamic Studies*, 7: 1–28.

DAMASKA, M. (1986), *The Faces of Justice and State Authority* (New Haven: Yale University Press).

DAVID, R. (1975), 'Introduction', in R. David (ed.) *International Encyclopedia of Comparative Law*, ii (Tübingen: J. C. B. Mohr), 3–13.

DEWEY, J. (1924), 'Logical Method and Law', *Cornell Law Quarterly*, 10/1: 17–27.

DOI, A. R. I. (1984), *Shari'ah: The Islamic Law* (London: Ta Ha Publishers).

DOUGLAS, A. and MALTI-DOUGLAS, F. (1994), *Arab Comic Strips: Politics of an Emerging Mass Culture* (Bloomington: Indiana University Press).

DUBY, G. (1988), 'Preface', in G. Duby (ed.), *A History of the Private Life, Vol II: Revelations of the Medieval World* (Cambridge: Harvard University Press), pp. ix–xiii.

DUGGER, C. W. (1997), 'U.S. Grants Asylum to Woman Fleeing Female Genital Mutilation Rite', *The New York Times*, 14 June, A1.

DUTTON, Y. (1999), 'Judicial Practice and Madinan *'Amal: Qaḍa'* in the *Muwaṭṭa'* of Mā lik', *Journal of Islamic Studies*, 10/1: 1–21.

DWYER, D. H. (1977), 'Bridging the Gap Between the Sexes in Moroccan Legal Practice', in A. Schlegel (ed.), *Sexual Stratification: A Cross-Cultural View* (New York: Columbia University Press), 41–66.

ECHO-HAWK, W. (1996), 'Native Worship in American Prisons', *Cultural Survival*, 19/4: 58–62.

EDGE, I. (1989), 'Egyptian Family Law: The Tale of the Jinn', *International and Comparative Law Quarterly*, 38/3: 682–5.

EISENBERG, M. A. (1988), *The Nature of the Common Law* (Cambridge, Mass.: Harvard University Press).

EL-HAKIM, J. (1971), *Le Dommage du source délictuelle en droit musulman* (Paris: Librairie Général de Droit et de Jurisprudence).

ENGEL, D. M. (1978), *Code and Custom in a Thai Provincial Court: The Interaction of Formal and Informal Systems of Justice* (Tucson: University of Arizona Press).

ESSAID, M. J. (1998), *Introduction à l'étude du droit* ([Rabat, Morocco]: Collection Connaissances).

FAULKNER, R. (1994), 'Evidence of First Amendment Activity at Trial: The Articulation of a Higher Evidentiary Standard', *U.C.L.A. Law Review*, 42/1: 1–46.

FEIFER, G. (1964), *Justice in Moscow* (London: Bodley Head).

FLUEHR-LOBBAN, C. (1987), *Islamic Law and Society in the Sudan* (London: Cass).

FORTE, D. F. (1993), 'Islamic Law in American Courts', *Suffolk Transnational Law Journal*, 7:1–33.

FOUCAULT, M. (1970), *The Order of Things: An Archaeology of the Human Sciences* (London: Routledge).

FRANKENBERG, G. (1985), 'Critical Comparisons: Re-thinking Comparative Law', *Harvard International Law Journal*, 26/2: 411–55.

FRIEDMAN, T. L. (1989), *From Beirut to Jerusalem* (New York: Doubleday).

GALANTER, M. (1981), 'Justice in Many Rooms: Private Ordering and Indigenous Law', *Journal of Legal Pluralism and Unofficial Law*, 19: 1–47.

GALLAGHER, C. (1959), 'New Laws for Old: The Moroccan Code of Personal Status', *American Universities Field Staff Reports, North Africa Series*, 5: 1–12.

—— (1963), *The United States and North Africa* (Cambridge, Mass.: Harvard University Press).

GARDNER, F. (1999), 'Yemen Killers Get Death Penalty', *The Independent* (London), 6 May, 14.

GATES, H. L., Jr. (1992), 'Black Demagogues and Pseudo-Scholars', *The New York Times*, 20 July, A15.

GEERTZ, C. (1968), *Islam Observed* (New Haven: Yale University Press).

—— (1973), *The Interpretation of Cultures* (New York: Basic Books).

—— (1979), 'The Bazaar', in C. Geertz, H. Geertz, and L. Rosen (eds.), *Meaning and Order in Moroccan Society* (New York: Cambridge University Press), 123–313.

—— (1983), *Local Knowledge: Further Essays in Interpretive Anthropology* (New York: Basic Books).

—— GEERTZ, H. and ROSEN, L. (1979), *Meaning and Order in Moroccan Society: Three Essays in Cultural Analysis* (New York: Cambridge University Press).

GELLNER, E. (1988), 'Trust, Cohesion, and Social Order', in D. Gambetta (ed.), *Trust: Making and Breaking Cooperative Relations* (Oxford: Basil Blackwell), 142–57.

GERBER, H. (1994), *State, Society, and Law in Islam: Ottoman Law in Comparative Perspective* (Albany: State University of New York Press).

GHANEM, I. (1982), *Islamic Medical Jurisprudence* (London: Arthur Probsthain).

GILMORE, D. D. (Ed.) (1987), *Honor and Shame and the Unity of the Mediterranean* (Washington: American Anthropological Association).

GITTES, K. S. (1983), 'The *Canterbury Tales* and the Arabic Frame Tradition', *PMLA (Publications of the Modern Language Association),* 98: 237–51.

GLUCKMAN, M. (1955), *The Judicial Process among the Barotse of Northern Rhodesia* (Manchester: Manchester University Press).

GOITEIN, S. D. (1960), 'The Birth Hour of Muslim Law?', *The Muslim World,* 50/1: 23–9.

—— (1967–83), *A Mediterranean Society* (Berkeley: University of California Press).

GOLDZIHER, I. (1981), *Introduction to Islamic Theology and Law* (Princeton: Princeton University Press).

GOODRICH, P. (1994), 'Antirrhesis: Polemical Structures of Common Law Thought', in A. Sarat and T. R. Kearns (eds.), *The Rhetoric of Law* (Ann Arbor: University of Michigan Press), 57–102.

GORDLEY, J. (1991), *The Philosophical Origins of Modern Contract Doctrine* (Oxford: Clarendon Press).

GOULD, S. J. (1978), *Ever Since Darwin* (New York: Norton).

—— (1985), *The Flamingo's Smile* (New York: Norton).

—— (1989), 'Judging the Perils of Official Hostility to Scientific Error', *The New York Times,* 30 July, E6.

GREGORY, S. S. (1994), 'At Risk of Mutilation', *Time,* 21 March, 45–6.

GREIF, A. (1989), 'Reputation and Coalitions in Medieval Trade: Evidence on the Maghribi Traders', *Journal of Economic History,* 49/4: 857–82.

—— (1993), 'Contract Enforceability and Economic Institutions in Early Trade: The Maghribi Traders' Coalition', *American Economic Review,* 83/3: 525–48.

GRIFFITHS, J. (1986), 'What is Legal Pluralism?', *Journal of Legal Pluralism,* 24: 1–55.

GRINSTEIN, J. (1996), 'Jihad and the Constitution: The First Amendment Implications of Combating Religiously Motivated Terrorism', *Yale Law Journal,* 105/5: 1347–82.

HADDAD, Y. Y. (ed.) (1991), *The Muslims of America* (New York: Oxford University Press).

—— (1993), *Mission To America: Five Islamic Sectarian Communities in North America* (Gainesville: University of Florida Press).

—— and Smith, J. I. (eds.) (1994), *Muslim Communities in North America* (Albany: State University of New York Press).

HAERI, S. (1989), *Law of Desire: Temporary Marriage in Shi'i Iran* (Syracuse, NY: Syracuse University Press).

HALLAQ, W. B. (1984), 'Was the Gate of Ijtihad Closed?', *International Journal of Middle East Studies,* 16/1: 3–41.

HALLAQ, W. B. (1987), 'The Development of Logical Structure in Sunni Legal Theory', *Der Islam,* 64: 42–67.

—— (1994), 'Murder in Cordoba: Ijtihad, Ifta' and the Evolution of Substantive Law in Medieval Islam', *Acta Orientalia [Copenhagen],* 55: 55–83.

—— (1997), *A History of Islamic Legal Theories* (Cambridge: Cambridge University Press).

—— (1999), 'A Prelude to Ottoman Reform: Ibn 'Abidīn on Custom and Legal Change', unpublished manuscript.

HAMMOUDI, A. (1993), *The Victim and Its Masks: An Essay on Sacrifice and Masquerade in the Maghreb* (Chicago: University of Chicago Press).

—— (1997), *Master and Disciple: The Cultural Foundations of Moroccan Authoritarianism* (Chicago: University of Chicago Press).

—— (Ed.) (2000), *Universalizing From Particulars: Islamic Views of Human Rights* (London: I. B. Tauris).

—— and Rosen, L. (1993), 'Islam Doesn't Sanction Female Circumcision', *The New York Times,* 5 February, A26.

HARRIS, E. (1995), *Guarding the Secrets: Palestinian Terrorism and a Father's Murder of his Too-American Daughter* (New York: Scribner).

HART, D. (1996), 'Murder in the Market: Penal Aspects of Berber Customary Law in the Precolonial Moroccan Rif', *Islamic Law and Society,* 3/3: 343–71.

HART, H. L. A. (1961), *The Concept of Law* (Oxford: Oxford University Press).

HASSAN, A. (1970), *The Early Development of Islamic Jurisprudence* (Islamabad: Islamic Research Institute).

HAYWOOD, J. A. and NAHMAD, H. M. (1993), *A New Arabic Grammar of the Written Language* (London: Lund Humphries).

HENKIN, L., PUGH, R. C., SCHACHTER, O., and SMIT, H. (1993), *International Law: Cases and Materials* (St. Paul: West Publishing Co.).

HERMASSI, A. and HMED, A. M. (1983), *Le Divorce dans le région de Tunis: Evolution et aspects psycho-sociologiques* (Tunis: U.N.F.T., Alliance des Femmes de Carrière Juridique).

HILL, E. (1987), *Al-Sanhuri and Islamic Law: The Place and Significance of Islamic Law in the Life and Work of Abd al-Razzaq Ahmad al-Sanhuri, Egyptian Jurist and Scholar 1895–1971* (Cairo: American University in Cairo).

HODGSON, M. G. S. (1974), *The Venture of Islam, Volume I: The Classical Age of Islam* (Chicago: University of Chicago Press).

HOEBEL, E. A. (1954), *The Law of Primitive Man: A Study in Comparative Legal Dynamics* (Cambridge, Mass.: Harvard University Press).

—— (1965), 'Fundamental Cultural Postulates and Judicial Lawmaking in Pakistan', *American Anthropologist,* 67/6, part 2: 43–56.

HOLLIS, M. (1998), *Trust within Reason* (Cambridge: Cambridge University Press).

HORDER, J. (1992), *Provocation and Responsibility* (Oxford: Clarendon Press).

HOROWITZ, D. L. (1994), 'The Qur'an and the Common Law: Islamic Law Reform and the Theory of Legal Change', *The American Journal of Comparative Law,* 42/2 and 3: 233–93, 543–80.

HOWARD, P. K. (1994), *The Death of Common Sense: How Law is Suffocating America* (New York: Random House).

HOWARD-MERRIAM, K. (1988), 'Egyptian Islamism and the Law: Connecting the "Private" and the "Public" ', *International Journal of Islamic and Arabic Studies,* 5/1: 77–96.

HYLAND, R. (1996), 'Comparative Law', in D. Patterson (ed.), *A Companion to Philosophy of Law and Legal Theory* (Oxford: Blackwell Publishers), 184–99.

IMBER, C. (1997), *Ebu's-su'ud: The Islamic Legal Tradition* (Edinburgh: Edinburgh University Press).

IQBAL, M. (Ed.) (1988), *Distributive Justice and Need Fulfilment in an Islamic Economy* (Leicester: Islamic Foundation).

ISEMAN, P. A. (1978), 'The Arabian Ethos', *Harper's*, 256/February: 37–56.

IZUTSU, T. (1966), *Ethico-Religious Concepts in the Qur'an* (Montreal: McGill University Press).

JEHL, D. (1999), 'Saddam Appeals for Arab Uprising', *International Herald Tribune*, 6 January, 1.

JENNINGS, R. C. (1979), 'Limitations of the Judicial Powers of the Kadi in 17th c. Ottoman Kayseri', *Studia Islamica*, 50: 151–84.

JOHANSEN, B. (1990), 'Le Jugement comme preuve: Preuve juridique et vérité réligieuse dans le droit Islamique Hanéfite', *Studia Islamica*, 72: 5–17.

—— (1993), 'Legal Literature and the Problem of Change: The Case of the Land Rent', in C. Mallat (ed.), *Islam and Public Law* (London: Graham & Trotman), 29–47.

—— (1995), 'Casuistry: Between Legal Concept and Social Praxis', *Islamic Law and Society*, 2/2: 135–56.

JONES, K. (1996), 'Trust as an Affective Attitude', *Ethics*, 107/1: 4–25.

JONSEN, A. R. and TOULMIN, S. (1988), *The Abuse of Casuistry: A History of Moral Reasoning* (Berkeley: University of California Press).

JUYNBOLL, T. W. (1910), 'Crimes and Punishment (Muhammadan)', in J. Hastings (ed.), *Encyclopaedia of Religion and Ethics*, iv (New York: Scribner), 290–4.

—— (1953), 'Ḳadhf', in H. A. R. Gibbs and J. H. Kramers (eds.), *Shorter Encyclopaedia of Islam*, xii (Leiden: E. J. Brill), 201.

—— (1961a), ''Adhāb', in H. A. R. Gibbs and J. H. Kramers (eds.), *Shorter Encyclopaedia of Islam* (Leiden: E. J. Brill), 15–16.

—— (1961b), ''Aḳila', in H. A. R. Gibbs and J. H. Kramers (eds.), *Shorter Encyclopaedia of Islam* (Leiden: E. J. Brill), 29–30.

KAHERA, A. I. and BENMIRA, O. (1998), 'Damages in Islamic Law: Maghribi Muftis and the Built Environment (9th–15th Centuries C.E.)', *Islamic Law and Society*, 5/2: 131–64.

KAMALI, M. H. (1991), *Principles of Islamic Jurisprudence* (Cambridge: Islamic Texts Society).

—— (1993), 'Freedom of Expression in Islam: An Analysis of Fitnah', *American Journal of Islamic Social Science*, 10/2: 178–200.

—— (1996), 'Islamic Commercial Law: An Analysis of Futures', *American Journal of Islamic Social Sciences*, 13/2: 197–224.

—— (1997), *Freedom of Expression in Islam*, rev. edn. (Cambridge: Islamic Text Society).

KAPCHAN, D. (1996), *Gender on the Market: Moroccan Women and the Revoicing of Tradition* (Philadelphia: University of Pennsylvania Press).

KARST, K. (1971), 'Rights in Land and Housing in an Informal Legal System: The Barrios of Caracas', *The American Journal of Comparative Law*, 19: 550–74.

KASSEM, H. (1972), 'The Idea of Justice in Islamic Philosophy', *Diogenes*, 79: 81–108.

KASSINDJA, F. (1998), *Do They Hear You When You Cry?* (New York: Delacorte Press).

KELLAL, A. (1958), 'Le Serment en droit musulman, École Malékite', *Révue Algérienne, Tunisienne et Marocaine de Législation et de Jurisprudence*, 74/1: 18–53.

KENNETT, A. (1968), *Bedouin Justice* (London: Cass).

KEPEL, G. (1997), *Allah in the West: Islamic Movements in America and Europe* (Stanford: Stanford University Press).

KERR, M. H. (1966), *Islamic Reform: The Political and Legal Theories of Muhammad Abduh and Rashid Rida* (Berkeley: University of California Press).

—— (1968), 'Moral and Legal Judgment Independent of Revelation', *Philosophy East and West*, 18/4: 277–83.

KHACHANI, M. B. (1998), 'Les Nouvelles Revisions du Code du Statut Personnel', in A. Belarbi (ed.), *Femmes et Islam* (Casablanca: Editions Le Fennec), 19–34.

KHADDURI, M. (1984), *The Islamic Conception of Justice* (Baltimore: Johns Hopkins Press).

KHALDUN, IBN (1958), *The Muqaddimah: An Introduction to History*, trans. Franz Rosenthal (New York: Pantheon).

KHAN, K. M. (1983), 'Juristic Classification of Islamic Law', *Houston Journal of International Law*, 6: 24–7.

KHAN, S. (1993), 'Canadian Muslim Women and Shari'a Law: A Feminist Response to "Oh! Canada" ', *Canadian Journal of Women and the Law*, 6: 52–65.

KORN, F. and KORN, S. R. D. (1983), 'Where People Don't Promise', *Ethics*, 93/3: 445–50.

KRESSEL, G. M. (1981), 'Sororicide-filiacide—Homicide for Family Honor', *Current Anthropology*, 22: 141–58.

KUHN, T. (1970), *The Structure of Scientific Revolutions* (Chicago: University of Chicago Press).

LAPANNE-JOINVILLE, J. (1957), 'Études de droit musulman malékite: Les présomptions', *Révue Algérienne, Tunisienne et Marocaine de Législation et de Jurisprudence*, 73/4: 99–113.

—— (1959), 'Le Code Marocain du Statut Personnel', *Révue Marocaine de Droit*, :97–9.

LAYISH, A. (1991), *Divorce in the Libyan Family* (New York: New York University Press).

LEVI, E. H. (1948), *An Introduction to Legal Reasoning* (Chicago: University of Chicago Press).

—— (1965), 'The Nature of Judicial Reasoning', *The University of Chicago Law Review*, 32/3: 395–409.

LEWIS, B. (1970), *Race and Color in Islam* (New York: Harper & Row).

—— (1984), *The Jews of Islam* (Princeton: Princeton University Press).

—— (1988), *The Political Language of Islam* (Chicago: University of Chicago Press).

—— (1993), *Islam in History* (Chicago: Open Court).

LIBSON, G. (1997), 'On the Development of Custom as a Source of Law in Islamic Society', *Islamic Law and Society*, 4/2: 131–55.

LIEBESNY, H. J. (1975), *The Law of the Near and Middle East* (Albany: State University of New York Press).

LIMPENS, J., KRUITHOF, R. M., and MEINERTZHAGEN-LIMPENS, A. (1983), 'Liability for One's Own Acts', in R. David (ed.), *International Encyclopedia of Comparative Law*, Vol. xi, Torts, ch. 2, s. 39 (Tübingen: J. C. B. Mohr), 20–2.

LINANT DE BELLEFONDS, Y. (1965), *Traité de droit musulman comparée, Tome I: Théorie générale de l'acte juridique* (Paris: Mouton).

LIPPMAN, M., MCCONVILLE, S., and YERUSHALMI, M. (1988), *Islamic Criminal Law and Procedure* (New York: Praeger).

LIPSON, L. and WHEELER, S. (Eds.) (1986), *Law and the Social Sciences* (New York: Russell Sage Foundation).

LUHMANN, N. (1979), *Trust and Power* (New York: John Wiley and Sons).

MCCARTHY, M. (1998), 'Scientists Reclassify All Plants', *The Independent* (London), 22 November, 1.

MCCLOUD, A. B. (1995–6), 'American Muslim Women and U.S. Society', *Journal of Law and Religion*, 12/1: 51–9.

MACDONALD, D. B. and CALVERLEY, E. E. (1971), 'Ḥaḳḳ', in B. Lewis, V. L. Ménage, C. Pellat, and J. Schacht (eds.), *Encyclopaedia of Islam,* iii (Leiden: E. J. Brill), 82–3.

MADHSHURAT JEMI'AT AL-HUQUQIYIN AL-MAGHEBIYA (1976), *Maḥākem al-Jemā'at wa al-Muqāt'aṭ* (Casablanca: Dar an-Nasher al-Maghrebiya).

MAHDI, M. (1957), *Ibn Khaldun's Philosophy of History: A Study in the Foundation of the Science of Culture* (Chicago: University of Chicago Press).

MAHMOOD, T. (1972), *Family Law Reform in the Muslim World* (Bombay: Tripathi).

MAINE, H. (1986), *Ancient Law* (Tucson: University of Arizona Press).

MAITLAND, S. (1990), 'Blasphemy and Creativity', in D. Cohn-Sherbok (ed.), *The Salman Rushdie Controversy in Interreligious Perspective* (Lewiston: The Edwin Mellen Press), 115–30.

MAKDISI, J. (1985a), 'Legal Logic and Equity in Islamic Law', *American Journal of Comparative Law,* 33/1: 63–92.

—— (1985b), 'An Objective Approach to Contractual Mistake in Islamic Law', *Boston University International Law Journal,* 3: 325–44.

—— (1990), 'An Inquiry into Islamic Influences during the Formative Period of the Common Law', in N. Heer (ed.), *Islamic Law and Jurisprudence* (Seattle: University of Washington Press), 135–46.

MALTI-DOUGLAS, F. (1988), 'The Classical Arabic Detective Novel', *Arabica,* 35: 59–91.

MANNAN, M. A. (1986), *Islamic Economics: Theory and Practice* (Cambridge, UK: The Islamic Academy).

MARGOLIOUTH, D. S. (1910), 'Expiation and Atonement (Muslim)', in J. Hastings (ed.), *Encyclopaedia of Religion and Ethics,* v (New York: Scribner), 664.

MARTIN, E. (1991), 'The Egg and the Sperm: How Science Has Constructed a Romance Based on Stereotypical Male–Female Roles', *Signs,* 16/3: 485–501.

MASUD, M. K. (1977), *Islamic Legal Philosophy: A Study of Abu Ishaq Al-Shatibi's Life and Thought* (Islamabad: Islamic Research Institute).

MATTEI, U. (1997), 'Three Patterns of Law: Taxonomy and Change in the World's Legal Systems', *The American Journal of Comparative Law,* 45/1: 5–44.

MAZRUI, A. A. (1989), *The 'Satanic Verses' or a Satanic Novel? The Moral Dilemmas of the Rushdie Affair* (Greenpoint, NY: The Committee of Muslim Scholars and Leaders of North America).

MEEKER, M. E. (1979), *Literature and Violence in North Arabia* (Cambridge: Cambridge University Press).

MERRY, S. (1988), 'Legal Pluralism', *Law and Society Review,* 1988: 869–96.

MESSICK, B. (1993), *The Calligraphic State: Textual Domination and History in a Muslim Society* (Berkeley: University of California Press).

METCALF, B. D. (ed.) (1996), *Making Muslim Space in North America and Europe* (Berkeley: University of California Press).

MEZ, A. (1937), *The Renaissance of Islam* (London: Luzac).

MILLIOT, L. (1918), *Démembrements du Habous* (Paris: Éditions Leroux).

—— (1920), *Récueil de jurisprudence chérifienne* (Paris: Editions Leroux).

—— (1924), *Récueil de jurisprudence chérifienne* (Paris: Éditions Leroux).

—— (1953), *Introduction à l'étude du droit musulman* (Paris: Librairie Récueil Sirey).

—— and LAPANNE-JOINVILLE, J. (1952), *Récueil de jurisprudence chérifienne* (Paris: Librairie Récueil Sirey).

MILLS, C. W. (1940), 'The Vocabulary of Emotions', *The American Journal of Sociology*, 5: 904–13.

MINISTÈRE DU PLAN, ROYAUME DU MAROC (1986), *Le Maroc en chiffres* (Casablanca: Impression Idéale).

MIR-HOSSEINI, Z. (1993), *Marriage On Trial: A Study of Islamic Family Law* (London: I. B. Tauris).

MOORE, K. M. (1995), *Al-Mughtaribun: American Law and the Transformation of Muslim Life in the United States* (Albany: State University of New York Press).

MOORE, S. F. (1972), 'Legal Liability and Evolutionary Interpretation: Some Aspects of Strict Liability, Self-help and Collective Responsibility', in M. Gluckman (ed.), *The Allocation of Responsibility* (Manchester: Manchester University Press), 51–108.

—— (1978), *Law as Process* (London: Routledge & Kegan Paul).

—— (1986), 'Legal Systems of the World', in L. Lipson and S. Wheeler (eds.), *Law and the Social Sciences* (New York: Russell Sage Foundation), 10–14.

MORÈRE, M. (1961), 'Le Procès criminel: L'Enquête sur 'la personnalité des inculpés' au Maroc', *Révue Marocaine de Droit*, 1961: 433–5.

MOTTAHEDEH, R. P. (1980), *Loyalty and Leadership in an Early Islamic Society* (Princeton: Princeton University Press).

—— (1993), 'Toward an Islamic Theology of Toleration', in T. Lindholm and K. Vogt (eds.), *Islamic Law Reform and Human Rights* (Oslo: Nordic Human Rights Publications), 25–36.

MUSLEHUDDIN, M. (1975), *Islamic Jurisprudence and the Rule of Necessity and Need* (Islamabad: Islamic Research Institute).

NEW YORK TIMES (1994), 'Wellesley Leader Rebukes Professor for Book on Jewish Conspiracy', *The New York Times*, 1 February, A18.

NEW YORK TIMES (1998), 'Virginia Board Approves Saudi School Plan', *The New York Times*, 6 March, A17.

NEWMAN, R. (1961), *Equity and Law: A Comparative Study* (New York: Oceana Publications).

NEWTON, N. J. (1995), 'Memory and Misrepresentation: Representing Crazy Horse', *Connecticut Law Review*, 27: 1003–54.

NIMER, M. (1997), 'The Muslim Experience of Discrimination in the United States', *The Journal of Islamic Law*, 2/1: 21–44.

OLGIATI, V. (1997), 'Le Pluralisme juridique comme lutte pour le droit: La folie théorique et méthodologique d'une récente proposition', *Canadian Journal of Law and Society*, 12/2: 47–74.

ÖRÜCÜ, E. (1996), 'Mixed and Mixing Systems: A Conceptual Search', in E. Örücü, E. Attwooll, and S. Coyle (eds.), *Studies in Legal Systems: Mixed and Mixing* (The Hague: Kluwer International), 335–52.

PACHA, A. I. (1944), *De la résponsabilité pénale en droit islamique d'apres la Doctrine Hanafite* (Paris: T.E.P.A.C.).

PAREKH, B. (1990), 'The Rushdie Affair and the British Press', in D. Cohn-Sherbok (ed.), *The Salman Rushdie Controversy in Interreligious Perspective* (Lewiston: The Edwin Mellen Press), 71–96.

PEARL, D. (1985–6), 'Islamic Family Law and Anglo-American Public Policy', *Cleveland State Law Review*, 34: 113–28.

PERISTIANY, J. G. (ed.) (1966), *Honor and Shame: The Values of a Mediterranean Society* (Chicago: University of Chicago Press).

PETERSEN, H. and ZAHLE, H. (eds.) (1995), *Legal Polycentricity: Consequences of Pluralism in Law* (Aldershot, England: Dartmouth).

POSPISIL, L. (1967), 'Legal Levels and Multiplicity of Legal Systems in Human Societies', *The Journal of Conflict Resolution*, 11: 2–26.

POULTER, S. (1986), *English Law and Ethnic Minority Customs* (London: Butterworths).

—— (1990), 'The Claim to a Separate Islamic System of Personal Law for British Muslims', in C. Mallet and J. Connors (eds.), *Islamic Family Law* (London: Graham & Trotman), 147–66.

POWERS, D. S. (1986), *Studies in Qur'an and Hadith: The Formation of the Islamic Law of Inheritance* (Berkeley: University of California Press).

—— (1990a), 'A Court Case from Fourteenth-Century North Africa', *Journal of the American Oriental Society*, 110/2: 229–54.

—— (1990b), 'The Islamic Inheritance System: A Socio-Historical Approach', in C. Mallot and J. Connors (eds.), *Islamic Family Law* (London: Graham & Trotman), 11–29.

—— (1994) '*Kadijustiz* or *Qadi*-Justice? A Paternity Dispute from Fourteenth-Century Morocco', *Islamic Law and Society*, 1: 332–66.

PRICE, S. (1980), 'Reciprocity and Social Distance: A Reconsideration', *Ethnology*, 17: 339–50.

PRICHARD, H. A. (1949), *Moral Obligation* (Oxford: Oxford University Press).

RAHMAN, F. (n.d.) 'Law and Morality in Islam' (unpublished).

REBSTOCK, U. (1999), 'Qadi's Errors', *Islamic Law and Society*, 6/1: 1–37.

RISPLER-CHAIM, V. (1993), *Islamic Medical Ethics in the Twentieth Century* (Leiden: E. J. Brill).

RITVO, H. (1997), *The Platypus and the Mermaid and Other Figments of the Classifying Imagination* (Cambridge, Mass.: Harvard University Press).

ROSEN, L. (1968a), 'A Moroccan Jewish Community during the Middle East Crisis', *The American Scholar*, 37/3: 435–51.

—— (1968b), 'The Structure of Social Groups in a Moroccan City', unpublished Ph.D. dissertation, Department of Anthropology, University of Chicago.

—— (1970), ' "I Divorce Thee": Moroccan Marriage and the Law', *Transaction*, 7/8: 34–37.

—— (1972), 'Muslim–Jewish Relations in a Moroccan City', *International Journal of Middle East Studies*, 3/4: 435–49.

—— (1980–1), 'Equity and Discretion in a Modern Islamic Legal System', *Law and Society Review*, 15/2: 217–45.

—— (1984), *Bargaining for Reality: The Structure of Social Relations in a Moroccan City* (Chicago: University of Chicago Press).

—— (1985), 'Intentionality and the Concept of the Person', in J. R. Pennock and J. W. Chapman (eds.), *Criminal Justice* (New York: New York University Press), 52–77.

—— (1989a), *The Anthropology of Justice: Law as Culture in Islamic Society* (New York: Cambridge University Press).

—— (1989b), 'Islamic "Case Law" and the Logic of Consequence', in J. Starr and J. Collier (eds.), *History and Power in the Study of Law* (Ithaca: Cornell University Press), 302–19.

—— (1989c), 'Responsibility and Compensatory Justice in Arab Culture and Law', in B. Lelre and G. Urban (eds.), *Semiotics, Self, and Society* (Berlin and New York: Mouton de Gruyter), 101–20.

—— (1995a), 'Have the Arabs Changed their Mind? Intentions and the Discernment of Cultural Change', in L. Rosen (ed.), *Other Intentions: Cultural Contexts and the Attribution of Inner States* (Santa Fe, NM: School of American Research Press), 178–200.

ROSEN, L. (1995b), 'Islamic Concepts of Justice', in M. King (ed.), *God's Law versus State Law: The Construction of an Islamic Identity in Western Europe* (London: Grey Seal Books), 62–72.

—— (1995c), 'Justice: Concepts of Justice', in J. L. Esposito (ed.), *The Oxford Encyclopedia of the Modern Islamic World*, ii (Oxford: Oxford University Press), 388–91.

—— (1995d), 'Law and Custom in the Popular Legal Culture of North Africa', *Islamic Law and Society*, 2/2: 194–208.

—— (ed.) (1995e), *Other Intentions: Cultural Contexts and the Attribution of Inner States* (Santa Fe, NM: School of American Research Press).

—— (1995f), 'Review of Norman Calder, *Studies in Early Muslim Jurisprudence*', *Law and History Review*, 13/1: 137–9.

—— (1996), 'Common Law, Common Culture, Commonsense: An Introduction to Arab Legal Reasoning', *POLAR: Political and Legal Anthropology Review*, 19/2: 1–6.

—— (1997), 'A la barre: Regard sur les archives d'un tribunal marocain (1965–1995)', in G. Boëtsch, B. Dupret, and J. N. Ferrié (eds.), *Droits et Sociétés dans le monde arabe: Perspectives socio-anthropologiques* (Aix-en-Provence: Presses Universitaires d'Aix—Marseilles), 87–99.

—— (1998), 'A Brief Stroll through Arab Society and Law', *The Key Reporter (Phi Beta Kappa)*, 63/1: 1–6.

—— (2000), 'Islam and Islamic Cultures in the Courts of the United States', in A. Hammoudi (ed.), *Universalizing from Particulars: Islamic Views of Human Rights* (London: I. B. Tauris).

—— (forthcoming), *The Culture of Islam: Continuity and Discontinuity in Contemporary Muslim Life*.

ROSENTHAL, F. (1975), *Gambling in Islam* (Leiden: E. J. Brill).

—— (1983), *'Sweeter Than Hope': Complaint and Hope in Medieval Islam* (Leiden: E. J. Brill).

—— (1997), 'The Stranger in Medieval Islam', *Arabica*, 44/1: 35–75.

ROYAUME DU MAROC (1975a), 'Dahir no. 1-74-339 of 24 joumada II 1394 (15 July 1974), reprinted from the Bulletin Officiel du Royaume du Maroc (3220), 17 July 1974, 1090–93', In *Annuaire de l'Afrique du Nord*, xiii (Paris: Centre National de la Recherche Scientifique), 756–64.

—— (1975b), 'Dahir no. 2-74-499 of 25 joumada II 1394 (16 July 1974), reprinted from the Bulletin Officiel du Royaume du Maroc (3220), July 17, 1974, 1094–95', in *Annuaire de l'Afrique du Nord*, xiii (Paris: Centre National de la Recherche Scientifique), 764–5.

—— (1990), *Annuaire statistique du Maroc* (Rabat: Direction de la Statistique).

—— (1992), *Annuaire statistique du Maroc* (Rabat: Direction de la Statistique).

—— (1993), *Code du Statut Personnel et des Successions (Loi no. 1-93-347; 10 septembre 1993)* (Casablanca: Librairies Al-Wahda Al Arabia).

RUTHVEN, M. (1984), *Islam in the World* (London: Penguin).

RUXTON, F. H. (1916), *Maliki Law* (London: Luzac).

SACCO, R. (1991), 'Legal Formants: A Dynamic Approach to Comparative Law, I and II', *The American Journal of Comparative Law*, 39: 1–34, 343–401.

SAHLINS, M. (1972), *Stone Age Economics* (Chicago: Aldine).

SALEH, N. A. (1986), *Unlawful Gain and Legitimate Profit in Islamic Law* (Cambridge: Cambridge University Press).

—— (1989), 'The Law Governing Contracts in Arabia', *International and Comparative Law Quarterly*, 38/4: 761–87.

SANTILLANA, D. (1931), 'Law and Society', in T. Arnold and A. Guillaume (eds.), *The Legacy of Islam* (Oxford: Oxford University Press), 284–310.

SANTOS, B. (1987), 'Law: A Map of Misreading; toward a Postmodern Conception of Law', *Journal of Law and Society*, 14: 279–302.

SAVORY, R. M. (1976), 'Law and Traditional Society', in id. (ed.), *Islamic Civilisation* (Cambridge: Cambridge University Press).

SCELLES-MILLIE, J. and KHELIFA, B. (1966), *Les Quatrains de Medjdoub le Sarcastique: Poète maghrébine du XVIe siècle* (Paris: G.-P. Maisonneuve et Larose).

SCHACHT, J. (1932), 'Islamic Law', in E. R. A. Seligman (ed.), *Encyclopaedia of the Social Sciences*, iv (New York: Macmillan), 344–9.

—— (1950), *The Origins of Muhammadan Jurisprudence* (Oxford: Clarendon Press).

—— (1956), 'Review of Louis Milliot, *Introduction à l'étude du droit musulman*', *American Journal of Comparative Law*, 5/1: 133–41.

—— (1957), 'Classicisme, traditionalisme et ankylose dans la loi réligieuse de l'Islam', in R. Brunschvig et al. (eds.), *Classicisme et déclin culturel dans l'histoire de l'Islam* (Paris: Besson-Chantemerle), 141–61.

—— (1964), *An Introduction to Islamic Law* (Oxford: Clarendon Press).

—— (1974), 'Islamic Religious Law', in J. Schacht and C. E. Bosworth (eds.), *The Legacy of Islam* (Oxford: Clarendon Press), 392–403.

—— (1986) in C. E. Bosworth, Evan Donzel, B. Lewis. and Ch. Pellat, *Encyclopaedia of Islam*, new edn. i., 177–80.

SCHLAG, P. (1996), 'Hiding the Ball', *New York University Law Review*, 71/6: 1681–1718.

SCHLEGEL, S. (1970), *Tiruray Justice* (Berkeley: University of California Press).

SCHLESINGER, R. B., BAADE, H. W., DAMASKA, M. R., and HERZOG, P. E. (1988), *Comparative Law* (Mineola, NY: The Foundation Press).

SCHWARTZ, R. (1986), 'Law and Normative Order', in L. Lipson and S. Wheeler (eds.), *Law and the Social Sciences* (New York: Russell Sage Foundation), 63–107.

SELIGMAN, A. B. (1997), *The Problem of Trust* (Princeton: Princeton University Press).

SERJEANT, R. B. (1964), 'The "Constitution of Medina" ', *Islamic Quarterly*, 8: 3–16.

—— (1978), 'The Sunnah Jāmi'ah, Pacts with the Yathrib Jews, and the Taḥrīm of Yathrib: Analysis and Translation of the Documents Comprised in the so-Called "Constitution of Medina" ', *Bulletin of the School of Oriental and African Studies*, 41/1: 1–42.

SHAPIRO, S. (1987), 'The Social Control of Impersonal Trust', *American Journal of Sociology*, 93/3: 623–58.

SIMPSON, A. W. B. (1973), 'The Common Law and Legal Theory', in A. Simpson (ed.), *Oxford Essays in Jurisprudence, 2nd Series* (Oxford: Oxford University Press), 77–99.

SKOVGAARD-PETERSEN, J. (1997), *Defining Islam for the Egyptian State: Muftis and Fatwas of the Dār al-Iftā* (Leiden: E. J. Brill) .

SLAUGHTER, M. M. (1993), 'The Salman Rushdie Affair: Apostasy, Honor, and Freedom of Speech', *Virginia Law Review*, 79: 153–204.

SLOANE, P D. (1988), 'The Status of Islamic Law in the Modern Commercial World', *The International Lawyer*, 22/3: 743–66.

SMIRNOV, A. (1996), 'Understanding Justice in an Islamic Context: Some Points of Contrast with Western Theories', *Philosophy East and West*, 46/3: 337–50.

SMITH, M. G. (1969), 'Some Developments in the Analytic Framework of Pluralism', in L. Kuper and M. G. Smith (eds.), *Pluralism in Africa* (Berkeley: University of California Press), 415–58.

SMITH, W. C. (1965), 'The Concept of Shari'a among the Mutakallimun', in G. Makdisi (ed.), *Arabic and Islamic Studies in Honor of H. A. R. Gibb* (Leiden: E. J. Brill), 581–602.

—— (1971), 'A Human View of Truth', *Studies in Religion*, 1: 6–24.

SOKAL, R. R. (1966), 'Numerical Taxonomy', *Scientific American*, 215/6: 106–16.

SOLOMON, R. C. and Murphy, M. C. (eds.) (1990), *What is Justice? Classic and Contemporary Readings* (New York: Oxford University Press).

SOLOVE, D. J. (1996), 'Faith Profaned: The Religious Freedom Restoration Act and Religion in the Prisons', *Yale Law Journal*, 106/2: 459–91.

SONTAG, S. (1990), *Illness as Metaphor and AIDS and its Metaphors* (New York: Doubleday).

SOUAG, M. (1976), 'La Justice et l'Injustice', *Lamalif*, no. 83: 41.

SPATZ, M. (1991), 'A "Lesser" Crime: A Comparative Study of Legal Defense for Men Who Kill Their Wives', *Columbia Journal of Law and Social Problems*, 24: 597–638.

STEINFELS, P. (1993), 'Clinton Signs Law Protecting Religious Practices', in *The New York Times*, 17 November, A18.

STEWART, F. H. (1994), *Honor* (Chicago: University of Chicago Press).

STONE, J. (1950), *The Province and Function of Law: Law as Logic, Justice and Social Control* (London: Stevens).

SUNSTEIN, C. (1993), 'On Analogical Reasoning', *Harvard Law Review*, 106: 741–91.

TAMANAHA, B. (1993), 'The Folly of the "Social Scientific" Concept of Legal Pluralism', *Journal of Law and Society*, 20/2: 192–217.

TOLEDANO, H. (1974), 'Sijilmasi's Manual of Maghribi 'Amal, *al-'Amal al-Muṭlaq*: A Preliminary Study', *International Journal of Middle East Studies*, 5: 484–96.

—— (1981), *Judicial Practice and Family Law in Morocco* (Boulder: Social Science Monographs).

TOOMEY, S. (1985), 'Eskimo Erotica? Traditional-Conduct Plea Wins Sex Charge Acquital', *National Law Journal*, 4 February, 6.

TUCKER, J. E. (1998), *In the House of the Law: Gender and Islamic Law in Ottoman Syria and Palestine* (Berkeley: University of California Press).

TUNC, A. (1974), 'La Réform du Droit des Accidents de la Circulation—l'Ordonnance Algérienne du 30 janvier 1974', *Révue International de Droit Comparé*, 26/2: 345–7.

—— (1983), 'Introduction', in R. David (ed.), *International Encyclopedia of Comparative Law*, vol xi, Torts, ch. 1, s. (Tübingen: J. C. B. Mohr), 1–180.

TURNER, B. (1997), *Islam and the African-American Experience* (Bloomington: Indiana University Press).

TURNER, B. S. (1974), *Weber and Islam: A Critical Study* (London: Routledge & Kegan Paul).

TYAN, É. (1926), *Le Système de résponsabilité delictuelle en droit musulman* (Beirut: Imprimérie Catholique).

—— (1945), *Le Notariat et le régime de la preuve par écrit dans la pratique du droit musulman* (Beirut: Université de Lyon, Annales de l'École Française de Droit de Beyrouth).

—— (1955), 'Judicial Organisation', in M. Khadduri and H. J. Lieberny (eds.), *Law in the Middle East*, i (Washington: The Middle East Institute), 236–78.

—— (1960), *Histoire de l'organisation judiciaire en pays d'Islam* (Leiden: E. J. Brill).

—— (1965), 'Diya', in B. Lewis, C. Pellat, and J. Schacht (eds.), *The Encyclopaedia of Islam*, ii (Leiden: E. J. Brill), 340–3.

UDOVITCH, A. L. (1970), *Partnership and Profit in Medieval Islam* (Princeton: Princeton University Press).

UNITED STATES SUPREME COURT (1949), 'Terminiello v. Chicago', *United States Reports*, 337: 1–37.

UNTERMAN, A. (1990), 'A Jewish Perspective on the "Rushdie Affair" ', in D. Cohn-Sherbok (ed.), *The Salman Rushdie Controversy in Interreligious Perspective* (Lewiston, NY: Edwin Mellen Press).

VAN CAENEGEM, R. C. (1987), *Judges, Legislators and Professors* (Cambridge: Cambridge University Press).

VANDERLINDEN, J. (1971), 'Le Pluralisme juridique: Essai de synthèse', in J. Gilissen (ed.), *Le Pluralisme juridique* (Brussels: Université Libre de Bruxelles), 19–56.

—— (1989), 'Return to Legal Pluralism: Twenty Years Later', *Journal of Legal Pluralism and Unofficial Law*, 28: 149–57.

VARGA, C. (1977), 'Utopias of Rationality in the Development of the Idea of Codification', *Archiv für Rechts- und Sozialphilosophie*, 11: 27–40.

VOGEL, F. E. and HAYES, S. L. (1998), *Islamic Law and Finance: Religion, Risk, and Return* (The Hague: Kluwer Law International).

WAKIN, J. A. (1972), *The Function of Documents in Islamic Law* (Albany: State University of New York Press).

WASHINGTON POST (1998), 'Intolerance in Loudoun', *The Washington Post*, 4 March, A20.

WATSON, A. (1974), *Legal Transplants: An Approach to Comparative Law* (Edinburgh: Scottish Academic Press).

WEBER, M. (1954), *Max Weber on Law in Economy and Society* (New York: Simon & Schuster).

WESTERMARCK, E. (1926), *Ritual and Belief in Morocco, Vol. I* (London: Macmillan).

—— (1930), *Wit and Wisdom in Morocco* (London: Routledge).

WHITE, J. (1996), 'Analogical Reasoning', in D. Patterson (ed.), *A Companion to Philosophy of Law and Legal Theory* (Oxford: Blackwell Publishers), 583–90.

WHITE, J. B. (1990), *Justice as Translation: An Essay in Cultural and Legal Criticism* (Chicago: University of Chicago Press).

WIGMORE, J. H. (1936), *A Panorama of the World's Legal Systems* (Washington: Washington Law Book Co.).

—— (1941), *A Kaleidoscope of Justice* (Washington: Washington Law Book Co.).

WOLF, E. R. (1951), 'The Social Organization of Mecca and the Origins of Islam', *Southwestern Journal of Anthropology*, 7/4: 329–56.

WOLGAST, E. (1987), *The Grammar of Justice* (Ithaca: Cornell University Press).

YAMANI, A. Z. (1968), *Islamic Law and Contemporary Issues* (Jidda: The Saudi Publishing House).

YNGVESSON, B. (1993), *Virtuous Citizens: Order and Complaint in a New England Court* (New York: Routledge).

ZEYS, E. and SAID, M. O. S. (1946), *Récueil d'Actes et de Jugements Arabes* (Algiers: Éditions Jules Carbonel).

ZIADEH, F. J. (1957), 'Equality (Kafa'a) in the Muslim Law of Marriage', *The American Journal of Comparative Law*, 6/4: 503–17.

—— (1960), ''Urf and Law in Islam', in J. Kritzeck and R. B. Winder (eds.), *The World of Islam: Studies in Honor of Philip Hitti* (London: Macmillan), 60–7.

—— (1990), 'Integrity ('Adālah) in Classical Islamic Law', in N. Heer (ed.), *Islamic Law and Jurisprudence* (Seattle: University of Washington Press), 73–93.

ZWEIGERT, K. and KOTZ, H. (1998), *An Introduction to Comparative Law* (Oxford: Oxford University Press).

Index